THE RISE *of* U. S. GRANT

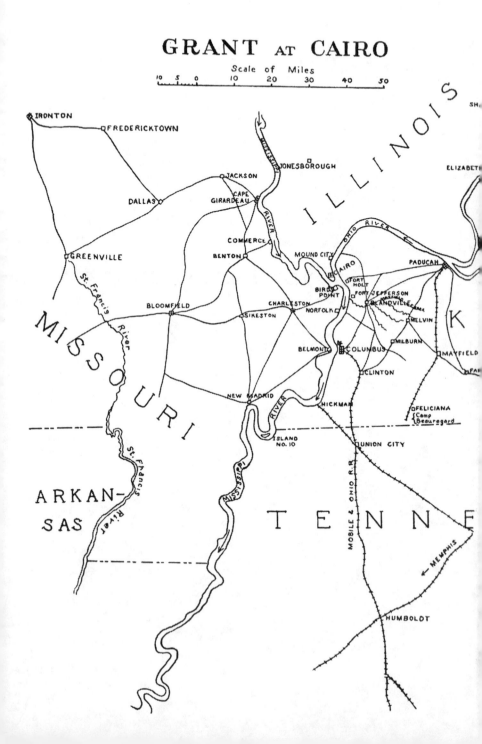

GRANT AT CAIRO
Scale of Miles
10 5 0 10 20 30 40 50

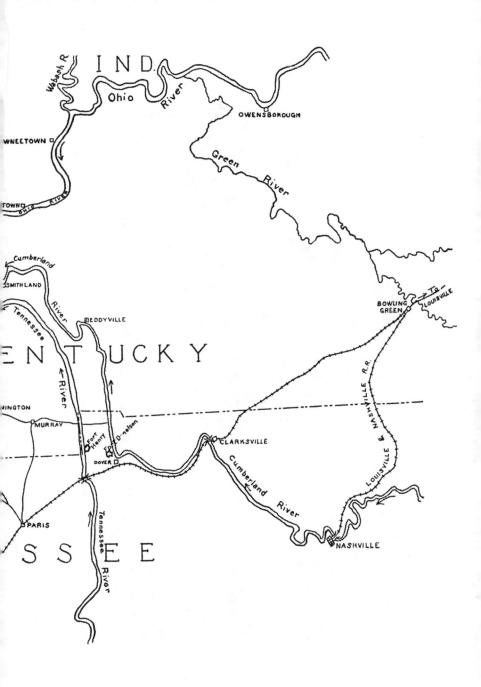

DEVEN EMORY MERRITT PARKE LOGAN BURNSIDE RAWLINS BLAIR DAVIS GRANGER
KILPATRICK CROOK WARREN MEADE SHERMAN HOOKER ORD SLOCUM HOWARD
CUSTER SHERIDAN MCPHERSON THOMAS GRANT HANCOCK TERRY SCHOFIELD

GRANT AND HIS GENERALS

(From the original wartime painting by Balling)

THE RISE

of

U. S. GRANT

By

A. L. CONGER

New introduction by Brooks D. Simpson

Illustrated with Photographs and Maps

DA CAPO PRESS • NEW YORK

Library of Congress Cataloging in Publication Data

Conger, A. L. (Arthur Latham), 1872–1951.
  The rise of U.S. Grant / by A. L. Conger; new introduction by
Brooks D. Simpson.—1st Da Capo Press ed.
      p.   c.m.
  Originally published: New York: Century Co., 1931.
  Includes bibliographical references and index.
  ISBN 0-306-80693-2 (alk. paper)
    1. Grant, Ulysses S. (Ulysses Simpson), 1822–1885. 2. Generals—
United States—Biography. 3. United States. Army—Biography. I. Title.
E672.C734   1996
973.7′ 3′ 092—dc20   95-26590
                                                                  CIP

First Da Capo Press edition 1996

This Da Capo Press paperback edition of *The Rise of U.S. Grant*
is an unabridged republication of the edition first published in
New York in 1931, here supplemented with a new introduction by
Brooks D. Simpson.

Published by Da Capo Press, Inc.
A Subsidiary of Plenum Publishing Corporation
233 Spring Street, New York, N.Y. 10013

TO

S. T. HUBBARD

INTRODUCTION

Why did Ulysses S. Grant prevail on the battlefield? What was the secret of his success as a general? Certainly he did not look the part—although perhaps the fact that we search for such outward signs of greatness says more about us and our willingness to be led astray by the superficial. Others have decided that the best way to come to terms with the problem of Grant's greatness as a general is to deny the proposition altogether. In some instances this strategy of denigration has proven far more successful than was the Confederate army in bringing him down. Many an armchair general, then and now, offers criticism upon criticism, reducing Grant to a plodding, unimaginative butcher who won by sure dint of superior resources despite operating in a haze of cigar smoke and alcohol. No doubt such conclusions are understandable when one considers the circumstances in which they're formulated. Waging war, after all, is not exactly difficult when done so after the fact by someone at home reclining in the safety of a chair or perched in front of a computer terminal. Nevertheless, a troubling question remains: if waging war is so easy, why have so few people been successful at it, and none more so than Grant? Only an impertinent realist would raise *that* point.

In fact, the stereotypical negative assessment of Grant's military career is grounded upon ignorance and myth. As a general he displayed imagination and daring, understood the need to move promptly and quickly, and overcame obstacles to claim victory several times—characteristics clearly displayed during the Vicksburg campaign. Other generals had access to the material resources and manpower of the North, yet still they failed; Grant knew how to use his resources to best effect while depriving the enemy of its own. In the end, even Robert E. Lee had to bow to his indomitable will.

Easy as it might be to refute simple-minded stereotypes about Grant's generalship, it is far more challenging to uncover what exactly explains his success—or the success of any general. Grant has proven easier to describe than he is to understand. One newspaper correspondent concluded that he was "altogether an unpronounceable man." Even those who had known him for years did not always fathom why he succeeded. Artillerist Charles Wainwright, who could never quite get over his infatuation with George B. McClellan, noted that "it is hard for those who knew [Grant] when formerly in the army to believe that he is a great man; then he was only distinguished for the mediocrity of his mind, his great good nature, and his insatiable love of whiskey."[1] How, then, does one explain his emergence as the man who led the Union armies to victory?

Colonel Arthur L. Conger set out to answer this question in *The Rise of U. S. Grant*. The result was one of the first studies to offer an informed appraisal of Grant's development as a commander. Judicious in his assessment of Grant and willing to highlight and explain shortcomings as well as successes, Conger offers an approach to his subject well worth emulating. Demonstrating a healthy skepticism about the accuracy of Grant's *Memoirs*, Conger turns to the published records of the conflict to uncover what happened—although he does not always realize that reliance on these materials can also mislead the scholar. Nevertheless, Conger remains one of the first historians to pose perceptive questions about Grant's generalship from the point of view of the military historian. It is no accident that those best trained in this area—from J. F. C. Fuller to Russell

Weigley—rank in the forefront of scholarship about Grant as a general.

Although the revival of Grant's military reputation is associated with Fuller, Conger had already offered a case for Grant's development as a commander. Unlike Fuller and others, who focused on his campaigns against Lee in 1864 and 1865, Conger decided instead to explore the first two years of Grant's career in the West. That choice was understandable for two reasons: few scholars had looked carefully at those campaigns, and Conger believed that Grant's experiences in the West would prove most helpful in the training of military officers. "Military history is the laboratory of the military profession," he declared. Historians had to analyze evidence to find out what happened; generals had to absorb, weigh, and interpret information before deciding what to do.[2]

Joining the faculty of the Army Staff College at Fort Leavenworth in 1907, Conger, whose college training took place at Harvard, not West Point, introduced the source method of military education, whereby students pored over documents and reports to find out what happened during a specific campaign. Among the campaigns he chose to subject to close analysis was Grant's capture of Fort Donelson. The legacy of that interest is apparent in this book to the point that one nearly loses sight of Grant altogether in Conger's reconstruction of the communications among Henry W. Halleck, Don Carlos Buell, and George B. McClellan—although this trio also tended to overlook Grant.[3] After years of study informed by a knowledge of military operations, Conger was able to challenge and in many cases refute criticisms of Grant's generalship at Shiloh; in turn, he offered some observations of his own that did not always place Grant in a favorable light. His interest in Grant anticipated the post-World War I writings of Fuller and B. H. Liddell Hart on Grant and Sherman, although his work did not appear until after theirs. If Fuller was interested in presenting Grant as the first of the great captains of modern warfare, Conger remained far more interested in showing how Grant encountered, then mastered, the problems of command as he made his way from colonel to general-in-chief.

Much has been made of Grant's unpromising start at West Point—perhaps too much. True, he graduated in the middle third of his class—21st of 39 graduates in 1843—but one's class rank measured compliance with regulations as much as it did performance in the classroom. Nor was West Point necessarily an ideal training ground for future military leaders. While it did a wonderful job of educating civil engineers, it offered little in the way of training officers to exercise command and to plan operations in the field. Moreover, much of what cadets learned in the 1830s and 1840s was woefully outdated by 1861. In discussions later in life Grant revealed that in fact he did have some knowledge of military history, but he knew that attempts to replicate what Frederick the Great or Napoleon did might well end in disaster. "I don't underrate the value of military knowledge," he once observed, "but if men make war in slavish observances of rules, they will fail. . . . Even Napoleon showed that, for my impression is that his first success came because he made war in his own way, and not in imitation of others. War is progressive, because all the instruments and elements of war are progressive." He added that "every war I knew anything about had made laws for itself"; that was the true lesson of military history.[4]

One might look to the Mexican War for signs of the future general. As regimental quartermaster for the Fourth United States Infantry, Grant learned the importance of keeping his men supplied and equipped; as commissary officer, he also kept them fed. Yet when it came time to fight, he always made his way to the front lines, demonstrating coolness and courage under fire in several engagements. Not afraid to take the initiative, he also improvised according to circumstances. During the final assaults on Mexico City, Grant directed a small squad to seize a church belfry, then helped them transport a disassembled cannon up the tower's stairs. Once reassembled, Grant's howitzer created chaos in the enemy's rear.

It would be left to Lloyd Lewis and others to describe Grant's pre-Civil War career in detail: Conger briefly passes over those formative years. Although Grant possessed a credible record of service, he never held a combat command. Nevertheless, he watched others. Zachary Taylor and Winfield Scott both left an impression upon Grant; he also learned much about his fellow officers, gaining knowledge that would be useful when he encountered them as his opponents years later. He once remarked that he was willing to be aggressive and take risks at Fort Donelson because he was already acquainted with the flawed skills and personality of Gideon J. Pillow, who helped direct the Confederate forces.

As colonel of the 21st Illinois in 1861, Grant showed that he could train soldiers and lead them in the field. He also learned that he could command men in combat. In early July he marched his men westward toward Palmyra, Missouri to relieve a supposedly besieged garrison, all the while wondering whether he was equal to the task of command under fire. The threat of battle proved premature. However, a week later the colonel received instructions to disperse a band of Confederates led by Thomas Harris, who were encamped at Florida, some two dozen miles away. As his men neared Florida, Grant grew uneasy once more: "[M]y heart kept getting higher and higher until it felt to me as though it was in my throat. I would have given anything then to have been back in Illinois, but I had not the moral courage to halt and consider what to do; I kept right on." When he came upon Harris's camp, he found it deserted.

"My heart resumed its place. It occurred to me at once that Harris had been as much afraid of me as I had been of him. This was a view of the question I had never taken before; but it was one I never forgot afterwards. From that event until the close of the war, I never experienced trepidation upon confronting an enemy, though I always felt more or less anxiety. I never forgot that he had as much reason to fear my forces as I had his. The lesson was valuable."[5]

It was a lesson worth imparting to others. Grant got an opportunity to do so on May 6, 1864 during the Battle of the Wilderness. For two days he and Robert E. Lee had engaged in a contest of thrust and parry in a dense thicket of undergrowth. As dusk approached on the 6th, Georgian John B. Gordon launched an attack on the Union right; the darkness concealed Gordon's inferior numbers and the Yankees broke. As news of the Confederate success filtered back to headquarters, veteran officers of the Army of the Potomac shook their heads knowingly. It was just one year and four days since Stonewall Jackson had pulled the same trick at Chancellorsville; James Longstreet had rolled up the Union flank in August 1862 at Second Bull Run—defeating yet another general from the West, John Pope. Whatever Grant's past record had been, they reasoned, he had not yet met Bobby Lee. Gordon's attack was sure to serve as a rude introduction. In its way, it did—the attack introduced the Army of the Potomac to Grant as no review or parade could.

As staff officers scurried about to direct reinforcements to counter the Confederate assault, Grant quietly sought information, issued orders, and then sat down and lit a cigar. He looked up to see a general approach him and excitedly announce, "General Grant, this is a crisis that cannot be looked upon too seriously. I know Lee's methods well by past experience; he will throw his whole army between us and the Rapidan, and cut us off completely from our communications." Grant stood and removed his cigar. "Oh, I am heartily tired of hearing about what Lee is going to do," he snapped. "Some of you always seem to think he is suddenly going to turn a double somersault, and land in our rear and our flanks at the same time. Go back to your command, and try to think what we are going to do ourselves, instead of what Lee is going to do." It was a view of matters that the Army of the Potomac had never taken before; it was one Grant would never allow them to forget.[6]

One facet of exercising command that is often overlooked by scholars—but not by Conger—is the importance of a general's staff. Staff officers bring the commander information; in turn, they are entrusted with relaying his orders, carrying out his directives, and administering the army. They have to interpret his intentions to subordinates and make sure that everyone understands his own role in the overall plan. As a brigadier general Grant appointed several trusted friends to his staff, the most famous being John A. Rawlins, who had known Grant before the war in Galena, Illinois. As the size of Grant's command expanded, so did his staff. The arrival of Joseph D. Webster and James B. McPherson in early 1862 marked the beginning of its professionalization. They would be followed by James H. Wilson, Orville E. Babcock, Cyrus B. Comstock, and Horace Porter—all young West Pointers of great promise. Most of the original staff members eventually left: they were no longer needed.

Grant used his staff not only to carry out his plans but also to help him formulate them. Evenings at headquarters often provided staffers with the opportunity to discuss various options. Grant listened as the pros and cons of each alternative were debated, rarely contributing his own perspective. Such conversations took place prior to the Vicksburg campaign; a year later, similar exchanges weighed the prospects for Sherman's plan to march to the sea. At times participants in these discussions claimed pride of authorship for Grant's plans, as if that in itself was sufficient to assure their successful implementation. Wilson credited himself with originating the Vicksburg campaign; another staff officer, Adam Badeau, later made it seem as if such discussions were essential to Grant's thought process. Staff officers "would systematically talk their ideas into [Grant's mind], for weeks, not directly, but by discussion among themselves, in his presence," Badeau bragged. "In the end, he would announce the idea as his own, without seeming conscious of the discussion; and would give the orders to carry it out with all the energy that belonged to his nature." Doubtless Badeau flattered himself, as he was wont to do: when he tried to take credit for writing Grant's *Memoirs*, the general fired him.[7]

There is far more to exercising command than planning campaigns and directing men in battle. Gathering intelligence about the enemy, arranging for food and supplies, drilling and equipping recruits—all are among the commander's responsibilities. Not everyone understood this. "There is a desire upon the part of the people who stay securely at home to read in the morning papers, at their breakfast, startling reports of battles fought," Grant remarked in 1861. "They cannot understand why troops are kept inactive for weeks or even months. They do not understand that men have to be disciplined, arms made, transportation and provisions provided." Commanders also had to manage subordinates and forge a command system; Grant excelled at this. As Charles Francis Adams, Jr. observed, "He handles those around him so quietly and well, he so evidently has the faculty of disposing of work and managing men, he is cool and quiet, . . . and in a crisis he is one against whom all around . . . would instinctively lean. He is a man of the most exquisite judgment and tact." Personal as well as professional considerations shaped these relationships. Thus Sherman, whose performance under Grant was not flawless, nevertheless earned his loyalty and respect, and returned it—allowing Grant to entrust him with directing a crucial diversionary movement during the Vicksburg campaign, even though he was fully aware that Sherman was not happy with the overall plan. In marked contrast was the relationship Grant endured with John A. McClernand, who schemed to displace his superior by discrediting him in gossipy letters to Lincoln. Aware of McClernand's friendship with the president—he once remarked that he couldn't afford to quarrel with someone that he was "compelled to command"—Grant kept a close eye on his subordinate and waited for the ideal opportunity to remove him. That chance came during the siege of Vicksburg when McClernand violated regulations by sharing his orders with a newspaper. McClernand's protests proved unavailing, for Lincoln realized that in the wake of victory Grant was untouchable.[8]

Although Grant did not excel in the study of military science at West Point—what there was of it—he demonstrated real talent in mathematics, so much so that he entertained thoughts of becoming a college professor. He always had a knack for breaking problems down to their basic components and then solving them. This pragmatic bent was reflected in his generalship, for he grasped the essentials of strategy and command as did few others. There was a directness to what he did, a grand simplicity that unwary critics have confused with simple-mindedness. In looking for greatness in Grant—and not finding it—these skeptics revealed that their own concept of what constituted greatness and military skill was flawed, if not altogether mistaken. Others came away from seeing Grant in action with a better understanding of what it took to be a successful commander. As one observer put it, "I thought I detected in the management what I had never discovered before on the battle-field—a little common sense. Dash is handsome, genius glorious; but modest, old-fashioned, practical everyday sense is the trump, after all." Grant himself was under no illusions about what he did. "The art of war is simple enough," he once remarked. "Find out where your enemy is. Get at him as soon as you can. Strike at him as hard as you can and as often as you can, and keep moving on."[9]

"Common sense"—that phrase recurs again and again in discussions of his generalship. William T. Sherman used it in a letter to Grant. "My only points of doubt were as to your knowledge of grand strategy, and of books of science and history," he wrote, "but I confess your common-sense seems to have supplied all this." Even Grant was known to employ the term. As a colonel he struggled to drill his regiment according to the book (the first time he had consulted a drill manual since West Point), only to discover that the complex maneuvers were too unwieldy to perform. A closer look revealed that the instructions were "nothing more than common sense and the progress of the age" applied to what he had endured at the military academy. "The commands were abbreviated and the movement expedited," he recalled. "I found no trouble in giving commands that would take my regiment where I wanted it to go and carry it around all obstacles. I do not believe that the officers of the regiment ever discovered that I had never studied the tactics that I used."[10]

If Grant's *uncommon* common sense explains much of his success as a military commander, so does his courage and self-confidence. He was brave under fire, but that alone is not the sort of courage one needs in a commander—and if Grant sometimes did not heed danger, he did not go looking for it either. Rather, it was his ability under pressure to respond to circumstances, to improvise, and to accept the fluidity of events as a given that served him well. One thinks of Grant's coolness under fire at Belmont, Fort Donelson, and Shiloh, or his willingness to adjust his plans of campaign in 1864 in response first to political pressure and then to setbacks elsewhere. Nothing seemed to shake him. Sherman told him that he marvelled at "the simple faith in success you have always manifested, which I can liken to nothing else than the faith a Christian has in his Saviour"—a fairly informed comparison in light of the intense religious faith of Sherman's wife. Sherman added that "when you have completed your best preparations, you go into battle without hesitation, as at Chattanooga—no doubts, no reserve; and I tell you that it was this that made us act with confidence." This was never truer than in the case of Sherman. He once confessed to another general to being "a damn sight smarter than Grant. I know a great deal more about war, military history, strategy, and grand tactics than he does; I know more about organization, supply, and administration, and about everything else than he does. But I tell you where he beats me, and where he beats the world. He don't care a damn for what the enemy does out of his sight, but it scares me like hell."[11]

If Sherman thus underestimated Grant's knowledge of military science and history, he did justice to Grant's character. Common sense, a faith in oneself, a willingness to master one's fears—these are essential qualities of the good commander. So are the abilities to filter out accurate information from rumors and reports, to assess one's opponent, to ensure cooperation and harmony among one's subordinates, and to keep an army supplied and fed. Grant may not have looked like a commander—at least not to those who saw George McClellan as the ideal model of one—but he was a great captain because of who he was and what he did. T. Harry Williams may have put it best:

There is no difficulty in composing a final
evaluation of Ulysses S. Grant. The summa-
tion can be as short as one of his own simple
statements. With him there need be no bal-
ancing and qualifying, no ifs and buts. He
won battles and campaigns, and he struck the
blow that won the war. No general could do
what he did because of accident or luck or
preponderance of numbers and weapons. He
was a success because he was a complete general and a complete character. He was so
complete that his countrymen have never
been able to believe he was real.[12]

BROOKS D. SIMPSON
Chandler, Arizona
April 1996

A noted Civil War scholar, Brooks D. Simpson is the author of
Let Us Have Peace: Ulysses S. Grant and the Politics of War
and Reconstruction, 1861–1868 *and* The Political Education of
Henry Adams.

NOTES

1. Bruce Catton, *Grant Moves South* (Boston, 1960), p. 272; Allan Nevins, ed., *A Diary of Battle: The Personal Journals of Colonel Charles S. Wainwright, 1861–1865* (New York, 1962), p. 329.
2. Carol Reardon, *Soldiers and Scholars: The U.S. Army and the Uses of Military History, 1865–1920* (Lawrence, KS: University Press of Kansas, 1990), pp. 34-35.
3. Ibid., pp. 69-75.
4. James Russell Young, *Around the World with General Grant* (2 vols.: New York, 1879), vol. 2, pp. 352-53, 615.
5. Ulysses S. Grant, *Personal Memoirs* (2 vols.: New York, 1885), vol. 1, pp. 249-250.
6. Horace Porter, *Campaigning with Grant* (New York, 1897), pp. 69-70.
7. Albert D. Richardson, *Personal History of Ulysses S. Grant* (Hart, CT, 1868), p. 296; Porter, *Campaigning with Grant* pp. 314-15; Adam Badeau, *The Military History of Ulysses S. Grant* (3 vols.: New York, 1868), vol. 3, pp. 140-45; Henry Adams, *The Education of Henry Adams* (Boston, 1973 [1918]), p. 264.
8. Grant to Jesse Root Grant, November 17, 1861, quoted in Brooks D. Simpson, "All I Want Is to Advance," *Gateway Heritage* 15 (Summer 1994), p. 15; Charles Francis Adams, Jr. to Charles Francis Adams, Sr., May 29, 1864, *A Cycle of Adams Letters*, ed. Worthington C. Ford, (2 vols.: Boston, 1920), vol. 2, pp. 133-34.
9. T. Harry Williams, *McClellan, Sherman, and Grant* (New Brunswick, 1962), pp. 85, 105.
10. William T. Sherman, *Memoirs of William T. Sherman* (2 vols.: New York, 1875), vol. 1, p. 400; Grant, *Personal Memoirs*, vol. 2, pp. 252-53.
11. Ibid.; Williams, *McClellan, Sherman, and Grant*, p. 59.
12. Ibid., pp. 109-10.

FOREWORD

STUDY of the Civil War period has a peculiar charm. A charm which, no doubt, is partly due to the completeness and easy accessibility of published data that give us a detailed picture of events; in this respect the war between the States has the advantage over wars of earlier date. But not least is it due to the fact that this was the last great war fought before the common use of the typewriter, when men still took time, from necessity as well as custom, to write in long hand precisely their matured thoughts.

In order to bring out this fragrance of the spirit of the time, the writer has let the actors in the drama speak for themselves wherever possible—not, indeed, from memoirs giving the dimmed and distorted, often quite false, impressions of later years, but from contemporaneously written messages and other papers.

When Fort Sumter fell, a man named Ulysses S. Grant was an obscure citizen of Galena, Illinois, without influential friends and lacking the reputation of success. Yet within three years this man rose to command the Union armies, and in four years had gained victory and dictated peace.

How can it be explained? What were the characteristics of such a man? By what method did he acquire his knowledge? Were his honors really earned or were they owed to chance?

In the hope of aiding those who, pondering the phenomenon of the man Grant, seek the answer to such questions, this book has been written.

CONTENTS

CHAPTER   PAGE

I   INTRODUCTORY 1

II   GRANT AND THE TWENTY-FIRST ILLINOIS 4

III BRIGADIER IN MISSOURI 11

IV THE CONFEDERATE FIASCO IN THE WEST 31

V   THE MISSISSIPPI 41

VI THE RÔLE OF KENTUCKY 50

VII GRANT AT CAIRO 60

VIII THE RAID ON BELMONT 81

IX THE AMENITIES OF WAR IN THE WEST 102

X   AFTER BELMONT 110

XI INCEPTION OF THE FORT HENRY PLAN 130

XII GRANT AND THE FORT HENRY PLAN 142

XIII FORTS HENRY AND DONELSON 155

XIV GRANT AND THE TRIUMVIRATE 178

XV GRANT IN OBSCURATION 193

XVI GRANT RESUMES COMMAND 214

XVII SHILOH—THE BATTLE 238

XVIII SHILOH—AND AFTER 257

XIX GRANT ENTERS A LARGER FIELD 276

XX VICKSBURG 285

XXI CHATTANOOGA 293

XXII GRANT AS STRATEGIST 306

XXIII GRANT'S FINAL CAMPAIGN 325

XXIV GRANT AND HIS ARMY COMMANDERS 348

XXV GRANT AND LEE 360

APPENDIX A: BELMONT IN THE MEMOIRS 365

APPENDIX B: BALLING'S "GRANT AND HIS GENERALS" . 378

A SHORT BIBLIOGRAPHY 379

INDEX 383

[xxiii]

ILLUSTRATIONS

GRANT AND HIS GENERALS (See pages 322 and 378) . . *Frontispiece*

FACING
PAGE

THE TRIUMVIRATE 178

MAJOR-GENERAL JAMES B. MCPHERSON 240

GRANT AT MEMPHIS 276

GRANT ON LOOKOUT MOUNTAIN 300

GRANT AND HIS GENERALS (See Appendix B) 322

GRANT'S ARMY COMMANDERS 348

GRANT AT CITY POINT, 1864 362

MAPS

PAGE

GRANT AND THE 21ST ILLINOIS 8

GRANT AT IRONTON 12

BELMONT 90

GRANT'S MARCH ON FORT HENRY 158

FORTS HENRY AND DONELSON 163

FORT DONELSON, FEBRUARY 13, 1862 166

FORT DONELSON, FEBRUARY 15, 1862 172

FORT DONELSON, FEBRUARY 15, 1862, 3 P.M. 175

SHILOH CAMPS 220

SHILOH (APRIL 6, 1862) 242

SHILOH (APRIL 7, 1862) 261

ENVIRONS OF CHATTANOOGA 302

THE RISE *of* U. S. GRANT

CHAPTER I

INTRODUCTORY

It is upon the serene and placid surface of the
unruffled mind that the visions gathered from the
invisible find a representation in the visible world.
—MAHATMA LETTERS.

FALLOW: plowed and left unseeded; said of land that has
been broken up by tillage but allowed to lie idle for a season
or more, that in future it may produce a better yield. Such, to
us who view in retrospect the striking contrasts in Ulysses Grant's
life, appears the existence he was leading as a mere clerk in a
small leather shop at the time the call to arms sounded which
ushered in the Civil War—an existence that must have seemed
all the more drab to him after the glamour and intensity of his
abandoned military career.

Accustomed to a simple life and inured to daily toil by his
early years in the country district he was chosen to represent at
West Point, he had experienced at the Military Academy new
drudgery, of course, but with it military pomp and glitter, and
association with keen young minds. A few years after his gradu-
ation, the fledgling officer found himself drawn into the vortex
of the Mexican War. This also meant drudgery and fatigue,
but in a nimbus of excitement and exhilaration; new lessons to
be learned, but no longer out of books; new problems, the failure
to solve which meant the forfeiture of the lives of men.

Too young and too low in rank to carry as yet the burden
of responsible decisions, he must none the less have gained a

mental concept of war, with its vital psychological problems, which future events were to prove to be more realistic and practical than the concept of many an older officer. Further, he saw and profited by the errors of his superiors—when such occurred—since younger officers with simpler responsibilities are always the first to detect and analyze wartime errors and their consequences.

Technically, he served as quartermaster-commissary and adjutant of his regiment and learned thus the rudiments of administration and supply—valuable assets for his later work in grappling with similar problems of greater magnitude in the more complex theater and amid the more acute conditions of the Civil War.

Honors, too, this earlier war brought him—two promotions by brevet, marks of the approbation of his superiors, but not unusual ones; it would have been unusual had he not had them, where so many were awarded. Nor were these brevets solely for staff duties: tactical experiences also came to him. At San Cosme he acquitted himself "most nobly," according to the official report.[1]

Of greater interest would it be to know if he had at this time gained that fixity of the "unruffled mind" which later was to reproduce so faithfully "the visions gathered from the invisible." Or was that one of the results of the fallow years which followed? On this, in fact on all other points, we lack contemporary evidence; no one, comrade or superior, suspected what the future was to bring "Uncle Sam Grant," as his fellow-cadets and his army friends called him. Nor do his Memoirs help us here, for they show us merely a man whose imagination colors his memory, and one who largely shares the sympathies and antipathies of his comrades.

---

[1] J. H. Smith, "The War with Mexico," Vol. I, pp. 162, 414. A. D. Richardson, "A Personal History of Ulysses S. Grant," p. 123.

In the spring of 1852, Grant's regiment, the 4th Infantry, after three years in the East following the Mexican War, was ordered to the Pacific coast, at the height of the gold rush and while in the minds of most people in that still far-away region ideas of law or order were scarcely more than memories. His young wife was unable to accompany Grant, and the desire to be back with her and their two children eventually led him, in 1854, to tender his resignation from the army. But the three years spent on the Pacific coast had their lessons for him. There he met men in the rough, saw life in the raw; and whatever of too great tenderness there was in him became not so much crushed out—for those who knew him best felt it always—as covered with a coat of steel, a coat he was to need time upon time in the Civil War.

Then followed seven lean years, the "fallow" period, dull and full of care, during which Grant developed a power of dogged endurance which was to mean much to his country. Had these years been spent in the monotonous grind of the small-garrison life of the period, with its perpetual, almost stupefying round of petty duties, he might have lost the naturally fine edge of his mind, and that discrimination which, as it steadily developed, proved so large an element in his Civil War successes.

Weighing all the factors, one cannot but feel that this prolonged fallow period was the best that could have come, both for the man and for his country.

CHAPTER II

GRANT AND THE TWENTY-FIRST ILLINOIS

In war men are nothing; the man is everything.
—NAPOLEON.

RICHARD YATES, Governor of Illinois, being a successful politician, was bound to be a good judge of men. Grant had come to him as a simple volunteer, asking nothing for himself—merely to be put to work. What executive can resist that appeal? The governor used him, and correctly estimating his poise, his common sense, and, despite a military education and experience, his freedom from military cant and pedantry, found a way to reward him for his services as virtually military secretary and chief clerk, as well as adviser, during the chaotic rush of the early mobilization period.

Congressman Washburne also was an admiring observer of the man's efficiency and balance, and while the governor gave Grant the highest rank at his disposal, that of colonel, the Congressman recommended him at Washington for appointment to the rank of brigadier-general. From the outset Grant inspired trust and confidence in all with whom he came in contact—civilian, military, and naval.

Grant's first contact with the 21st Illinois came when he mustered the regiment—as presumably he did other regiments—into the service of the State, at Mattoon, May 15, 1861. A month later the governor appointed him colonel of the regiment and he took command of it at Camp Yates, Springfield, Illinois. Twelve days later the regiment was mustered into the service of the United States—thirty-six officers and something over nine hundred men. The following Wednesday, July 3, Grant began his march on Quincy, Illinois, a distance of one hundred miles. His orders were to proceed by rail, but, for the instruction and hardening of his officers and men, he asked and obtained permission to march instead. The effect on the colonel himself was no doubt equally salutary. The lean years of civilian life through which he had passed could not have failed to leave their mark in dampening his spirit of independence, of initiative. He needed the experience of being once more "in the saddle," breathing the higher air of leadership, to regain his self-assurance.

We can picture him in the early dawn mounting his horse to observe the regiment breaking camp, then the troops filing past him as the ten companies, ninety men strong, swing into the road to take up the day's march. He sees the camp ground policed and rides along the column to its head. There is no band yet organized. Toward mid-afternoon he trots ahead to select the new camp site, near but not too near some town.

The stopping-places on this march are nowhere mentioned, but it is suggested by the enlistments, in his regiment, of six new men from and near Naples, Illinois, and by the one desertion he had there, that he crossed the Illinois River at that point. The march was continued to about three miles beyond the Illinois,[1] when orders reached the colonel to return with his regiment to the river and there await a steamer to take it down to St. Louis. He waited three days, but the steamer did not come.

In the meantime a comedy was taking place twenty-five miles southwest of Quincy. On July 10 the Confederate—or, rather, the Missouri—general Tom Harris, playing the rôle of guerrilla leader, had burned the railway station and some railway cars and

[1] Reports of the Adjutant General (Illinois), Vol. II, p. 214.

coaches at Monroe, Missouri. Colonel R. F. Smith, of the 16th Illinois, with seven companies and one gun, entered the town and placed his command, for safety, in the seminary. The next morning (July 11) General Harris came back with more guerrillas and two guns and attacked. The amusing part is that in the ensuing battle of raw levies no one was killed on either side.[2] Two innocent bystanders, however, citizens of Monroe, lost their lives.[3]

News of the Monroe "battle" reached higher headquarters, and Grant with the 21st Illinois was ordered to raise the siege. Trains were sent from Quincy to Naples, to carry his regiment forward, since the distance was too great to be made, as speedily as was desired, by marching. Before he reached Monroe, however, another battalion of Colonel Smith's own 16th Infantry, at Palmyra, had secured a train and steamed into Monroe, which so disheartened Tom Harris and his crew that his men began to leave and by nightfall had vanished. Grant's regiment was no longer needed.

But, possibly owing to this incident, the 21st was diverted from reinforcing either Ironton, Missouri, or Cairo, Illinois—fortunately for Grant, perhaps, as events turned—and assigned to guarding the Hannibal and St. Joseph Railroad which stretched east and west across northern Missouri, from Hannibal on the Mississippi to the Missouri at St. Joseph. Hurlbut was ordered "to hold this railroad" and posted three regiments along it (July 16 and 17). The 21st presumably had the right—the east—end of the line, since Grant in his Memoirs mentions a fruitless march, during this period, from Salt River, near Hannibal, to Florida, Missouri, in search of a handful of "rebels" under the wily Tom Harris. After describing his fears in anticipation of meeting the

---

[2] "War of the Rebellion: Official Records," No. 3, p. 40.
[3] "St. Louis Republican," July 13, quoted by Moore in "The Rebellion Record," Vol. II, p. 270.

enemy, and his relief at finding Tom Harris had decamped, he says: "It occurred to me at once that Harris had been as much afraid of me as I had been of him. This was a view of the question I had never taken before; but it was one I never forgot afterward." [4]

The northern Missouri experience for the 21st Illinois lasted four weeks—from July 10 to August 7. On July 18, General Pope took command of the northern district and by July 23, Grant must have had part of his command at Mexico, Missouri, since he enlisted a man from there.

On July 29, Grant got his first personal mention in the official records,[5] in being assigned by the district commander, General Pope, to command the Sub-district of Mexico, from Centralia on the north to Montgomery City on the south. This was decidedly a compliment, as Mexico was Pope's own headquarters town, where he wanted his best regiment and best man as regimental commander.

This period was one of useful learning: how to guard, how not to guard lines of rail communication in unfriendly or semi-hostile country, lessons which were to prove most valuable after Shiloh; how to deal with civilian inhabitants, friendly or otherwise. Pope made many mistakes of the sort, mistakes which Grant must have noted, for later, when in a like position, he avoided them.

Grant must soon have inspired his chief with a feeling of full confidence, for on August 5, Pope sent him to St. Louis, to General Frémont, commander of the department, with this letter of introduction:

I send down Colonel Grant, of the Twenty-first Illinois Volunteers, to inform you more fully than can be done by letter of the

4 "Personal Memoirs of U. S. Grant," Vol. I, pp. 200, 201.
5 W. R. 3:415.

policy I am pursuing here and its effects upon the people. He can also give full information concerning all matters of interest in this region. . . . Colonel Grant is an old army officer, thoroughly a gentleman, and an officer of intelligence and discretion.[6]

Grant was directed by Pope to return to Mexico "at once by special engine."[7]

The same day, presumably after this interview, Frémont's Special Orders, No. 26, directed Pope to "report to these Head-quarters immediately and bring one of his best regiments with him."[7] Two days later Special Orders, No. 35, reads: "Colonel Grant's regiment having arrived in this city, will proceed to Jefferson Barracks." This is the last of the half-dozen or so references to "Colonel Grant's regiment" in the war records.

[6] W. R. 114:201.
[7] W. R. 111:499.

Here we take leave of Grant the regimental commander. The regiment, indeed, went with him to Ironton—his first command as brigadier—but his own stay there was short, while the regiment remained and did not again come under his immediate command. But it is interesting to note that this regiment had a distinguished career and was known for its hard fighting, as became one which had looked to Grant for its first two months of training and leadership in the war. The story of its discipline and character is told by its losses in two battles:

	Killed	Wounded	Missing	Total
Stone's River	57	187	59	303
Chickamauga	22	70	146	238

The losses at Chickamauga were proportionately greater, as regiments in the Civil War had few replacements. Colonel Alexander, who succeeded Grant as regimental commander, was killed at Chickamauga, leading a charge of his regiment.

Brief as was Grant's career as a regimental commander—less than two months—it should not be accounted a mere convenient stepping-stone to higher rank, but as a vital and necessary part of his training.

There are two key positions in military organization, that of captain and that of colonel. The captain has the problem to solve of wielding his hundred or more men—many of them half educated, some of them rough, used to few restraints—into a psychological unity, responsive to his will; if he really succeeds, his company will want most to do precisely what he wills it to do, laying aside or overcoming the natural impulses arising from fear, fatigue, hunger, and the like.

The colonel's problem is far more complex and subtle. He no longer has the advantage of the prestige of an officer which the captain has in handling enlisted men. He is dealing with subordinates who are brother officers, as well educated and as accomplished technicians as he himself. He must support the better captains in their company training, and guide and assist those less able. He must prevent friendly rivalry between companies from growing into jealousy. Above all, he must preserve harmony among the officers of his regiment and create a regimental spirit which will inspire every officer and man to lay aside personal consideration and, when called upon, devote to his country's cause every ounce of effort he can summon.

All this requires a man of strong will-power, brains, tact, and experience. There can be little question that, with the practical knowledge gained during the Mexican War and his two years as company commander on the Pacific coast, Grant made a good colonel; the regiment's subsequent history is a testimonial to the spirit he infused into his men. That the experience as colonel is an essential one in the making of a great commander is almost axiomatic. It has often happened in our history that men have been appointed general officers from civil life or from staff branches who have never exercised command of both a company and a regiment, sometimes not even of a company. Such generals conduct operations under a severe handicap. Only a leader who understands the problems confronting his colonels and his captains can reach through them to the hearts of his men and pull victory out of defeat, at a Belmont, a Donelson, a Shiloh.

CHAPTER III

BRIGADIER IN MISSOURI

*In war one must consider that nothing has been
done so long as there remains anything to do.*
—TURENNE.

B Y Frémont's order [1] of the morning of August 8, Grant was
to proceed with his regiment to Pilot Knob (Ironton, Missouri) and take command of the forces already there, three regiments; to entrench, scour the country, send out spies, prepare for the contingency of a sudden movement, and report daily.

The same day he reached Ironton and assumed command. His daily reports tell the story of his activities and his thoughts, as he had not yet been taught by bitter experience to keep his own counsel. "I arrived here yesterday," he wrote on August 9. "Since that time I have studied the nature of the ground it may become necessary for me to defend, the character of the troops, and the means to do it with." [2]

Here we recognize the "regular": first the analysis of the terrain, his own forces, and his means of defense; next we expect to see him consider "the enemy," and we are not disappointed. "From all that I have yet learned," he continued, "from spies and loyally disposed citizens, I am led to believe there is no force within 30 miles of us that entertains the least idea of attacking this position, unless it should be left so weak as to invite an attack."

[1] W. R. 3:430.
[2] W. R. 3:432.

Thus in his very first officially recorded report in the war is indicated one of his most striking characteristics—his disposition to question the enemy's intentions and to doubt the offensive character of those intentions. At times this is to lead him into trouble; the tendency is basically essential for the independent commander,

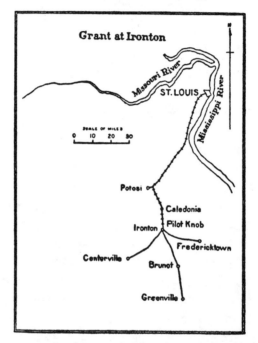

but to have too much of it, not held in leash by reason or intuition —as was the case with Pope and Hood in the Civil War—is to invite disaster.

But is Grant worldly-wise to tell his superior that the post is in no danger of attack? Is it likely to bring a speedy response to requisitions for needed supplies, equipment, and more troops to augment his command and make of it an effective field force? Scarcely! In this report selflessness and impersonality are evidenced. Grant does not here and never does—in the war, at least

—consider his own future, but only the cause of the country. That cause demands that the superior be correctly informed regarding the situation, and Grant informs him precisely as he sees it.

It was the panicky appeals of Frémont, Halleck, and others for more troops, more troops, that finally accumulated for Grant's use about Cairo, Illinois, the force that was to wreck the Confederate defense of the Mississippi. But Grant never made such an appeal himself, because he was never panicky and it never occurred to him to act or write from purely personal motives.

Coming now to his own troops, Grant speaks again as the regular and is under no illusions:

It is fortunate, too [that the enemy has no idea of attacking], for many of the officers seem to have so little command over their men, and military duty seems to be done so loosely, that I fear at present that our resistance would be in inverse ratio to the number of troops to resist with.

One regular officer to season three regiments is not much; however, when that regular is also the commander he can do a great deal, and Grant writes with entire self-confidence to reassure Frémont: "In two days more, however, I expect to have a very different state of affairs and to improve it continuously."

Next he takes up the conditions in the surrounding country:

Spies are said to be seen every day within a few miles of our camp; marauding parties are infesting the country, pillaging Union men, within 10 miles of here. At present I can spare no force; in fact, have no suitable troops to drive these guerillas out and afford to Union citizens of this place or neighborhood the protection I feel they should have.

Lastly, with respect to his needs for the "contingency of a sudden movement," mentioned in Frémont's orders of August 8, he reports:

Artillery and cavalry are much needed,[3] and the quartermaster's department is yet quite deficient. The number of teams would scarcely suffice for the use of this as a military post without making any forward movement, and the horses of those we have are many of them barefoot and without forage.

"But," adds this man who not only has been quartermaster of his regiment in the Mexican War, but knows what the authority of a general officer is and how to use it, "I have taken steps to remedy those latter defects."

The analysis of this first of Grant's officially recorded letters shows us a man frank, clear-sighted, critical, master of the situation, of his command, of himself, and with the ability to express his thoughts clearly and tersely. It is a letter of great promise; the writer is likely to travel far, if he lives and preserves his simplicity and his balance.

His report of the day following gives additional information regarding the enemy which Grant is "disposed to think reliable. General Hardee is at Greenville [forty miles south of Ironton] with 2,000 men, and six or eight field pieces, with 1,000 more troops thrown forward . . . near Brunot."

In modern general staffs one of the chief sections, intelligence, is devoted mainly to securing, classifying, and analyzing information regarding the enemy. In the Civil War, each general had to be his own "G-2" or go without—except McClellan, who had Allan Pinkerton of detective fame, to his own discomfiture in the Peninsula. Many were the generals who failed primarily because they could not appreciate the situation about them and had no organized staff section to study it and keep them informed. A man who comprehends existing conditions may of course still go wrong, but if he utterly misunderstands them, as McClellan and so many others did, it is almost a miracle if he does not go

---

[3] These, only Frémont can supply, if he chooses to do so!

wrong. How Grant acquired his faculty for weighing and judging, we have no data to show, but at the very outset he had it
and never failed to preserve in the back of his head the latest
revised estimate of the enemy's "position"—meaning: strength,
position, intentions.

The second report (August 10) suggests that, Ironton being
"a healthy locality," some newly organized regiments might be
sent there for "drill and discipline." This would enable Grant to
use the riper troops for scouting parties. He is feeling his oats
a bit. He again, "urgently" this time, recommends that cavalry
and artillery be sent him; but provides an alternative: if "equipment complete for one hundred mounted men could be spared
. . . they could be efficiently used." In other words, he would
make his own cavalry!

In his third report (August 11) the two days in which he expected to get his command in hand being now up, he begins to
act aggressively:

Since my report of yesterday, in addition to the ordinary picket
guards established, one company has been sent toward Caledonia,
two companies . . . for the protection of the railroad, four companies to Potosi [Missouri], the mounted Home Guards and two
spies, to ascertain the position, &c., of the Confederate troops.[4]

He then relates some experiences with marauders, and adds
regarding a point in his instructions which he failed to report
on before: "Nothing scarcely can be done toward fortifying this
place, for the want of tools to work with. This matter has not
been reported before, because two companies of engineers were
expected, and with them all tools required."

Fortifying always was Grant's bête noire! His very soul craved
action, not defense, not even an active defense—though he had to
learn that much at least.

4 W. R. 3:130.

On August 12, Grant reported the results of further scouting and asked about the censorship of the mails—another function, nowadays, of the general-staff intelligence section which then fell to the commanding generals personally—and added: "I am entirely without orders for my guidance in matters like the above, and without recent Acts of Congress which bear upon them." [5]

The commander making war in his own country has, indeed, many troublesome questions to decide regarding the civilian population. In deciding them he seldom receives "guidance," unless he goes wrong; when he usually is removed. General Grant never needed guidance in these matters.

On the same day we find his first recorded instructions to a subordinate, a major commanding an "expedition to Potosi," which throws an amusing side-light on certain of Grant's problems and on his canny solution of some of them:

Press into service as many teams as you want from secessionists, who will be pointed out by Union men of character, and march up by way of ——. You will do all you can to capture the party of rebels who are infesting the country through which you pass, but be careful about crediting reports you receive from citizens. When it is necessary to get provisions for your men, you will take them from active secessionists, if practicable; if not practicable, from Union or law-abiding citizens, giving an order on the post commissary here for the pay. Compel persons whose teams you press to send teamsters to take the teams back. You have my private instructions how to conduct this pressing business so as to make it as little offensive as possible. [6]

Also on the same day (August 12) Frémont sent a letter of instructions to Grant. For the purpose of keeping both his flanks open, Grant was directed "to send one column to Centreville and another to Fredericktown" and take possession of both places. At the same time he was "required to send out, with all necessary precaution, a moving column on the road to Greenville, whose duty it will be to ascertain the enemy's forces, movements and intentions." [7]

Frémont also stated that he was sending a regiment and fifty Illinois cavalry to occupy Potosi, which station would be under Grant's command.

Obviously, Frémont in his order for the occupation of Centerville, twenty-five miles to the southwest, and Fredericktown, twenty miles east, with green troops under improvised officers, and with a hostile force equal to Grant's own only twenty-five miles south—a force commanded by a trained ex-regular, Hardee—was committing the "favorite tactical sin of the beginner," dispersion. What should Grant do? Should he obey, and sin also, or hedge and play safe?

What he might have done had the circumstances remained the same we can only guess. But the very night that Frémont wrote his letter the Confederates occupied Fredericktown with three thousand troops, while Grant learned "reliably" that Hardee with five thousand men—Grant now had four thousand—was advancing on Ironton. Grant made no detachments, but prepared for defense and wrote calmly to Frémont: "I express you the facts [stated above], and leave it to the general commanding whether in his judgment more troops should not be sent." [8]

Frémont was not so calm when he received this letter. He had scarcely yet recovered from one disaster—General Lyon's defeat and death near Springfield, Missouri, on August 10—and now another appeared headed his way. Perhaps his conscience troubled him, as it should have, because instead of responding to

[7] W. R. 3:436.
[8] W. R. 3:440. The letter is of course, according to custom, addressed to Frémont's adjutant-general.

Lyon's [9] appeal for reinforcements when the latter found himself greatly outnumbered, Frémont had put his reserve troops on transports and gone puttering with them down Cairo way,[10] serving no useful purpose.

This time he ordered reinforcements—two regiments and two guns—to Grant and telegraphed a frantic appeal to the President: "General Grant, commanding at Ironton, attacked yesterday at 6 by a force reported at 13,000. Railroad seized by the enemy. . . . Will you issue peremptory orders to [the governor of Ohio] and other governors to send me instantly any disposable troops and arms?" [11] An amusing request for a department commander to make to the President of the United States. But, save the President, few of these earlier Civil War characters seem to have been blessed with a sense of humor.[12] Perhaps that was why so many broke under the strain.

Where did Frémont get his information, "Grant . . . attacked yesterday at 6 by . . . 13,000"? Not from Grant and not from any document in the official records. We can only surmise that he may have listened to and acted on some rumor; not having received the caution which Grant gave his subordinate: "Be careful about crediting reports you get from civilians."

None the less, this apparently foolish telegram from Frémont was to affect seriously the future of Grant and the course of the war; for the regiments sent in response to it—governors were notified by the War Department to forward all available forces! —were to make possible the creation and seasoning of a strategic reserve at Cairo which was eventually to lead to a successful issue for Grant and the Union at Donelson and Shiloh.

    [9] W. R. 3:408, 424.
    [10] Frank Moore, "The Rebellion Record: A Diary of American Events," Vol. II, p. 467.
    [11] Aug. 14, W. R. 3:441.
    [12] President Lincoln replied, Aug. 15: "Been answering your messages ever since day before yesterday." W. R. 3:443.

Getting back to the facts, we find the situation at Ironton on this day, August 14, unchanged. Grant wrote: "Since my report of yesterday, two spies have come in and report the position of the enemy about the same as yesterday. . . . To-night I have sent out toward Fredericktown, Colonel Hecker, with all his regiment not otherwise on duty. . . . " Some response, though in a modified way, to Frémont's instructions of the twelfth.[13]

On August 15, Grant noted the arrival of two regiments of reinforcements and at once ordered out two regiments (one of them the 21st Illinois) to advance on Brunot, by two different roads. He stated that he expected to go with his own former regiment. Whether he did or not, there is nothing to indicate save that after the evening of August 16 he made no further report to Frémont from Ironton. In the report of that date he says the regiment sent toward Greenville is twelve miles out on the road and is to be reinforced. Eight companies are at or near Fredericktown.

Grant, however, issued one more routine order at Ironton, on August 18, on which day General Prentiss appeared with instructions from Frémont to take over the command. The adjutant-general explained afterward that the order was issued under the misapprehension that Prentiss ranked Grant. It is possible that Frémont, having presumably seen more of Prentiss than of Grant, felt that he would prefer him at the danger-point. It is not clear whether Grant was expected to remain under Prentiss at Ironton or go elsewhere. By military custom at that time he could not serve under a junior, hence he reported back to Frémont at St. Louis, and applied for leave of absence to return home.

To Grant his relief, and the way it came about, was a piece of rank injustice as unexpected as a stab in the back. To have done his utmost; to have in ten days brought order, discipline,

---

[13] W. R. 3:442.

and organization out of the chaos at his station; then, just as he
was beginning active operations in the field—operations which
his own exertions and work alone had made possible—to find
himself, suddenly and without explanations, superseded, was
bitter. Yet it is often by such blows that is shaped the character
of those ultimately to be favored of fortune.

General Frémont did not approve of letting Grant take a leave
at this time. On August 7, when the newly promoted brigadier
reported to him, Frémont's eyes had been cast Mississippi-ward.
He had then but recently returned from Bird's Point, Missouri,
opposite Cairo on the Mississippi, and his thoughts were preoccupied with delivering or warding off blows in that direction.
Perhaps because of this he appears to have taken a merely
academic interest in the operations of General Lyon in western
Missouri, as something which did not directly concern himself.
Rude was his awakening, therefore, when, on August 10, Lyon's
forces met defeat and Lyon himself was killed. Frémont was
shocked into realization that something had to be done in the
West!

He had not yet learned fully to appreciate Grant; nor was he
ever to discover, as did Halleck, the possibility of riding on
Grant's shoulders to the post of Lincoln's chief of staff in
Washington; but he saw the man as obviously a good general, if
not as a brilliant one, and so, to stem the tide of the victorious
Confederate and Missouri State troops in southwestern Missouri,
and at the same time to safeguard the most important city (next
to Kansas City) on the Missouri River, Grant was sent to command at Jefferson City. In order, however, not to disturb the
territorial assignments of districts previously organized, he was
placed under the jurisdiction of Pope, commanding the troublesome northern half of Missouri.

Grant's instructions from Pope are not of record. Presumably they were orally given at Pope's headquarters, still in St. Louis; but they can be surmised from Grant's correspondence during the week that he remained at his second post.

Here at Jefferson City, there was no tactical situation to deal with, such as had existed at Ironton—unless we wish to consider the firing of guerrilla raiders into railroad trains such—but there was the same lack of organization that Grant had found at his earlier post and the remedying of which was his first and chief concern. He wrote on August 22:

During yesterday I visited the camps of the different commands about this city, and selected locations for troops yet to arrive. I find a great deficiency in everything for the comfort and efficiency of an army. Most of the troops are without clothing, camp and garrison equipage. Ammunition was down to about ten rounds of cartridges and for the artillery, none . . .

There are no rations to issue. The mules sent some time since are guarded in a lot, no effort being made to get them into teams, and a general looseness prevailing.

I have fitted out an expedition of 350 men to scour the country around where the cars were fired into day before yesterday. . . . The party in pursuit will subsist off of the community through which they pass. Stringent instructions have been given as to how supplies are to be got. From reports received here the whole of this country is in a state of ferment. They are driving out the Union men and appropriating their property. The best force to put this down would be mounted Home Guards [14] . . .

and he adds recommendations concerning their organization.

Nowhere in the war records are there to be found any complaints from Grant regarding personal hard knocks unfairly received; any attempts to justify himself—in other words, to build up a purely "paper record" of efficiency, a practice so common in

[14] W. R. 3:452.

all armies. Nor could one dream from the above letter that Grant had just been taken from a front-line command, facing an actively maneuvering, if not a fighting enemy, and sent to what was relatively a rear area, and in a manner which no soldier could help but feel was a stigma upon his good name, whatever the motive. We must admire this self-control, and still more must we admire the intense concentration with which the man at once took up his new problem, dealing with it all the more effectively for his experiences at Ironton.

The eagle eye which had envisioned in a day's time the exact status of his military command, and the mind which had immediately understood the nature of the civilian problem within his assigned territorial limits, had missed no important point. Indeed, his proposed solution of the civilian problem—so radically different from Pope's—showed that he was neither blinded by the policy of his superior nor afraid to suggest to him a saner method.

The writer of such a letter may be no genius, but it cannot be denied that he shows himself a practical man, of quick perceptions, of common sense, and of cool, balanced judgment.

Grant's next report, of August 23, added the view of the practical man on the ever insistent harping of his superiors upon "fortification." Obviously trench-digging was not the initial note to be struck in the building of a victorious, a conquering army; and to build such, and build it quickly, was just what the North must do, or fail in its objective—the desired reunion of the States.

I am not fortifying here at all [he says]. With the picket guard and other duty coming upon the men of this command, there is but little time left for drilling. Drill and discipline are more necessary for the men than fortifications. Another difficulty in the way of fortifying is that I have no engineer officer to direct it; no time to attend to it myself, and very little disposition to gain a "Pillow notoriety" for a branch of the service that I have forgotten all about.

Here his indignation, which can fairly be characterized as "righteous," almost carries him beyond the bounds of traditional military courtesy in addressing his superior! His report of August 25 indicates that his spy service was beginning to be effective:

From a spy who came in yesterday I learn that [hostile] companies are being organized in all the counties west of here. Some of these bands are acquiring considerable proportions. Many troops have crossed the Missouri River from the north within the last two weeks, and are joining the forces on this side.[15]

The real Grant of later days comes out in the words, "If I had sufficient force, all that could be stopped."

His last full report from Jefferson City covers a wide range of subjects, including spy reports and arrests of citizens under suspicion. There is fair indication, however, that Grant was not one of the witch-burning type, for, after describing the return of a detachment with parties arrested for firing on passing railroad trains, he added: "But from all the evidence they were the most innocent men in the county. I had them liberated." [16]

Also, as evidence that the eye of the one-time quartermaster is never too much occupied with civilian affairs, operations, instructions to subordinates, and administration to keep watch on his transportation facilities, we find:

I am getting teams broken in as rapidly as possible. I have to report that the harness sent here is entirely too light and very inferior in quality. The chains are so light and brittle that they snap with the least strain. I have been compelled to order the purchase of new traces here.[17]

15 W. R. 3:454.
16 W. R. 3:463.
17 W. R. 114:217.

Grant made one more report [18] before he was recalled to St. Louis to take charge of affairs in a larger field; but it was brief and shed no added light on his mind.

The purpose in giving these extracts is, primarily, to portray —as much as possible in his own words—the real Grant as he was entering upon his wartime career, and only secondarily to set forth the relatively unimportant events in Missouri at that time, though of these the reports in their entirety present a rather good delineation. As the war went on, Grant wrote less and less in quantity, though his powers of expression constantly improved. In the Cairo period, particularly, we find no such striking picture of him as flashes from these earlier letters.

There only remains to be added that if the Grant who emerges from them be compared with the other officers of Civil War fame, in either of the opposing armies, similarly revealed, he stands head and shoulders above them all, with the possible exception of Lee. That he did not earlier rise to the chief command-in-the-field was due to a series of events so peculiar as to lead to the surmise that some beneficent directing Power deemed it better for the final and enduring peaceful reunion of the then divided States that the war should not end too quickly, as with Grant sooner at the head it might have done.

When General Prentiss was ordered to Ironton on August 15, he was directed to make secure the St. Louis-Ironton Railroad, make reconnaissances on Greenville, occupy Fredericktown and Centerville, "open communication with St. Genevieve and Cape Girardeau, and keep the same open by constant scouting parties." [19]

Evidently Frémont had confidence in Prentiss's ability! But

18 Aug. 28, W. R. 3:465.
19 W. R. 3:443.

what Prentiss actually accomplished, we do not know, as his reports—if such were made—are not recorded. Frémont wrote Prentiss again, on August 20, saying he had had no report from him, informing him that a Confederate force (three thousand to five thousand strong) was moving from Charleston on Commerce, and directing him to "detach a force of your command sufficient, in concert with our troops at Cape Girardeau, to prevent the enemy from taking possession of Commerce and inter▾pting the free navigation of the Mississippi."

Five days later, on August 25, Frémont again addressed Prentiss at Ironton to the effect that "four thousand rebels are fortifying Benton, Mo.," and directing him "to move forthwith" with all his "disposable force to Dallas." From that point he was to coöperate with other forces sent out from Cape Girardeau, under Colonel Smith, "all to be united under your command." [20]

Prentiss, in pursuance of these orders, left Ironton on the morning of August 27, as Frémont was informed—not by Prentiss himself but in a pathetic letter from Colonel Bland, left in command there. [21]

Whether Frémont was displeased over the dearth of reports from Prentiss or had come to doubt the military capacity of that officer or wanted a firmer hand in control of the Cape Girardeau operation, we can only surmise. In any case, Grant was suddenly recalled to St. Louis on August 28, given the same information regarding the "four thousand rebels" reported as fortifying Benton, received copies of the orders previously given to Prentiss and Smith, and was instructed to proceed to Cape Girardeau, assume command, act in accordance with all the foregoing dispositions, and "when the junction with the forces of General Prentiss is effected, you will take command of the combined forward move-

20 W. R. 3:453.
21 W. R. 3:462.

ment." [22] Nor was he to escape from the customary instructions to fortify: "Finally, I recommend you to do everything to promote the work of fortification commenced at Cairo, Bird's Point, Cape Girardeau and Ironton."

Frémont's orders also informed Grant of another expedition (under Colonel Waagner, chief of artillery at Cairo) to seize Belmont with Colonel McArthur's regiment and from there to move also on Charleston "with the view of coöperating with the forces from Ironton and Cape Girardeau towards Benton," an expedition destined indirectly to throw the State of Kentucky into the arms of the Union. But of that later.

As a military operation, considering the distances, no more fatuous combined movement could have been conceived. Secrecy was impossible. If the Confederate leader had had, as was reported, a force of four thousand men at Benton, he could have taken his time in choosing whether to attack one of the advancing columns or retreat. If, as proved to be the case, Benton were occupied by a mere picket, it was like sending three men each armed with a hammer to swat a fly!

Grant arrived at Cape Girardeau in the late afternoon of August 30, and found that Colonel Marsh and a detachment of all arms—four battalions, two guns, fifty troopers—had marched the evening before on Jackson, Missouri, taking two days' rations. Colonel Marsh had found no enemy in Jackson and had heard nothing of the column under General Prentiss.

Grant's first measure was to organize for Marsh's command a wagon-train containing three days' additional rations. His first report deals with the military situation, with the precise number of teams, wagons, harnesses, mules, and with the fortifications which he had inspected that afternoon and judged as "being pushed forward with vigor." Apparently even he was convinced that at this point fortifying was in order.

[22] W. R. 3:141.

Prentiss appeared on September 1, his command evidently having reached Jackson in five days, an average of twelve miles a day—good time for raw troops. Then arose a question of precedence, amusing to us now, and possible only in an unmilitary or semi-military nation, but interesting on account of the contrast between the conduct of Prentiss here and that of Grant when superseded in command at Ironton.

It will be recalled that Prentiss had been informed by Frémont in the initial order for the movement that when the columns met he, Prentiss, should command the whole. On August 28, when Frémont decided to send Grant to Cape Girardeau he caused a letter to be despatched to Prentiss informing him:

Brigadier-General Grant has been directed to proceed to Cape Girardeau, assume command of the forces there, and coöperate with the troops moving from Ironton. When you were ordered to Ironton and took the place of General Grant, it was under the impression that his appointment was of a later date than your own. By the official list published it appears, however, that he is your senior in rank. He will, therefore, upon effecting a conjunction with your troops, take command of the whole expedition.[23]

Had this letter reached Prentiss, his action on meeting Grant might have been other than it was; but, written the day after his column left Ironton, it probably had not reached him, and in consequence he, expressly directed in the orders of August 25 which he had received, to "take command of the whole on the conjunction of the forces at or near Benton," was not disposed to yield that command to a brigadier whom he had previously displaced in a front-line command.

Prentiss, an Illinois militiaman, had been a lieutenant and a captain in the Mexican War. He had begun the Civil War as colonel of the 7th Illinois, but soon after was made a militia brigadier-general of the "three-months" troops. His commission

23 W. R. 3:142.

as Brigadier-General of Volunteers dated from May 17, as did Grant's. But as he had actually been de facto a brigadier months before Grant, it was, not unnaturally, difficult for him to see why Grant should now rank him. The story is best told in Grant's own words:

(1) From headquarters, Cape Girardeau, Missouri, September 1, 1861, to Frémont:

General Prentiss has just arrived. Will move the column under his command to Sikeston as soon as possible. I will go to Bird's Point and take command there, and push out from that point.

(2) From headquarters United States Forces, Cairo, September 2, to Frémont:

I left Cape Girardeau at 10 o'clock this morning. General Prentiss raised the question of rank, and finally refused to obey my orders. Last night he tendered his resignation, after being refused a leave of absence, but said he would command as directed until your decision. To-day he positively refused, and reported himself in arrest. I have placed Colonel Cook in command. . . . I will forward by to-morrow's mail a copy of all orders issued to General Prentiss, together with charges.

(3) From headquarters District of Southeastern Missouri, Cairo, September 3, to Brigadier-General B. M. Prentiss, Cape Girardeau:

Having received from General Frémont orders for you to proceed to St. Louis, I of course decline placing you in arrest. Having sent charges to headquarters, Department of the West, against you, as in duty bound, I send you a copy of them. In justice to myself I must say that in this matter I have no personal feeling, but have acted strictly from a sense of duty, and, should it be General Frémont's wish, am perfectly willing to see the charges quashed and the whole matter buried in oblivion. A sacrifice of my own feelings is no sacrifice when the good of the country calls for it.

Some of the despatches sent here for telegraphing by one of the newspaper correspondents accompanying you were of such a character, and so detrimental to the good of the service, that I felt it my duty to suppress them.[24]

Prentiss was restored to duty by Frémont, employed for a time in Missouri, sent by Halleck to report to Grant shortly before Shiloh, commanded a division, and was captured by the Confederates in that battle. Later he was exchanged, and was eventually detailed as a member of the famous court-martial to try the case of Major-General Fitz-John Porter.

As for Grant, it may be pointed out that while he had "right" on his side in the Prentiss matter, the fact that Prentiss twice changed his mind with regard to obeying the other's orders suggests that had Grant been a little more tactful in dealing with the first general officer to come under his command, so distressing an incident might not have occurred. He was so intensely patriotic and so truly disinterested, that he was always ready to ignore, in his official capacity, his own personal feelings; and, particularly in his earlier career, he expected the same impersonality in others. He eventually came to realize that however loyal the run of men may be to a high and noble cause, in most cases there are likely to occur weak moments when personal considerations override. When this happens, a little diplomacy is better than a court-martial. As a first lesson in the need for tact in the exercise of higher command the Benton incident was no doubt not without its value to Grant.

The Prentiss affair and other pressing matters caused Grant to postpone and finally to abandon the projected advance on Sikeston. Here was once more a favorable turn, for the North, of the wheel of Fortune; had the movement been carried into execution, Grant would presumably have been away from his post of command at one of the crucial moments of the war, when prompt action by the local Union commander was most essential to ultimate success.

In what has gone before no attempt has been made to give the whole picture of which Grant's operations formed a part—this not only from lack of space but because until he reached Cairo, Grant had in no sense played a vital part in the war. Our interest in his earlier career is mainly personal as we note the development of his character and of his understanding of the basic principles of military operations and leadership. But on September 4, 1861, when he assumed command of the District of Southeastern Missouri with headquarters at Cairo, Illinois, he stepped from the circumference of the Western circle to its center. To understand his rôle there, it will be necessary to consider briefly some of the conditions confronting him in his new post.

CHAPTER IV

THE CONFEDERATE FIASCO IN THE WEST

> It seems incredible, and yet it has happened a
> hundred times, that troops have been divided and
> separated merely through a mysterious feeling of
> conventional manner, without any clear perception
> of the reason.—CLAUSEWITZ.

IN looking back on any war it is always easy to be wiser than
the participants. But in assigning blame for mistakes, it is well
to bear in mind that most may be classified under one of three
heads:

(a) Mistakes due to acting on erroneous information.
(b) Mistakes due to acting upon wrong principles, or the
failure to apply correct principles properly.
(c) Mistakes due to poor judgment.

No one can be blamed for action based on wrong information, especially if he has done his best to discover the facts. Nor
can he be blamed for poor judgment. All men cannot be expected
to have equally good judgment, and all we can ask of any commander is that he shall do his best. But what we have a right to
expect from the trained executive in any line of human endeavor
is that he shall act upon well-known and accepted principles
when these apply to the case in hand.

Such a principle is that of unity of command in any given
theater of war. Yet even here it may be said in extenuation of
President Davis's course of action that it was probably not so

much lack of knowledge of the military principle involved as it was a failure to perceive that the Mississippi Valley constituted, in its entirety, a single military problem and not a half-dozen.

There is this also to be said: preoccupied with affairs in the East, he might quite naturally have forgotten that the time had arrived when the initial separate military efforts by the individual seceding States should be better coördinated. It may be, however, that President Davis, himself a West Point graduate and a regimental commander in the Mexican War, was a trifle cautious in delegating authority and trusted overmuch to his own knowledge of military matters.

The personalities who exercised the half-dozen separate commands were also, unfortunately for the outcome desired, not able to act in concert; nor did they always show good judgment, though for that we cannot blame Mr. Davis, since in war a leader cannot fashion or remake his subordinates; the most he can do is to juggle a bit so as to bring the strong man opposite the hard job where success will count most.

Davis's first measure was to divide the Mississippi River into two departments: Department No. 1, with headquarters at New Orleans (General Twiggs); Department No. 2, headquarters at Memphis (General Polk).

Department No. 2 embraced only the western part of Tennessee (west and south of the Tennessee River) and eastern Arkansas (east of the Black River). Up to July 23, the Tennessee State troops had not yet been turned over to the Confederacy, though their commander, Major-General Pillow, had agreed to move across the Mississippi to New Madrid, Missouri, and place himself, with six thousand Tennesseeans, under Polk's orders. Also at New Madrid were three thousand Missourians, Southern sympathizers who had been organized by General M. Jefferson Thompson, whose status it is hard to define. He generally acted under orders from Polk and Pillow, but appears to have disobeyed them in obedience to orders from the deposed Governor or Vice-Governor of Missouri.

Here, then, were three distinct commands on the upper Mississippi itself: Polk, Pillow (for Pillow deliberately disobeyed Polk when he felt like it), and Thompson. The remainder of the State of Arkansas was scarcely better organized: Brigadier-General Hardee was given command of that portion of the State west of the White and Black rivers and north of the Arkansas River to the Missouri line. Nominally he was under Polk, but Polk had little more influence with him than with Pillow. His troops were four thousand Arkansans; his mission, "to watch over and protect the country within the limits referred to, also that part of Missouri contiguous thereto."

Brigadier-General McCullough had been assigned as early as May 13 to command the "Indian Territory lying west of Arkansas and south of Kansas." His command was to consist of one regiment of foot, from Louisiana; one regiment mounted, from Arkansas; one regiment mounted, from Texas—which however, did not arrive till late summer. His mission was "to guard that [Indian] territory against invasion from Kansas or elsewhere."

It appeared on his approach to the aforesaid territory that the Indians objected to being protected. They had declared their neutrality in the war and, while sympathetic toward the South, were prepared to fight any intruder. Hence McCullough held his command in western Arkansas and twice applied for command of the territory, but apparently was never formally assigned to it. Finally he crossed into Missouri on the request of the governor of that State and played rather a brilliant rôle in the two campaigns in July and August, in the second of which, at Wilson's Creek, General Lyon was killed.

Lastly among the Arkansas commands came the brigade of

three thousand State militia under the militia Brigadier-General Pearce. He and McCullough were operating much together, but they were mostly at loggerheads, as "allies" frequently are. When, eventually, Pearce's brigade was ordered mustered into the Confederate service minus General Pearce who was not wanted, his men all disbanded and went home. Pearce was blamed for this defection, but he says pathetically of his men:

They had been in the Army from two to five months and had never received any pay or clothing, and when the board said they could honorably leave the service and left it to their choice, being naked and barefooted, the natural impulse to each individual was, "I must go home." [1]

Also to be counted among the eight commands in the Mississippi Valley was the National Guard of the State of Missouri, commanded by General Price, often by Governor Jackson in person. It consisted of anywhere from three thousand to fifteen thousand men, according to circumstances.

Hopeless as this organization was from a scientific point of view, the situation might yet have been saved for the Confederacy had the various commanders been militarily efficient, or even had they been imbued with that fine spirit of mutual coöperation which so often saves divided commands. Thus to complete the picture of the Confederate forces in the theater of war into the center of which (at Cairo) General Grant suddenly found himself apparently fortuitously pitched on September 2, we must consider briefly the training, experience, and characteristics of these men.

General David E. Twiggs had been a general in the United States Army, in command of the Department of Texas, and had voluntarily surrendered his command to the State authorities when Texas "seceded," for which action he had been summarily dis-

[1] W. R. 3:716.

missed from the service. A man who has betrayed one trust is scarcely likely to prove worthy of another; and in addition Twiggs was old and infirm and could hardly leave his chair. He was relieved in the fall of 1861, but the lack of a strong directing hand in the chief Confederate city of the West, New Orleans, during the crucial mobilization days of the war, was of itself enough to foreshadow the early disaster which overtook the Confederacy in this theater.

Major-General Leonidas Polk, Episcopal Bishop of Louisiana, was fifty-five at the beginning of the war. He had been graduated from West Point Military Academy in 1827 and had entered the service as a lieutenant, but resigned after a few months, to study for the ministry. After his ordination poor health compelled him to travel for a year and eventually, unable to stand the regular work of a parish, he settled down to the active management of a farm in Tennessee. In 1838 he was elected Missionary Bishop of the Southwest and traveled extensively through the region, with which no one was better acquainted than he. He was elected Bishop of Louisiana in 1841, but still found time to engage in sugar- and cotton-raising in addition to his diocesan work.

Thus Polk had been all his life an active outdoor man and a man of affairs, and also knew from his West Point years the rudiments of drill and discipline. He had not sought to enter the military service, but had gone to Richmond to visit the Louisiana troops in his episcopal capacity and while there had called on President Davis to urge that a competent general be sent to take charge of the Mississippi Valley. To this Davis responded by offering the command to Polk himself. He was influenced in this not only by the fact of Polk's West Point education—though the President took that very seriously, having had the same, himself—but by the facts that Polk had had a many-sided experience as an executive, knew the country, and had a wonderfully commanding personality. And notwithstanding his total lack of practical military experience or knowledge of the technique of operations, he was by no means the poorest of the Confederate generals.

Major-General Gideon J. Pillow began the war as commander of the militia forces of the State of Tennessee. He was the same age as General Polk, fifty-five, a lawyer by profession. During the Mexican War he had gained command of the Tennessee Volunteers as brigadier-general, and had been the stormy petrel of both Taylor's Monterey campaign and Scott's march to the capital. He is described as a trim, agile man with a handsome face and restless black eyes, a consummate politician of the intriguing sort, but never a soldier. He was governed chiefly by his emotions; each day brought him fresh ideas which he set forth in an unending series of letters, with numerous and flowery reasons why he no longer should do what he had yesterday proposed doing, but instead, something else. With him everything was to take place to-morrow, never to-day, and there were always countless excuses to postpone action.

Mr. Sam Tate of Memphis, in an appealing letter to his Congressman on August 23, says:

> Our army matters here are in a terrible condition . . . Polk and Pillow are at loggerheads—Polk giving a command and Pillow countermanding it . . . Pillow, I learn, is acting on his own hook; . . . denies Polk's authority to give him orders. . . . He says he intends to fight his own fight first before he joins command with Hardee or anyone else.[2]

Judging from Pillow's own letters as given in the records, this contemporary portrait of him does not appear overdrawn.

Brigadier-General William J. Hardee, regular officer, had served as captain in the Mexican War and had written a book on

2 W. R. 4:396.

tactics. But he was old, unresourceful, and lacking in initiative. It was he who commanded the Confederate forces in front of Grant at Ironton, forces with which he did nothing but organize petty raids. He was a fair subordinate but as a commander he always had reasons why he could not march to help out a neighboring column and why he could do nothing himself because no one would come to help him. His influence in this theater of war was almost nil.

Brigadier-General Benjamin McCullough, forty-seven years old, was a Tennesseean who had migrated to Texas. He enlisted in the Texas Artillery Corps in 1836 and later made a brilliant record as a captain of rangers in the Mexican War. Wherever he may have learned it, he knew his art of war better than Grant at the start; but he was not a West Pointer and so his ability was mistrusted by President Davis, although at Wilson's Creek he won the only striking success that the Confederates ever gained west of the Mississippi.

Regarding General N. Bart Pearce the records give little information, save that he terminated his three months' career as general of the Arkansas militia distrusted by both his governor and the Confederate War Department. Nevertheless it may be urged in his behalf that at least he showed a spirit of coöperation—a spirit which seemed absent in both Hardee and Pillow—joining his command to that of McCullough.

General Sterling Price was commander of the Missouri State militia, composed of Southern sympathizers and organized by Governor Jackson's orders for the avowed purpose of fighting for the Southern cause. He was a really able man, as his subsequent career showed, but at the start had little knowledge of the technique of command.

Brigadier-General M. Jefferson Thompson, a citizen of St. Joseph, Missouri, conceived the idea of establishing inside the

Confederate lines a rendezvous for exiled Missourians who desired to enlist in the Southern cause. He did so and was made
their commander. He proved himself a veritable genius in minor
harassing operations, and had he been intelligently used and
directed he might possibly have become the Stonewall Jackson
of the West. Unfortunately for his side, such was not the case.
During the crucial period his command was for the most part
at Bloomfield, Missouri, in front of Pillow and diagonally in
front of Hardee. Pillow assumed the rôle of director of Thompson's operations, and what Thompson managed to accomplish,
despite the incoherent blasts of orders and counter-orders from
Pillow, does him the greatest credit. The fact that he with his
three thousand men neutralized much of the time the efforts of
three to five times that number of Union troops showed the
possibilities of the case. It may be recalled that the combined
movement of the Ironton and Cape Girardeau troops—to take
charge of which Grant was sent by Frémont to Cairo—was
entirely based on the hope of catching Thompson!

This frittering away of the military means of combat in small
uncoördinated commands, each with virtually a passive-defensive
mission, was building a house of cards fated to be toppled over
the moment a strong man appeared on the opposite side. Even
had the Northern and Southern forces been equal, the flimsy
Southern structure was bound to collapse at the first strong stress
at any point. That this did not happen sooner was due to the
lack of any Northern general to cognize and take advantage of
the opportunity presented, until Grant was sent to the front line.
That he did not bring this to pass before he did was due not
to hesitation on his part, but to the indecision and lack of vision
of his superiors, Frémont and Halleck—and in Halleck's case
perhaps also to a slight distrust of Grant's real ability, a distrust
which was not dissipated until after Vicksburg, if even then.

But lack of coördination was not the only instance of poor Confederate management in the West. The Western theater bore a striking resemblance to the Eastern in one respect: it would have been possible to use the State of Arkansas for inroads against Missouri precisely as the Shenandoah Valley was so successfully used by the Confederacy for threats against Maryland, Pennsylvania, and the Northern capital.

Arkansas itself the North could not penetrate with any considerable force. The only railroads in southern Missouri were the St. Louis-Ironton and the St. Louis-Rollo. From these points to the Arkansas frontier was farther than any force larger than could live off the country would be able to supply itself over the poor roads. On the other hand, the South had the best of military lines of communication, for those days, in the Arkansas and White rivers, the latter navigable at all times to within sixty miles of the Missouri frontier. But while Arkansas was too sparsely settled to permit a hostile invading army to live off the country, Missouri was quite otherwise. In addition, a Southern invading force in Missouri had the great advantage that a very large percentage of the population was in sympathy with the Confederacy. Then, too, there was the Missouri (Confederate) militia.

But to all these possibilities the Confederate leadership appears to have been quite blind. It wished Missouri to join the Confederacy, but it never would extend to that State a helping military hand, a gesture which could have been so easily made and would have been so potent in its results.

The Confederacy wanted Arkansans as soldiers, and troops were raised in Arkansas, but their leaders were imbued with the conviction that these troops were solely for the defense of the State and were not to be ordered out of it. How easy it would have been to show them that the best, the only effective, defense of Arkansas was to make Missouri a Confederate State *in fact,* as it already was largely in feeling!

When a reader of the official records of the war ponders on what would have been the probable results of such a Southern policy—in the light of what was actually occurring on the Northern side—he can only smile and wonder how long, in such case, the war would have lasted. Certain it is that the North's Western Department, hard pressed in Missouri, would have had no spare troops for Grant or any other leader in forays against Belmont, Henry, or Donelson.

CHAPTER V

THE MISSISSIPPI

It shall flow unvexed to the sea.
—WARTIME SLOGAN.

THE popular view in looking back on the Civil War is that it was in the main a war of sentiment: on the part of the seceding States, for the institution of slavery and for that vague doctrine known as "States' rights"; on the part of the North, for preservation of the Union and the abolition of slavery. Sentiment was indeed a contributing factor, but behind the sentiment was the economic urge—one might even say economic necessity—as it appeared to both of the participating parties.

In the South the economic reasons, valid and otherwise, for abandoning the Union and setting up a new confederation were fairly uniform, since the interests of the Southern States were largely common interests. In the North the case was different. The Northwestern States had one set of reasons for prosecuting the war, the Middle Western and the Atlantic States quite different reasons, to them just as valid. None of the various Union groups cared very much for the war aims of the other groups, nor were any of them purely altruistic; they were fighting to make their own particular region a better habitat for its dwellers and their children.

To the States of the Northwest the Civil War was a contest for control of the Mississippi as a trade route. At the present day it is difficult for us to appreciate the importance of the river as it appeared to the people of these States in 1861, for to-day this same river is of quite minor consequence to them. That a change of axis of trade routes has taken place is in large measure due to the economic history of the Civil War itself.

The boldest imagination of 1861 could scarcely have conceived of Chicago as the grain mart of the West, or of the Chicago-New York railroad lines as arterial highways of trade between the agricultural Northwest and the outside world. Railroads did exist, but at that time the main lines ran not east and west, but north and south, connecting the ports on the Great Lakes with the Mississippi and its tributaries, chiefly with the Ohio River. Many canals further supplied this commercial need. There were, indeed, lines connecting in a loose-jointed way and with a multiplicity of gages New York and Chicago, but their rates were high and their carrying capacity was small, and until the stress of war conditions brought them prosperity these struggling lines were far from being the financial successes that the roads were which served as feeders to the great Mississippi route.

The east and west routes carried, it is true, passengers and valuable freight, but prior to the Civil War the bulky farm products of the Northwest had just one possible and at the same time profitable outlet, and that was the Mississippi; at least, such was the view of it in 1861. By this route only could the grain of the Northwest be shipped to the "Cotton" States, to the Atlantic States, to Europe. Hence the closing of the route seemed to the people of the Northwest a veritable catastrophe.

As early as January 26, 1861, we find the legislature of Minnesota passing a series of resolutions, the first six of which are highly rhetorical, such as "the constitutional majority must always rule" . . . "any attempt to dissolve . . . the Union . . . is without excuse," etc. Not until we come to the seventh do we discover the underlying and practical reason for the preceding six:

7. *Resolved,* That we never will consent or submit to the obstruc-

tion of the free navigation of the Mississippi River, from its source to its mouth, by any power hostile to the Federal Government.

The people of Wisconsin were similarly ready to fight, and for equally substantial reasons. In the special session of the legislature convened in May to authorize the raising of State troops for the war, Governor Ramsey's strongest argument was this:

"The vast lumber and mineral interests of Wisconsin, independent of her commanding produce and stock trade, bind her fast to the North border and Northwestern States, and demand, like them, the free navigation of the Mississippi and all its tributaries, from their highest navigable waters to their mouths."

Responding to this strongest of local appeals, the legislative "War Bill" authorized the raising of five regiments in addition to the three called for by the Federal Government, and further authorized the governor to keep always a "reserve of two regiments" beyond what were required for national defense.

Regarding the degree of popular enthusiasm in the North for the war, it is interesting in this connection to note that in the measure of its intensity, the percentage of the population which was enrolled in the three years' volunteers, these Northwestern States stood highest.

PERCENTAGE OF POPULATION ENROLLED IN THREE YEARS'
VOLUNTEERS

State	Per Cent	Chief economic interest
Illinois	.077	
Indiana	.07	
Iowa	.07	Agricultural
Minnesota	.06	
Wisconsin	.05	
Pennsylvania	.058	Manufacturing
New York	.045	Commercial
New England	.042	Manufacturing and Commercial

Of course in the North as in the South the public leaders had strong influence in directing public opinion. There can be no doubt that both Lincoln and Davis knew their Mississippi fairly well. Both were born in Kentucky and both had navigated the Mississippi—Lincoln in his youth as a flatboatman. But Lincoln, from his later residence in Illinois, was better able to weigh the influence of the Mississippi "urge" on the Northwest than was Davis, who had moved to the State of Mississippi.

The early policy of the Confederacy was originally to use the threat of closing the Mississippi rather as a club with which to force the Northwestern States to acquiesce in the South's peaceful withdrawal from the Union; yet it was precisely this threat that fomented the war spirit in the northern and central West to its highest pitch and made any compromise impossible. Some must have foreseen the inevitability of this result, for the first Confederate Congress at its initial meeting passed a resolution disclaiming any intention to interfere with the free navigation of the Mississippi; but it failed to carry weight.

The official records give an interesting report of the "sounding" of the Union prisoners captured at Belmont, December 14, 1861—

as to the opinion of the people of the West relative to the free navigation of the Mississippi after the war is over. Whilst we found some of them advised of the action of the first meeting of the Confederate Congress others expressed themselves as having joined the army under the belief that the Union must be restored in order to their enjoying such free navigation.[1]

The significance of this evidence appears to have been missed by the Confederate leaders, engrossed as they quite naturally were in affairs nearer to the seat of government of the new con-

[1] W. R. 114:542.

federation. However, even at that time, it was almost too late to repair mistakes of policy.

That Lincoln fully realized the importance—nay, the necessity—of the North's not only holding the upper Mississippi at all costs but also gaining possession of the lower Mississippi, is clearly evident. This was necessary in order to keep the States of the Middle West and Northwest in line for the war and also—as General Scott pointed out in his, at that time, so often derided "Anaconda Plan"—because pressure successfully applied there would bring the North the greatest substantial results and likewise would most effectively cripple the South.

The Lincoln despatches, from Sumter on, show that the President's first thought, after Washington itself, was the safety of Cairo, Illinois, any threat to which never failed to produce prompt action by Washington in forwarding to that point troops, guns, or armored craft. This constant vigilance was perhaps still more clearly demonstrated by the fact that, after McClellan had proved his incapacity in the Peninsular Campaign, and it was decided to bring one of the two successful Western commanders to command in the East, it was the obviously second-best, Pope, who was detached, while the spectacularly victorious Grant was kept in the West to work out his and the Union's destiny on the Mississippi. To one able to read between the lines it is evident that Lincoln, however much he may have been censured by wartime and later critics for his inability to keep "important secrets," appears to have kept his chief "secret"—his policy—rather well, and we find it expressed in all its perfection not in words but in deeds.

That Grant himself, breathing as he had been, during the years of excitement over the "Southern question," the hopes, prejudices, and fears of his fellow-Illinoisans, appreciated the scope and meaning of the Mississippi, there can be no question.

From the very first day that an offensive by his Cairo command was in any way possible, we find him in his direct fashion urging his superior to permit him to strike either directly at the first serious obstacle on the Mississippi, the Confederate fortifications at Columbus, Kentucky, or indirectly at some neighboring point.

When Grant came to Cairo he found at his disposal gun-boats, built and building, which virtually assured naval control of the Ohio, Mississippi, Cumberland, and Tennessee rivers. Although it is true that this advantage must be credited in part to the superior resources of the North, in money and material and in better ship-building facilities, yet the main fact that stands out in the "Official Naval Records of the War of the Rebellion" is that the prompt and practical utilization of such resources and facilities by the Federal Government in the early months of the summer and in the autumn of 1861, and the failure of the South to use her corresponding resources, gave the Union commander in the West, who already held there all the trump cards—more money, more munitions, more and better troops—also the joker. For the river navy was precisely that. It could support in the West any offensive on or along a river where alone an offensive could be profitably made, and could block effectually any possible enemy offensive on or near the Mississippi.

In the South, just as the chief emphasis on the military side was laid on the operations in the East, so in the naval activities the needs stressed were privateers, possession of the coastal ports, and, generally speaking, measures affecting foreign commerce. That the Confederacy's "Golden West" was to be doomed to isolation for the lack of a few good river gunboats quite escaped official consideration.

Not until four months after the fall of Fort Sumter were any means of river combat, other than shore batteries, provided for. On August 9, General Twiggs, commanding at New Orleans, wrote:

I understand that the Lincoln Government is making formidable preparations for the devastation of the Valley of the Mississippi and a descent upon New Orleans. I am told that they are building and equipping a powerful fleet of iron-clad gun-boats. . . . There are at this place some six floating docks of immense strength, which are capable of being converted into floating batteries of tremendous power. . . . These docks can be towed up to any point on the river where the channel is narrow and be made an impassable barrier to the vessels of the enemy.[2]

On August 24, Twiggs's recommendation was strongly approved by the Confederate Secretary of War and ordered put into immediate execution, but even this was only a passive-defensive measure. Yet the ship-building capacity of the New Orleans yards alone was nearly double that of Cincinnati, Louisville, and St. Louis combined. It was not until another five months had passed that, on January 9, 1862, a corps for "service on Western waters" was provided for by the Confederate Congress.[3]

Federal action in this respect had been much speedier. On May 14, a month after the attack on Sumter, Welles, Secretary of the Navy, referred to the War Department a letter from James B. Eads, of St. Louis, proposing to convert river steamers into gunboats. The question was submitted to General McClellan, commanding at Cincinnati, who was, after consulting with Mr. Eads and an officer to be sent out by the Navy Department, to "take order for the proper preparation of the boats."[4] Two days later Commander John Rodgers of the United States Navy was

[2] W. R. 111:722, 731.
[3] W. R. 111:770.
[4] "Official Records of the Union and Confederate Navies in the War of the Rebellion," No. 22, pp. 277, 280.

sent to McClellan as naval adviser for this work, and a most capable officer he proved to be.

On June 8, three weeks from the time of his arrival at Cincinnati, Commander Rodgers reported the purchase of the first three river steamers for conversion into gunboats at a cost of $100,000, including the expense of conversion. Money well spent. These first three boats, the *Tyler,* the *Lexington,* and the *Conestoga,* were all in commission and virtually under Grant's command from the time of his arrival at Cairo. It was not only a very useful fleet, it was also inspiring. It breathed the spirit of initiative, of the offensive. It raised the morale of Union officers and men and depressed that of the Confederate forces, precisely as would be the case to-day with one army possessing complete air supremacy over its opponent.

Commander Rodgers's activity continued, and later he was transferred as naval adviser to Frémont, when the latter took over the river problem on McClellan's transfer to Washington. Frémont and Rodgers between them built and converted gunboats, authorized and unauthorized, until Union river command—in the absence of adequate Confederate preparation—was completely assured. As the flotilla grew in size, Frémont asked for a naval officer of higher rank than Rodgers to command it and Captain A. H. Foote was sent, arriving in St. Louis just after Grant reached Cairo.

One cannot but feel that this appointment was unfair to Rodgers, who had borne the burden of the difficult construction and organization of the navy's stepchild, the river fleet. But it was perhaps fortunate for Grant, for Foote possessed exactly the bold dashing spirit, eager for combat, which was to combine so well with the general's rugged determination. Foote may also be credited with giving Grant excellent advice, and, later on, securing Halleck's approval of what was to be their great mutual adventure—Henry-Donelson! Furthermore, both put the national interests ahead of any personal interests and therefore we find them in their joint operations acting in perfect mutual understanding, confidence, and harmony.

CHAPTER VI

The Rôle of Kentucky

Purchase but their neutrality, thy sword
Will, in despite of oracles, reduce
The rest of Greece.
—GLOVER.

MR. STEPHENS, in a speech at Savannah, Georgia, soon after his installation as Vice-President of the Confederacy said: "That they [the border States] ultimately will join us, be compelled to do so, is my confident belief; but we can get on very well without them, even if they should not."

Among the greatest weaknesses of the Confederate war-directing power was its ignorance of the economic factors and their influence on the struggle. No more striking example of this could be conceived than is found in the latter part of the statement by Mr. Stephens.

Of the three border States Maryland, Kentucky, and Missouri, Kentucky was, as regards military resources, of by far the greatest importance. In addition, its strategic location doubled its value to either of the warring sections, since if Kentucky went with the North, Missouri could not be held by the Confederacy, even were that State to secede. Also, with Kentucky in Union hands western Tennessee was threatened, and with it control of the Mississippi as far south as Vicksburg. On the other hand, the South, were Kentucky on its side, would have there the means to carry on offensive warfare in Missouri and to threaten an offensive against Indiana, Ohio, and western Pennsylvania—Pittsburgh, at least. Such a threat would have proved the best of safeguards for Virginia and the East, since, in the face of it, the troops of the menaced States could scarcely have been diverted, on the scale they were, to the eastern theater.

With Kentucky neutral, as it began by being, the advantage was altogether on the side of the Confederacy—especially in view of the Southern policy of sending all the best Confederate troops possible to Virginia—for the South could then safely guard the Mississippi with relatively small forces on the northern boundary of Tennessee, while the North would still be obliged to hold considerable forces in readiness within easy reach of the Ohio River, to provide for eventualities.

Before taking up the seemingly trivial events which caused Kentucky to enter the war on the side of the North and thus to give Grant his opportunity to lay strong hands on one vital, strategic point in that State, Paducah, it may be well to pause for a brief glimpse of the war resources of the two contending parties, with a glance in passing at the probable effect on the balance of power had the border States also seceded, in order to make clear the full significance of these events:

WEALTH (CENSUS OF 1860) IN MILLIONS

Southeastern Confederate States (east of the Mississippi)	2,748
Southeastern Confederate States (with Virginia and Tennessee)	4,035
Southeastern Confederate States (with trans-Mississippi States)	5,202
Southeastern Confederate States (had Maryland, Kentucky, and Missouri joined)	6,544
Northern Free States	9,413
Northern Free States (with Maryland, Kentucky, and Missouri)	10,957

It will be seen by this table that had the border slave States joined the Confederacy, the wealth of the opposing sides would have been in the ratio of two to three, instead of one to two and as it later became (after the trans-Mississippi States were cut off), two to five. As, however, these figures include on the part of the South a two-billion dollars' valuation of the slaves, a better picture of the fluid wealth is given by the bank statistics, which virtually double the ratio, being one to four of bank capital and one to five of bank deposits.

As the cost of the war to the North was actually a billion and a half, or one seventh of its 1860 estimated resources, it will be easily realized how difficult, financially, was the meeting of the Southern budget requirements.[1]

In the matter of man-power the table on the opposite page tells the story.

We see that, notwithstanding Mr. Stephens's confident assertion, had the border States joined the Confederacy, the relative man-power advantage of the North would have been hardly more than two to one, instead of the preponderating four to one. Without Kentucky and western Tennessee, the Confederacy was unable to feed itself properly or ration its armies adequately; it could not find horses for its mounted arms, make uniforms for its soldiers, supply needed arms and ammunition, or provide locomotives and rolling stock for its railroads.

[1] There was, indeed, one way in which the South might have financed the war. In the first year, when the optimism of the Southern leaders over the prospect of ultimate success was shared by the ruling classes of Europe, President Davis sent a mission to France and England to negotiate a loan. The foreign bankers, learning in advance of their coming, threshed out the matter of a loan and decided to float for them a bond issue of a half-billion dollars—a large sum for those days. When the mission made its application for a mere paltry fifty-million loan the European bankers almost refused to lend it to them, as it showed such short-sightedness of financial policy on the part of the Confederate leadership. The loan was made, however, and at once oversubscribed. Had the loan been ten times that amount, as the foreign bankers wished to make it, there was every probability, not only of future loans to back it up, but of ultimate foreign governmental participation in some form. But with the Confederate defeat at Donelson, the opportunity passed, and the Confederate credit continued to fall with each fresh Northern victory in the Mississippi Valley; for war and finance are so closely related that the one is inexplicable without an understanding of the other.

COMPARATIVE MAN-POWER

(Census of 1860)

North

	Population in thousands
New England	3,110
Total Eastern States	10,528
Central and Midwestern States	7,698
Kentucky	919[2]
Missouri	1,063
Total North, as fought	20,210

South

Eastern States	4,344
Trans-Mississippi States	1,102
Total South, as fought	5,446
Border slave States	2,498
What might have been!	7,944

As one examines the statistics, the conclusion becomes inevitable that had Kentucky played the same rôle in the West that Virginia did in the East, or even had it remained neutral and allowed its resources to be drawn upon by the Confederacy, the history of the Civil War would have made very different reading and might even have had another ending.

President Davis, on August 28, wrote to assure Magoffin, the Governor of Kentucky, that his Government "neither intends, nor desires to disturb the neutrality of Kentucky." [3] We may judge of what were Governor Magoffin's projects from the fact that the commander of the State militia, General Buckner, visited

---

[2] Kentucky enrolled a larger percentage of its population in the Union armies than did some of the New England States.

[3] W. R. 4:396.

Richmond on the third of September and sought "in advance of the action of her [Kentucky's] Governor, to have such co-intelligence with the Confederate authorities as will enable him to act effectively when the opportune moment arrives." [4]

So well was General Buckner able to satisfy the Southern authorities of Kentucky's trend, that the War Department at Richmond gave him a letter to General Zollicoffer in East Tennessee; to Governor Harris of Tennessee, at Nashville; and to General Polk at Memphis. In it the recipients were instructed to "converse with him so freely, that he may anticipate the assistance which Kentucky may expect in the hour of her need from the forces and other means of the Confederate States." But before the official head of the Kentucky State troops had time to perfect arrangements which should facilitate the easing of his State into the war on the Confederate side, the whole scheme was ruined by the invasion of her "sacred soil" by some troops of General Polk, who occupied Columbus, Kentucky, on September 5.

The cause of this sudden blow, the repercussions of which were to prove so disastrous to the Confederacy, lay in events at Cairo on General Grant's arrival at his new post of command. In connection with the combined movement upon Benton, Frémont's orders of August 28 had informed Grant that Colonel Waagner was to be sent with a regiment and two gunboats to Belmont "to destroy the fortification erecting by the rebels, keep possession of that place, and move thence, in concert with the two regiments [from Bird's Point] towards Charleston, with the view of coöperating with the forces from Ironton and Cape Girardeau towards Benton." [5] Pursuant to this order Colonel Waagner occupied Belmont, lying directly across the river from Columbus, on September 2.

[4] W. R. 4:400.
[5] W. R. 3:141, 142.

Grant had remained at Cape Girardeau from August 30 to September 2, arranging for the proposed combined movement on Benton and trying without avail to soothe the ruffled feelings of General Prentiss. On the second, however, he proceeded to Cairo, the headquarters of his new command. In view of the defection of General Prentiss, the combined move on Benton was ordered suspended, and on the third Grant wrote Colonel Waagner to "retain possession of Belmont until otherwise directed." But the very next day the general reported to Frémont that on the representation of Commander Rodgers, the senior naval commander at Cairo, he deemed it advisable to withdraw the troops from Belmont.[6]

In the meantime, however, Southern sympathizers in Columbus had lost no time in informing General Polk of Colonel Waagner's expedition to Belmont, with such alarmist details as convinced Polk that the Union movement across the river was an active threat against the town of Columbus on the Kentucky shore. Polk promptly despatched Pillow with his command of Tennessee troops by steamer to Columbus, which was occupied on September 5, Pillow having landed and stopped for the night of September 3–4 at Hickman, just north of the Kentucky line.

To the authorities at Richmond this movement was as unexpected as it was unwelcome. The Confederate Secretary of War telegraphed Polk on the fourth: "News has reached here that General Pillow has landed his troops at Hickman, Kentucky. Order their prompt withdrawal from Kentucky."[7]

Harris, Governor of Tennessee, also telegraphed him the same day: "Just learned that Pillow's command is at Hickman. This is unfortunate, as the President [Davis] and myself are pledged to respect the neutrality of Kentucky. I hope they will be with-

6 W. R. 3:147, 148.
7 W. R. 4:180.

drawn instantly, unless their presence there is an absolute necessity."

To Harris, Polk replied, in justification of the landing at Hickman, that "in consequence of the armed position of the enemy, who had posted himself with cannon and intrenchments opposite Columbus, the general [Pillow] was forced to land at Hickman to avoid his cannon."

To President Davis, Polk wrote on September 4:

The enemy having descended the Mississippi River some three or four days since, and seated himself with cannon and intrenched lines opposite the town of Columbus, Kentucky, making such demonstrations as left no doubt upon the minds of any of their intention to seize and forcibly possess said town, I thought proper . . . to direct a sufficient portion of my command, both by river way and by land, to concentrate at Columbus. . . . This demonstration on my part has had the desired effect. The enemy had withdrawn his force even before I had fortified my position. It is my intention now to continue to occupy and keep this position.

As we of to-day know, of course, Grant's withdrawal of his troops from Belmont was in no way connected with or influenced by the Confederate movement, but Polk's explanation and his assertion of the apparent success of his movement satisfied President Davis, who telegraphed back, also on the fourth, "The necessity justifies the action."

The pity of it, looking at it from the Confederate point of view, was the utter futility of Pillow's incursion. Not even the most obvious temporary advantages so easily to be had were gained by it. Were the neutrality of Kentucky to be violated at all—despite the pledges of President Davis and the Governor of Tennessee—then the troops should, manifestly, have been in readiness to cross the frontier simultaneously at all convenient points and occupy the entire State before the Union troops could make a counter-move. Had Polk been commanding the entire State of Tennessee, it is possible he might have thought of such a concerted movement, for, judging from his reply to Governor Harris, he was entirely uninformed regarding the policy of the Richmond Government toward Kentucky. Further, he appears to have been led to believe by his correspondents in Columbus that such action as he took would be welcome to the people of Kentucky, or, as he writes, "at least this portion of Kentucky."

However, he was not in command of the entire State of Tennessee, but only of the strip west of the Tennessee River, and, his whole attention being centered on the passive defense of the Mississippi itself, he naturally enough coveted the commanding bluffs at Columbus as sites for his river-defense guns, either unaware of or ignoring the effect of his action on the political issues, and its far-reaching and disastrous military consequences.

The political results came swiftly. On September 12 the Kentucky Senate and House of Representatives passed a resolution requiring Governor Magoffin—who had been so anxious to jockey his State over to the Confederate side—"to issue a proclamation ordering off the Confederate troops." This proclamation caused much anxious correspondence among the political and military leaders of the Confederacy, but its demand was not complied with. Kentucky entered the war on the side of the Union, thereby dooming the South to a hopelessly unequal struggle.

To the North the military advantages resulting from Polk's precipitate action were scarcely less important than the political. Volunteers for the Union army were in fact already being recruited and organized in Kentucky, but these constituted mere recruit camps and in no wise yet could be considered as troops, though Governor Magoffin had protested to President Lincoln against their presence. But now that a Confederate army had entered the State, the most pacifically inclined adherent of the policy of neutrality could not logically object to the Union army's doing the same thing for the purpose of driving out the invading forces.

Grant was quick to see this point and immediately took advantage of it. On September 5 he telegraphed from Cairo to the Speaker of the Kentucky House of Representatives: "I regret to inform you that Confederate forces in considerable numbers have invaded the territory of Kentucky, and are occupying and fortifying strong positions at Hickman and Chalk Bluffs." [8] And, not content with merely reporting the matter, he immediately moved on Paducah, where we find him on the sixth, issuing a proclamation to the people of the town. It was on this expedition that he first came into contact with Captain Foote, the newly arrived commander of the Northern river flotilla, who, having reached Cairo on the evening of the fifth, accompanied the gunboats.

Grant's action was taken not without asking leave of his superior, Frémont, but without waiting to receive the latter's approval. As was so often to be the case, his clear-sighted envisioning of the factors and possibilities in the situation precluded any doubt in his mind of its wisdom. Sure that he was right, he acted on his own responsibility, upon his return informing Frémont fully of his action.

Grant's measures for the occupation were exemplary. He issued a statesman-like proclamation to the inhabitants, informing them that he had come "as a friend" to "defend you against this [invading] enemy"; seized all the military supplies on hand; and did not fail to have the telegraph files and letters in the post-office examined for intelligence regarding the enemy.

After the seizure of Paducah, Polk began to regret his over-hasty action. He wrote to Governor Magoffin on September 8:

[8] W. R. 109:188.

Since I have taken possession of this place [Columbus] I have been informed . . . that certain representatives of the Federal Government . . . are making it a pretext for seizing other points. . . . I am prepared to say that I will agree to withdraw the Confederate troops from Kentucky, provided that she will agree that the troops of the Federal Government be withdrawn simultaneously.[9]

Too late he saw the danger and sensed that he himself had opened wide the door that led to the conquest, by the North, of the entire Mississippi Valley. It was one of those mistakes of the early mobilization period which could not be repaired in the entire course of the war.

[9] W. R. 4:185.

CHAPTER VII

GRANT AT CAIRO

We must be pleased to come down to such warfare as consists in a mere threatening of the enemy.—CLAUSEWITZ.

UPON his return to Cairo from the seizure and occupation of Paducah, Grant received the first of his rebuffs as a subordinate commander, of which he was to have so many. His telegram to the Speaker of the Kentucky House of Representatives had been brought to the attention of Frémont, who, not unnaturally, did not like to have his subordinates playing politics and therefore had his "military secretary" inform Grant that "Brigade and other commanders are not to correspond with State or other high authorities in matters pertaining to any branch of the public service."

It was one of those directives unpleasant not so much in themselves, as in the manner in which they are expressed. That Grant was galled by it appears from the way in which he mentions the incident in his Memoirs. To be sure, he seldom forgot personal indignities and, after the manner of his day, was slow to forgive them.

Frémont at the same time sent C. F. Smith, whom he had just had appointed brigadier, to command at Paducah. While the letter informing Grant that Smith at Paducah would not be under him was worded in a manner evidently intended not to accentuate the idea of reprimand—"to enable you to continue personally in command of our forces at Cairo, Bird's Point, Cape Girardeau and Ironton" was the euphemism with which it began [1]—the order itself indicates that Frémont was still displeased either at the bold action of Grant in making the seizure before receiving authorization for it, or with his presumption in acquainting the Kentucky legislature of the Confederate "invasion," or perhaps both. In any case, the division of authority was decidedly unsound. That no ill effects resulted from it was due to the fact that Grant and Smith were both men who put public service ahead of all personal considerations. Yet even so, had Polk chosen to advance northward between the Tennessee and Mississippi rivers, the divided command on the Union side would have given him a decided advantage.

Grant, upon his return from Paducah, at 4 P.M. on September 6, gave instructions for forwarding reinforcements to that town and went himself to Cape Girardeau and Jackson, Missouri, which were still occupied, to see what forces could be spared from there.[2]

On the eighth Grant sent his chief of artillery, Colonel Waagner, who appears to have been an excellent scout, with the gunboat *Lexington,* to reconnoiter Columbus. They drew fire from artillery posted on the banks, and returned after drawing two "gunboats" in pursuit.[3]

Later in the day Grant received information that five hundred Confederate cavalry, sent by Polk from Columbus, were within seven miles of Fort Holt, on the Kentucky shore across from Cairo; also that the Missouri general Jeff Thompson was reconnoitering opposite, on the west bank of the Mississippi. This was an invitation not to be ignored; Grant at once ordered Colonel

---

[1] W. R. 3:471.

[2] W. R. 4:198, 256, 258.

[3] W. R. 3:167. Just what these "gunboats" were like is not clear. They were presumably partly converted river boats, armed but unprotected against return fire. Commander Rodgers had already encountered them early on the morning of Sept. 4, while on a reconnaissance to Hickman, and it was largely his report of their efficiency that decided Grant to order the withdrawal of the inadequate Union force occupying Belmont.

Hecker's regiment from Fort Holt in pursuit, and also despatched troops under Colonel Waagner to Norfolk, after Thompson.[4] When Grant later heard that Hecker had succeeded in getting in the rear of the Confederate cavalry, he sent a regiment, and subsequently six additional companies, to bag them. Elated at the prospect, the next morning he confidingly shared the good news with Frémont: "Colonel Hecker has got in the rear of 500 cavalry, Kentucky side. Colonel Ross' regiment is in front, and six companies of Turchin's will go to their assistance. We occupy Norfolk."

Frémont replied with this wet blanket: "Dispatch about Hecker not understood. Keep strictly within your orders in reference to the Kentucky movements." [5]

Grant retorted: "Colonel Hecker has been no further in Kentucky than you directed." Frémont's orders on the seventh had prescribed: "The heights commanding Fort Jefferson and Blandville should be occupied." Blandville, as it happened, was precisely seven miles from Fort Holt! [6]

Apparently, however, the Confederate cavalry escaped from the infantry attempting to surround it, since we find no further mention of the matter, nor any written reports of the affair by any of the column commanders.

Also on the eighth Grant sent a detachment from Bird's Point under command of Colonel Waagner to occupy Norfolk, and despatched a gunboat, the *Lexington,* Commander Stembel, to support it.[7] On the ninth Colonel Waagner reconnoitered a few miles southward from Norfolk, supported by the *Lexington,* but reported to Grant that he had heard the enemy at Belmont was advancing to attack him, and also that the Confederate Navy was

---

[4] W. R. 3:479, 480.
[5] W. R. 3:481.
[6] W. R. 3:476, 480.
[7] N. R. 22:326.

showing fight. Grant promptly ordered reinforcements to Waagner and despatched the gunboat *Conestoga* to back up the *Lexington*.[8] To get an additional regiment to reinforce General Smith at Paducah, he withdrew the regiment at Jackson, no longer needed there, in view of the general shift of the forces to the south.

In his report of events to Frémont on September 10, Grant wrote:

> This morning Colonel Waagner started from Norfolk . . . to reconnoiter towards Belmont . . . They went as far as Beckwith. . . . Found no regular force, but had one man wounded and lost one horse by shots from the pickets of the rebels. The gunboats, however, penetrated farther and found large numbers of cavalry on the Missouri shore and . . . artillery. . . .
>
> The gunboat *Yankee* could not be induced to come far from a battery on the Kentucky shore. Captain Stembel, however, succeeded in bursting a shell in her wheelhouse, disabling her. . . . The batteries on shore were silenced.[9]

In the conclusion of this report, Grant voiced for the first time the urge to battle so characteristic of him from now on, and, speaking not only for himself but for his troops, wrote:

> All the forces show great alacrity in preparing for any movement that looks as if it was to meet an enemy, and if discipline and drill were equal to their zeal, I should feel great confidence even against large odds. . . . If it were discretionary with me, with a little addition to my force I would take Columbus.

Here in its germ is the spirit of Belmont, of Donelson, of the Wilderness. It is gratifying to note that Frémont for once appeared pleased with Grant; he answered: "Dispatch received. Push forward actively on the Missouri side. Move the gunboats

8 W. R. 3:480, 481.
9 W. R. 3:168.

cautiously in concert with the troops on shore, and confine yourself
to holding the positions we have taken in Kentucky." [10]

Encouraged by this response, Grant on the eleventh wrote to
Waagner, still at Norfolk: "Renew your reconnaissance of yesterday, pushing as far down the river as practicable, and annoying
the enemy in every way possible. . . . The gunboat *Conestoga*
will act in conjunction with you. Should you make any important
discoveries, inform me as early as possible." [11]

There are no reports of this reconnaissance, and perhaps none
was made. Higher commanders sometimes overlook, in their enthusiasm for reconnaissances, that whereas infantry soldiers will
cheerfully do their sixteen miles per day, and more, going in a
continuous direction, yet when they have gone eight miles forward
and eight back on two consecutive days without finding anything,
they do not welcome orders to repeat the forward-and-back movement the third day. Colonel Waagner, with the troops, knew this,
however, and perhaps wisely gave them a rest day.

Grant appears to have put in the day questioning an intelligent
deserter about affairs at Columbus and made a lengthy report to
Frémont of the information obtained. He must also have looked
into the needs of his supply department, for he added: "I would
respectfully urge the necessity of having clothing of almost every
description, particularly shoes, blankets and shirts, forwarded
here immediately. Tents also are required." [12]

Last, but not least, we find him for the first time calling for
more troops: "Cavalry is much needed . . . also more batteries
of light artillery. All the reinforcements that can be spared for
this post, of every arm of the service, would be welcome."

The next day, September 12, Grant suggested to Frémont by
telegraph: "Cannot the troops moved from this place to Paducah

or a part of them be returned?   More troops are needed here."
To which Frémont replied: "I will send you more troops. Keep
me informed minutely." [13]

On the same day Frémont, perhaps repenting of the over-
quiescent policy on the Kentucky shore imposed on Grant by his
despatch of the tenth, sent him the following model of all that
a military directive ought not to be:

> Fort Jefferson, just as this time, desires a battery. Be careful to
> find out all about the roads, taking all natural advantages for the
> advance as well as the retreat on the Mayfield Creek line from the
> Mississippi to Level (or Sevel, or the like), if the enemy cannot be
> prevented from crossing at Belmont, and should they move that way
> inform me, and be present with a force on the Missouri as well as the
> Kentucky shores.[14]

Grant evidently gathered from the above order, following as
it did Frémont's promise of more troops, that his superior now
desired renewed activity in Kentucky, because, while he despatched
two regiments to reinforce Colonel Oglesby, in command at Norfolk, he detached Colonel Waagner, who had been conducting
the reconnaissances in Missouri, instructing Oglesby: "Throw out
pickets to keep you constantly informed of the movements of the
enemy, but make no movements with the main body of your command without further instructions, unless it should be necessary
for protection." [15]

The same evening he informed Frémont: "To-day our scouts
have not been able to discover anything of the enemy. A reconnaissance has been made of the roads around Fort Jefferson and
I shall take possession of it day after to-morrow with most of the
force at Fort Holt."

Grant's report also contained the latest intelligence of the

[13] W. R. 3:488, 489.
[14] W. R. 3:489.
[15] W. R. 3:488, 489.

enemy, gathered from a newspaper, renewed his request for supplies and ordinance, and concluded with the following interesting
but not altogether mature proposal:

I am of opinion that if a demonstration was made from Paducah
towards Union City, supported by two columns on the Kentucky
side from here, the gunboats, and a force moving upon Belmont,
the enemy would be forced to leave Columbus, leaving behind their
heavy ordnance. I submit this to your consideration, and will hold
myself in readiness to execute this or any plan you may adopt.

As a tactical proposal, for distinctly raw troops commanded
by untrained and untried leaders, this cannot be considered sound.
A year later Grant himself would have laughed at such an idea.
Yet, considering the trepidation felt by Polk six weeks later during the Belmont affair, who can say that as a psychological bluff it
might not have worked? However, it was not to be put to the test.
Whatever Frémont might have thought of the suggestion in ordinary circumstances, he was too busy at the time he received it—
trying to extricate the unfortunate Mulligan and his command,
besieged by Price at Lexington, Missouri—to consider it at all.

On September 13, Grant made preparations for an active re-
newal of reconnaissances the day following. He sent Oglesby
from Norfolk "down the river as far as you can safely go" and
W. H. L. Wallace from Bird's Point toward Charleston,[16] and
possibly was personally directing movements on the Kentucky side
of the river, since we find no written record of orders for or
reports from them. He summed up the result in a message to
Frémont on the fifteenth: "Reconnaissances . . . yesterday dis-
close the fact that the enemy have broken up their camp above
Belmont, also that they have no force from there to some distance
beyond Charleston." [17]

16 W. R. 3:491.
17 W. R. 3:494.

Further riding his theory of the twelfth that the enemy had a faint heart, Grant continued, "I believe they are leaving Columbus; whether marching upon Paducah or leaving Kentucky altogether I will try and determine to-morrow." The message concluded by stressing once more the need for supplies, ordnance, and, this time, money!

Under date of September 15, in a report from Frémont to Cameron, we find the first return of Grant's Cairo command:

Cairo	5 regiments	4,826
Forts Holt and Jefferson, Kentucky	4 "	3,595
Bird's Point and Norfolk, Missouri	4 "	3,510
Cape Girardeau and Jackson, Missouri	1 regiment	650
Mound City, Illinois	1 "	900
	15	13,481

With seven posts to be guarded, and all but two open to Confederate attack, this, even with naval superiority on the river, was not much. Polk had on September 7 at Columbus thirteen and a half regiments of infantry to Grant's fifteen, fourteen troops of cavalry to Grant's seven, and six batteries of light artillery to Grant's three—a much better rounded force than Grant's, and nearly all disposable for the field, except for transportation facilities, with respect to which both commands were about equally hampered.

The difference was that while Grant was tugging at the leash to take the field and attack, Polk appears to have been quite content to play the passive-defensive rôle adopted by President Davis as the general initial policy for the Confederacy; and the mental attitude of the commanders imparted itself—as it always does in some mysterious way—to their respective forces.

However, taking into account Paducah with its garrison of seven thousand men, the scales would not have been so evenly

balanced had it not been for the divided Union command. On
the Confederate side the same weakening division of command
had on September 2 been in part rectified by Special Orders, No.
141, which extended General Polk's department "to embrace the
State of Arkansas and all military operations in the State of
Missouri." [18]

Frémont's promise to Grant of September 12 to send him
more troops was not kept, for two days later the general-in-chief,
Winfield Scott, telegraphed Frémont: "Detach 5,000 infantry
from your department to come here without delay . . . The
President dictates," and Frémont, not knowing where else to get
them, on the fifteenth detached two of his best remaining regiments from Grant, who had already deprived himself of his best
by selecting them for the seizure of Paducah. Had Grant been
a philosopher, he might have consoled himself with the reflection
that there was no general of his time who could get along better
than he, if not altogether without troops, at least with troops of
inadequate training, discipline, and equipment. In any case, we
cannot but admire his soldierly acceptance of the situation, without remonstrance, and his continuing to do his utmost with the
combat means at his disposal.

In order not to interfere with his planned reconnaissances,
Grant on the fifteenth sent two regiments from Cairo, to replace
the two ordered away from Fort Holt by Frémont, and directed
more reconnaissances for the sixteenth—infantry to occupy Fort
Jefferson and cavalry under Colonel Waagner to reconnoiter
toward Blandville; Oglesby, as previously, toward Belmont. He
reported the result to Frémont on the evening of the sixteenth:
"Reconnaissance to-day shows no enemy between Charleston
and two miles above Belmont. None on the Kentucky shore
within two miles. Our troops occupy Fort Jefferson." [19]

[18] W. R. 3:691.
[19] W. R. 3:491, 494, 495, 497.

But on the seventeenth, a Sunday, thinking things over, Grant began to feel the pinch resulting from the loss of the two regiments. He decided to withdraw his outlying post at Elliott's Mills, Kentucky, and expressed his feelings in a letter to C. F. Smith:

I regret exceedingly that I am unable to spare you any troops in the present emergency. A most extraordinary movement took place here yesterday, which will compel me to contract my present limits, particularly on the Kentucky shore. I have received orders, and have sent off two of the best regiments under my command; where, can only be surmised.

But, ever generous in dealing with his one-time instructor at West Point, he added: "I send you a battery of artillery, which may be of material service." This was all the more a striking proof of friendship because artillery was precisely the arm most needed by Grant for his own command as well as by Smith for his.

Owing to his reduced forces, the next few days were quiet ones for Grant and his command. The gunboats, however, continued actively to patrol the river.[20]   On September 20 he reported: "There has been nothing in the movements of the enemy for the last few days that I could learn worthy of note. They now seem to be falling back from Mayfield upon Columbus, Kentucky."[21]

The same day he wrote to Smith, and after informing him of the loss of Colonel Waagner—his only really experienced subordinate—who had been taken by Frémont as his chief of artillery, said:

I had no plan to submit to you for action; but Colonel Waagner, having been very active in the reconnaissances which I have ordered from time to time, some of them extending near Columbus, I have talked to him of the plan I would approve or recommend if we were

20 N. R. 22:339.
21 W. R. 3:501.

in a situation to advance. At present, however, the force is scarcely more than a weak garrison.

On the twenty-first it occurred to Grant, with his shrunken command, to use his naval control of the Mississippi River to strengthen the advanced forces for reconnaissance work. Accordingly, he transferred Oglesby with half the troops at Norfolk to back up Lauman in a movement south from Fort Jefferson (below Columbus, on the Kentucky shore), and used the gunboats in support.[22] He reported: "The result proved the Confederates to be in and around Columbus. No outposts are occupied by them nearer to us."

This time, however, Polk was stirred to retaliation. Lauman reported the day following that Confederate cavalry had attacked his outposts, adding, "If possible, send us some addition to our cavalry force, and I pledge you they won't approach our pickets again with impunity." [23]

The same day (the twenty-second) Grant suffered another loss in offensive power, though this time only a temporary one. Two of his gunboats were ordered up the Ohio River on patrol duty to Owensboro, Kentucky, reported to have been seized by the Confederates.

On the twenty-third the general heard that the Confederates were crossing from Columbus to the Missouri shore. Having two days before borrowed half the Norfolk troops to reinforce Lauman, he now reversed the process and sent Lauman to reinforce Norfolk.[24] He reported on the twenty-fourth:

I have no new move of the enemy to report. I still continue active reconnaissance and have, I believe, driven the enemy back to Columbus and Belmont. Every day our advance scouts come in sight of parties of rebels, but they always retreat upon sight of our troops.

22 W. R. 3:502, 4:199.
23 W. R. 4:200.
24 W. R. 3:504, 505.

I have withdrawn all the troops from Fort Jefferson and strengthened the command at Norfolk. Should re-enforcements be sent here, however, I will retake that position. It was only abandoned this morning.

To this letter Frémont replied on the twenty-sixth:

I will . . . re-enforce you with two new regiments as soon as possible. By this means you will be enabled, in concert with Brigadier-General Smith, to control the rebel forces on the Kentucky and Missouri shores. Should the enemy expose a weak point on either side of the river, you may inflict upon him a combined blow; but at present I am not in favor of incurring any hazard of defeat. [25]

We cannot blame Frémont for his cautious attitude when we recall that the defeat of Lyon at Wilson's Creek had just been followed by the inglorious surrender of Colonel Mulligan at Lexington. He had had nothing but reverses to report in his department.

The last days of September were quiet ones for the District of Cairo. Grant, quick to learn, had recovered from the notion that a daily reconnaissance in force, to keep the enemy within his Columbus-Belmont bounds, was necessary, and was content to glean information through cavalry and patrols. Oglesby, scouting south from Norfolk, had two minor affairs with cavalry—on the twenty-sixth and the twenty-eighth—in both of which he was successful; but there was nothing new learned worthy of report.[26]

Grant wrote Frémont on the twenty-ninth: "Everything here is quiet and no rumors to disturb it," and since it was quiet, he, taking thought for the well-being of his command, added:

The cold season is now so nearly at hand, that it is time to think of providing winter quarters for the garrison. Log huts could be

[25] W. R. 3:507.
[26] W. R. 3:197, 198.

cheaply built, but even they would call for the outlay of some money. Credit will not do at this place longer. I understand that the credit of the Government has been already used to the extent of some hundred thousand dollars, and no money ever paid out. This causes much murmuring among the citizens, and unless the paymaster is soon sent to pay off the troops, the same may be expected from the soldiers. I would respectfully urge, therefore . . ."[27]

But, though Grant had heard no disquieting rumors, one had reached the ever credulous Frémont, who on the twenty-eighth wrote from Jefferson City: "It is reported that the rebels have evacuated Columbus and crossed over to Belmont, to attack Cape Girardeau or Ironton. Should that be the case," outlying posts are to be abandoned; Bird's Point reinforced, and—what in Frémont's orders appears inevitable—a "demonstration is to be made against Charleston." [28]

Grant received this on September 30 and the same day had intelligence of his own that Thompson was advancing on Charleston. He therefore wrote Oglesby, still at Norfolk, on the first of October [29] : "Despairing of being immediately re-enforced, I deem it the better part of valor to be prudent. You will, therefore, move your entire force back upon Bird's Point," and the same evening further notified him: "From information received . . . Thompson will probably march upon Charleston to-morrow, on his way north. Move out with 1,000 infantry and all the cavalry you can spare and intercept him." [30]

At the same time he wrote to allay Frémont's fears:

I have to-day concentrated my command at this place [Cairo], Bird's Point and Fort Holt. The work of placing these points in a strong defensive condition will be prosecuted with all our force. There is no enemy on the Missouri side of the river from Cape

27 W. R. 3:509.
28 W. R. 3:507.
29 W. R. 3:511.
30 W. R. 3:510.

Girardeau to New Madrid, except Jeff. Thompson's force at Belmont. I had troops in Charleston last evening. All quiet there.

Part of the information contained in Grant's message was from a gunboat reconnaissance, the *Conestoga* having at length returned from its tour up the Ohio River.

Notwithstanding Grant's reduced forces and the rumors of Confederate advances, his poise does not appear to have been really disturbed. He wrote Frémont on October 4:

I have nothing reliable from the enemy further than that Jeff. Thompson has broken up his encampment at Belmont and gone to New Madrid, Mo. No doubt it is with the view of going north from there, but whether any other force goes with him I have no positive information. My impression is, there is no concerted plan to attack this place, Cape Girardeau, or Paducah, for the present.[31]

On the sixth he added:

For the last two days I have had no reliable intelligence of the movements of the enemy. The gunboats have been out of order, so as to be unable to make reconnaissances, and one of my spies, from whom I expected a full and accurate report, has not returned. Our scouts report nothing of importance. I have ordered a force of 1,200 men to Charleston. . . . My own opinion is that the enemy have no present intention of moving on Cape Girardeau. I think Paducah is more likely the point.[32]

Subsequent events more than justified Grant in his impression. The day following, the "accurate" spy evidently returned, filled to the brim with the same sort of propaganda successfully disseminated by General Albert Sidney Johnston both in Columbus and at Bowling Green, Kentucky, where it deceived Sherman and afterward Buell. Grant wrote:

Information which I am disposed to look upon as reliable has reached me to-day that the Confederates have been re-enforced at

31 W. R. 3:519.
32 W. R. 3:523.

Columbus to about 45,000. In addition to this they have a large force collected at Union City, and are being re-enforced every day. They talk boldly of making an attack upon Paducah by the 15th of this month.[33]

So much for the propaganda-fed spy report! It is gratifying to find Grant's critical faculty—or intuition—operating in this instance also and causing him to add: "My own impression, however, is that they are fortifying strongly and preparing to resist a formidable attack, and have but little idea of risking anything upon a forward movement." A complete reading of the minds of Johnston and Polk, however he may have gained it. What could promise better for the making of a higher commander?

The report continues concerning affairs in his immediate sector: "Jeff. Thompson and Lowe are no doubt occupying positions at Sikeston and Benton. If the cavalry here were fully armed and equipped, they could be easily driven out. There is no use going after them with any other arm." No more sending, by Grant, of infantry to bag cavalry! One more lesson in military art learned and digested.

On October 9, Grant reported the result of an inspection of the defenses of Cape Girardeau, which he found satisfactory, and added that "information to-day confirms the belief that Cape Girardeau is only threatened by Thompson and Lowe," that is to say, that there are no other Confederate troops operating in that vicinity.[34]

On the eleventh Grant received the further information: "Thompson with his troops has gone west to Bloomfield or farther."[35]

This so eased his mind respecting an attack on Cape Girardeau

33 W. R. 3:199.
34 W. R. 3:529.
35 W. R. 3:531.

that he overlooked the fact that this information concerned vitally the commander at Ironton—the nearest Union command to the west, and his own former post of command—and he therefore reported it to Frémont by letter instead of by telegraph, and also failed to suggest its importance to the Ironton commander. This was the more unfortunate because Frémont was in western Missouri and the letter could reach him only after some days, if at all. This oversight may have been the result of too great absorption in matters close at hand, and concern for the welfare of his men.

The letter continues: "I sent the gunboats . . . down near Columbus to-day, not so much for the purpose of reconnoitering as to protect a steamer sent after wood belonging to Hunter, who is with the Southern Army. About 100 cords were brought up." He might not be able to secure money to build huts for his men, but at least they should have firewood as long as it could be taken from "rebels" with the aid of a gunboat or two.

As a result of Grant's unfortunate neglect to warn or have warned the commander at Ironton, the Confederates were left with a free hand in that direction. Jeff Thompson, marching northward with his five hundred mounted men, struck the line of the St. Louis and Ironton Railroad at Big River bridge, twenty-five miles north of Ironton, on the fifteenth, captured the infantry guard, and destroyed the fine "three-span bridge." His infantry meanwhile had marched to Fredericktown, where he hoped to assemble enough armed Missourians who were Confederate sympathizers to enable him to attack Ironton. But in this hope he was disappointed.

Frémont was at this time in southwest Missouri, conducting operations against Price. The adjutant-general at St. Louis ordered Grant on the sixteenth to send out a detachment from Cape Girardeau to assist Carlin, the commander at Ironton, in cutting off Thompson at Fredericktown. Grant did so, and Colonel Plummer, commander of the column sent, had the satisfaction of attacking Thompson, who had taken up a defensive position south of Fredericktown, inflicting on him substantial losses and seriously lowering the morale of his men.[36]

On the Confederate side, it was a case of sending a boy to do a man's job. A couple of good regiments, easily available from Columbus, would have enabled Thompson to capture Ironton and inflict heavy damage. That General Johnston hoped much from this expedition is shown by his endorsement on Thompson's first report: "Two smart and successful affairs, resulting in the accomplishment of an object which has been for some time much desired."

Early in October, Hardee's five thousand men from northern Arkansas had been brought by Johnston to Columbus and from there despatched to reinforce Buckner at Bowling Green, Kentucky, whither Johnston himself went on the thirteenth. On the sixteenth Sherman, commanding in central Kentucky, telegraphed this information to Grant and requested him "in connection with General Smith, to make a demonstration on Columbus." [37] Grant promptly wrote Smith, sending Sherman's despatch, "If you have any plan to propose, I am ready to coöperate to the extent of my limited means." Apparently Smith was no more receptive to the idea than Grant appears to have been, for nothing of record came of it.

On October 17, Grant reported:

For the last few days the reports I get from the enemy are so contradictory that I feel but little like reporting. I am satisfied, however, that Hardee, with five regiments has joined Buckner; also that a large force has crossed to the Missouri shore—this latter chiefly, I think, to gather the large crop of corn now maturing.

[36] W. R. 3:202, 236.
[37] W. R. 3:536.

He concluded: "I would like to visit St. Louis and Springfield strictly on business for this command. I have frequently reported our deficiency in many of the necessaries to a complete outfit, and want to give my best efforts to remedy the evil."

Clearly, if needed arms, shoes, uniforms, tents, and bedding were to be had, either from the State authorities of Illinois or from department headquarters, Grant purposed to go and get them. Grant's "supplies trip" was of short duration, for on the twenty-second he sent a note to Captain Walke [38] from Cairo, and, returning on the evening of the twenty-fourth, reported the next morning: "My mission to Springfield was only partially successful. The governor has neither artillery nor small-arms at his disposal." [39] But if he obtained no arms, he at least got some of the other necessary supplies required by his men.

The same day (October 25) Grant wrote to Smith that he had learned of a Confederate cavalry recruit camp near Eddyville, Kentucky, forty-five miles up the Cumberland River. Smith promptly sent three companies of infantry with a gunboat and broke up the camp. [40] So much, at least, could be done to create a diversion to help Sherman.

On October 27, Grant made the last report of record for the month, a report which indicates that he had a very clear picture of the weakness of the enemy opposite him:

Such drafts have been made on the force at Columbus lately for the Green River country [Bowling Green] and possibly other parts of Kentucky, that if General Smith's and my command were prepared it might now be taken. I am not prepared, however, for a forward movement. My cavalry are not armed nor my artillery equipped; the infantry is not well armed, and transportation is entirely inadequate to any forward movement. [41]

[38] N. R. 22:376.
[39] W. R. 3:556.
[40] W. R. 3:556; W. R. 4:215, 219; N. R. 22:379.
[41] W. R. 3:556.

Once more he is yearning for action, but his eyes are not yet open, as they will be later, to the possibility of operating by river, using steamers in lieu of land transport; nor does he realize that, great as are his deficiencies in arms, those of the enemy are still greater.

And yet, after reading the old-time records, we cannot but feel that the Grant of the October phase of Cairo is, as compared with the Grant of the month before, a rapidly and steadily maturing and mellowing general. There is, of course, still much in common; but, while the September Grant was straining every nerve, wearing out both himself and his men, demanding the impossible in order to obtain the possible, the October Grant has more poise and a much more balanced view. His information service is well organized, and he himself has learned to evaluate its reports so that he is not in the main deceived by enemy propaganda; and he has mastered one all-important secret of success, namely, to conserve the strength of his men in non-essentials in order to obtain the limit of the possible in crises when the expenditure will count the most. We also see him devoting more and more of his time and energy to the equipping and rounding out of his force as a field command.

In this connection it is significant that on October 14, in General Orders, No. 11, he had organized his command into five tactical brigades.[42] His return of strength present on October 31 was 11,161—two thousand less than that reported on September 15. Yet it is beyond question that the eleven-thousand-strong garrison of October 31 was a more formidable fighting force than the thirteen-thousand force of the month before.

Meanwhile, what were the conditions existing in the Confederate force opposed to Grant?

On September 2, Polk's command was extended by War De-

[42] W. R. 3:533.

partment orders "to embrace the State of Arkansas and all military operations in the State of Missouri." [43]

On September 10, General Albert Sidney Johnston was assigned to command Department No. 2 [44] and assumed command at Nashville.

On the sixteenth Johnston, after ordering General Buckner to seize and hold Bowling Green, Kentucky, went to Columbus, and made that his headquarters until October 13. By Johnston's orders of September 21, Polk was assigned to command the first territorial division of Department No. 2, which division embraced the State of Tennessee west of Nashville, and that part of Kentucky west of the Cumberland. While his western territorial limits were "the western bank" of the Mississippi River, he was none the less "charged with the defenses of the Mississippi."

Thus by a curious coincidence the making of the Cumberland the dividing line between departments, by the North, was repeated by Johnston in making it the boundary between the territorial divisions of his very large department.

The Confederate records of Polk's command for this period which have been preserved are very meager. It appears, however, that Jeff Thompson was sick early in September [45] and during the time his mounted command of five hundred men was at Belmont it undertook no large-scale operations to oppose Grant's reconnaissances. The withdrawal from Mayfield which Grant reported on the sixteenth appears to have been caused by a shortage of water for the troops. The chief reasons for Confederate inaction were, however, the lack of arms and ammunition, and the necessity felt by Polk of devoting all his energy to preparations for defense of Columbus, Island No. 10 (in the Mississippi

[43] W. R. 4:399.
[44] This embraced Tennessee, Arkansas, and "all that part of the state of Mississippi west of the New Orleans, Jackson and Great Northern Central Railroad; also the operations in Kentucky, Missouri, Kansas and the Indian Country immediately west of Missouri and Arkansas." W. R. 4:405.
[45] W. R. 3:698.

River), and New Madrid. The lack of a river navy was keenly
felt. Polk wrote on September 25:

> The gunboats the enemy have now in the Mississippi River are
> giving us most serious annoyance, and I find it indispensable, to
> check their movements and to protect our transports, to have an
> armed boat under my command. Without its aid our operations
> would be very seriously obstructed, if not to an extent paralyzed.
> As a necessity, therefore, I have purchased a strong river boat . . .
> and have sent it to New Orleans to be cut down and prepared for an
> armament.[46]

From the time of Johnston's arrival on September 18 at
Columbus, discipline and morale began to improve, and, while
he does not seem to have considered seriously operations against
Grant's command—the gunboats were too much of a handicap
for that—he was keen to initiate an active campaign in Missouri;
particularly after learning of Price's capture of Lexington, in that
State, on September 20.[47]

In general, Polk's policy for the Mississippi Valley, approved
and adopted by Johnston, may be summed up in the phrase "let
sleeping dogs lie." Johnston is quoted by Governor T. C. Reynolds as having said while at Columbus: "For a long time to
come there will be no operations on this line if I can prevent
them. We have no powder."

Thus Grant's success in his first few weeks at Cairo was in a
sense easily won. He had shown commendable enterprise, but
looking behind the scenes on the corresponding Confederate command it is easy to see that the same results might have been
obtained with the expenditure of far less troop energy. However,
it must not be forgotten that all the expeditions hither and yon
provided fine experience for the troops.

[46] W. R. 3:707.
[47] W. P. Johnston, "Life of A. S. Johnston," pp. 325, 327; also orders to
Thompson, W. R. 3:709.

CHAPTER VIII

THE RAID ON BELMONT

*It seems to be a law, inflexible and inexorable,
that he who cannot risk cannot win.*
—JOHN PAUL JONES.

FRÉMONT, still at Springfield, and preoccupied with affairs in southwestern Missouri, had sent to Grant, on November 1, the rather startling order:

You are hereby directed to hold your whole command ready to march at an hour's notice, until further orders. . . . You are also directed to make demonstrations with your troops along both sides of the river towards Charleston, Norfolk and Blandville, and to keep your columns constantly moving back and forward against these places, without, however, attacking the enemy.[1]

Grant is also notified that similar instructions have been sent to Smith.

On November 2, Grant was assigned a somewhat more concrete mission: "Jeff. Thompson is at Indian Ford of the St. François River, 25 miles below Greenville with a force of 3,000." It is to be noted that in this exploit Thompson appears to be giving Grant's command a wide berth! "Colonel Carlin has started with force from Pilot Knob [Ironton]. Send a force from Cape Girardeau and Bird's Point to assist Carlin in driving Thompson into Arkansas." [2]

With this more definite order Grant at once complied, sending

[1] W. R. 3:267.
[2] W. R. 3:268.

Oglesby from Bird's Point after Thompson, with a reinforced brigade, and ordering Plummer at Cape Girardeau to send a regiment to cover Oglesby's communications. In his report dated November 17 he wrote: "On the 5th a telegram was received from headquarters Saint Louis, stating that the enemy was re-enforcing Price's army from Columbus by way of White River, and directing that the demonstration that had been ordered against Columbus be immediately made." [3]

But who sent this message and what instructions it actually contained is not clear, since it is not found in the records. Adjutant-General McKeever telegraphed to Frémont on November 9: "General Grant did not follow his instructions. No orders were given to attack Belmont or Columbus." [4]

On November 5, Grant had informed Smith of his plans:

In pursuance of directions from headquarters Western Department I have sent from here a force of about 3,000 men all armed, towards Indian Ford on the St. Francis River, and also a force of one regiment from Cape Girardeau in the same direction. I am now, under the same instructions, fitting out an expedition to menace Belmont, and will take all the force proper to spare from here—probably not more than 3,000 men. If you can make a demonstration towards Columbus at the same time with a portion of your command, it would probably keep the enemy from throwing over the river much more force than they now have there, and might enable me to drive those they now have out of Missouri. The principal point to gain is to prevent the enemy from sending a force to fall in the rear of those now out from this command. I will leave here to-morrow night and land some 12 miles below. [5]

Whatever his final instructions may have been, it is beyond question that Grant had been more and more tugging at the leash

---

[3] W. R. 3:268. See Appendix for true date of this report.
[4] W. R. 111:507.
[5] W. R. 3:273.

to be let go at Columbus, and that this desire had been whetted by contacts with his colleagues of the sister-service, the navy commanders of his gunboats, who were equally impatient.

Captain Foote and apparently the rest of the naval officers had had all along a much more aggressive attitude toward the Confederates than had Frémont. As early as September 8, just after the occupation by Grant of Paducah, Foote wrote to G. V. Fox, Assistant Secretary of the Navy, "Were they [the new gunboats] ready now, I would endeavor to obtain authority from General Frémont to go with them, and he sending troops, to dislodge Pillow at Columbus before they become strongly entrenched." [6] That Grant was of the same mind is shown by his despatch to Frémont of September 10, reporting a naval reconnaissance down the river: "If it were discretionary with me, with a little addition to my present force I would take Columbus."

On October 23, Foote visited Cairo and Paducah and we find him writing Commander Porter on that date:

If we had control of matters here I would like to act toward the enemy, but we are only a force under orders from the commanding army officer of the West, and we cannot move except under instructions from that source. . . . I would gladly myself take the three gunboats and go down to Columbus with a military force had I the authority to do it, but as it is, we must wait the action of the military.[7]

Again, in an endorsement of November 6, he wrote, "I, myself, when last in Cairo consulted with the commanding general in relation to going down to attack Columbus with two gunboats and 4,000 men, remarking to him that the boats were ready and I would go down with them." [8]

On November 9, Foote stated that he had requested Grant to "inform me by telegram, at St. Louis, whenever an attack on

[6] N. R. 22:322, 330.
[7] N. R. 22:377, 378.
[8] N. R. 22:397.

the enemy was made requiring the coöperation of the gunboats, that I might be here [at Cairo] to take them into action." [9] Grant, according to Foote, promised this, and on the ninth "expressed his regret that he had not telegraphed as he had promised, assigned as the cause that he had forgotten it, in the haste in which the expedition was prepared, until it was too late for me [Foote] to arrive in time to take command."

Commander W. D. Porter's report sent from St. Louis on November 15 adds to this:

> On the 13th of October last I made a reconnoissance of the enemy's force and batteries at the Iron Bluff [Bank] near Columbus, Ky. I took drawings and plans and ascertained that the enemy were throwing troops across the Mississippi River on the Missouri shore. On my return to Cairo I laid these plans before General Grant . . . and urged upon him the necessity of attacking their troops with a combined army and naval force. [10]

Thus the impetus for the attack down the river, for which orders from the headquarters of the Western Department at St. Louis are entirely lacking in the records, may well have been planted in Grant's mind by Foote, Porter, and others; but Grant's own desire to fight and the urge from within his own force were no less strong. All he needed was an excuse and this the mysterious and unrecorded telegram from St. Louis on the fifth, which we cannot trace to any source, may have furnished.

Grant, despite the "haste" which he gives as an excuse to Foote, appears to have made his preparations for Belmont with deliberation and with great secrecy regarding destination. His telegraphic orders from St. Louis were received, he tells us, on November 5, yet it was not until 6 P.M. on November 6 that the naval commander, Walke, received instructions for a reconnais-

9 N. R. 22:399.
10 N. R. 22:430.

sance "down the river," and as "convoy to some half dozen transport steamers." [11]

Grant took no chances of having information leak through subordinates. Though he had quite definitely ordered Colonel Oglesby—who three days before had been sent with a column on Sikeston, Missouri—to turn "toward New Madrid, halting to communicate with me at Belmont," and had more fully confided in his trusted friend and fellow-commander General Smith at Paducah, he does not appear to have communicated his ultimate intentions or plans to any of his immediate subordinates at Cairo.

The five regiments chosen for the expedition were put aboard the river boats on the afternoon of November 6, between four and five o'clock, floated after six o'clock a few miles down-stream, and anchored for the night about nine miles from Cairo, off the Kentucky shore. Aside from the fact that two days' rations were ordered to be taken, which must have aroused many excited conjectures, apparently there was nothing to give even an inkling of the destination or the purpose of the expedition.

Grant's only recorded written order issued for this affair was sent out at 2 A.M., dated "On Board Steamer Belle of Memphis, November 7." [12] This organized the five regiments, battery, and two troops into two brigades to be commanded respectively by General McClernand and Colonel Henry Dougherty, and directed the command to move at 6 A.M. in this order: (1) gunboats; (2) 1st Brigade; (3) 2d Brigade. The entire force was to be landed on the Missouri shore above Belmont at a point to be selected by Captain Walke, the senior naval officer present, whence "orders will be communicated for the disposition of the entire command."

[11] N. R. 22:400.
[12] N. R. 22:402; W. R. 3:270.

By 8:30 A.M. all the transports had reached the point selected, two and a half miles from Belmont, and the landing was effected without interruption. McClernand, seemingly without further orders from Grant, formed his (1st) brigade into march column, sending the cavalry ahead to reconnoiter the road, and moved out, followed by Dougherty, on Grant's order. By Grant's direction five companies from Dougherty's brigade were left as guard for the transports. This guard, a detachment from each of the two regiments composing Dougherty's brigade—or, as Grant terms it in his fourth report, "reserve"—was, however, by an order communicated through an aid, moved out by a road along the river to a ravine nearer Belmont, where it came under the fire of Confederate guns on the Kentucky shore though it suffered no losses.

According to his own report, it was McClernand who selected the place for deployment of the command, a mile from the landing, between a corn-field and a dry slough. Here the five regiments were formed in line and, in accordance with the tactical ideas of the day, two companies from each of the ten-company regiments were sent out as skirmishers.[13]

What, meanwhile, was happening on the Confederate side? Belmont had been occupied by one regiment of infantry, a battery of six guns, and two troops of cavalry. As soon as General Polk learned of Grant's landing he sent four regiments and a battery across the river as reinforcements, with Pillow to take command. Thus the first phase of the engagement was fought with five regiments, a battery, and two troops on each side. Pillow's account states his strength as somewhat under 500 per regiment, for the five regiments, but as probably Tappan's regiment, already in Belmont, was somewhat over 500, we may esti-

---

[13] The two 2d Brigade regiments, however, had only 7 and 8 companies respectively, as the transport guard had been taken from these.

mate the Confederate infantry strength at 2,500. A Memphis paper gives the total Confederate strength as 2,700. Grant's total strength was 3,114, but, allowing for the transport guard, the cavalry, and the artillery, the two forces engaged must have been about equal in numbers.

However, three factors operated in Grant's favor: First, his Illinois and Iowa backwoodsmen—frontiersmen in the truest sense—were probably superior as soldier material. Secondly, two of his regiments and their commanders had already had field experience. Colonel Dougherty (22d Illinois) had before this commanded his regiment in a successful action at Charleston, Missouri, as early as August 20, in which he, a lieutenant-colonel, and two captains were wounded; and again near Norfolk on September 27. Colonel Lauman (7th Iowa) had been under Grant at Ironton in August, had commanded for a time at Fort Jefferson, and had conducted or participated in numerous operations against parties of the enemy in both Kentucky and Missouri.

It was certainly no small advantage to Grant to have, in what was to develop into almost wholly a regimental commanders' fight, two regiments which for that day might well be considered "veteran regiments," already practised in combat and campaign, especially as against the enemy's inexperienced and less well-trained and well-equipped troops. But the most favorable factor for him was that he was on the offensive—always inspiriting to troops, especially to those new to the profession of arms—while Pillow was on the defensive and played even that rôle very badly. The sense of superiority in Grant's men was augmented by the backing of the Northern river fleet, which had been all along so unquestionably dominating the upper reaches of the Mississippi.

The regiment on the extreme right of the line of deployment—the 27th Illinois, Colonel Buford—found in front of it a shallow pond, so that its skirmishers were sent southward around the edge; and when the command for a general advance was given, Buford with commendable initiative determined to follow a road he was assured led "to the rear of Belmont." For the time being, however, he was completely out of touch with the remainder of the command, except Dollin's cavalry, which "appeared" on his left and obeyed his orders to "go forward and discover the enemy." [14]

In the center, the remaining regiments of the 1st Brigade went forward along the main road to Belmont, followed by McClernand and Grant. On the left, the two regiments of the 2d Brigade, preceded by skirmishers, advanced also, on the left of the main Belmont road, without encountering any enemy, but impeded and delayed by dense fallen timber.

Colonel Dougherty, the brigade commander, meeting no enemy on his front, but "hearing firing on the right" and doubtless influenced by the hard going—also with praiseworthy initiative—changed direction, marching by the right flank and crossing in the rear of the 1st Brigade regiments until he could advance to the sound of musketry, so as to come in on the right of those two regiments. Unfortunately the result of this well-intended movement was that it eventually led to great confusion and mixing of units and to a gap between Logan's regiment, the 31st Illinois, and Lauman's, the 7th Iowa.

The two-hundred-odd skirmishers sent forward by Pillow proved not enough to stay the Union advance through the woods to the Confederate "Camp Johnston," which had been established in a clearing close to the river. Up-stream from it lay three cornfields; down-stream, a wide stretch of fallen timber partially converted into abatis. Colonel Tappan, commanding the infantry regiment, the 13th Arkansas, and the camp, on receipt at 7 A.M.

[14] W. R. 3:284.

of information from Polk of the Union landing up the river had promptly sent out his two troops to reconnoiter and disposed his regiment and six guns to defend the camp, posting two guns to cover each of the three roads over which the enemy might come.

Pillow, arriving an hour later with his four Tennessee regiments, adopted Colonel Tappan's defensive line about four hundred yards from the river and placed his reinforcements right and left of the 13th Arkansas, which was concentrated to the right of the center; but the guns he also concentrated in the center, commanding the main and probable road of the Union advance.

By 10:30 A.M. the Confederate skirmishers had been driven in and the Union skirmishers were feeling their way to develop the enemy's main line, when Pillow, lacking in both discretion and patience, ordered a "bayonet charge," to "drive those rascals out." The Confederate line was a strong one, being in the open a hundred to two hundred yards from the edge of dense woods.[15] This was far enough, with the muskets then in use, to be beyond effective range from the enemy in the edge of the woods; so the common-sense view is that had Pillow been content to wait he would have had every advantage. His men had cover, having had time to prepare hasty trenches; the Union troops, while covered in the wood, would have to come out and expose themselves in order either to attack or to bring an effective fire to bear upon the Confederate line.

Pillow's line had good lateral and rear communications which facilitated the exercise of control. On Grant's side any exercise of control was impossible, because of the dense woods and also because his command by this time was scattered and badly disorganized. Not only were brigades and regiments mixed, but also officers and men in the various units, except in the 27th Illinois (Buford), which was by itself on another road.

15 Except the right regiment, the line of which extended into the woods.

In these circumstances it is doubtful if, had Pillow remained in his chosen position, the Union attack could have been effectively made. But Pillow's "charge" threw away these advantages. His men advanced fifty to seventy-five yards, to near the edge of the woods, and there halted. Some of the regiments remained in their advanced positions half to three quarters of an hour; others

fell back almost at once, the command to retire being passed along the line without any one's knowing where it originated. This early retirement left gaps in the line and sapped the morale of those remaining forward in the open, firing at close range against an enemy under cover and finding themselves subjected to flanking fire as the gaps in the forward line increased in size and number.

It is uncertain whether of the Federal troops more than the advance skirmish lines had reached the edge of the woods at the time this so-called bayonet charge was made. No Union reports mention it. They merely state that three stands were made by the enemy: one by the four companies of advanced skirmishers; one near the edge of the clearing; and the third, the hardest to overcome, near the main camp. Even so, the final line might have held had Pillow left the two guns where Tappan placed them, commanding the southernmost road along which Buford was advancing against the left Confederate regiment, which was the first to give way and whose giving way proved the signal for the break.

Another Confederate advantage wasted was the fact that the extra ammunition, which is always so easily handled on the defensive and which had been sent across the river expressly for the battle, was not distributed, but dumped on the river bank, where it evidently was not easily accessible when the need for it arose.

But while all these shortcomings of the defense made Grant's success easier—if it is not too much to say possible—of attainment, we cannot but admire the élan of the Northern men, even though they were aided by the sense of pursuing an already beaten and retreating enemy, an élan which carried them forward in a victorious assault in the open after an advance through more than a mile of dense woods.

No European commander of conscript troops, however well trained, would expect his men to be capable of it, and well might Grant write the next day, as he did to his father: "The victory was complete. It has given us confidence in the officers and men of this command that will enable us to lead them in any future engagement without fear of the result." [16]

[16] Moore III:288.

Shortly after noon the camp fell, the Confederate troops retreating to the river bank. The goal was reached and Grant, his officers, and his troops, filled with an exultation easily understood, paused, quite humanly but unwisely, to gather in what they conceived as the fruits of victory. McClernand led his men in "three cheers for the Union," to which, his report tells us, "the brave men around me responded with the most enthusiastic applause."

How critical the situation still was, no one in the Union forces appeared to realize. Had Grant kept out a reserve, now would have been the time to employ it in following up the retreating enemy; as he lacked one, the circumstances called for immediate re-forming and reorganizing of his badly mixed and mingled regiments. Instead, he gave the order to burn the camp or, in the words of his report, "for destruction of everything that could not be moved." Nor was the order given to a designated unit, but apparently to every one.

Grant woefully failed to remember from his Mexican War experience the weakness of the American soldier, amounting almost to a passion, for souvenirs, especially battle souvenirs! And therefore immediate pursuit was not undertaken; and, to make matters worse, in the course of the looting and burning many of the troops got out of hand.

The Confederate outlook while the Northern troops were looting their camp was discouraging, yet not hopeless. Organizations on that side also were mixed, and in addition the men were panicky. The scene on the river bank is described by Captain Trask of the Confederate steamer *Charm,* engaged in bringing reinforcements across the river:

Upon landing, at 12 M., on the Belmont side . . . we found the landing obstructed by our disorganized forces, who endeavored to board and take possession of our boat, and at the same time cry-ing: "Dont land!" "Dont land!" "We are whipped!" "Go back!" &c. We, however, succeeded in landing six companies of Colonel Marks' regiment, when the disorganized troops previously spoken of made a rush on our boat and forced me to give the order to take the boat from the landing.[17]

But by this time two other regiments of Confederate rein-forcements had already been landed. The earliest of these to arrive, the 2d Tennessee, Pillow had kept in reserve on the river bank and now utilized to cover the withdrawal and reorganiza-tion of his broken regiments. The next two, the 11th Louisiana and 15th Tennessee, he sent up-stream to make a flank and rear-ward attack on the Union regiments busy looting Camp Johnston.

Polk, in observation across the river, had at last become con-vinced that the only danger threatening his command that day was at Belmont, and he was taking strong measures. "Lady Davis," the Confederate heavy "pivot" gun on the heights, fired two rounds on Grant's men in the burning camp and then jammed. More effective were two field batteries placed during the morning on the Kentucky heights immediately opposite Camp Johnston. Now these batteries had an objective at a range of less than one thousand yards and opened fire. They silenced Grant's artillery, a part of which was firing on the steamer bringing Con-federate reinforcements across. They also, however, aided Grant in a way, driving his disorganized men from the camp and thus making it possible to bring them under some semblance of control for the struggle to follow.

It must have been toward 2 P.M. when the Union force was gotten in hand and began its retreat. Just where the subsequent fighting occurred is not clear from the reports. Parts of three of the Confederate regiments which had fought in the morning battle had moved up the river bank and been joined to the two

[17] W. R. 3:363.

reinforcing regiments of Colonels Marks and Tyler in a fresh attack somewhere on the flank of Grant's line of retreat. It was a bitter pill, after the initial thrilling success, to have to run away under fire. It meant more than disappointment. It meant heavy casualties in killed, wounded, and prisoners. But, owing to Grant's failure better to use the crucial hours from twelve to two o'clock, no other course was now possible.

It was at best a disorganized retreat, and most of the Union losses were incurred at this time, especially in the 7th Iowa, which lost 26 killed, 93 wounded, and 137 missing, mostly prisoners.

The Confederate infantry engaged during the battle and in the retreat comprised ten regiments, though the last two of these caught up with Grant's troops only after the reëmbarkation of all except Buford's regiment and stragglers who had been cut off.

The navy seem to have been fairly disinterested observers in the matter of the reëmbarkation of Grant's troops. Commander Walke in his report writes:

When nearly all our troops had reëmbarked and were about ready to start, a sudden attack was made upon the transport vessels by a large [Confederate] force coming in from above. Our gunboats being in good position, we opened a brisk fire of grape and canister and five shells, silencing the enemy with great slaughter.[18] After the transports were safely underway we followed them, throwing a shell occasionally to repel the enemy approaching to the banks. When a few miles up the river, we met one of the transports, *Chancellor,* with Brigadier-General McClernand aboard, who stated that some of their men were left behind, and asked that we might return with our gunboats and see if we could find them. We did so, the *Lexington* accompanying us, and between us succeeded in securing nearly all that was left behind [Buford's regiment], together with about forty prisoners, including some badly wounded.[19]

[18] The "great slaughter" was, actually, twelve wounded.
[19] N. R. 22:401.

The chief interest in Belmont lies in its being the first of the series of blows struck by Grant against an enemy capable and desirous of striking back, the series which ended with Appomattox. Strategically—in a narrow sense—it was difficult to justify; tactically foolhardy, yet psychologically a necessity. Up to this time, both in Kentucky and Missouri, the Confederates had had the initiative. Now Grant seized it and kept it.

It is easy from our present knowledge to pick flaws in Grant's tactics. Yet it is not only idle but unjust to blame either the general or his contemporaries for these, since in his time there was an entire absence of any tactical literature or instruction worthy the name. Probably no Civil War officer had ever heard of a "map problem," "tactical walk," or "war-game." The faulty deployment—of so large a force—in a single line; the absence of a real reserve; the failure properly to organize and to direct the attacking force, were all traceable to instructions in or omissions from the authorized drill regulations of the day, "Casey's Tactics." What Grant later learned, he learned by recognizing his own mistakes. This is evidenced not only by his conduct in subsequent operations but by the shaping of his official reports.

Undoubtedly much of his initial success at Belmont was due to the very boldness of conception of the undertaking, but also and perhaps equally to the initiative, enterprise, and ability of the five regimental commanders. Dougherty was incapacitated by his wounds, else more would certainly have been heard of him; but the others all rose to distinction in the war. Grant naturally chose his best regiments for the expedition, and the best regiments are always those having the most efficient colonels.

By the Confederates, Belmont was, correctly enough for propaganda purposes, hailed as a signal victory. They had been assailed at a vulnerable point, and the temporary loss of the defensive position adopted by their troops and the destruction of a regimental camp had been more than offset by the subsequent entirely successful counter-attack which had driven the enemy in more or less confusion from the field.

The policy that had been adopted by the Confederate Government in the beginning was one of non-aggression, but of vigorous defense of their own territory. Hence, considering the affair, as they did, an attempt to break the line of their Mississippi defenses, they could, and not without justice, point with pride to the fact that just as they had successfully parried the first Northern thrust at the heart of Virginia at Bull Run, so they now with equal success had countered the first blow on the Mississippi. While the two combats were scarcely comparable in size, with regard to forces engaged, public opinion did not always measure results by the number of battalions employed.

Yet this Southern official claim does not ring quite true; nor is it borne out by a closer examination of the consequences. As has been partially shown in a previous chapter, President Davis expected that both Kentucky and Missouri would join the Confederacy. In the hope, apparently, of hastening the taking of this wished-for step, by the governments of the two States, he forbore too long to lend active assistance to the Confederate partizans in them or to attempt operations to gain military control. He must have failed to picture to himself what would be the hopeless situation economically of the Confederacy should the two States, particularly Kentucky, be wholly lost to it.

As the North gained a stronger and stronger grip on Missouri he did approve the allotment of a half-million dollars to assist the State (Confederate) militia, and he did send regular Confederate troops across the Arkansas border to assist Price and Governor Jackson in the Wilson's Creek campaign against Lyon. But in the main his mind was on affairs in the East, and the flower of the troops raised in the West was from the beginning drawn eastward. When the possibility of employing guerrilla tactics in Missouri was suggested to him he quite definitely deprecated the idea.

With regard to Kentucky, as we have seen, he regretted Polk's action in violating the declared neutrality of that State by occupying Columbus; but, though he later acquiesced in the holding of the points seized, he failed to realize the full consequences of the change in circumstances. Having full confidence in the ability of Albert Sidney Johnston, assigned to command the Confederate Western Department on September 10, he gave the general a free hand in the management of affairs in that area.

Johnston reached his Western Department—extended by President Davis to include all of Tennessee, Arkansas, Kentucky, and Missouri—shortly after the occupation of Columbus, Kentucky, and at once threw all available reserves into an invasion of central and eastern Kentucky, to rescue from the Northern grip what he could of the resources of that State. His main army he built up on the line of the Louisville and Nashville Railroad, and though he did not then assume personal command of it, it consumed most of his time and attention. Polk had been his room-mate at West Point and always his devoted friend. He quite naturally, therefore, left Polk to deal with the Mississippi and trans-Mississippi problems in his own way.

Polk, hampered as he had been by the caliber of his chief subordinates, Pillow, Cheatham, Price, and Thompson—Hardee had been taken by Johnston for his main army—and also by his lack of material and funds, had carried on very well.

The general conditions immediately prior to Belmont are well summed up by Commander Porter. In command of the gunboat *New Era,* he had spent a month at Paducah and cruised 850 miles along the Mississippi, Tennessee, and Cumberland rivers, and in his report to Commodore Foote on his return to St. Louis on November 6, he wrote: "I found all of the United States troops lying inactive behind intrenchments, while the enemy are active in every direction with a force not more than half the number of the United States forces." [20]

The opinion of the naval officer observing land operations is always of value, because he is able to speak not only with the authority of one who has had professional training, but with a certain detachment of interest. Nor does close examination reveal the case to have been otherwise than as Porter described it. Such a state of affairs could not fail to depress the morale of the Union soldiers and improve that of the Confederates. That it existed is not to be attributed to the failure of local detachment commanders such as Grant and Smith, but rather to the rigid orders of the department commander, Frémont, who withheld authority for the proper exercise of initiative.

With Belmont the tide turned, though this was not at first evident. Soldier opinion and public opinion both looked, indeed, for a Confederate follow-up operation. Grant himself is said to have expected an attack on Fort Holt, a low-lying fort on the Kentucky shore opposite Cairo, Illinois, and only a full day's march from Columbus, with no intervening obstacles. But nothing happened. There were, as we to-day know, many reasons why. Polk did not feel competent to undertake a field expedition himself and had no subordinate officer suitable to command one; material and transportation were lacking; troops had been detached; there was no naval force able to cope with the Northern river flotilla. Regarding this last deficiency, however, it is interesting to note that the Confederates evidently failed to appreciate the fact that at Belmont they had with a mere field battery kept the Union gunboats at bay up the river.

[20] N. R. 22:397.

One easily understood cause of the Confederate inactivity in this theater subsequent to Belmont was that Polk himself had been injured and temporarily disabled by the bursting of the big gun "Lady Davis" at Columbus. For days following, nothing was done. By the time the general recovered, the best of his troops had been drawn eastward by Johnston.

Yet the main cause of passivity was undoubtedly that, notwithstanding what the Southern press and propagandists might say, the Confederate morale in the West had really suffered. Propaganda and claimed victories may dupe statesmen and people alike, but not the soldiers concerned. They know! Perhaps the best compliment the Union force at Belmont ever received was Polk's despatch to President Davis the night after the battle, magnifying Grant's force two and a half times—to 7,500 men.[21]

That despatch might deceive the President, but the Confederate soldiers actually engaged knew that Grant had not had more men than the defenders at Camp Johnston. They knew that, man for man, they had been beaten, and that with their own number made double by reinforcements—ten regiments to Grant's five—the most they had been able to do was to drive the enemy back on his transports. Stripped of all camouflage, this was the truth, this was why they were no longer keen to fight. Polk himself, whatever he might claim, perhaps even believe on the night after the battle, was bound, as the hard facts gradually intruded themselves, to feel the same about it.

How different the picture at Cairo the next day! There the men were tired but jubilant. They had their trophies, their battle souvenirs—costly to others if not to themselves, in life and limb —to gloat over, tales of their experiences in their initial battle to exchange; and their reflections and comments could only be:

[21] Moore III:287.

"We licked our own numbers! And when they sent reinforcements to surround us we licked those fellows too! We're better men than they are and we know it and they know it! But—moral!—don't ever stop to loot till you're sure the battle is all over."

Other elements contributed to the impairment of the Confederates' self-confidence. The long-drawn-out investigation by Polk; the interrogation of officers on the subject of Pillow's exercise of command; Pillow's resignation—later withdrawn—all helped produce the impression, among officers and men alike, that the Confederate command in the battle had somehow been wrong.

Belmont had given to President Lincoln, whether he yet knew it or not, one of those assets beyond price, a general who had the trust and allegiance of his men. Grant had gone into battle with his troops, had braved the same dangers, had had his horse shot from under him and mounted another. All these things, it is true, he might have done and not have won their confidence. But more than his physical presence was the released dynamic force that swept with him into the battle, and, whatever the feelings of his troops toward him before the engagement, there was welded during it that subtle bond which made them from that hour "Grant's men."

The bond between comrade and comrade that is forged by the "baptism of fire" on the battle-field establishes one of the most beautiful of human relationships. Still more beautiful, perhaps because rarer, is the tie that results from a sense of real, one must say "spiritual," team-work between a commander and his men. Pétain and Hindenburg created it in the World War; so did Lord Roberts in South Africa, and Oyama in Manchuria; so also Lee in the Civil War; McClellan too, though only temporarily. Men will do anything in their power for him who has exercised spiritual leadership over them in a great cause. It was this sort of loyalty that elected Grant President.

A semblance of such loyalty can be fostered for a time by more or less artificial means, as McClellan and others have understood very well. Grant scorned artificiality. His carelessness in dress, for example, though it rather appealed to his backwoodsmen of the West, offended the Army of the Potomac, taught by McClellan how to expect a general to appear before them. In neither case did Grant care. He valued the substance, not the shadow.

After Belmont, Grant felt that he owed it to his men to let them know his appreciation; that he knew what they felt, and liked it. His order read to them on November 8 at retreat undoubtedly came from his heart and cemented the bond between him and them:

The general commanding this Military District returns his thanks to the troops under his command at the battle of Belmont on yesterday.

It has been his fortune to have been in all the battles fought in Mexico by Generals Scott and Taylor save Buena Vista, and he never saw one more hotly contested or where troops behaved with more gallantry.

Such courage will insure victory wherever our flag may be borne and protected by such a class of men.

To the brave men who fell the sympathy of the country is due, and will be manifested in a manner unmistakable.[22]

[22] Moore III:285, 286; N. R. 22:398.

CHAPTER IX

The Amenities of War in the West

> I deplore in this war the lack, in some of the
> combatants, of the old knightliness with which
> war formerly was waged.
> —Von Hindenburg (1919).

AS early as October 14, Polk had sent two of his officers, under a flag of truce, to Grant at Cairo, proposing an arrangement for the exchange of prisoners. To this Grant had replied, rather brusquely, that he could of his "own accord, make none." His reply continued: "I recognize no Southern Confederacy myself but will communicate with higher authority for their views. Should I not be sustained I will find means of communicating with you." [1]

Grant's view was not "sustained," for he caused McClernand, post commander at Cairo, to write "The Commanding Officer, Columbus, Ky.," on October 22:

The chances of the present unhappy war having left in my hands a number of prisoners . . . I have for special reasons as well as in obedience to the dictates of humanity determined unconditionally to release them . . . Colonel Buford, of the 27th Regiment of Illinois Volunteers, is charged by me with the delivery of said prisoners [three] . . . under the protection of a white flag. [2]

Not to be outdone in courtesy, Polk replied to this:

I have received your note . . . responding to the overtures made by me to General Grant some days since on the subject of exchange of prisoners; and although your mode of accomplishing it waives

[1] W. R. 114:511.
[2] W. R. 114:512.

the recognition of our claims as belligerents I am not disposed to insist on an unimportant technicality when the interests of humanity are at stake.

I accept the release of the three prisoners tendered me being as your note implies all of those of the Confederate army in your possession. In return I have pleasure in offering you the sixteen of those of the Federal army in my possession.

Hoping that in the prosecution of the unhappy conflict in which we are engaged we shall never lose sight of the claims of generosity on those who direct the operations of the armies of our respective Governments,

I have the honor to be, etc.

Buford's report gives us a most pleasing picture of his interview with Polk:

The General received my suite [of five] with cordiality; and we were introduced to General Pillow and . . . many other officers. He remained on the Steamer *Charm,* with our tug alongside, for four hours, while the prisoners were being got ready . . . during which time the most friendly conversation was enjoyed.

My party were hospitably entertained. I ventured to propose the sentiment "Washington and his principles," which was repeated with hearty approbation.

Generals Polk and Pillow expressed a high appreciation of your character . . . The Conference ended without an unfriendly word or occurrence.[3]

Captain Polk, son of the Confederate general, also gives an account of the toast incident, amusing in its different coloring: "The gallant colonel, raising his glass, proposed, 'George Washington, the Father of his Country.' General Polk, with a merry twinkle in his eye, quickly added: 'And the first Rebel!' The Federal officers, caught in their own trap, gracefully acknowledged it by drinking the amended toast." [4]

[3] Moore III:234.
[4] "Battles and Leaders of the Civil War," Vol. I, p. 357.

Evidently encouraged by the success of Colonel Buford's mission, Grant sent his aid, Captain Hillyer, on a similar errand, on October 30. Hillyer also was received by Polk, aboard the *Yazoo*.

Thus the way had been well prepared for Grant to write Polk on November 8, the day after Belmont:

In the skirmish of yesterday in which both parties behaved with so much gallantry many unfortunate men were left upon the field of battle who it was impossible to provide for. I now send in the interest of humanity to have these unfortunates collected and medical attendance secured them. I at the same time return sixty-four prisoners taken by our forces who are unconditionally released. Colonel Webster . . . goes bearer of this and will express to you my views upon the course that should be pursued under circumstances such as those of yesterday.[5]

Polk, according to a paragraph in the "Boston Evening Transcript" of December 6, 1861, on reading the word "skirmish," exclaimed "Skirmish! Hell and damnation! I'd like to know what he calls a *battle*." [6]

But Polk had received new instructions and could no longer exchange prisoners without referring to higher authority. However, he sent a staff officer to meet Colonel Webster and it was arranged that a Union working party should visit the battle-field, "where they were employed for the remainder of the day in caring for the wounded, some of whom were found yet there, and in burying the dead." Thirteen wounded Union men were brought back by Colonel Webster.

A correspondent of the "Chicago Tribune," "B. R. K.," writes as a postscript to his Cairo letter of November 8:

The *Memphis* returned at midnight. The expedition that went down upon her with flags of truce, report the whole number of our dead found and buried by them on the field of battle at eighty-five.

[5] W. R. 114:515.
[6] Moore III, P., 71.

. . . All [the wounded] that were left on the field the night of the battle were well cared for, and experienced the kindest treatment from the rebel surgeons. All the troops have been withdrawn to Columbus. Nothing was to be seen on the Belmont side yesterday, but the party burying the dead and a company of cavalry, searching the woods for dead and wounded.[7]

Two days later, on the tenth, Grant wrote Polk again, addressing him this time by name, and not simply as before, as "Commanding Officer, Columbus, Ky.":

General: It grieves me to have to trouble you again with a flag of truce but Mrs. Colonel Dougherty whose husband is a prisoner with you is very anxious to join him under such restrictions as you may impose, and I understand that some of your officers expressed the opinion that no objections would be interposed. I will be most happy to reciprocate in a similar manner at any time you may request it.[8]

Polk acknowledged this note:

It gives me great pleasure to grant her the opportunity of rendering such grateful service and I hope through her attention the colonel may be restored to such a condition of health as is compatible with the loss he has been obliged to sustain.[9]
Reciprocating your expressions of a readiness to interchange kind offices, I remain . . .

Grant went down, himself, on the twelfth [10] for a personal interview with Polk on his flag-of-truce boat. Of this meeting Polk says in a letter to his wife two days later:

My interview with General Grant was, on the whole, satisfactory. It was about an exchange of prisoners. He looked rather grave, I

---

[7] Moore III:293. To those who know the propaganda of the World War only, about the treatment of the captured, it cannot but be astonishing not that the fact of kind treatment should exist but that the press should have so stated it.
[8] W. R. 114:517.
[9] Owing to wounds received at Belmont his leg had to be amputated.
[10] W. R. 114:519.

thought, like a man who was not at his ease. We talked pleasantly and I succeeded in getting a smile out of him and then got on well enough. I discussed the principles on which I thought the war should be conducted; denounced all barbarity, vandalism, plundering, and all that, and got him to say he would join in putting it down. I was favorably impressed with him; he is undoubtedly a man of much force. We have now exchanged five or six flags [of truce], and he grows more civil and respectful every time.[11]

On November 12, Polk had written to Grant, informing him that he had received discretionary powers regarding the disposition of prisoners and that he had concluded to return all Grant's wounded, one hundred and three in number.[12]

Grant, replying to this, expressed himself as happy to know that the matter had been left to Polk's discretion; that evening the two met at the conference just described, and arrived at an understanding regarding the further exchange of prisoners. Unfortunately, this understanding, being oral, soon led to differences of opinion and to more correspondence.

Colonel Buford, once more sent under a flag of truce, wrote General Polk on November 29:

I feel constrained to inform you that General Grant and the officers who attended him with the flag of truce understood that he should liberate all the prisoners under his control and that you should do the same.

He is of the opinion that he sent you more sound, healthy men than you returned him wounded men. In relieving you of the wounded he did you a service and leaves an obligation due from you.[13]

This view of Grant's, hard as it sounds, is interesting as the germ and reason for his refusal in 1864, as Lieutenant-General

[11] B. and L. I:356, 357.
[12] W. R. 114:518.
[13] W. R. 114:526.

Commanding the Armies of the United States, to make any further exchange of prisoners with the Confederate armies.

Buford's letter concludes, speaking frankly from the heart of a regimental commander:

My earnest desire for the liberation of mine of the 27th Regiment is unabated. It preys upon me. I desire you to return the ninety-eight prisoners sent to Memphis and express to you the belief that your magnanimity will be suitably acknowledged.

Let us have one more meeting and talk of peace.

Your friend,
N. B. BUFORD,
Colonel 27th Regiment Illinois Volunteers.

The reason for this complaint was that nearly all the prisoners brought away by Grant from Belmont had been unwounded, while Polk had almost as many of Grant's wounded as Grant had prisoners altogether. Not unnaturally, Polk sent back the Union wounded first, and when it came to the rest, Grant had none to exchange for them, until Henry and Donelson tipped the scales in the other direction. During November Grant gave up 124 for 114 returned by Polk, who reported on November 16 that he still had 100, "sent to Memphis for safe keeping." [14]

Ultimately a cartel was arranged: "When the same grade cannot be given . . . give two of the next grade below, that is for one colonel give two lieutenant-colonels, or four majors, or eight captains, &c." [15]

The correspondence between Grant and Polk continued up to February 4, 1862—two days before the attack on Fort Henry—and covered a wide range of subjects. [16]

[14] W. R. 114:541.
[15] W. R. 114:536 *et seq.*
[16] W. R. 114:515–547.

The courtesies exchanged between these belligerent gentlefolk of the old school were by no means limited to military matters, or to consideration for the wives of officers alone. Grant wrote Polk on December 5:

I also permit Mrs. —— of Evansville, Ind., to accompany the flag in the hope that you will permit her daughter, Mrs. Harris, of Columbus, and her son, a boy of some fourteen years of age, to visit her in the truce boat. This lady also desires to bring back her son. In this behalf I do not intercede knowing nothing of any of the parties. Being disposed myself to visit as lightly as possible the rigors of a state of war upon non-combatants, I have permitted this lady to go to you to plead her own cause.[17]

One result of the personal interview of November 12 between Grant and Polk was the return by Polk of "Francis M. Smith, hostler of General Grant [captured at Belmont], sent in accordance with the agreement . . . to the effect that Colonel Tappan's colored servant, George, should be returned to him."

In the World War the old-time amenities were somewhat lost to view. Certainly on the battle-fields in France nothing could have happened to be compared to the following incident related by the correspondent of the "Chicago Journal," writing from Cairo the day following Belmont, who says:

At the last session of Congress, Colonel Foulke parted from Colonel [J. V.] Wright [Colonel of the 13th Tennessee Regiment], a member from Tennessee, and used this expression: "Phil, I expect the next time we meet it will be on the battlefield, and I want to ask one favor of you; if you get me or any of my men, I want you to use us well, and if I get you or any of your men, I will do the same!" Yesterday they met in battle, and the very first prisoners, sixty in all, that were taken belonged to Colonel Wright's command, and his old friend, Colonel F., took them. . . .

Colonel Foulke was asked by a Lieutenant at Columbus if he

17 W. R. 114:528.

was not the Colonel who drove Colonel Wright and his command. He told him he was. The Lieutenant then told Colonel F. that twenty guns were aimed to pick him off, when Colonel Wright saw him and ordered his men not to shoot at him as he was his friend.[18]

Colonel Marcus J. Wright, commanding one of the Confederate regiments engaged in pursuing the Union force at Belmont in the afternoon, gives us another example of an amenity which is the more interesting as being the only glimpse of Grant's movements or doings on that afternoon, except his own statements, unsatisfactory as evidence, in his 1865 and subsequent accounts. Writing in 1888, on the Battle of Belmont, Colonel Wright, describing the pursuit by his regiment, says:

Within a half mile from where we started we came near a double log house, about one hundred yards from the road, and which was occupied by the Federals as a hospital. At the gate were two Federal officers mounted on fine stallions. . . . At this juncture, two officers —one with an overcoat on, the other with his overcoat on his arm— came out of the hospital and ran towards a corn-field, jumping the fence and disappearing. When they first appeared, a number of my men of the 154th regiment cocked their guns and made aim at them.

General Cheatham at once directed me to order their guns to a shoulder and not to fire on stragglers, as his orders were to attack the troops seeking the transports. The order was given and there was no firing on them. On the day after the battle, General Cheatham met, under a flag of truce, Colonel Hatch, who was General Grant's quartermaster. Colonel Hatch, in his conversation with General Cheatham, told him that the two officers who ran out of the hospital were General Grant and himself, and that both were surprised that they were not fired on. General Cheatham, in a few days afterwards, met General Grant on a flag-of-truce boat, and he fully confirmed Colonel Hatch's statement.[19]

<hr/>

[18] Moore III:292. The correspondent of the "Memphis Appeal" (*idem* 296), writing from Columbus on November 10, also gives a version of this incident.

[19] "Southern Historical Society Papers," No. 16, p. 82.

CHAPTER X

AFTER BELMONT

> In war the general alone can judge of certain
> arrangements. It depends on him alone to conquer
> difficulties by his own superior talents and resolu-
> tion.—NAPOLEON.

HUNTER, interim commander of the Western Department
after Frémont, was himself in western Missouri, and the
records do not show any correspondence between him and Grant,
or that he exercised any influence upon events at Cairo. Nor at
Cairo were there any happenings of note save the frequent visits
of flag-of-truce boats and arrangements for the exchange of prisoners, previously mentioned.

On November 18, Jeff Thompson was ordered by Polk on a
cavalry raid to break through Grant's outpost-net west of the
river, and to waylay a certain passing steamer between Cairo and
St. Louis. In response to the order he wrote: "I will, with pleasure, undertake the expedition, but I have no hopes that I can
remain long enough in ambush to catch any particular boat. I
will do my best, and if I cannot get the one desired I will get
some other." [1]

The chief interest in the affair is given it by a mention in the
Memoirs of an attempt to hold up a steamer on which Grant was
expected to be a passenger, which may possibly refer to this
expedition.[2]

[1] W. R. 3:368.
[2] Grant I:217.

Thompson succeeded in holding up the steamer *Platte City,* capturing and releasing on parole two officers of the 2d Cavalry (Union). Grant learned of this hold-up the same day and took immediate steps for a vigorous pursuit; and Thompson, though he was not caught, was discouraged from making any further attempt. Soon after this the enlistments of Thompson's men in the Missouri militia expired and, the endeavors to get them to reënlist for the Confederate service being mostly unsuccessful, he of necessity ceased for a time to play a rôle of any consequence.

On November 21, Grant received General Halleck's order of the nineteenth assuming command of the Western Department, re-named the Department of the Missouri, and in acknowledgment made him a report which gives a clear picture of his outlook on that date.

After describing what his district comprises, Grant first takes up *"the Enemy"*:

Since the affair of Belmont, on the 7th instant, quite a number of Northern men have made their escape from the South, not a few of them soldiers. From this source I have got what I believe a reliable statement of the strength of the enemy; the position of his batteries; number of his troops, &c.

There are now at Columbus forty-seven regiments of infantry and cavalry, two companies of light artillery, and over one hundred pieces of heavy ordnance. All the statements I have received corroborate each other. In addition to these there are at Camp Beauregard, on the road about half way between Mayfield and Union City some 8,000 more, of all arms . . .

The enemy are working night and day upon their fortifications, and the greatest consternation has prevailed for the last ten days lest Columbus should be attacked. Finding they are let alone, they may be induced to act on the offensive if more troops are not sent here soon. A gunboat [Confederate] reached Columbus the night of the 19th instant, and another is expected within a few days.

Then *"Own Forces"*:

The condition of this command is bad in every particular except discipline. In this latter I think they will compare favorably with almost any volunteers. There is a great deficiency in transportation. I have no ambulances. The clothing received has been almost universally of an inferior quality and deficient in quantity. The arms in the hands of the men are mostly the old flint lock repaired . . . and others of still more inferior quality.

Here speaks the realist!

My cavalry force are none of them properly armed . . . Eight companies are entirely without arms. . . .

The Quartermaster's Department has been carried on here with so little funds that Government credit has become exhausted. I would urgently recommend that relief in this particular be afforded.[3]

This is scarcely an optimistic view of affairs. Grant, indeed, points out the Confederate weaknesses and fears, but he presents no plan of operations even should he be reinforced and his deficiencies in arms and supplies made good.

His report of the day following, November 22, indicates that he is becoming more economics-conscious, and is taking steps to make effective within his jurisdiction that economic pressure which in the end, by judicious application, was to become so important a factor in the ending of the Civil War, as was the case later in the World War. He wrote:

I have frequently reported to the Western Department [4] that the line of steamers plying between St. Louis and Cairo, by landing at points on the Missouri shore, were enabled to afford aid and comfort to the enemy. I have been reliably informed that some of the officers, particularly the clerks of these boats, were regularly in the employ of the Southern Confederacy, so called. The case of the *Platte Valley*, a few days since, confirmed me in this belief. I have

[3] W. R. 7:442.
[4] Frémont had taken no heed of such reports.

heretofore recommended that all the carrying trade between here and St. Louis be performed by Government, charging uniform rates. I would respectfully renew the suggestion, and in consideration of the special disloyalty of Southeastern Missouri I would further recommend that all commerce be cut off from all points south of Cape Girardeau.   There is not a sufficiency of Union sentiment left in this portion of the State to save Sodom.   This is shown from the fact that Jeff. Thompson or any of the rebels can go into Charleston and spend hours or encamp for the night on their way north to depredate upon Union men, and not one loyalist is found to report the fact to our pickets, stationed but $1\frac{1}{2}$ miles off.[5]

Halleck endorsed this but half-heartedly to the provost marshal at St. Louis, General Curtis, directing him to "carry into effect the recommendations of Brig. Gen. U. S. Grant . . . as far as you may deem necessary and practicable." [6]

Curtis, however, did not deem it necessary.   Perhaps he had been irritated by a rather undiplomatic letter he himself had received a few days before from Grant, protesting against the giving by Curtis of too many indiscriminate safe-conducts through Cairo, and concluding: "I shall in future exercise my own judgment about passing persons through my lines, unless the authority comes from a senior and one who exercises a command over me." [7]   In other words, he would no longer respect the safe-conducts of Curtis!

Grant sought also to tighten up on other parts of his lines and on November 26 instructed the commanding officer at Caledonia, Illinois, to

prevent all crossing of citizens and all intercourse between the people of Kentucky and the Illinois shore.   All persons known to be engaged in unlawful traffic between the two States will be arrested. . . . Particular caution is enjoined, however, in making seizures, to

[5] W. R. 8:373.
[6] W. R. 8:375.
[7] W. R. 3:571.

see that no hardship is inflicted upon innocent people. The greatest
vigilance will be observed to prevent contraband trade or intercourse
between the two States.[8]

A week later he took another fling at Curtis in a letter to
Halleck dated December 2:

The *J. D. Perry* has arrived, having landed at Price's [on the
Missouri side], putting ashore a large amount of freight. I understand that the authority to do so was given by the provost-marshal
of St. Louis. There is great danger of losing our boats by making
these landings . . . I have ordered the captain of the *J. D. Perry*
to disregard all orders to land on the Missouri shore between Cape
Girardeau and this place, unless given by the commanding officer
of the department or myself.[9]

Two days later the general added, a bit ironically:

I would respectfully report that the goods landed at Price's landing
. . . were moved directly to Hickman, Kentucky, and New Madrid,
Missouri [Confederate garrisoned towns]. I learned these facts too
late to capture the goods and the teams used in their transportation.
Eighty barrels of this freight were whiskey; a character of commerce
I would have no objection to being carried on with the South, but
there is a possibility that some barrels marked whiskey might contain
something more objectionable.[10]

As we hear no more such complaints from Grant, it may be
assumed that Halleck did something to remedy matters. Curtis
was shortly after sent to southwestern Missouri, where he carried
on very successfully.

With regard to more strictly military matters, we find Grant
on November 27 making his first report to Halleck on enemy
activities, briefly and to the point: "The rebels are fortifying New Madrid; have 500 negroes at work. A party of our

8 W. R. 7:449.
9 W. R. 7:465.
10 W. R. 8:404.

cavalry was yesterday in Belmont. No enemy found on the Missouri side." [11]

On the twenty-eighth he expressed concern over the non-arrival of expected reinforcements to his gunboat fleet and explained:

The rebels have one gunboat at Columbus, and are now expecting a fleet of them from New Orleans, under command of Captain Hollins. The arrival of this fleet without the floating means here of competing with them will serve materially to restore the confidence and feeling of security of the enemy, now, from best accounts, much shaken. [12]

On the twenty-ninth he added:

Information from Columbus to-day is to the effect that the rebels have three gunboats. They are small, carrying but four guns each. . . . The State of Mississippi has called for 10,000 State troops for sixty days to assist in the defense of Columbus. There seems to be a great effort making throughout the South to make Columbus impregnable. I get this information from the Memphis Appeal of the 28th . . . I give the information for what it is worth. [13]

Grant was exercising more and more his critical faculty. The information given in his last three reports was entirely accurate. The Governor of Mississippi called for ten thousand militia, but succeeded in raising only five thousand, under General Alcorn, and of this we shall hear later.

The three Confederate gunboats made their first appearance before Fort Holt on December 1, exchanging shots with the fort's batteries. [14] Grant sent his gunboats in pursuit, but the Southern boats were too fleet for them and got away. Grant in his report

[11] W. R. 8:383.
[12] W. R. 7:455.
[13] W. R. 7:460.
[14] Report of Dove, N. R. 22:448; of Cook, W. R. 7:7.

of December 1 [15] made a constructive recommendation for increasing the hospital facilities at Cairo, "in advance of the demand," and for securing more storage space for commissary supplies. He also mentioned the welcome receipt of "invoice and bill of lading" of "4,000 stand of French muskets with accouterments complete," and added, "These, with the 4,000 stand of improved arms, which I understand are to be sent for General McClernand's brigade, will supply the command, or nearly so."

The previous deficiency must certainly have been exasperatingly great. The last of December the enlisted strength present, of infantry and cavalry, was thirteen thousand; yet it had taken eight thousand small arms to "supply the command, or nearly so"!

On December 2 the general reported his measures to provide winter quarters for his troops, and inclosed a letter—since lost—from Colonel Ross regarding, among other matters, a "change of cavalry." Of this Grant said: "The cavalry complained of belong to Gen. Sigel's brigade, and such complaints have been made against them for their marauding propensities that I would recommend mustering them out of service." [16]

He evidently had no sympathy with the great American passion for "souvenirs"—possibly less since his Belmont experience. He wrote to Colonel Ross:

You will require Colonel Murdoch to give over to the quartermaster all property taken by them from citizens of Missouri. Such as may be reclaimed by the owners you will direct to be returned . . . I know your views about allowing troops to interpret the confiscation laws; therefore no instructions are required on this point. One thing I will add: In cases of outrageous marauding I would fully justify shooting the perpetrators down if caught in the act—I mean our own men as well as the enemy.[17]

[15] W. R. 7:462.
[16] W. R. 7:464.
[17] W. R. 8:404.

Grant intended to have no more of that. Only a short time before, on November 26, he had written to Colonel Oglesby on this subject:

You will cause an immediate investigation to be made of the property now illegally held by officers and soldiers of your command. All officers found with captured property, taken at Belmont or on your recent expedition . . . will be placed in arrest, and soldiers so holding will be put in confinement. Conduct of such an infamous character has been reported to me as to call for an investigation. If incorrect, it is well that the matter should be set right. If true, the guilty should be punished in order that the innocent may not suffer for the acts of others.[18]

It can well be imagined that with all these administrative matters to attend to, matters which were so well and so firmly handled, Grant had but little time for drawing up plans of campaign for forces not yet in hand or even in prospect. He was always a practical man, dealing with the daily tasks and problems that confronted him. He was also logical, not afraid to draw the plain, blunt conclusion from his data. He wrote Halleck on December 3, regarding two regiments sent by the Governor of Illinois to Shawneetown, one hundred miles up the Ohio River from Cairo, which Grant had temporarily supplied:

Troops are highly necessary at Shawneetown, not only to protect the citizens from marauding parties of secession troops, who are now collecting hogs and cattle and horses on the opposite [Kentucky] side of the river, but will serve to keep open navigation of the Ohio, and to prevent much of the smuggling now going on. Under these circumstances I would respectfully ask if it would not be well to extend the limits of this military district to the Wabash and give it limits north in this State. If this is not done, I would at least recommend that some command be required to take in these troops, where they can look for supplies, and so that they may be properly retained.

[18] W. R. 8:369.

Constant complaints are coming here from citizens of Crittenden and Union Counties, Kentucky, of depredations that are being committed by troops from Hopkinsville, and as the troops at Shawneetown have a steamer at their command, they may make excursions across the river that might be improper. There are large quantities of stock of all kinds being driven from these counties to the Southern Army, and quite a trade is being carried on in salt, powder, caps, and domestics. I have reported these facts . . . to Gen. Buell.[19]

Buell had succeeded Sherman in command of the Union forces in central and eastern Kentucky.

On December 5, Foote, promoted to commodore, reported his arrival at Cairo with some of the long-expected new river iron-clads, not yet in commission but receiving their armament. He telegraphed to Halleck on the sixth: "There is less prospect of an attack from Columbus than I expected when in St. Louis" [20] and in a letter to Secretary Welles he explained that he had reached this conclusion after interviewing "a clever observing officer who was yesterday at Columbus under a flag of truce." [21]

On December 6, Grant ordered a cavalry dash to be made from Bird's Point to Belmont, to spike some guns said to be there under a small guard.[22] There is, however, no report of the result. What operations there were appear to have been made more and more on either oral orders or memoranda not preserved. This is indicated at least by the messages to McClernand and Wallace on the eighth that: "owing to the inability of the gunboats to coöperate, the proposed expedition to New Madrid is postponed," which is all we know about it! [23]

The same day Grant reported his latest intelligence to Halleck:

I have just got in a man who spent yesterday in Columbus. He reports the enemy strongly fortified there, with fifty-four pieces of

19 W. R. 7:472.
20 N. R. 22:453.
21 N. R. 22:452.
22 W. R. 8:410.
23 W. R. 8:416.

heavy ordnance. . . . In addition to this they have ten batteries of light artillery, with forty-seven regiments of infantry and cavalry, all armed. There is not the slightest intention of attacking Cairo, but the strongest apprehension exists that Columbus is to be soon attacked. I believe that I have full means of keeping posted as to what is going on south of this point and will keep you fully informed.[24]

For the next four days the records give us not a word of Grant or his command. But on December 13 the general made preparations for active defense of Bird's Point, by having the troops sleep under arms, placing four regiments on the transports in readiness to reinforce any point threatened and asking the navy to coöperate.[25] What the cause was we can only surmise from a Confederate report made on this date by Jeff Thompson to Polk:

I inclose you a letter from the captain of my scout near Charleston, which is rather discouraging, compared with the events of the evening before. My men attacked them, the enemy, before, and brought in 2 men, 5 muskets, 15 blankets, &c.; but they paid me for it last night. Unless something unexpected transpires between now and night, I intend to take a moonlight ride after them myself and hope then to give a good account of them . . . I send you also a letter taken from one of the prisoners.[26]

The inclosed letter from the captain of scouts reads:

Dec. 12: The Northerners were out yesterday scouting the country west of Charleston as far as Bertrand. They took 12 citizens prisoners in that vicinity, and they came in contact with our pickets, 6 in number; 4 at one place, which they captured, the other 2 at another place, and made fight, and succeeded in killing 1 Northerner, slightly wounding another and killing 1 horse, and made their escape into the swamp. Their forces amounted to 200 cavalry and about the same of infantry. The infantry was left at Charleston

24 W. R. 7:482.
25 W. R. 8:430–433.
26 W. R. 8:711.

while the cavalry scouted. . . . They say they are going to scout the country out or run us out of it.

The second inclosure is undated and unsigned. In view of the capture of twelve citizens the day before, its presence in a Union pocket is not so surprising. It begins:

Mr. [sic] Polk: Sir: I have just returned from St. Louis, and I learned that they have chartered 40 steamboats, to be at Cairo on the 10th of this month; but the river is so low that they cannot get all their gunboats down. They will have some twelve or thirteen gunboats, and three hundred guns, and they say they can take Columbus with 40,000 men most easy. They will come down to you. I think they will have seventy-five regiments or more. They haven't over 6,000 at Camp Holt. I don't know how many guns they have there and at Bird's Point. I don't know as they won't let me go to their cannon. I think I will be able to go where I please soon. I will get more information soon. They are close after me at this time.

Whatever the origin of this letter, it probably did not prove soothing to Polk in his already tremulous condition.

Nothing came of the affair reported by Thompson, but it showed in strong light a Grant keen to fight, resourceful, and, if a fight came, prepared to put his last man into it, as befits a commander of lesser forces. It might be added that had Grant taken one half the measures of precaution the night before Shiloh that he took on the evening of December 13, the result would not for so long have hung in the balance. But perhaps the fact that he felt a bit sheepish in the gray dawn of December 14, when nothing happened to justify his many precautionary measures—in the eyes of his men, at least—may not have been without its influence in causing him to steel himself later on against over-safeguarding. Verily, there is no teacher like experience in these matters, and fortunate are those able to profit from the experience of others. So far as Grant was concerned, he had to wait for Shiloh to impress upon him that in tactical situations an ounce of prevention is sometimes worth a pound of cure.

In the latter part of December we find him grappling more and more with the economic problems. On December 17 he writes Halleck:

I received a dispatch a few days ago that quinine was being shipped from St. Louis via the Ohio and Mississippi and the Illinois Central Railroad to Duquoin, where it was received by special agents and transported across land to the Mississippi River, thence through Missouri, south. I sent up a detective, who captured 100 ounces, together with evidence that it was destined for Memphis, and that the agent was to receive $500 for his trouble if he succeeded in getting it through.[27]

Except for the small remuneration involved for the conveyer this reads like a bit of modern bootlegging history!

A few days later Grant wrote Oglesby at Bird's Point:

Understanding that a heavy trade is being carried on between points north of Bird's Point and Charleston, Mo., and south by means of teams, I am desirous of breaking it up. To this end you will send to-morrow or Monday [December 23] a sufficient force, say two squadrons of cavalry . . . to the neighborhood of Belmont, with directions to proceed back on the main travelled road towards Charleston, taking possession of all teams loaded with produce or goods destined for the South and send them back to Bird's Point. The object of this expedition, it is hardly necessary for me to inform you, should be kept entirely secret.[28]

The day after this letter—on December 22—Grant tightened the net on the Illinois side. He wrote McClernand:

A trade is being carried on between Jonesborough and the Mississippi River, thence with the Southern Army by way of Neely's Landing. I want Captain Stewart's company to go to the neighbor-

27 W. R. 8:440.
28 W. R. 8:453.

hood of the mouth of Big Muddy and, if practicable, break up the traffic. There is also a number of armed desperadoes in that vicinity that I hope may be broken up. . . . I will see Captain Stewart before he starts, and give him all the information in my possession on the subject.[29]

The same day Grant reported this to Halleck, with the additional information that as the men composing Captain Stewart's company of cavalry which was being sent "to the scene of these infractions of the law" had been "raised in the neighborhood of Jonesborough," he had hopes "of breaking up this traffic and this body of men." [30]

Unimportant as this comparatively small curtailment of the economic flow of goods to the Confederate States and armies may seem at first glance, it cannot be too strongly emphasized that Grant, through his experiences in dealing with the problem on a small scale, in his immediate sector, not only was preparing himself to study and solve the greater economic problems in the whole theater of war later on, but was also, in no small measure, directly facilitating the immediate tactical victories soon to be gained by himself and others in the Mississippi Valley, in the spring campaigns of 1862 then in preparation.

Grant's administration and supply difficulties during this period were far from being easy of solution. On January 12 he wrote Halleck:

I have placed Capt. ———, assistant quartermaster in arrest . . . This was done on notice from Washington that charges would be preferred. . . . Every day develops further evidence of corruption in the quartermaster's department, and that Mr. ———, chief clerk, if not chief conspirator, is at least an accomplice. I have ordered his arrest and confinement.[31]

29 W. R. 8:457.
30 W. R. 7:510.
31 W. R. 7:545.

A week later, while Grant was in the field with his troops, his chief quartermaster, Captain Baxter, made a stirring appeal to a quartermaster in St. Louis, on January 21:

What does Government intend to do? This department has been neglected in every way. No funds; no nothing, and don't seem as though we ever would get anything. Everybody, high and low, in this district is discouraged, and I assure you I had rather be in the bottom of the Mississippi than work night and day as I do without being sustained by Government. I have written to St. Louis and Washington and it avails nothing, and if my whole heart and soul was not in the cause I would never write another word on the subject, but let matters float, I assure you; and a few days will prove my assertion, that unless Government furnishes this department with funds, transportation, &c., the whole concern will sink so low that the day of resurrection will only raise it. Laborers have not been paid a dime for six or seven months; don't care whether they work or not. If they do, don't take any interest in anything. Government owes everybody and everything, from small petty amounts to large. Liabilities more plenty than Confederate scrip and worth less. Regiment after regiment arriving daily. Nothing to supply them with, and no funds to buy or men to work. No transportation for ourselves or anyone else.

To tell you the truth we are on our last legs and I have made my last appeal in behalf of Government unless it's to a higher power, for it will kill any man and every man at the head of departments here the way we are now working. Is it possible that General Halleck does not know the situation of affairs here? If you think not, I hope you will inform him at once, for if he should come here he will be astonished and annoyed to find us in such a condition. The general commanding and myself have done our best to bring about better results, but our wants are not supplied or even noticed.

Respectfully, your friend, in haste . . .[32]

In haste, certainly, but highly descriptive! The friend took the letter to Halleck, who endorsed it to McClellan "for his perusal," adding, "These letters show the condition of affairs not only at Cairo but throughout the department."

Happily, this sorry plight was soon thereafter remedied. Foote, who knew Quartermaster-General Meigs, took a hand and gave Baxter a personal letter of introduction to Meigs. Armed with this, Baxter went to Washington and, to judge from after reports, did not return empty-handed.

From these extracts it will be seen that, as is frequently the case in war, the enemy was not Grant's only, and often not his chief, source of concern at Cairo. Undeniably, all these valiant struggles against odds, this working doggedly under difficulties, was serving to develop in Grant resourcefulness and strength of character. Both of these he was to need later on in his larger fields even more than he now needed government funds and supplies. Yet nothing, surely, could more vividly reflect his already existent powers of endurance under pressure, his utter singleness of purpose, than the above letter from his subordinate, Quartermaster Baxter.

Until Belmont, Grant's active service, from the time his regiment left Illinois, had been under the gay and picturesque General Frémont. Part of the time, both as colonel and brigadier, Grant had been under Pope's immediate command. Then, as during his entire war career, he displayed the most exemplary spirit of loyalty, entire candor, and desire to coöperate and comply to the fullest extent possible with the plans and wishes of his immediate superior. Nor did he give the slightest indication, during the war, of a questioning or faultfinding attitude toward them or toward their official conduct. This was in striking contrast to the spirit of many of the general officers of his time, who were lacking either in his solidity of character or in his earlier advantages of military training and discipline.

Particularly was it noteworthy that Grant—in this also sharply differing from so many Civil War generals—observed scrupulously the time-honored adage to let one's superior's superior severely alone, except when directly called on by him to answer questions.

We have no record of Frémont's having seen Grant after the latter received his commission as brigadier, though probably he gave the general some personal instructions at the time of sending him to command at Cairo. But Frémont did not thereafter visit Cairo, his attention (until his relief from command of the Western Department on November 2) being taken up with affairs in other parts of Missouri, nor is there record of Grant's having visited St. Louis after that. It is evident from the records that affairs in the District of Southeastern Missouri gave Frémont less concern than those of most of the remainder of his department, and his despatches show a constantly increasing reliance upon Grant.

Whether or not Frémont would have approved of Grant's action at Belmont, had he returned to St. Louis in command on November 6, instead of en route East, is hard to say. As events turned, it did not matter.

Many of Grant's more or less partizan biographers have put forth the view that Halleck began his wartime dealings with Grant by being prejudiced against him—possibly through having learned of the cloud under which Grant was said to have resigned from the regular service on the West coast in 1854—and that he ended by being jealous of him and his successes. Such partizans, moreover, can find but little merit in any of the deeds of this very strong and efficient administrator, whose ability and services contributed so largely to the restoration of the Union. In view of this harshness toward Halleck, which appears to have become traditional with Grant's biographers, it is of special interest to examine the development of the relations between the two leaders.

It is true that at the outset there was no cordiality evidenced in their correspondence. Halleck, so far as the records show, does not appear to have replied to or even acknowledged many of the numerous letters and reports of Grant, cited above, and the communications he did send were signed by his adjutant-general, "by command," instead of by Halleck himself as were his messages and letters to Pope, Prentiss, Curtis, and others of his immediate subordinates nearer at hand. Grant's earlier letters were not addressed to Halleck in person, as were those of the others mentioned, but to the adjutant-general, as required by the formal military custom of the time. No particular significance is to be attributed to this, since Grant and Halleck were both old-time regular officers and, never having been more than mere acquaintances, would hardly have departed from military routine.

Another item in favor of the commonly accepted theory might seem to be the fact that, a few days after his arrival in St. Louis, Halleck, wanting information which he might have secured from either Grant at Cairo or Smith at Paducah, addressed the following to Smith:

It is reported that General Hardee, with 8,000 men, is about to cross the Ohio between the Wabash and Cumberland, to destroy the Ohio and Mississippi and Illinois Central Railroad. Others say that he is to be re-enforced by General Polk and attack Paducah. Keep me advised of the enemy's movements.[33]

Although it is true that the contents of this message did vitally concern Grant, as well as Smith, it might naturally appear proper to the newly arrived Halleck to address it to the man nearest the region, especially if he did not know of Grant's better intelligence service and deeper understanding of conditions.

[33] Nov. 22, W. R. 7:444.

Still another incident which might on the surface appear significant occurred in the middle of December. A group of Southern prisoners of war, duly "exchanged," had been sent from St. Louis to Cairo for Grant to turn over to General Polk, at Columbus. Grant returned them to St. Louis with the following explanation: "On the strength of a telegraphic dispatch received from St. Louis that the prisoners arriving here yesterday were impostors, I have ordered them back to St. Louis." [34]

Halleck telegraphed Grant, over his own name this time: "By what authority did you send back exchanged prisoners? They are not under assumed names. All were identified here before exchange." [35]

Grant's reply to this is not of record, but he evidently quoted in it the following despatch:

St. Louis, December 15, 1861.

GENERAL GRANT:

The *D. G. Taylor* left here at 1 P.M. to-day. Stop her and send back all the Camp Jackson men. They all have assumed names.

W. H. BUEL, *Colonel.*

Halleck replied to Grant the same day: "No such man as W. H. Buel, Colonel, known at these headquarters. It is most extraordinary that you should have obeyed a telegram sent by an unknown person and not even purporting to have been given by authority. The prisoners will be immediately returned to Cairo."

The day after, Halleck added: "The person who sent the telegram about the prisoners has been discovered and placed in confinement. He has no authority whatever. You will hereafter be more careful about obeying telegrams from private persons countermanding orders from these headquarters." [36]

[34] Dec. 17, W. R. 114:120.
[35] Dec. 19, W. R. 114:121.
[36] Halleck to Grant, Dec. 20, W. R. 114:122.

There is no denying the fact that the second message offended Grant's sense of dignity. His lengthy reply and explanation clearly show that.[37]

But to read into the circumstance that Halleck, the wealthy and successful man of affairs, the friend of General Scott and the President, was taking this occasion to show his contempt for the unbefriended, little known, and—in civil life, at least—unsuccessful Grant, requires a vivid imagination. It is at least equally likely that Halleck, in his momentary exasperation and precisely because he regarded Grant—who, like himself, was a former regular officer—as a trusted equal, spoke his mind bluntly. Grant evidently needed to learn that particular lesson; Halleck would help him to learn it thoroughly. Strong men in acute crises do not mince words, and their opinion of people is usually more accurately indicated by their actions than by what they say about them or to them.

Halleck's real regard for Grant was proved beyond all question, by his enlarging of Grant's command on the very day he sent the last of the above three messages,[38] not only giving to Grant the territorial limits in southern Illinois that the latter had recommended on December 3, but putting under him the whole of western Kentucky, including C. F. Smith's command.

Halleck, whatever his faults, was an able administrator and quick to recognize successful administrative talent in those under him. As one reads the reports of the time, of the state of affairs elsewhere, and Halleck's own correspondence, it becomes patent that Grant's Cairo command was, if not the one bright spot in Halleck's department, at any rate the one which caused him the least concern.

Had the combining of the two districts—Cairo and Paducah—

---

[37] W. R. 114:121.
[38] S. O., No. 78, W. R. 109:201.

taken place immediately on Halleck's arrival, it might be adjudged a mere bit of logical administrative consolidation, but coming as it did after a month's observation of Grant's handling of his command, there can be no question that it was a positive token of Halleck's esteem for the general and respect for his ability. For whatever the exigencies of the moment might demand in the way of temporary measures in northern or western Missouri, it was only opposite Cairo that there existed any Confederate force really formidable, and in that direction only that future operations could promise material success for the Union cause.

From the time of this consolidation of the Cairo and Paducah districts, Grant takes his place as the commander of the vanguard of the Federal main column in the West.

CHAPTER XI

INCEPTION OF THE FORT HENRY PLAN

> In every situation the principal strategical requirements must be clearly defined and all other things must be subordinated to these considerations.—FREDERICK THE GREAT.

THE fortuitous circumstance that Grant was the one to seize Paducah, and later Smithfield, led to that part of Kentucky west of the Cumberland River being included in the territorial limits of the Western Department, while the rest of Kentucky was incorporated in the Department of Ohio.

This adoption of the Cumberland as a territorial sector line between military departments did not anticipate the fact that the Cumberland was to become one of the three most important lines of advance and of supply for Northern troops in the year 1862. The military high commanders of the initial period were too engrossed in their immediate concerns of mobilization and organization to take stock of this circumstance, though it did not escape the ever watchful eye of the President.

Halleck evidently did begin to dream as early as December 2 of more active operations than pursuing Missouri guerrillas, for we find him then asking McClellan: "Can't you send me a brigadier general of high rank capable of commanding a *corps d'armée?* . . . Grant cannot be taken from Cairo . . . I dare not trust the 'mustangs' with high commands in the face of the enemy."

"Mustangs" evidently means non-West Point generals, of

whom there were many. Grant here is evidently deemed valuable as a sit-tight defender, but not yet recognized as sufficiently ornamental to command a corps. As to the line of the larger offensive operation, indicated by the desire for a *corps d'armée*, the letter gives no inkling save the natural inference that it was not one which would preclude a possible hostile attack on Cairo.

The day following, Halleck wrote in answer to a request from McClellan for information, "I have not been able, and shall not for some time be able, to give any attention to the gunboats," [1] indicating that an offensive along any of the possible river lines was a subject for future, not present, consideration by him.

Again pressed for information, he telegraphed McClellan on the sixth: "Information respecting gunboats will be telegraphed as soon as it can be obtained . . . Our army is utterly disorganized . . . We are not prepared for any important expedition out of the State; it would imperil the safety of Missouri." [2]

In a letter of the same date he wrote, "This, General, is no army but rather a military rabble!"

The relations between Halleck and McClellan, while courteous—though there was a little bluntness at times on Halleck's part—were never cordial. Quite intimate, on the other hand, were the bonds of friendship between McClellan and Buell, who addressed each other as "My dear Buell," . . . "My dear friend," in place of the more formal salutations usual in military correspondence.

As early as November 22, 1861, we find Buell writing McClellan regarding his plans for an offensive against Bowling Green, "It will be important that Halleck shall strike at the same time that I do, and I think you will agree that his blow should await my preparation." [3]

[1] W. R. 8:402.
[2] W. R. 8:408.
[3] W. R. 7:444.

More definitely, on the twenty-seventh, he added, with regard to movements against Nashville: "In conjunction with either of these should be the movement of two flotilla columns up the Tennessee and Cumberland . . . A strong demonstration should at the same time be made on Columbus by the Mississippi." [4]

McClellan answered Buell's letter of the twenty-second on the twenty-fifth, saying, "I hope to place at your disposal early next week two divisions from Missouri." [5]   And on receiving his second letter, wrote, on November 29:

Your welcome letter received . . . I now feel sure that I have a "lieutenant" in whom I can fully rely . . . Your views are right.

I have telegraphed to-day to Halleck for information as to his gunboats. You shall have a sufficient number of them to perform the operations you suggest. I will place C. F. Smith under your orders and replace his command by other troops.

Inform me some little time before you are ready to move, so that we may move simultaneously. [6]

On December 5, McClellan again wrote Buell:

Give me at once in detail your views as to the number and amount of gunboats necessary for the water movement, the necessary land forces, &c. Would not C. F. Smith be a good man to command that part of the expedition? When should they move? [7]

Buell replied on the tenth, outlining his plans:

I have not seen Smith for seven years, and am afraid to judge him. I have never rated him as highly as some men. The expedition [up the rivers] requires nothing more, as matters now stand, than ordinary nerve and good judgment and ability to command men. The troops ought of course to be the best . . . The object is not to fight great battles and storm impregnable fortifications, but

[4] W. R. 7:451.
[5] W. R. 7:447.
[6] W. R. 7:457.
[7] W. R. 7:473.

by demonstrations and maneuvering to prevent the enemy from concentrating his scattered forces . . . I suppose that 10,000 men, with
two batteries, would not be too great an estimate for each of the
rivers, if the enemy should do all that he probably can do.[8]

Defective as is this proposal, as a strategic plan, it yet has the
merit of being the first, on the Northern side, directed at penetrating the weak point in the Confederate northwestern line of
defenses.

McClellan, even before receiving the last letter, had written
Halleck on the tenth, in answer to the latter's "military rabble"
letter: "I am sorry to learn the very disorganized condition of
the troops . . . Can you yet form any idea of the time necessary to prepare an expedition against Columbus or one up the
Cumberland and Tennessee Rivers, in connection with Buell's
movements?" [9]

Halleck answered this letter on the sixteenth and wrote again
on the nineteenth,[10] but devoted himself to a lengthy description
of his many troubles in Missouri instead of answering McClellan's
questions. Finally, on the twenty-sixth, he wrote: "If I receive
arms in time to carry out my present plans in Missouri, I think I
shall be able to strongly re-enforce Cairo and Paducah for ulterior
operations by the early part of February." [11]

The same day (December 26), Grant sent Buell his order
defining the limits of his own command, and added, "The object
is that you may know its extent and to express to you a desire
to coöperate with you as far as practicable," [12] a letter which was
apparently never answered.

Between McClellan and Buell only formal communications
passed in the latter part of December, while McClellan was too

[8] W. R. 7:488.
[9] W. R. 8:419.
[10] W. R. 8:437, 448.
[11] W. R. 8:463.
[12] W. R. 7:516.

sick to do much planning, until the twenty-ninth, when Buell again brought up the subject of operations on the rivers:

It is my conviction that all the force that can possibly be collected should be brought to bear on that front of which Columbus and Bowling Green may be said to be the flanks. The center, that is, the Cumberland and Tennessee where the railroad crosses them, is now the most vulnerable point. I regard it as the most important strategical point in the whole field of operations.[13]

That this center, rightly judged "the most important strategical point," should lie on the sector line dividing the two great departments in the central West was a most serious fault of organization, rendered the more serious by the incapacity through sickness of McClellan, the commanding general, through whose active supervision lay the only prospect of proper coördination.

The President, correctly sensing that all was not right and that something must be done about it, telegraphed and wrote directly to the two department commanders on December 31: "General McClellan is sick. Are you [Halleck and Buell] in concert?" [14]

The two replies are characteristic of the two men.

From Buell: "There is no arrangement between General Halleck and myself. I have been informed by General McClellan that he would make suitable disposition for concerted action." [15]

From Halleck: "I have never received a word from General Buell. I am not ready to coöperate with him. Hope to do so in few weeks. Have written fully on this subject to Major-General McClellan. Too much haste will ruin everything."

Mr. Lincoln replied to these on January 1: "General McClel-

---

[13] W. R. 7:521.
[14] W. R. 7:524.
[15] W. R. 7:526.

lan should not yet be disturbed with business. I think you better get in concert at once. I write you to-night." [16]

Halleck and Buell were now forced to act. Buell telegraphed the President, "I have already telegraphed General Halleck with a view to arranging a concert of action between us and am momentarily expecting his answer."

Halleck's communication to Buell of January 2 did not sound promising:

I have had no instructions respecting coöperation. All my troops are in the field except those at Cairo and Paducah, which are barely sufficient to threaten Columbus, &c. A few weeks hence I hope to be able to render you very material assistance, but now a withdrawal of my troops from this State is almost impossible. Write me fully.[17]

On January 3, Buell in reply gave Halleck his estimate of the enemy's situation, an estimate which was fairly sound, and told him what he wanted done:

The attack upon the center should be by two gunboat expeditions, with, I should say, 20,000 men on the two rivers . . . The mode of attack must depend on the strength of the enemy at the several points and the features of the localities. It will be of the first importance to break the railroad communications . . . bridges over the Cumberland and Tennessee. . . .

I say this much rather to lay the subject before you than to propose any definite plans for your side. Whatever is done should be done speedily, within a few days. The work will become more difficult every day. Please let me hear from you at once.[18]

Halleck answered the letters of both Lincoln and Buell on January 6. To the President he gave many excuses and summed up, "I am in the position of a carpenter who is required to build a bridge with a dull ax, a broken saw, and rotten timber." [19] But

[16] W. R. 7:526, 926.
[17] W. R. 7:527.
[18] W. R. 7:528.
[19] W. R. 7:532, 533.

one cannot escape the impression that his real objection is that the bridge proposed is one to lead to a great military success for Buell, not Halleck!

To both the President and General Buell, Halleck stated that he had "only about 15,000 at Cairo, Fort Holt and Paducah," and could in consequence send only about 10,000 men to assist Buell. This statement is erroneous, as there were nearly 15,000 in the District of Cairo even before Paducah was added to Grant's command, on December 20,[20] and over 6,000 additional at Paducah and Smithland; but the error may have been caused by Halleck's failure to notice that Grant's return of strength of December 31 did not include C. F. Smith's troops, although they were then already a part of Grant's command.

Halleck concluded both letters with the theoretical objection to the operation proposed by Buell that it "is a plain case of exterior lines . . . which leads to disaster ninety-nine times in a hundred."

Lincoln endorsed on this letter: "It is exceedingly discouraging. As everywhere else, nothing can be done."

The impression that Halleck in these letters either is not honest with his two correspondents or, which is perhaps more likely, is somewhat fickle-minded, is strengthened by the fact that on the same day, January 6, he wrote Grant, ordering a "demonstration in force" toward Columbus with the objective "to prevent reinforcements being sent to Buckner," at Bowling Green.

The day following (the seventh) Mr. Lincoln again cracked the whip, telegraphing the two commanders: "Please name as early a day as you safely can on or before which you can be ready to move southward in concert. Delay is ruining us." [21]

Halleck replied: "I have asked General Buell to designate a

<hr>

[20] W. R. 7:525, 544.
[21] W. R. 7:535.

day for a demonstration to assist him.   It is all I can do till I get arms." [22]

The records contain no replies from Buell to either despatch. It is possible that he felt himself unready to name a day or that he may have felt that, McClellan being once more recovered and in correspondence with all concerned, any action by himself was unnecessary.

McClellan, much improved by January 2, saw the President, who evidently impressed on him the need for haste, for he wrote Halleck on January 3 not to lose a moment's time in preparing an expedition to be sent up the Cumberland River of one or two divisions, with a simultaneous demonstration against Columbus and perhaps a feint on the Tennessee River; all this to prevent Confederate reinforcements from being sent to Bowling Green.[23]

Halleck replied to McClellan on the ninth, inclosing his order of the sixth, to Grant, for the demonstration, giving a detailed account of his own various operations in Missouri and stating in conclusion:

> If a sufficient number of troops are to be withdrawn from Missouri at the present time to constitute an expedition up the Cumberland, strong enough . . . we must seriously peril the loss of this State.   I can make with the gunboats and available troops a pretty formidable demonstration, but no real attack.   The gunboats are not yet ready, but probably will be within a week or two.   With good luck here . . . we can by the early part of February throw some 15,000 or 20,000 additional troops on that line.[24]

And he added, beginning a little of the "buck-passing" so familiar to readers of military history: "If you insist upon my

22 W. R. 109:203.
23 W. R. 7:527.
24 W. R. 7:539.

doing this now, your orders will be obeyed, whatever may be the result in Missouri."

The next day Halleck, as if to quash any idea McClellan might still have of detaching troops from his department to assist Buell, repeated his warning and put it in the form of a telegram, on the tenth:

Do you insist upon my withdrawing troops from Missouri for the purpose indicated in your letter of the 3d instant? If so, it will be done, but in my opinion it involves the defeat of the Union cause in this State. I will write more fully what I have done and can do to assist D. C. Buell.[25]

McClellan answered this on the thirteenth with a neat little calling down, but passing the buck right back:

I do not think you had read my letter of the 3d with much care when you sent the telegraphic reply . . . If you can spare no troops it is only necessary to say so . . . There is nothing in my letter that can reasonably be construed into an order, requiring you to make detachments that will involve the defeat of the Union cause in Missouri.[26]

The same day McClellan wrote Buell, "Halleck is not yet in condition to afford you the support you need when you under-take the movement on Bowling Green."

The friction between the two departments, a natural result of the desire to gain and keep control of all the good troops possible, is well illustrated by the following telegram from Buell to the adjutant-general on the eleventh: "Raw troops do not add much to our strength for active operations. Why not send them into garrison at Cairo and Paducah, and let the older troops take the field, as the Confederates are doing? I refer to the Illinois regiments ordered here."[27]

25 W. R. 7:543.
26 W. R. 7:547.
27 W. R. 7:545.

This dagger-thrust—the attempt to steal Halleck's best troops, so long as Halleck would not use them in coöperation—the adjutant-general promptly referred to Halleck with the question: "Does it meet your views?"

Halleck's reply, if he made one, is not of record, yet it is perhaps significant that the same day (the eleventh) he telegraphed Grant, who had been ordered to make a demonstration against Columbus on the sixth, but later had been told to postpone beginning it until Buell could be heard from as to the date it was desired, "I can hear nothing from Buell, so fix your own time for the advance." [28]

Some use had to be made of the troops, lest they be detached. Grant's troops (at Cairo) had become "veterans" by the hard-fought Battle of Belmont, while Smith's command (at Paducah) Halleck himself officially reported in the best discipline and order of any in the department.[29]

Halleck, however, was quite as willing as Buell to get troops from another department if he could. He wrote McClellan on January 14:

I regret very much that the two regiments of Illinois cavalry have been sent to Kansas. There can be no pressing necessity for their services there, while here they would have been invaluable, and, moreover, would have enabled me to send five or six infantry regiments to Cairo and Paducah, to coöperate with General Buell by a demonstration in the enemy's rear.[30]

This can hardly be called quite candid, as Halleck, three days before, had told Grant, "Fix your own time for the advance."

In another letter of the same date Halleck informed McClellan of Grant's reconnaissance and added, "I have no doubt [it] will

[28] W. R. 7:544.
[29] W. R. 7:929.
[30] W. R. 8:501.

keep them [the Confederates] in check till preparation can be made for operations on the Tennessee or Cumberland."

In the meantime McClellan, in a kindly way, had been trying to speed up Buell. He wrote him on January 13: "You have no idea of the pressure brought to bear here upon the Government for a forward movement. It is so strong that it seems absolutely necessary to make the advance on Eastern Tennessee at once." [31]

Buell gave the orders for this and, as if to make it possible, Zollicoffer, the Confederate general in eastern Kentucky, obligingly attacked Thomas at Mill Springs on January 19 and was decisively defeated. However, nothing further could be done over the poor roads.[32]

On January 20, Halleck, recovering from a week's sickness with the measles, gave McClellan his project for the conduct of the war in the West, "hastily written out, but the result of much anxious inquiry and mature deliberation." He wrote:

> The idea of moving down the Mississippi by steam is, in my opinion, impracticable, or at least premature . . . A much more feasible plan is to move up the Cumberland and Tennessee, making Nashville the first objective point. This would turn Columbus and force the abandonment of Bowling Green. . . . But the plan should not be attempted without a large force, not less than 60,000 effective men.[33]

McClellan made no reply to this letter, but on January 29 telegraphed both Halleck and Buell: "A deserter just in from the rebels, says that . . . he heard officers say that Beauregard was under order to go to Kentucky with fifteen regiments from the Army of the Potomac." [34]

Halleck replied to this on the thirtieth: "Your telegraph

[31] W. R. 7:547.
[32] W. R. 7:568.
[33] W. R. 8:509.
[34] W. R. 7:571.

respecting Beauregard is received. General Grant and Commodore Foote will be ordered to immediately advance, and to reduce, and hold Fort Henry, on the Tennessee River."

Thus, as often happens in war, was precipitated through a "soldier rumor" repeated by a deserter one of the most important campaigns in bringing about the reëstablishment of the Union.

CHAPTER XII

Grant and the Fort Henry Plan

Therefore, far from making it our aim to gain upon the enemy by complicated plans, we must always rather endeavor to be beforehand with him by the simplest and shortest.—Clausewitz.

MEANWHILE Grant's outlook was materially changed by the inclusion of C. F. Smith's troops at Paducah and Smithland under his district command. Hitherto he had faced the enemy along the course of a single river, the Mississippi, and its two banks. Now he had three hostile forces to consider; or, rather, a pool of hostile forces which might advance against him by any one of three river routes—the Mississippi, the Tennessee, or the Cumberland. On the other hand, he himself might advance against the enemy by any one of these same three rivers. If so, which should it be, and why, and what the consequences of success? of failure? Naturally, the influence of the navy on any plan, offensive or defensive, would be great; consequently the views of the naval commanders concerning what they could do to best advantage or not do at all became all-important. The problem did not formulate itself to Grant quite so abruptly as this, yet we see the new point of view taking shape with comparative quickness in his mind.

The fleet of gunboats was not yet armed and manned in sufficient numbers to insure the dominant naval control of the rivers which was essential for success, in a serious attack. But fortunately for Grant, he was in the meantime to be afforded the opportunity to test his troops, his staff (such as he had), his supply departments, and, last but not least, himself and his methods of command and liaison, in a practice maneuver, supported by the navy with five gunboats, in the face of the enemy and in a theater resembling that in which he was so shortly after to conduct similar operations against an active enemy. A genuine boon! It is interesting to note how this became possible.

McClellan's letter to Halleck of January 3 began with the statement, "It is of the greatest importance that the rebel troops in Western Kentucky be prevented from moving to the support of the force in front of General Buell," and after describing the Tennessee-Cumberland movements desired, it contained the positive warning, "Not a moment's time should be lost in preparing these expeditions." [1]

Halleck, taking these instructions very seriously, emanating as they did from the Commanding General of the Army, felt that something must be done and at once. He could not, without abandoning western Missouri to Price, send enough troops up the Tennessee or Cumberland to accomplish much. But he could always fall back on a demonstration. Accordingly, he wrote a directive to Grant to conduct what would now be termed "camouflage operations" between the Tennessee and Cumberland rivers, using troops from both Cairo and Paducah, and of course the gunboats. [2]

The day following, Halleck received a despatch from the President to "name a day" for a concerted movement with Buell, [3] and, having passed on to Buell the responsibility for so doing, Halleck felt, despite McClellan's insistence on the necessity for haste, that it would be better to delay Grant's camouflage campaign until he received a reply from Buell.

[1] W. R. 7:527.
[2] W. R. 7:534.
[3] W. R. 7:535.

Grant received Halleck's instructions on the eighth and, after consulting with C. F. Smith, evolved a commendable skeleton plan allowing for variations from day to day according to the information received, since both he and Smith were to take the field with the troops and they could rely on each other for coöperative action in case of hostile collision.

Grant, in reporting his plans, on January 8, to Halleck, stated, "The continuous rains for the last week or more have rendered the roads extremely bad, and will necessarily make our movements slow," but added with characteristic optimism, "This, however, will operate worse upon the enemy, if he should come out to meet us, than upon us." [4]

Just *how* the mud would be worse for the enemy than for him, Grant did not explain. No doubt he reasoned that Polk, having for the most part "impressed transportation," could not get supplies over the bad roads as well as the Federal troops could with their army wagons, built to meet every condition of weather.

Grant expected to begin his movements on the ninth by transporting troops from both Cairo and Bird's Point to the Kentucky shore. However, he had to telegraph Halleck on January 9, "The fog is so dense that it is impossible to cross the river. This will defer any movement for one day." [5]

Halleck, still waiting for Buell to "name a day," telegraphed Grant in reply, "Delay your movement until I telegraph," [6] but, perhaps tired of waiting for Buell, the next day telegraphed again, "I can hear nothing from Buell so fix your own time for the advance." [7]

As a matter of fact, Grant's cavalry had already crossed over to Fort Holt and marched out before the fog closed in and thus

4 W. R. 7:538.
5 W. R. 7:540.
6 W. R. 7:543.
7 W. R. 7:544.

furnished a complete screen for the movements of the infantry, which were begun on the eleventh.

The plan was, in substance, for a right column commanded by McClernand to descend the Kentucky shore of the Mississippi from Fort Holt to Blandville, supported by three gunboats; while a left column under C. F. Smith, supported by two gunboats on the Tennessee, was to march south from Paducah on Mayfield— where the columns were to unite in case of need—and subsequently on Murray; the idea being to threaten an advance, first against Columbus, secondly against Fort Henry. A brigade, commanded by General Paine, was to follow the right column as a general reserve.

The infantry of the right column was out eleven days and marched seventy-five miles "over icy or miry roads," according to McClernand's report,[8] while the cavalry marched a hundred and forty miles. Smith's column, which had farther to go, was out fourteen days and the march culminated in his taking a personal look at Fort Henry, from one of his gunboats, and reporting that in his opinion "two iron-clad gunboats would make short work of Fort Henry."[9]

Grant made no complete report on the affair, but his partial report on January 17 gives a picture of his own activities and observations:

On this day [that is, on January 15] I visited all the different commands except the one at Elliott's Mill [the reserve], and returned for the night to Coathe's Mill. Written instructions were left with General McClernand . . . Reconnaissances were made by our troops to within 1½ miles of Columbus and to below the town along the railroad. All was quiet, and as yet no skirmish has taken place, unless it was with General McClernand's command, which I do not think likely to-day.

[8] W. R. 7:71.
[9] W. R. 7:72; 561.

Yesterday [January 16], having my forces between me and the enemy, I made a reconnaissance of about 35 miles, taking my staff and one company of cavalry with me. I find that the Mayfield Creek is fordable at but few points from its mouth up as far as I went, and at these points the water is up to the saddle-skirts and the banks very steep.[10]

What could be more modern than Grant's taking his escort— after finding no hostile interference with the general scheme—on a "staff ride" during the maneuver? A bit trying for the younger gentlemen of the staff to have to prove the depth of fords in icy January weather; no wonder Grant had the reputation of being hard on staff officers! The report continues:

To-day [January 17] I have reconnoitered the roads south of the [Mayfield] Creek and to the Mississippi River at Puntney's Bend. Having ridden hard during the day, and finding that I should be late returning, I sent a note to Captain Porter, of the Navy, requesting him to drop down to Puntney's Bend and for a steamer to accompany him to bring myself and escort up to Fort Jefferson. On turning the point in sight a rebel gunboat was discovered and a cavalry force of probably 100 men on shore. I got in probably twenty minutes after the rebel cavalry had fled.

This simple statement shows Grant to be possessed of one faculty essential for a successful commander—still more strikingly than it proves his powers of physical endurance—namely imagination! Grant clearly is checking up at every moment: "Is there now anything that requires to be done, and if not what is the best use to make of the staff and myself?"

Superficially the report seems to indicate that Grant was devoting his whole attention to the planning of future operations against Columbus, but a phrase in Smith's report, "the appearance of the work [Fort Henry] corresponds, as far as could be

10 W. R. 7:557.

discovered, with the rough sketch that General Grant has seen in my quarters at Paducah," [11] seems to indicate that the two generals had discussed the matter and decided that Smith should study the Fort Henry possibilities while Grant worked out plans for an attack on Columbus.

Smith's statement, "I think two iron-clad gunboats would make short work of Fort Henry," makes it clear to Grant that in that quarter lies the quickest and surest success, and, evincing another quality essential to successful leadership, flexibility, he drops and forgets his own plan, made with the expenditure of so much time and labor, and adopts that of another, which is better and safer.

To account for the lack of hostile activity encountered by Grant during the winter months, it is necessary to turn again to the Confederate side.

In a letter to the Missouri general Price on November 28, Polk said:

I have strengthened this position [Columbus] until I regard it as safe from any assault the enemy may make against it.

I am now concentrating here a strong force and am fortifying New Madrid.

I have also at my disposal the gunboats belonging to Commander Hollins' fleet, so that we are getting into a position to aid you above.

I shall be governed by circumstances as to my movements, but feel that you should not allow the enemy to rest or move from St. Louis southward.[12]

That begins and ends the outlook of the good bishop-general. His attention fixed on the passive defense of Columbus and the Mississippi, he hopes that others—Price in this instance—will keep the troublesome enemy from coming southward, but if not,

[11] W. R. 7:561.
[12] W. R. 8:698.

he feels, with his guns and fortifications and newly acquired fleet, "safe from any assault the enemy may make."

Far different was the outlook of his superior, the scholarly Johnston, who had sent Polk this directive but a week before, on November 22, 1861:

> Fort Columbus being completed, your force will now be free to maneuver in reference to the movements of the enemy, and to act as a corps of observation to prevent the siege of the place, and should be so handled as to avoid being caught between the enemy and the river and surrounded and cut off from the magazine and re-enforcements.[13]

What this meant—namely, the use of a fortress as a pivot of maneuver—the good bishop lacked the military background to understand.[14] Johnston in his endeavor to fix it in Polk's mind, during his own stay at Columbus (September 18 to October 13), had had the ground reconnoitered for a camp outside the circle of fortifications—"Beauregard" it was called—and had put in it some of Polk's best troops, Bowen's division, to form the nucleus for a mass of maneuver when the time came, in conjunction with Fortress Columbus as the pivot.

On December 10, Johnston amplified this idea, and, after describing the probable movements of the enemy via the Tennessee and Cumberland rivers, went on to say:

> Fort Columbus, now being completed, cannot, I think, be taken by assault . . . Now, if this be true, your army outside is left free to maneuver in reference to the movements of the enemy, and ought to be so handled as to prevent, by its successive movements, the introduction of the enemy's force into the country in such manner as to deprive you of support and supplies.[15]

---

[13] W. R. 7:690.

[14] It is but fair to add that Polk was still suffering with shell-shock from the explosion of the big gun on Nov. 12 and may not have seen the letter until some time afterward. He did not resume command of the division till Dec. 4. W. R. 7:736.

[15] W. R. 7:752.

Events were to show within a week how completely the significance of Johnston's plan had failed to penetrate Polk's mind. On December 18, Johnston called on Polk for five thousand of his "best infantry," to be sent to Bowling Green.[16] Polk's first reply was to protest against compliance, saying he expected an attack in the next four days, whereupon Johnston, on December 19, revoked the order.[17] But a few days later the unfortunate idea occurred to Polk that, while he could not spare any men from the fortifications of Columbus, he could dispense with his mass of maneuver, the use of which he did not understand anyhow. So he telegraphed Johnston on December 24: "Do you still want support? Answer."[18]

Johnston answered, "Yes, ten thousand or more, if possible, without delay of a day."

Polk telegraphed, "I have resolved to send you Bowen's command . . . and will replace his forces at Feliciana [Camp Beauregard] by four regiments sixty days' men from Mississippi."

In other words, the élite troops designated by Johnston as the nucleus of the mass of maneuver were to be replaced by probably the most amusing but militarily useless body of temporary militiamen that ever encumbered a country road—Alcorn's Mississippi brigade. Had not Johnston been at the time so deeply occupied with affairs in his immediate front, he must have seen from this that something besides sending written orders to the division headquarters of the Mississippi-Tennessee-Cumberland river-front was required if his policy was to be carried out. But in the pressure of events near at hand it was not until January 12, when Polk notified Johnston that he expected an attack from Cairo within three or four days and found his only troops outside the fortifications were one thousand cavalry and General Alcorn's

[16] W. R. 7:773.
[17] W. R. 7:774.
[18] W. R. 7:790.

men, that Johnston realized his intentions had not been understood by his subordinate.[19]

As the reports of Grant's movements began to be received, and no action was taken by Polk along the line desired, Johnston telegraphed on the nineteenth, "Did you receive my letter of December 10?" and called attention to "the suggestions made in that letter." [20]

The reports from what was left of Johnston's planned mass of maneuver are of interest as showing why Grant's men on the reconnaissance encountered little save bad weather.

Lieutenant-Colonel Miller, commanding the one thousand cavalry, reported to General Polk from headquarters at Camp Beauregard, at seven o'clock on January 21:

The accompanying dispatches [lost!] you will read with painful interest. My command is mostly in; but few of our wagons have arrived. We are now here for the winter, as the roads are mostly impassable. Our arrangements should be made accordingly. Can nothing, general, be done to stop the invader? It will be a dark day when the soil of Tennessee is polluted by his footstep. O, for a brigade now here to fall upon him! My command is distressingly small, as our late scouting and moving through sleet, snow and ice has sickened men and crippled unshod horses.

I will do what I can to harass and cripple the enemy. Cannot two good regiments of infantry be called from below somewhere and placed under a practical judicious brigade officer? With them and the advantage of the roads [21] and season (which is equal to two regiments) we can stop the ruthless invader. You must devise, and subordinates execute. I will keep you constantly advised of the movements of the enemy and will try to do my duty.

P. S. I have no pen, ink, or envelopes. Please send the post-boy.[22]

[19] W. R. 7:829.
[20] W. R. 7:839.
[21] Like Grant, Miller sees the condition of the roads in his favor!
[22] W. R. 7:841.

As to the new infantry of the mass of maneuver, we have no reports of it during this period, but can infer from the description by its commander a month earlier, December 21, what it was like:

My command is mostly armed with double-barrel sporting pieces of a good class. I have ammunition for two-thirds of the command and expect soon to be supplied. . . . I shall endeavor to ask nothing from the Confederate Government but subsistence for my troops, hospitals for my sick, lumber to protect my men from the chilling earth, and the privilege of fighting as a Mississippi brigade with its general officer, who shall, with the command, be subject alone to the orders of the major general commanding.[23]

Polk says a few weeks later (on January 11) that General Alcorn's men "are armed with every variety of weapon. They are sick with measles, raw and undisciplined. This brigade cannot be expected to be very effective." [24]

How much of this state of affairs Grant knew and how much he guessed, we have little to show, but it is easy to see that he returned from his reconnaissance more contemptuous than before of the enemy in his front—in fact more so than was good for him, as later events were to show—and in consequence anxious to begin real offensive operations. To do this he had to get Halleck's consent. He had applied for permission to go to St. Louis, "on business" [25] on the sixth, but before the request could be acted on, orders for the demonstration necessarily postponed it until Grant's return from the field on January 25.

On the twenty-second Halleck telegraphed Grant "permission to visit headquarters," and the general apparently made his visit on the twenty-sixth or the twenty-seventh.

Judging from Grant's statements in his Memoirs, his conversa-

23 W. R. 7:783.
24 W. R. 7:826.
25 W. R. 7:534.

tion with Halleck was uncomfortable for both men. It is easy
for the reader, knowing what he knows, to see why. At his desk
sat Halleck, engrossed in his month's bombardment of letters and
telegrams from the President, McClellan, and Buell on the subject
of a Tennessee-Cumberland river expedition, of which bombardment he had neither the time nor the inclination to inform his
subordinate. On the other side of the desk sat Grant, burning
to inform Halleck how desirable and easy it would be, as demonstrated by recent events, to reach out and grab Fort Henry, but not
knowing how to begin and unfortunately beginning at the wrong
end—ignorant, of course, of all of Halleck's many reasons for
already desiring to make the move at the earliest moment possible.

But the coloring which Grant's account gives the interview
cannot in the light of the records be accepted. He says, "I had
not uttered many sentences before I was cut short as if my plan
were preposterous." [26]

Grant became very bitter against Halleck later on, and this
statement must be questioned. The solution which seems best to
fit the documents is that Grant began with "reasons" for taking
Fort Henry. The badgered Halleck naturally did not want these;
he knew more reasons for taking Fort Henry than Grant had
ever dreamed of. The only question was, could it be done?

He asks, "How do you know you can take it?"

All Grant can answer is, "Smith says it can be done with two
gunboats!"

Halleck returns: "What does Foote say about that?"

That is a bombshell, for Grant has not specifically asked
Foote, who has considered only the attack on Columbus.

Halleck naturally cannot order without knowing the view of
the gunboats' commander and says: "Go back and consult with
Foote and let me know by telegraph what you and he both think

[26] Grant I:235.

about it after your consultation. You can write me your reasons later."

That seems the simple explanation of these two telegrams, so characteristic of the senders:

To Halleck from Foote, Cairo, January 28: "Commanding General Grant and myself are of opinion that Fort Henry, on the Tennessee River, can be carried with four ironclad gunboats and troops to permanently occupy. Have we your authority to move for that purpose when ready?" [27]

To Halleck from Grant, Cairo, January 28: "With permission, I will take Fort Henry, on the Tennessee, and establish and hold a large camp there." [28]

To assume (as indicated by the Memoirs) that Grant instigated Foote to telegraph, and telegraphed himself after being rebuffed, in the sense of his account, or for the purpose of going over the head of or forcing the hand of his immediate commander, is to assume that the Grant of 1862 was not the well-disciplined and perfectly subordinate Grant that the contemporary evidence in every instance shows him to be. We must therefore distrust such a tale whether it emanates from the Grant of later years—shown everywhere in his Memoirs as of uncertain memory—or from any other source.

Yet his letter confirming and enlarging on his telegram may well have been a very hard letter to write, smarting as he was under Halleck's retort: "You need not tell me about the *advantages*. I know all about those! What I want to know is, does Foote say he can do it. You can telegraph me about what Foote says," and, softening a bit, perhaps, "Write me about the advantages!"

On January 29, Grant wrote:

In view of the large force now concentrating in this district and

27 W. R. 7:120.   28 W. R. 7:121.

the present feasibility of the plan I would respectfully suggest the propriety of subduing Fort Henry, near the Kentucky and Tennessee line, and holding the position. If this is not done soon there is but little doubt but that the defenses on both the Tennessee and Cumberland Rivers will be materially strengthened. From Fort Henry it will be easy to operate either on the Cumberland, only 12 miles distant, Memphis, or Columbus. It will, besides, have a moral effect upon our troops to advance them toward the rebel States. The advantages of this move are as perceptible to the general commanding as to myself, therefore further statements are unnecessary.[29]

The interesting elements in this letter are his again presenting "the moral effect on the troops" and the fact that he does not point out or even hint at the strategic consequences to be expected of the capture of Fort Henry and Fort Donelson—the abandonment of Bowling Green and Columbus by the Confederates—which in his Memoirs he claims to have foreseen. That he should not have foreseen them is not at all discreditable. The perfecting and control of his immediate command had scarcely left him time for envisioning future possible events in a larger field. He was not yet Commander of the Armies, nor even Commander in the West. As a district commander, he saw an enemy fort in his front which his gunboats could silence and his men could take and hold. It would raise morale and be an advantage for further operations. He so reported. What more can one ask of a district commander? That he be a prophet?

It will be recalled that at the same time with these messages from Grant and Foote, or while Halleck was pondering them, came McClellan's message, mentioned in the last chapter. That was all Halleck needed to turn his Cairo dogs of war—army and fleet—loose. On January 30 he telegraphed Grant the order: "Make your preparations to take and hold Fort Henry. I send you written instructions by mail."[30]

[29] W. R. 7:121.   [30] W. R. 7:121.

CHAPTER XIII

FORTS HENRY AND DONELSON

When the hostile army is in disorder the favorable occasion offers. Then the commander, without loss of an instant, must direct, with the utmost rapidity and vehemence, the nearest force at hand, against the weakened place in the opposing formation. These are the strokes that gain battles and decide campaigns.—COUNT DE SAXE.

DESPITE the experience Grant had had in transporting troops by river steamers, gained at Belmont and in subsequent operations, his movement on Fort Henry appears slow. Not yet having a properly organized staff, in the modern sense, he had to attend personally to many details. Consequently, it was not until the evening of February 2, three days after the receipt of his authorization to proceed, that the first transports left Cairo. The general himself did not start up the river until the evening of the third, trusting to McClernand, now commanding his 1st Division under the reorganization effected for the movement, to select the landing-place for the troops.

It is with no wish to blame Grant that this tardiness is remarked. Had he had a general-staff operations section which had previously "studied" not only a Fort Henry movement, but other likely or possible moves, and had the necessary orders for each been ready for issue, the start could have been made in as many hours as the general took days. But it would be distinctly unreasonable to expect of him that, amid all his other problems and difficulties of administration and supply—Captain Baxter's letter, already quoted, enables us to realize in a measure some of the latter—he should have daily set aside certain hours to prepare plans for hypothetical expeditions which might never be made. *Sufficient unto the day are the problems thereof* is the only possible rule for an untrained man lacking a staff and feeling his way in a situation fraught with as many difficulties and uncertainties as was Grant's. Fortunately, in the World War, against another class of enemy, our generals did have trained general-staff officers and a moderately rational staff organization.

When Grant did reach the landing-place selected by McClernand, below Fort Henry, on the morning of February 4, he did not approve of it, it being too far distant—ten miles—from the fort,[1] and the move to a landing-site six miles nearer consumed a day's time for again embarking and disembarking the command. Since the boats had to return and make a second trip to bring up the remainder of the troops, the day of the fifth was spent in reconnaissances; not very fruitfully, it seems, for the information obtained appears meager.

In Grant's order for the movement against Fort Henry on the sixth we see reflected the lessons learned from his Belmont experience. At Belmont, there had been no preliminary reconnaissance. At Fort Henry, Grant sent his chief of staff, Colonel Webster, under escort of a detachment of infantry and cavalry, to reconnoiter Fort Henry, its "approaches and accessibility" and its "position and various external relations."[2]

At Belmont, there had been a right column by chance; and it had proved a valuable adjunct to the success of the attack on the camp. At Fort Henry a right column was provided in orders —Smith's division (less one brigade) to ascend the west bank of the Tennessee and attack the redoubt (Fort Heiman) on the com-

[1] W. R. 7:127; Moore IV:69.
[2] W. R. 7:128.

manding heights overlooking Fort Henry. There was the added urge for this measure in Grant's memory of his discomfiture at Belmont in being driven from the captured camp by hostile artillery fire from the opposite bank.

At Belmont, there had been no reserve; at Fort Henry one was provided—in fact, though not so called in the order,[3] the 3d Brigade, 2d Division (Smith's), which was to be retained on the east bank and utilized according to circumstances.

At Belmont, Grant had mixed in the forefront of the fight, and became one of the fugitives; here, he remained back with the reserve,[4] leaving it to McClernand with his 1st Division (two brigades) to conduct the principal column which was, a little vaguely, "to prevent all reinforcements to Fort Henry or escape from it; also to be held in readiness to charge and take Fort Henry by storm promptly on receipt of orders."

In the light of Grant's previous experience, the order for the advance against Fort Henry is as good as could be expected. Its glaring faults are the failure to take stock of space, time, and road conditions—it had rained heavily the night of February 5–6—and its undue dispersion, by detaching two fifths of his command on what proved to be a wild-goose chase west of the river, a blow in the air.

The movement was to start at 11 A.M. Foote gave the land columns an hour and a half start and then opened fire with his seven gunboats. It was not time enough; McClernand's column took four hours to reach the fort; Smith's reached Fort Heiman on the opposite bank only after nightfall.

The unequal fight, in the meantime, had lasted but an hour and a quarter. Against the twelve bow-guns of the four armored gunboats in advance, the fort had only eleven effective guns. The

[3] F. O., No. 1; W. R. 7:585.
[4] "Boston Journal" narrative, Moore IV:72.

largest of these, a ten-inch Columbiad, jammed and the only rifled cannon in the fort burst; the others proved ineffective. The ill-disciplined and untrained infantry garrison, Heiman's regiment, posted to man the land-side defenses of the fort, was seized with panic and fled early in the fight to the nearest place of refuge they knew, Fort Donelson, twelve miles distant eastward on the

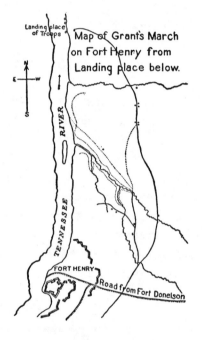

Cumberland River. One cannot but admire the gallantry of the Confederate commander, General Tilghman, in continuing the fight as long as he did, and his chivalry in remaining to share the surrender with his brave but untrained gunners.

At 3 P.M. a chagrined and crestfallen Grant finally rode into the captured fort. His first measure was to board the flag-ship, to congratulate Foote on his brilliant success. His next thought was for his report to Halleck. In this, Grant showed that he had at once recognized his first fault; for he began it with an apology for his late start, explaining it by saying that his "forces were not up at 11 o'clock last night when" his "order was written." [5] The explanation, however, does not make it clear that he as yet realized that the failure to bag the garrison of Fort Henry did not come from his 11 A.M. start but was caused by his failure to synchronize the land and naval attacks by doing a little reckoning of road-space and marching time.

The report further begs the question: "Had I not felt it an imperative necessity to attack Fort Henry to-day, I should have made the investment complete and delayed [the gunboat attack] until to-morrow, so as to have secured the garrison."

But Grant was right when he added: "I do not now believe, however, that the result would have been any more satisfactory." It would, indeed, have been too much to expect of Albert Sidney Johnston to risk fifteen thousand of his all too scanty infantry in Fort Donelson if Grant had shown himself able to surround and capture the one-thousand-strong garrison of Fort Henry.

Grant's chief sin in his attack order—undue dispersion of his force in the absence of more definite intelligence of the enemy—was, however, not to be taken advantage of by the enemy's passive-defensive measures; hence Grant had to wait to learn that lesson, at greater cost, at Donelson and Shiloh.

How different would have been the outcome had General Polk, within whose district lay both Fort Henry and Fort Donelson, understood and acted on Johnston's directives with regard to the utilization of Columbus as a pivot of maneuver and his effectives as a mass of maneuver! Polk had at Columbus three organized divisions, in addition to the "Columbus garrison." [6] In infantry strength they were probably at least equal to Grant's two

[5] W. R. 7:124.
[6] Confederate Returns, W. R. 7:853, 854.

divisions and in cavalry and artillery units they were stronger. Had Polk availed himself of his railroad facilities to transport this corps to either bank of the Tennessee River, when he received Heiman's message of February 4 informing him that "the enemy is landing troops in large forces on this [east] side of the river within three miles of the fort," [7] Grant would have had cause bitterly to regret this unwise splitting of his forces, and there might have been a "Part II" of the capture of Fort Henry which would have read very like the Union retreat from Belmont. But Polk neither saw his opportunity nor really understood the tenor of Johnston's instructions.

The striking feature of Grant's Fort Henry report is its conclusion, remarkable alike for its boldness of purpose and its shortsightedness. One is almost inclined to believe that it was quite impromptu—certainly it was not well considered—and that Grant, stung by the fact that his army had sadly fizzled at Fort Henry and left to the navy, in consequence, the honors of accomplishing unaided the surrender, felt he must needs announce by way of atonement something his army would accomplish in a day or two. His report reads:

I shall take and destroy Fort Donelson on the 8th and return to Fort Henry [8] with the forces employed, unless it looks feasible to occupy that place with a small force that could retreat easily to the main body. I shall regard it more in the light of an advance grand guard than as a permanent post. [9]

Had the general at almost any later period of his career been confronted with the latter part of his report and a request to explain what he meant by it and how he meant to do what he said, even his facile mind would have quailed at the effort.

[7] W. R. 7:858.
[8] So much he telegraphs (W. R. 7:124). The remainder is in his written report.
[9] W. R. 7:125.

Judging from the above despatch, Grant on February 6 had little conception of the difficulties awaiting him at Fort Donelson with regard to terrain; what the naval contingent could do to assist; when they could do it; his supply problem, acute because of the limited land transportation available, four teams per regiment; and not least what the enemy might do in the meantime.[10]

With regard to terrain Lieutenant Phelps, commanding the gunboat *Conestoga,* had made numerous reports on Fort Donelson, copies of which, if not actually furnished Grant, could have been his for the asking.[11] In the latest of these the superior strength of the batteries at Fort Donelson is pointed out and the value of mortar-boats for attack is stressed for "clearing the battery on Jackson's Hill, where the gunboats would fire to great disadvantage." [12] But he appears not to have consulted Foote, either to learn the results of naval reconnaissances or to inquire when the navy could furnish whatever coöperation was possible on the Cumberland. Foote's orders for the Tennessee River expedition to proceed "as soon as the Fort shall have surrendered" to intercept the railroad-bridge crossing of the Tennessee, and then "proceed as far up the river as the stage of water will admit and capture the enemy's gunboats and other vessels" had been issued on February 2, unquestionably with Grant's knowledge and acquiescence, since that was one of the main objects of the combined expedition.[13]

These three gunboats despatched up the Tennessee left Foote with only four, of which one, the *Essex,* had been badly injured in the Fort Henry engagement and the others more or less damaged. Thus the simplest calculation would have shown Grant that he could not count on Foote's having the gunboats assembled

[10] G. O., No. 7; W. R. 7:579.
[11] Dec. 13, N. R. 22:461; Jan. 3, N. R. 22:485; Jan. 21 (2), N. R. 22:512, 514.
[12] N. R. 22:513.
[13] N. R. 22:537.

at Cairo to ascend the Cumberland before the tenth (in fact, they left there only on the evening of the eleventh)[14] and that minus the gunboats he could send neither transports nor supply boats up the Cumberland, without which he lacked the necessary wagons to ration his command overland, even if he had the necessary troops for the operation.

To sum it up, Grant evidently had not the faintest inkling of the man-sized task which awaited him at Donelson, but pictured it as a ripe apple ready to fall as soon as he should appear with a handful of troops to give the tree a shake.

Richardson, who first met Grant at Fort Henry, records this interview with him, evidently on February 7:

I stepped into the General's office on the steamer to say "Good-bye."

He replied: "You had better wait a day or two."

"Why?"

"I am going over to attack Fort Donelson to-morrow."

"Do you know how strong it is?"

"Not exactly, but I think we can take it; at all events, we can try."[15]

Realities soon awakened Grant from his dreams. By the seventh all the gunboats but one were gone—three up the river, three to Cairo for repairs. The prisoners and the sick and wounded had to be provided for, and extensive captured stores to be looked after—a matter to which Grant gave scant attention and which resulted in scandals he subsequently admitted were not without foundation.[16]

[14] N. R. 22:579.

[15] Richardson, "Personal History of Ulysses S. Grant," p. 217.

[16] W. R. 11:14. In his report of Mch. 18 (W. R. 11:45) Grant wrote: "I have found that there was much truth in the report that captured stores were carried off from Fort Henry improperly." His discomfiture over this discovery was doubtless added to by the fact that two members of his staff joined with two of the regimental commanders (two of the four being mentioned in the charges) shortly after, at Fort Henry, in presenting him with a sword "manufactured at great expense; the handle is ivory mounted with gold . . . inclosed in a fine rosewood case." Moore III:Diary 56.

While Grant was dealing with his many problems on the seventh he sent Lieutenant-Colonel McPherson, engineer officer on Halleck's staff—who had been loaned to him for this campaign— with cavalry to reconnoiter the road to Fort Donelson. McPherson

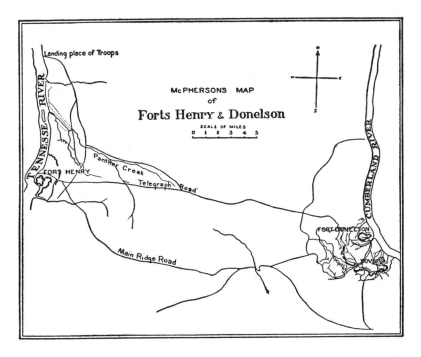

went within one and a half miles of the fort and brought back twelve field-guns abandoned by the Confederates' Fort Henry garrison in its retreat.[17]

Any remaining idea Grant may have had of "taking Donelson on the eighth" was dispelled by the bad weather. On the eighth he reported to Halleck:

At present we are perfectly locked in by high water and bad roads, and prevented from acting offensively, as I should like to do . . . I contemplated taking Fort Donelson to-day with infantry

[17] Cullom to Halleck, W. R. 7:597.

and cavalry alone, but all my troops may be kept busily engaged in saving what we now have from the rapidly-rising water.[18]

He himself used the rainy day to make a personal reconnaissance twenty miles up the Tennessee, presumably to assure himself that the work of demolishing the railroad bridge had been properly accomplished.

On the ninth the weather moderated sufficiently to enable him to accompany the cavalry on a second reconnaissance to Fort Donelson; in this a number of prisoners were secured from whom he learned that Pillow—his opponent at Belmont—had that day reached Donelson and assumed command of the fort.[19]

That evening, on his return, Grant found time to write his sister:

Before receiving this you will hear by telegraph of Fort Donelson being attacked . . . You have no conception of the amount of labor I have to perform. An army of men all helpless, looking to the commanding officer for every supply. Your plain brother has as yet no reason to feel himself unequal to the task, and fully believes that he will carry on a successful campaign against the rebel enemy. I do not speak boastfully but utter a presentiment.[20]

By the tenth he was again the realist dealing with actualities. He had given up the idea of an infantry and cavalry coup de main against Fort Donelson and settled down to await the coöperation of the navy.[21]

He wrote Foote, still at Cairo repairing his gunboats:

I have been waiting very patiently for the return of the gunboats under Commander Phelps, to go around on the Cumberland,

---

[18] W. R. 7:596.

[19] It was perhaps fortunate for Grant that Forrest, the famous Confederate cavalry leader, did not reach Fort Donelson till the day following, the 10th; thereafter cavalry reconnaissances on Fort Donelson were not so easy.

[20] Letters of U. S. Grant quoted in "Donelson Campaign Sources," p. 206.

[21] W. R. 7:600.

whilst I marched my land forces across to make a simultaneous attack upon Fort Donelson. I feel there should be no delay in this matter, and yet I do not feel justified in going without some of your gunboats to coöperate. Can you not send two boats from Cairo immediately up the Cumberland?

He must nevertheless have reached the end of his patience, because the same day he set a date for the movement and issued "warning orders" to prepare his troops to march to Fort Donelson on the twelfth, and to designate forces to remain and guard Fort Henry.[22]

Difficulties nearly always yield to proper method and study, and it is a satisfaction to find that Grant's measures for the movement across to the Cumberland indicate that he had recognized and corrected his mistakes in the earlier movement, against Fort Henry.[23] He utilized the two available roads which were within supporting distance; he marched the stronger column on the better road; to gain time, in order to reach Fort Donelson before dark on the short February day, the brigade to form the advance-guard was moved to a bivouac five miles out on the afternoon before the march was to begin; and, last but not least, the general commanding found his place, where he belonged, at the head of the principal column, where he could receive early information, and best control the deployment of his command.

The day for the march, February 12, proved sunny but "cool and invigorating."[24] The troops were in the best of spirits and the advance proceeded like clockwork. By one o'clock the hostile outposts were encountered and driven back, and by half-past three Grant found his advanced skirmish lines facing the main outer works of Fort Donelson. The artillery, however, was not yet

[22] F. O., Nos. 7 and 8; W. R. 7:601.
[23] F. O., No. 11; W. R. 7:605.
[24] See accounts in "New York Times" and "Missouri Democrat," quoted in Moore IV:170–176.

posted to enable an assault to be ordered in the remaining hours
of daylight. Consequently the troops were put in position for the
night by extending the lines in an endeavor to prevent the
Confederates from escaping, and instructed to sleep on their arms,
the air being "mild and genial" and the "bright moon" and many
"camp-fires" enlivening the scene.[25]

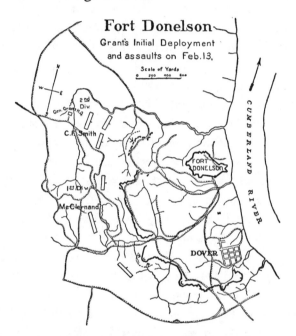

The original Fort Donelson was a small bastioned work on a
hilltop commanding the Cumberland River; it did not contain
guns of large caliber with which to engage the Union gunboats,
those being placed lower down the hillside in two water batteries,
one containing three, the other nine guns.

This hill-work being too small for the enlarged garrison which
Johnston had determined to place there after the fall of Fort

[25] Moore IV:177.

Henry, open trenches were constructed on a higher commanding ridge a half-mile to the west and extending from an impassable backwater on the north for two miles southward across Indian Creek and eastward for a third mile to the river, and inclosing the village of Dover on the lower ground near the river, a mile south of the original bastioned fort. The fort proper contained temporary barracks for about a brigade. Other than this there was no shelter for the garrison except that afforded by the few buildings in the village, quite inadequate.

The entire surrounding country was cut by steep ravines with dense wooded growth. In front of the Confederate trenches, in the outer trace, this had been more or less cut to clear a field of fire and construct a rude abatis.

Such was the work, garrisoned by the equivalent of about thirty infantry regiments, which Grant approached on February 12 with two divisions, twenty-four regiments, though his reinforcements brought up by river and by land from Fort Henry increased his force two days later to thirty-six regiments; the probable proportions of the opposing forces being five to four in favor of the Confederates for the first two days; after that six to five in favor of the Federal troops.

Grant wrote in his report for the thirteenth, "No attack was made, but the investment was extended on the flanks of the enemy and drawn closer to his works, with skirmishing all day." [26]

He appears to have had other hopes, judging from his message to Commander Walke, who arrived that morning with the *Carondelet,* ahead of the rest of the flotilla: "If you will advance with your gunboats at ten o'clock A.M., we will be ready to take advantage of every diversion in our favor." [27]

[26] W. R. 7:159.
[27] N. R. 22:594.

Walke did what he could with one gunboat, by advancing and firing 184 shell at long range into the fort. On the land side, McClernand made an ill-organized attack on a redoubt opposite the center of his line with three regiments, which failed with heavy losses; while on the Union left, Lauman's brigade of Smith's division became involved and also suffered heavily.[28] On the remainder of the front the activity in both armies was limited to artillery duels and picket firing.

Deep concern was felt by the Union commanders over the non-arrival of the main flotilla and transports with reinforcements and supplies. Rations were getting short and the mild weather of the first two days was followed by sleet and snow on the evening of the thirteenth. This was hard on the men, who had no tents, and many of whom were inadequately clothed. The troops in the front lines were not allowed fires, and several of the regimental reports speak of keeping the men "standing under arms all night," because there was no other course open to them.

Foote with his flotilla and the transports reached the landing-place north of the fort at midnight on February 13–14. Yet not many of the Union troops had breakfast the next morning and with the few wagons and bad roads it took most of the day to get rations to them, especially to McClernand's men on the right. With many of his troops hungry and all of them cold and wet, Grant wisely desisted from an attack, though skirmishers were pushed forward, and some artillery firing conducted.

Grant attempted to extend his lines to the south and east to reach to the bank of the Cumberland, south of Dover, in order to cut off all escape of the garrison by land. To accomplish this he inserted the reinforcements organized as a 3d Division under General Lew Wallace in the center and moved the 1st Division

[28] W. R. 109:9.

(McClernand's) to the right as far as it would reach in single line of regiments, without either supports or reserves.

This failing to reach to the river, Grant took the seemingly unwise measure of detaching McArthur's brigade of the 2d Division, which Smith had been treasuring as a reserve, the only one in the three miles of front, and sent that to the extreme right. This extension enabled McClernand to cover all the roads southward from the fort except the river road, which was three feet under water and impassable except for cavalry.

Grant's measure of responsibility for McClernand's faulty dispositions is difficult to determine. His headquarters were quite properly located in a little cabin in rear of Smith's division on the Fort Henry road. To what extent he rode the lines, if at all, there is nothing to indicate. In his earlier career he nearly always looked out for supply measures first, and very likely he considered, on February 14, that getting food to the hungry troops and seeing Foote to arrange for the naval attack were more important than supervising the tactical organization of McClernand's divisional line. If so, he may not have realized the weakness of McClernand's formation, devoid as it was of adequate flank protection, supports, or reserves. On the other hand, he may have known it and recognized the danger but felt over-confident that the enemy could not or would not undertake a sortie. In any case, this faulty alignment was destined to bring about the first great test of his calmness and equipoise in the face of seeming disaster.

But in the meantime, at three o'clock on the afternoon of the fourteenth, urged by Grant, Foote attacked with all his gunboats the two Confederate batteries commanding the river. Like the Fort Henry engagement, the attack lasted an hour and a quarter, but the result was otherwise. The story is told simply in the despatches of Floyd, the Confederate commander, to Johnston:

No. I

The enemy are assaulting us with a most tremendous cannonade from gun-boats abreast the batteries, becoming general around the whole line. I will make the best defense in my power.

No. II

The fort cannot hold out twenty minutes. Our river batteries working admirably. Four gun-boats advancing abreast.

No. III

The fort holds out. Three gun-boats have retired. Only one firing now.

No. IV

The gun-boats have been driven back. Two, it is said, seriously injured. I think the fight is over to-day.[29]

Grant has been blamed by some for not assisting the naval attack, or attempting at least to take advantage of it as a diversion to secure desirable points on the land side. But the fact is that he did have a most comprehensive plan for naval and land coöperation. On the north and west sides of the outer Fort Donelson no attack in coöperation with the navy was possible, on account of the high intervening ridge. But on the southern end, where the ground was lower, the flotilla, as soon as it had passed the water batteries, was to "take a position opposite and near the town of Dover, and shell the rebels out of their intrenchments near the river, we [the army] at the same time sweeping around with our right and taking possession of a portion of their works, cutting them off from the greater part of their supplies, and driving them back upon our center and left, which were strongly posted to prevent their escape."[30]

[29] W. R. 110:274.
[30] W. R. 7:163.

It may well have been that Foote's eagerness to pass above the river batteries and carry out Grant's plan brought about his own defeat; because had he "stood off" another quarter of an hour down the river where the longer-range fire of the gunboats was effective and where the fire of most of the twelve guns of the Confederates was ineffective, he would in all probability have silenced the land batteries. But as it was—the land batteries being thirty-two feet above the water-level—as the fleet advanced, its shell either buried themselves in the parapet or passed harmlessly overhead, while the effect of the land guns on the gunboats proved much more damaging at the shorter ranges. Even so, Foote reports:

Notwithstanding our disadvantages, we have every reason to suppose [that this attack] would in fifteen minutes more, could the action have been continued, have resulted in the capture of the two forts bearing upon us, as the enemy's fire materially slackened and he was running from his batteries when the two gunboats helplessly drifted down the river from disabled steering apparatus.[31]

This view is confirmed by Confederate writers.[32]

The repulse of the fleet was, naturally, as cheering to the Confederates in the fort as it was depressing to Grant and his men. In a council of war of the general officers of the defenders, —Floyd, Pillow, Buckner, and Bushrod Johnson—it was determined to follow up the victory gained over the gunboats by an attack the next morning, to break up and drive off the besieging army. The favorable point for initiating this was unerringly chosen—McClernand's right flank, unsupported and "in the air."

The attacking columns, led by Pillow, began their assault at

---

[31] W. R. 7:166.
[32] S. H. S. P. 13:165; W. R. 7:388, 401.

daybreak on February 15. Surprise was impossible, as the Union troops not in formation were sleeping under arms and could form in a moment. But the Union forces were caught at a disadvantage, because of the lack of "distribution in depth" at least in the right division, and of anything adequate in the nature of re-

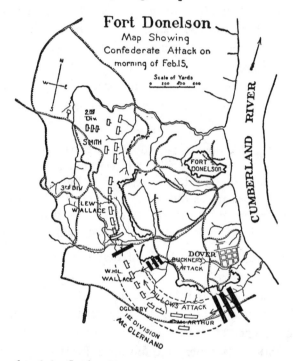

serves for the right flank. Yet the skill and experience of subordinate leaders and good discipline of the troops—among the best and oldest in Grant's army—prevented the ensuing retirement to the left from becoming a stampede. The extreme right brigade —McArthur's—borrowed from Smith's reserve, met and parried the first shock. Next came Oglesby's, containing two veteran regiments—one of them Logan's—which had fought at Belmont. The next, that of W. H. L. Wallace, another experienced brigade commander, shortly to become division commander. Though the Confederates might gain ground from brigades such as these, yet it would cost them dearly in time and casualties.

McClernand's report of the attack did not reach Grant, who had gone to the gunboats to consult Foote, wounded in the battle of the fourteenth.

About eight o'clock McClernand sent messages to the other division commanders, begging for reinforcements. Lew Wallace, the nearer of the two, sent him a brigade which further slowed up, though it did not stop, the Confederate advance.

After four hours of fighting, McClernand's division, including the brigade sent him by Lew Wallace, had been driven from the field; some of it in disorder, most of it out of ammunition. Four of Grant's ten infantry brigades were, so to speak, out of commission. But of the seven Confederate brigades which had been engaged in the attack, scarcely enough men to form one brigade remained. Such is the disruptive effect of the battle-field on inexperienced troops.

Pillow did, indeed, try to reorganize his men, and continued the entirely proper attempt to roll up the Union lines by attacking toward noon the flank of the center division of Lew Wallace. But his men had reached the limit of their endurance and he did the only thing possible in the circumstances—left three regiments to hold the ground gained, and ordered his scattered and skeletonized commands back to the fort to reorganize.[33]

---

[33] Ropes and other theorists have blamed Pillow for this order, assuming he should have retreated on Clarksville instead. Such a criticism is absurd. Most of Pillow's men had been under arms and without food ten hours, in the fighting four hours. They were scattered through a mile or more of thick woods and many could not be reached by any orders, while few would have obeyed any order except to go back where there was food. Sometimes orders must be given contrary to the real wish of the prudent commander; for example, he may not wish to retreat, but he realizes that if he does not, his command will break and scatter anyway and he will lose all control; whereas if he retreats he can get it in hand and again offer effective resistance. Such was the case here.

We must now return to Grant, who had gone early on February 15 to the gunboats to consult Foote. It had been agreed between them in conference that the two damaged gunboats should return to Cairo for repairs and that the general would intrench and await further reinforcements and the return of the gunboats before attacking.

Upon his return, which must have been toward noon, Grant found his 1st Division badly beaten and part of it demoralized through the heavy losses in officers.[34]   But the fact that the Confederates were not continuing the attack, despite the enormous advantage they had gained, was to Grant significant.   Pillow and Buckner were not fools: if they were not pushing home their success, it meant that they had nothing left to push with.

As a mathematical problem, it was simple.   The Confederates had in the fort (including the cavalry) thirty regiments, of which twenty had been engaged in the attack; Grant had thirty-six regiments, of which as yet only sixteen had participated in the fight. It was high time to bring some of the twenty remaining regiments into play.

The obvious thing to do was to order an advance "all along the line," but two reasons forbade that: first, some of the new reinforcements were raw and their commanders inexperienced; secondly, the difficulties of terrain on parts of the line were very great owing to the steep hillsides and dense undergrowth.   Therefore the wise course was to select favorable points where the best of the commanders and troops could be brought into play to take advantage of the Confederates' momentary weakness following the breakdown of the attack in which the major part of their forces had been engaged.

To the reader of the story, after the event, it seems as if any

[34] Two of McClernand's brigades (9 regiments) had lost 13 officers killed and 45 wounded, an average loss of more than 6 per regiment. W. R. 7:167, 168.

one could do that much. Yet on the ground and at the time it was by no means easy. McClellan, four months later, before Richmond, when attacked by Lee under similar conditions, ordered his army—four times Grant's in size—to retreat to the James.

It would be interesting if we could follow Grant's course in this first of the great crises of his career; where he went, what

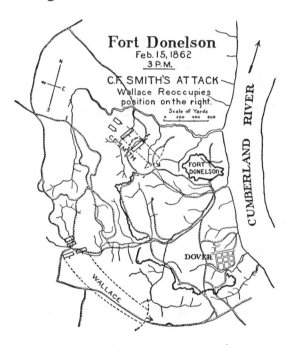

he saw, with whom he spoke; but the only information we have that is worthy of credence is that toward 3 P.M., and probably before 2 P.M., he personally gave Smith orders to assault the Confederate works on the left, and shortly after ordered McClernand and Wallace to recapture the ground lost on the right, sending them another reserve brigade of Smith's to assist in doing it.

Both attacks succeeded and the Confederate garrison, completely worn out by its four days of exposure and zealous efforts, succumbed, to surrender the next morning, less the two senior generals, Floyd and Pillow, who escaped by boat with four Virginia regiments, and also less Forrest's cavalry, most of which picked its way out along the flooded river bank. Thus may be changed, in the space of a few hours, a sorry defeat into a decisive victory.

Three phases of Grant's conduct on this day demand mention: first, his cool and unerring judgment of the enemy's strength and situation; secondly, his versatility in adopting new plans and measures to meet sudden and unexpected changes in the state of affairs; thirdly, his complete self-forgetfulness and sense of loyalty to his men, which resulted in their being spared the panic that a few hours later overtook the Confederate forces. His troops looked to Grant to point the way out in the hour of need; their trust was his inspiration and he did not fail them; yet he remained simple, natural, and unaffected, with a complete absence of any grand manner about him.

Richardson gives us a pleasing picture of him at this time:

His unassuming modesty, and a certain quiet earnestness, which seemed to "mean business," won greatly upon me, but kindled no suspicion that he was the Coming Man. My fancy painted that expected hero in the good old colors, as quite the opposite of this prosaic brigadier. In my mind's eye I saw him charging at the head of his body-guard in the supreme moment of battle, while he cried, "God and the Union!" and flaming out in proclamations which rang through the land like a trumpet—all in the high Roman fashion.

But every general of whom I predicted greatness, failed to achieve it. Meanwhile, I saw more of Grant, sitting beside him around nightly camp-fires, at the most trying period of his life. Even then I defended him a little haltingly, against bitter assailants. I held him a pure man, an energetic fighter, but by no means one of the few, the immortal names.

At last, educated to humility of opinion through "the long, dull anguish of patience," it dawned upon me that he was winning great successes, because he was a great general—rising into the key position of the national batteries, solely because he was our gun of heaviest metal and largest caliber.[35]

Is it surprising that what the trained news-writer—who by his very profession is compelled to be a keen student of human nature—did not see in Grant at this time, so many of the general's military seniors and associates should also have failed to perceive in him—the "Coming Man"?

[35] Richardson, Preface, page vi.

CHAPTER XIV

GRANT AND THE TRIUMVIRATE

> War is the province of uncertainty. Three-fourths of those things upon which action in war must be calculated are hidden more or less in the clouds of great uncertainty. Here, then, above all other, a fine and penetrating mind is called for, to grope out the truth by the tact of its judgment.—CLAUSEWITZ.

THE "concert" between the departments of Buell and Halleck, urged on them by the President on January 1, resulting as it did in what, to Halleck's mind at least, was the somewhat premature attack on Fort Henry, eventuated in a political and strategic combination which none of Grant's seniors—Halleck, Buell, and McClellan—anticipated or were ready to turn to their personal advantage. Halleck, by far the cleverest of the three, was easily the winner in the duel of despatches that ensued.

We must now return to January 30, when Halleck telegraphed McClellan of the "immediate advance" on Fort Henry. In his accompanying letter he had the wit to say, "As Fort Henry, Dover, &c., are in Tennessee, I respectfully suggest that that State be added to this department." [1]

The same day he notified Buell: "I have ordered an advance of our troops on Fort Henry and Dover. It will be made immediately." [2] Buell replied at once: "Please let me know your plan and force and the time, &c." With this request it was difficult to comply. Halleck had no general plan in which the open-

[1] W. R. 7:571.
[2] W. R. 7:574.

From B. & L.

Henry Wager Halleck
(1815–72)

From B. & L.

Don Carlos Buell
(1818–98)

From B. & L.

George Brinton McClellan
(1826–85)

THE TRIUMVIRATE

ing of the Tennessee would be the first step and he did not know Grant's strength or the length of time it would take him to reach Fort Henry. However, he answered on the thirty-first, dodging the issue as best he could: "Movement already ordered to take and hold Fort Henry and cut railroad between Columbus and Dover. Force about 15,000; will be re-enforced as soon as possible. Will telegraph the day of investment or attack." [3]

Buell, who, if lacking in imagination, nevertheless had brains, and wished to avoid personal blame in case the attempt failed, returned immediately:

Do you consider active coöperation essential to your success, because in that case it would be necessary for each to know what the other has to do? It would be several days before I could seriously engage the enemy, and your operation ought not to fail. The operation which was suggested in my letter yesterday [4] would be an important preliminary to the next step.

Halleck, having still no idea of Grant's plans for or actual movements in the operation, was nonplussed; he must either admit his lack of knowledge or tell Buell to mind his own business. He chose the latter course, but he worded his reply with all the lawyer's instinct for postponement of any issue, and with superb tact:

Coöperation at present not essential. Fort Henry has been re-enforced, but where from I have not learned. The roads are in such horrible condition as to render movements almost impossible on land.[5] Will write you fully my plans as soon as I get your letter of the 30th ultimo. Write me your plans, and I will try to assist you.[6]

[3] W. R. 7:574.

[4] The destruction of railroad bridges on the Tennessee River and seizure of the Confederate steamboats at Tuscumbia. W. R. 7:573.

[5] They were so reported by Smith on the reconnaissance of Jan. 11–25. They were not nearly so bad at this time, but Halleck had to appear to have some news from the front.

[6] W. R. 7:576.

Buell's letter of January 30 was received on February 2. Halleck answered at once, but by letter [7] to gain more time, and throwing no more light on Grant's expedition. On February 1, Buell sent McClellan his own plans, adding:

While you were sick, by direction of the President I proposed to Halleck some concert of action between us. He answered, "I can do nothing; name a day for a demonstration." Night before last I received a dispatch from him, saying, "I have ordered an advance on Fort Henry and Dover. It will be made immediately." I protest against such prompt proceedings, as though I had nothing to do but command "Commence firing" when he starts off. However, he telegraphs me to-night that coöperation is not essential now.[8]

In other words, Buell had a grievance, but whatever happened, no one could now blame him.

On February 3, Buell threw a whole bombshell of bad news at Halleck, advising him to have the gunboats run by the forts at night and destroy the railroad bridges above the forts, and adding:

Without that I should fear the force you name could not hold both points. It will not do to be driven away. You had best count on meeting a re-enforcement of 10,000 from Bowling Green at this time, besides what may arrive from Virginia with Beauregard, who is said to bring fifteen regiments with him.[9]

On February 5, Halleck telegraphed the commanding officer at Cairo, "Send troops forward to General Grant as rapidly as possible." [10]

As Grant had taken twenty-three regiments with him and left eight regiments at Cairo and its outlying posts,[11] Halleck began

[7] W. R. 7:578.
[8] W. R. 7:933.
[9] W. R. 7:580.
[10] W. R. 109:206.
[11] W. R. 7:581, 579.

to feel a bit shaky. The same day he telegraphed McClellan: "Bombardment of Fort Henry now going on. [At least Halleck hoped so!] Our troops have landed three miles below." [12]

He also, but less definitely, informed Buell: "Our advance column is moving up the Tennessee—twenty-three regiments. More will soon follow." He asked, "Can't you make a diversion in our favor by threatening Bowling Green?" [13]

Buell answered: "My position does not admit of diversion. My moves must be real ones, and I shall move at once unless . . . It must probably be twelve days before we can be in front of Bowling Green." [14]

Discouraged, Halleck turned again to McClellan, repeating to him Buell's good advice of the third—"You had best count on meeting a re-enforcement of 10,000 from Bowling Green"—in the form of a definite report "that 10,000 men have left Bowling Green by railroad to re-enforce Fort Henry. Can't you send me some infantry regiments from Ohio? Answer." [15]

McClellan at once repeated to Buell Halleck's telegram, and added: "If report true [of ten thousand reinforcements], can you not assist by a demonstration in direction of Bowling Green? Communicate with Halleck and assist him if possible. Please reply." [16]

Buell replied: "I am communicating with him . . . No demonstration is practicable. I will send him a brigade." [17] In another message he added, "I hope General Halleck has weighed his work well." [18]

McClellan, meantime, had answered Halleck's last message: "Have telegraphed Buell to communicate with you . . . Please communicate fully with Buell and with me." [19]

[12] W. R. 7:583.
[13] W. R. 7:583.
[14] W. R. 7:583.
[15] W. R. 7:583.
[16] W. R. 7:584.
[17] W. R. 7:584.
[18] W. R. 7:585.
[19] W. R. 7:584.

Halleck had now done everything he could think of, save one; he learned that T. A. Scott, the Assistant Secretary of War, was at Indianapolis, and telegraphed him, "I want all the infantry regiments at Cairo you can possibly send me there."

February 6 dawned and while the actual bombardment of Fort Henry was not yet begun, the bombardment of despatches between the higher headquarters still went on—despatches at cross-purposes and with innumerable repetitions.

Halleck telegraphed McClellan, "Unless I get more forces, I may fail." [20]

McClellan demanded of Buell: "If road so bad in your front, had we not better throw all available force on Forts Henry and Donelson? What think you of making that the main line of operations? Answer quick." [21] And later, scenting a promotion in prospect there for his favorite: "Ought you not to go in person? Reply, and if so, I will inform Halleck."

Buell was now thoroughly exasperated, not at all realizing that his own excuses to McClellan for not going forward himself had led to inciting messages from McClellan to Halleck and so had been the direct cause leading to Halleck's hastily begun movement. He therefore, without restraint, spoke his mind in his reply:

This whole move, right in its strategical bearing, but commenced by General Halleck without appreciation—preparative or concert— has now become of vast magnitude. I was myself thinking of a change of the line to support it when I received your dispatch. It . . . is hazardous. I will answer definitely in the morning. [22]

Halleck and Buell, meantime, were haggling over the brigade of reinforcements which Halleck asked Buell to send up the Cum-

[20] W. R. 7:586.
[21] W. R. 7:587.
[22] W. R. 7:587.

berland. "They can land near Dover," Halleck said. Buell replied: "Do you say send the brigade up the Cumberland River to land near Dover? Is not the enemy in possession of the route across from Dover? Please describe Grant's position and the enemy's." [23] These were embarrassing questions for Halleck to answer, for of course he knew nothing as yet of Grant's position.

As the day closed, Halleck, still without news from Grant, felt he must say something more to McClellan. It is difficult to decide from his message whether it was a threat of failure if he were not reinforced or a promise of what could be gained if he were. He telegraphed: "If you can give me, in addition . . . 10,000 men, I will take Fort Henry, cut the enemy's line, and paralyze Columbus. Give me 25,000 and I will threaten Nashville and . . . force the enemy to abandon Bowling Green without a battle." [24]

On the seventh news of the capture of Fort Henry at last reached higher headquarters.[25] McClellan and Buell sent Halleck their congratulations. McClellan added: "Please thank Grant and Foote and their commands for me," which Halleck forgot to do, though he himself congratulated Foote—not Grant—on the ninth.[26]

Stanton, the new Secretary of War, sent Halleck his congratulations the next day: "Your energy and ability receive the strongest commendation of this Department. You have my perfect confidence and may rely upon the utmost support in your undertakings." [27]

The three higher headquarters were now faced with a new situation which none of them was ready to solve, though more than a week had passed since Grant was ordered to start. While

[23] Feb. 6, W. R. 7:588, 589.
[24] Feb. 6, received 10 P.M., W. R. 7:587.
[25] W. R. 7:590–592.
[26] N. R. 22:547.
[27] W. R. 8:547.

he, with the bit in his teeth, was going ahead, they continued to exchange views about the next step to be taken and what general should be chosen to command the forces for a further advance. Nobody realized—except, perhaps, President Lincoln—that probably the best rough-and-ready commander they had was already on the spot and running the show.

McClellan proposed to Halleck on February 7: "Either Buell or yourself should soon go to the scene of operations. Why not have Buell take the line of Tennessee and operate on Nashville, while your troops turn Columbus? Those two points gained a combined movement on Memphis will be next in order." [28]

McClellan throughout sought to protect the interests of his friend Buell. He laid the same proposal before Buell,[29] who, however, was not sufficiently alert mentally to face the requirements of the altered situation and replied: "I cannot, on reflection, think a change of my line would be advisable . . . I hope General Grant will not require further re-enforcements." Evidently grudgingly, he added, "I will go, if necessary." [30] Which reminds one of the quartermaster-general who remarked to Colonel Roosevelt, in the midst of the Spanish-American War, "I had a perfectly organized department until the war came and busted up everything."

Halleck proposed much the same thing to McClellan; he wanted Buell's troops, but not Buell, for an advance up the rivers. He added: "If you agree with me, send me everything you can spare from General Buell's command or elsewhere. . . . I am sending everything I can rake and scrape together from Missouri." [31]

He was indeed, fortunately for the outcome. He even suc-

[28] W. R. 7:591.
[29] W. R. 7:593.
[30] W. R. 7:593.
[31] Feb. 7, W. R. 7:591.

ceeded in borrowing several regiments from Hunter's Department of Kansas.[32]

On February 8, Halleck received McClellan's proposal of the day before and answered at once, reiterating his call for Buell's troops, but, to head off Buell's coming with them to take command, adding, "I shall go to Fort Henry on Monday or Tuesday." [33] Halleck, being senior to Buell, would be in command if both went to the front. He did not really want to go, however, because he wrote a letter the same day suggesting that the Western departments be united under his command, and that either Hitchcock or Sherman be assigned to command the river movement.[34] Grant ranked Hitchcock as brigadier, but Halleck requested that Hitchcock be made major-general.

Buell was still vacillating. He telegraphed McClellan, "I am concentrating and preparing, but will not decide definitely yet." [35]

To Halleck he revealed his quandary:

Your position on the Tennessee involves two questions in which I am concerned: First, a new plan of campaign; second, the rescue of your column, if it should come to that. The first I have had in my mind, and may depend very much on your further success. The second will leave me no option but to use every man not necessary for defense here to effect the object, if possible. If General Grant should be beleaguered so as to be in danger, you will of course inform me of it.[36]

A glorious opportunity for Buell—should it come—to raise the siege of Grant, himself besieged in Fort Henry! One wonders if the wish was father to the thought.

On the ninth Halleck heard that Hitchcock, who was in Wash-

[32] W. R. 7:636.
[33] W. R. 7:594.
[34] W. R. 7:595.
[35] Feb. 8, W. R. 7:594.
[36] Feb. 8, W. R. 7:937.

ington, had been appointed major-general.[37]   He expressed his
elation to General Cullum, his chief of staff, sent to take charge
at Cairo: "McClellan gives hopes of adopting my plan entire,
by sending a part of Buell's army to the Cumberland. If so,
look out for lively times." [38]

During all this period Halleck was hard pressed for information to pass on of what was happening on the Tennessee. No
word came through from Grant, although he, according to his
later statement, was writing Halleck every day. The practice of
sending liaison officers to lower staffs, expressly to pass up information, had not yet come into vogue. Yet Halleck must say
something, so he despatched the following to McClellan on
the tenth:

Colonel Holt and others say that troops cannot move by land in
Kentucky before well into April. If sufficient forces are sent to
the Cumberland, we can by that time be in the heart of Tennessee.
Give us the means and we are certain to give the enemy a telling
blow.[39]

McClellan and Buell the same day [40] exchanged messages
about the alteration of muskets, but the subject of operations was
not mentioned; neither realizing, apparently, that it was their fat
also which was on the griddle.

On Tuesday, February 11, Halleck finally concluded to divide
the spoils of his enterprise with Buell. He telegraphed to him:
"Gunboats will be ready to ascend the Cumberland by the last of
the week . . . Can't you come with all your available forces
and command the column up the Cumberland? I shall go to the
Tennessee this week." [41]

Perhaps Halleck was urged to this step by misgivings aroused

[37] McClellan to Halleck, Jan. 29, W. R. 7:930.
[38] W. R. 7:598.
[39] W. R. 7:599.
[40] W. R. 7:601, 602.
[41] W. R. 7:605.

by a message the same day from the Assistant Secretary of War, who was in Cairo: "Is General Grant strong enough and quite ready for the Cumberland and Donelson movement? Position is said to be strong, and we should be strong enough to be very certain of success." [42]

Buell found Halleck's invitation tempting. He informed McClellan: "I will advance up the Tennessee or Cumberland with a portion of my force, leaving the rest to operate against Bowling Green . . ." The decision was not, however, whole-hearted; there were numerous conditions: "The movement . . . is difficult . . . It should be thoroughly supported . . . The rivers must be made absolutely secure by gunboats . . . There ought to be five gunboats to each river . . . Broader ones ought to be got up at once . . . Paducah should be held by not less than 10,000 men . . ." and last, but not least, he suggested that McClellan "be prepared any day to throw strong re-enforcements into these movements." [43]

One is glad when reading this that President Lincoln had at least one general in his army who was able and willing to deal with conditions as they existed and not insisting that they be made over the way he would prefer to have them!

In replying to Halleck, however, Buell seemed even less sure:

I shall determine on my ultimate movements the moment I have something in regard to your position on the Tennessee River . . . It seems to me you cannot well direct your re-enforcements up the Cumberland River. Is it certain that they can form a junction by that route? They certainly can by the other. [44]

As is often the case with those most troubled by doubts of what they themselves should do, Buell had the strongest convictions concerning how others should act.

[42] W. R. 7:604.
[43] Feb. 12, W. R. 7:938.
[44] Feb. 12, W. R. 7:607.

Halleck answered: "Gunboats have destroyed everything on the Tennessee to Florence, in Alabama . . . Expedition started up the Cumberland last night . . . It is reported that 40,000 rebels are at Dover and Clarksville." Not really cheering news to a hesitating Buell. "If you conclude to land the column on the Cumberland, come at once, with your spare forces."

He explained in another message the need for sending part of Grant's forces around by the Cumberland.[45]

Buell acknowledged these despatches the same day, saying, "Will move on the line of the Cumberland River or Tennessee River, but it will take ten days at least to effect the transfer of my troops," and asking: "Why is it necessary to use the Cumberland? Where are the reinforcements to land? Where form a junction? And by whom are they commanded? Have you any map of the ground?"

Thus passed, in the rear at the higher headquarters, the day of Grant's march from the Tennessee at Fort Henry to the Cumberland, on Fort Donelson!

On February 13, the day of the first tentative assaults, the spry-witted Halleck informed Buell, who said it would take him "ten days to transfer his forces": "The attack will be made on Fort Donelson to-day . . . or if not to-day certainly to-morrow. Would it not be possible to make a cavalry demonstration on Bowling Green? . . . I have no maps other than the general ones in book-stores." [46]

Once more Halleck repeated his offer, evidently not prepared to place any large bets on Grant's chances, and willing to shunt the responsibility on the shoulders of another: "Why not come down and take the immediate command of the Cumberland col-

[45] W. R. 7:608.
[46] W. R. 7:609.   Sherman was on this date assigned to command at Cairo. W. R. 8:555.

umn yourself? If so, I will transfer Sherman and Grant to the Tennessee column."

Neither was McClellan betting. On February 13 he enjoined Buell: "Watch Fort Donelson closely. I am not too certain as to the result there."[47] To Halleck he was really helpful. He authorized him to "suspend movement of any troops en route or under orders for Kansas" and to report the facts, and added, "I am anxious about Fort Donelson."[48] Halleck replied on the fourteenth, emboldened to suggest: "Can't you spare some troops from the Potomac? I am not strong enough if the enemy concentrates on me."[49]

From these telegrams it appears that Grant alone was not worrying. His message of this date to Halleck declared, "I feel every confidence of success and the best feeling prevails among the men."[50]

The thought of having to detach troops from his own Army of the Potomac was one McClellan never could face. When Halleck demanded that, McClellan at once turned again to Buell to ask what reinforcements had already been sent.[51]

Buell replied at 6 P.M. the same day: "One brigade from Kentucky and eight regiments from Ohio and Indiana. I have made preparation and start myself on Monday with two divisions . . . General Grant cannot any longer be in danger . . . The only apprehension I have now is for his gunboats."

Real intuition, because at that hour the gunboats had fallen down-stream, defeated in their attack, damaged, with Foote, their commander, wounded!

Reassured by Buell's message about Grant, McClellan, in a calm mood, the same evening responded to Halleck:

[47] W. R. 7:608.
[48] W. R. 8:555.
[49] Feb. 14, 5 P.M., W. R. 7:612.
[50] W. R. 7:613.
[51] W. R. 7:612.

What disposition do you intend to make of Hitchcock? If you do not go in person to the Tennessee and Cumberland, I shall probably write Buell to take the line of the Tennessee, so far as Nashville is concerned [52] . . . It may well be necessary to throw a large portion of the troops up the Tennessee, in which case he is entitled to their command.[53]

McClellan was ever thoughtful for the interests of his favorites. But the idea of losing part of his territorial command to Buell was as distasteful to Halleck as that of losing detachments from the Army of the Potomac was to McClellan. Halleck's reply to this is not given; perhaps in the pressure of events he overlooked it—or at least the disconcerting parts.

February 15 was Grant's hardest day at Fort Donelson, the day of the Confederate attack. Halleck, of course, knew nothing of that, but must have the last word and if necessary invent news. In one message he wrote: "Everything looks well. [Far from the fact!] Grant says we can keep them in till mortar-boats arrive. Commodore Foote will immediately return from Cairo with two more gunboats. Troops are moving very rapidly to Fort Donelson." [54] Had he said, "*around* Donelson under Confederate attacks," he would have come nearer the truth.

At 11 A.M., he fabricated another message: "I have no definite plan beyond the taking of Fort Donelson." So much is credible, but one who has read the reports of the discomfiture of Grant's forces on the fifteenth has to smile when Halleck concludes, "The siege and bombardment of Fort Donelson are progressing satisfactorily." [55]

Shortly after, Halleck learned from Buell of the evacuation of Bowling Green by the Confederates.[56] He became less con-

[52] It is likely that the message is garbled, Nashville being on the Cumberland.
[53] Feb. 14, W. R. 7:614.
[54] Feb. 15, W. R. 7:616.
[55] Feb. 15, W. R. 7:616.
[56] W. R. 7:621, No. 1.

fident and appealed to McClellan: "I must have more troops.
It is a military necessity." [57]   At 8 P.M., after studying Buell's
plan to advance, after all, on Nashville, sending one division,
Nelson's, by the Cumberland,[58] Halleck protested to McClellan:
"This is bad strategy—his forces should come and help me." [59]
McClellan replied: "Your idea is in some respects good.   But
. . ." and approved Buell's plan.[60]

The same evening, it occurred to McClellan to ask Grant to
"telegraph in full the state of affairs with you," [61] but this message seems not to have reached Grant.

On the sixteenth Halleck had some real news to communicate [62]—the fighting of the previous three days; but he put a good
face on it, with a little added romancing, and still insisted that
Buell's army should be sent to join Grant.

At 10 A.M. on the seventeenth Halleck was still begging
McClellan: "Do send me more troops.   It is the crisis of the war
in the West," [63] but three hours later he began a new song in a
major key: "Make Buell, Grant and Pope major-generals of volunteers and give me command in the West.   I ask this in return
for Forts Henry and Donelson." [64]

Strangely enough, it never occurred to one of the Triumvirate
that any credit was due Grant for the Donelson success.   Halleck
was still, on the eighteenth, coaxing Buell: "Come down to the
Cumberland and take command.   The battle of the West is to be
fought in that vicinity.   You should be in it as the ranking general in immediate command.   Don't hesitate." [65]

[57] Feb. 15, 3 P.M., W. R. 7:616.
[58] Buell to Halleck, Feb. 15, W. R. 7:621, No. 2.
[59] Feb. 15, 8 P.M., W. R. 7:617.
[60] Feb. 15, 11 P.M., W. R. 7:617.
[61] W. R. 109:212.
[62] Halleck to McClellan, W. R. 7:624.
[63] W. R. 7:627.
[64] W. R. 7:628.
[65] W. R. 7:632.

On the nineteenth, replying to McClellan's question as to what he wanted of Hitchcock, Halleck said: "Hitchcock will take command here . . . I think Hunter . . . will command the central column." [66]

The same day Halleck recommended C. F. Smith for major-general. "Honor him for this victory." [67]   He thanked Hunter, commanding the Department of Kansas, for his assistance which "enabled us to win the victory.   Receive my most heartfelt thanks." [68]   But for Grant, not a word of personal thanks,[69] only the grudging recommendation for promotion to major-general, but *after* Buell, so that he should remain junior to him.

None the less a reward came, unasked by Grant, and not recommended by any sponsor.   President Lincoln, who had been closely watching the campaign,[70] upon news of the surrender promptly nominated Grant—and Grant alone—as major-general and the Senate as promptly confirmed the appointment.

[66] W. R. 7:636.
[67] Halleck to McClellan, W. R. 7:637.
[68] W. R. 7:636.
[69] Halleck did, indeed, three days later, issue a General Order, congratulating Foote, Grant, and their "brave officers and men" for the victories on the Tennessee and Cumberland.   W. R. 7:638.
[70] Lincoln to Halleck, Feb. 16, W. R. 7:624.

CHAPTER XV

GRANT IN OBSCURATION

Friction is the only conception which in a general way corresponds to that which distinguishes real war from war on paper.—CLAUSEWITZ.

NO one can compare the actual situation at Forts Henry and Donelson with Halleck's ideas of what he wanted done there and what he thought was being done, without realizing that Grant's world of reality and Halleck's figment of that world were as far apart as Mars and Jupiter.

If Halleck had sent a staff officer to the front each day—as is now the practice—to stay twenty-four hours, then return and report; if he had even had a liaison officer there to do nothing but keep him informed, the gulf of misunderstanding might have been bridged. On the other hand, had Grant ever had staff experience at a higher headquarters—as Lee had had with Scott in Mexico—he would have taken steps to protect himself by a better staff organization, a systematized courier service, message centers, the numbering of messages, the sending of important messages in duplicate by different routes to provide against loss; and the breach would at least not have become so wide.

But under the actual conditions there was only one hope of restoring harmony, which was for Halleck to go to the front—as he had, himself, proposed to McClellan—and by twenty-four hours of contact with the reality reconstruct from the bottom up his mental conceptions. Unfortunately, because of the heavier burdens thereby shifted to President Lincoln's shoulders and be-

cause these initial delays and lack of coördination undoubtedly
lengthened the war, unfortunately, too, for the peace of mind of
both Halleck and Grant, he did not go and the gulf was not
bridged.

Let us now see how the differences came about.

Halleck's instructions to Grant of January 30 provided for:

1 Sending forward with the least delay possible all available
   forces, leaving behind suitable garrisons.
2 Going up the Tennessee—as far as practicable by steamer.
3 Taking and holding Fort Henry.
4 Troops to land below the fort and invest the land side.
5 (Optional) a heavy Union battery on the opposite side of the
   river.
6 The obstruction (but not the destruction) of railroad bridges
   above the fort.
7 The building of a telegraph line from Paducah to Fort Henry.

These instructions—except the fifth, which proved unnecessary—accord so literally with what Grant did as to suggest that
he had, himself, proposed the plan to Halleck in their interview
on January 27.[1]

On February 1, Halleck warned Grant: "Don't cumber up
. . . with too large a train. . . . Move rapidly . . . by steamers,
to reduce the place before . . . re-enforcements can arrive." [2]

This also fits into the picture: Grant had the steamers, had
not the field transportation, and could do nothing else anyhow.

The next day, however, Halleck added what to Grant was a
new idea: "I think a column should move from Smithland [at

    [1] See Grant to Halleck, Jan. 31, in W. R. 7:575; and Grant to Smith, Feb. 1,
ibid. 7:578.
    [2] W. R. 7:577.

the mouth of the Cumberland] between the rivers if the road is practicable. Nearly all your available cavalry could take that route and be supplied, at least partly, by the boats." [3]

This was a wide departure from the previous plan, and doubtless suggested to Halleck by his study of Napoleonic campaigns. It involved innumerable delays, and slowing up of the movement. What was Grant to do? No reply from him is to be found. Possibly the message was not received, for he left Cairo the same day.

This idea had, however, been a pet baby of Halleck's. On January 24 he had written to Smith—not Grant or through Grant—to send a full description of the Smithland-Dover-Fort Henry roads,[4] and that was doubtless the report he was waiting for on the twenty-ninth when he telegraphed Foote: "Am waiting for General Smith's report . . . As soon as that is received will give order. Meantime, have everything ready." [5]

But of this Grant knew nothing, since both communications had been addressed to Grant's subordinates direct and over his head. Yet on this is based Halleck's first grievance against Grant—that he was ignoring instructions.

On the seventh Halleck addressed "Brigadier General Grant or Flag-Officer Foote: Push the gunboats up the river to cut [?] the railroad bridges. Troops to sustain the gunboats can follow in transports." [6]

This, apparently, was inspired by the suggestion of Buell, backed by McClellan. It countermanded the previous order not to destroy the bridges but only to render them impassable. Again the order came too late; the three gunboats had already left Fort

[3] Feb. 2, W. R. 7:579.
[4] W. R. 7:930.
[5] N. R. 22:525.
[6] W. R. 7:591.

Henry on their three days' cruise up the Tennessee. However, Grant complied by sending cavalry to destroy the Tennessee bridge of the Paris-Dover Railroad.[7]

Halleck seems to have been overflowing with ideas on February 8. He ordered Grant to "destroy the bridge at Clarksville," over the Cumberland, forgetting the injunction in the Scriptures, if you would spoil a strong man's house, *first* bind the strong man—in this case Fort Donelson. "Shovels and picks will be sent you to strengthen Fort Henry." "The guns" of Fort Henry were to be "transferred" for land-side defense; "slaves of secessionists" were to be impressed. (There were no slaves, nothing but wild woods.) The slaves were to be "kept under guard and not . . . allowed to escape. Where supplies are taken from Union men, they should be paid for . . . where from secessionists . . ." Minutiæ of instructions not flattering, to say the least, to Grant's intelligence. "Cut the enemy's telegraph lines," and lastly, "Keep me informed of all you do." [8]

What was Grant to do about these directions? Give up the attack on Donelson and by stopping to fortify Fort Henry invite the enemy to come and attack him? Or should he go ahead, let trifling matters wait? Naturally, there was but one answer to that. Grant made it on the eleventh: "Every effort will be put forth to have Clarksville within a few days. There are no negroes in this part of the country to work on fortifications." [9]

Meanwhile Halleck had repeated on the tenth: "Destroy bridge at Clarksville. Run any risk to accomplish this. Strengthen land side of Fort Henry and transfer guns to resist a land attack. Picks and shovels are sent." [10]

Absorbed as he was in his interchange of messages with

[7] Grant to L. Wallace, W. R. 7:619.
[8] W. R. 7:595.
[9] Grant to Halleck, W. R. 7:604.
[10] Halleck to Grant, W. R. 7:600.

McClellan and Buell, and having, apparently, no idea of where Clarksville, Dover, Fort Donelson, and the bridges really were, Halleck had of course no realization of what absurd reading his message made; while Grant, knowing nothing about how the Triumvirate were squabbling over the division of his raiment, could not understand what it was all about.

The same day, February 10, both Grant and Halleck were sending orders to Foote—happily, not in this instance contradictory—to take his gunboats up the Cumberland.[11]

On the twelfth Grant reported his departure from Fort Henry for Donelson.[12]   On the thirteenth he despatched from Donelson: "Send all troops to arrive to Fort Henry . . . One gunboat should be there." [13]

This message could not but make it appear to Halleck, who did not know the circumstances, that Grant either was weakening or had left Fort Henry inadequately guarded.

On the fourteenth Grant sent two telegrams and one letter to Halleck and another to Cullum for Halleck.   In the last he said, "Appearances indicate now that we will have a protracted siege here," and called for land transportation and for ammunition for his heavy artillery.[14]

Grant made no report on the fifteenth, but news of the fighting reached Halleck from other sources, and it of course irritated him to have no word from the commanding general except the messages of the fourteenth, all too brief for Halleck's purposes.   Had Grant telegraphed the substance of his more descriptive letter of the fourteenth, it would have helped Halleck greatly in his dickering with McClellan and Buell, by giving him some real news to pass on.

[11] Halleck to Cullum, and Grant to Foote, W. R. 7:600.
[12] W. R. 7:612.
[13] W. R. 7:609.
[14] W. R. 7:613.

From the tenth to the sixteenth of February, Halleck paid
Grant the compliment of not burdening him with further instructions. Luckily; for Grant had a hard job to handle and only needed
to be let alone. It was scarcely fair to him, however, that Halleck
should give him no inkling on the seventeenth, after learning of
the surrender, of the further intentions arrived at by the Triumvirate. This neglect was all the more marked because Halleck
on that date sent Sherman—assigned as commander of the District
of Cairo, while Grant was made commander of the District of
West Tennessee [15] —a rather full outline of his plans:

All troops from Kentucky [i.e., all the troops of Buell] will be
sent up the Cumberland. All others will be stopped at Paducah
to await further orders. Watch Beauregard's movements from Columbus and report by telegram your forces at Paducah; also report
all you can stop there. I am not satisfied with present success. We
must now prepare for a still more important movement. You will
not be forgotten in this.[16]

Had this information—virtually to the effect that Buell was
now to take over operations on the Cumberland, while Halleck
had big plans in mind for operations on the Tennessee or Mississippi according to developments—had been communicated to
Grant, much friction would have been avoided. It is all too obvious, however, that Halleck, unable to appreciate the man's fast
developing powers of generalship and ability to command, regarded Grant merely as an office boy, already given too much
authority in being sent to the bank to make a deposit, and who,
having made it, should now sit quietly on his bench and await
further orders.

Up to this time, indeed, Grant had not shown marked far-
sightedness. He had announced on January 31 that after taking

[15] Halleck to Cullum, Feb. 14, W. R. 7:614.
[16] Halleck to Sherman, Feb. 17, W. R. 7:629.

Fort Henry he would leave Smith or McClernand there "to command after my return," [17] evidently expecting to return to Cairo at once, just as he had returned there after the seizure of Paducah. And when, on the spot, his vision grew to include the capture of Donelson, he did not see beyond that point, but stated, "I shall take and destroy Fort Donelson on the 8th and return to Fort Henry." [18]

Had the Donelson affair been merely a duplication of the Henry, as Grant probably thought at the time it would be—a speedy surrender of the fort with its heavy guns and a handful of men, after an hour's naval bombardment—such a course on his part would have been eminently sensible. But the surrender at Donelson of a force comprising at least half of the available Confederate troops in the middle Tennessee theater of war, created a totally different outlook for him, and one which would entirely have justified his saying, "I shall take Nashville on the eighteenth"! And he could have contended with justice that in doing so he was still within his assigned district.

The opportunity passed, however—not through any mending of the broken joints in the Confederate armor, but because of Halleck's peremptory order of the eighteenth to Grant: "Don't let gunboats go higher up than Clarksville. Even there they must limit their operations to the destruction of the bridge and railroad, and return immediately to Cairo, leaving one at Fort Donelson." [19]

This order—which explained nothing—coming as it did just as the rich harvest of easy captures of enemy towns, forts, guns, men, and military stores was opening before his gaze as a consequence of his capture of Donelson, must have seemed to Grant

---

[17] Grant to Halleck, W. R. 7:575.
[18] W. R. 7:124.
[19] W. R. 7:633.

as a blow in the face, all the more so as it was Halleck's first word after Grant's outstanding success.

On the nineteenth, Grant, not yet having received Halleck's order of the eighteenth, wrote Cullum: "Clarksville [which also had Confederate riverside batteries] is evacuated, and I shall take possession of it on Friday [the twenty-first]. . . . If it is the desire of the general commanding department, I can have Nashville on Saturday week." [20]

The same day he telegraphed Sherman: "Send all re-enforcements up the Cumberland. I shall occupy Clarksville . . . and Nashville . . . if it meets the approval of General Halleck. I have written him to that effect." [21]

Sherman of course knew, what Grant had no means of knowing, that not even the occupation of Clarksville met with Halleck's approval.

On February 20, Halleck telegraphed McClellan: "I must have command of the armies in the West. Hesitation and delay are losing us the golden opportunity. Lay this before the President and Secretary of War. May I assume command? Answer quickly." [22]

McClellan replied coolly to this demand: "Buell at Bowling Green knows more of the state of affairs than you at St. Louis. . . . I shall not lay your request before the Secretary until I hear definitely from Buell." [23]

Rebuffed but not silenced, Halleck appealed to Stanton, the Secretary of War, for supreme command in the West: "One whole week has been lost already by hesitation and delay . . . Give me authority, and I will be responsible for results." [24]

Stanton replied: "The President . . . does not think any

---

[20] W. R. 7:637.
[21] W. R. 7:638.
[22] W. R. 7:641.
[23] McClellan to Halleck, Feb. 21, W. R. 7:645.
[24] Feb. 21, W. R. 7:655.

change . . . at present advisable. He desires and expects you and General Buell to coöperate fully and zealously with each other." [25]

From McClellan came a second rebuff to Halleck on the twenty-first: "You do not report either often or fully enough. Unless you keep me fully advised, you must not expect me to abandon my own plans for yours." [26]

Halleck was now thoroughly roused. Regarding as due solely to himself the credit for the Henry-Donelson victories, he felt not only that he was not receiving the reward which he merited, in the shape of an enlarged and reinforced command, but that all his scheming toward that goal was going awry, and instead there was laid on him the blame for faults for which, in his opinion, his predecessor Frémont and his own subordinates were mainly responsible. Such a situation is one of the tests of the really great commander. He passes on the credit to his lieutenants, but what blame there may be he assumes and carries on his own shoulders. The petty-minded commander reverses the process. In this respect Halleck writes his own indictment, as will be shortly seen.

On February 21, Foote, from Paducah, seconded Grant's Nashville proposal. Addressing Cullum—for Halleck—he wrote:

General Grant and myself consider this a good time to move on Nashville . . . We were about moving for this purpose when General Grant, to my astonishment, received a telegram from General Halleck not to let the gunboats go higher than Clarksville; no telegram sent to me . . . Please ask General Halleck if we shall do it. [27]

Foote sent Grant Halleck's answer the next day: "Halleck is waiting instructions from the War Department and Kentucky, and directs that everything remain *in statu quo*." [28]

[25] Feb. 22, W. R. 7:652.
[26] W. R. 7:646.
[27] N. R. 22:622.
[28] Feb. 22, N. R. 22:624.

Also Foote wrote his wife what he thought about it: "I am disgusted that we were kept from going up and taking Nashville. It was jealousy on the part of McClellan and Halleck . . . I shall report McClellan and Halleck to the [Navy] Department, and soon there will be a row." [29]

Foote was right about the men to blame, but mistaken, as is evident from the complete record, regarding their motive. McClellan was looking only toward conserving the interests of his "one lieutenant he could trust," Buell, and Halleck desiring only to gain more power for himself.

February 23 being Sunday, Halleck had time to consider and decided to let Foote and Grant go up the Cumberland.[30] Perhaps, also, Secretary Stanton's message that the President desired and expected coöperation made him a bit uneasy about not helping Buell take Nashville.

Two days later Halleck learned of Buell's being in or before Nashville, and countermanded his order, directing: "Grant will send no more troops to Clarksville . . . Smith's division will come to Fort Henry." [31]

On the twenty-fourth Nelson's division of Buell's army, originally intended as a reinforcement for Grant, but now ordered to rejoin Buell by way of the Cumberland, on transports, reached Donelson and reported to Grant. Grant sent it on to Nashville with orders to debark at the city.[32] Buell, who with his leading troops had reached the river, opposite Nashville, was furious, and fearful lest the enemy, who had abandoned Nashville, might return and attack Nelson before his main body arrived. In consequence, the same day that Halleck countermanded his order for a Cumberland advance, Buell both requested and ordered Smith's

[29] N. R. 22:626.
[30] Halleck to Sherman and Foote, W. R. 7:655.
[31] Halleck to Cullum and Sherman, copy sent Grant, Feb. 25, W. R. 7:667.
[32] W. R. 7:662.

division to come temporarily to his support at Nashville;[33] and Grant, still not having received Halleck's order of the twenty-fifth, sent Smith's division to Nashville on the twenty-sixth, and on the twenty-seventh went there himself to confer with Buell.

It was a simple case of wartime friction to be expected in a theater so large, without telegraphic communication and even a properly organized courier service. But Halleck, lacking any real war experience, and no doubt unaware that the misunderstanding was mainly chargeable to the failure of himself and his own poorly organized staff to keep Grant properly informed—in part also, perhaps, to his two changes of plan, on the twenty-third and twenty-fifth—grew angry with Grant and when, on March 1, he first learned of Smith's movement he demanded heatedly of Cullum, still at Cairo: "Who sent Smith's division to Nashville? I ordered them across to the Tennessee, where they are wanted immediately. Order them back. What is the reason that no one down there can obey my orders? Send all spare transports to General Grant up the Tennessee,"[34] where Halleck supposed Grant to be, in accordance with his order of the twenty-fifth, instead of where Grant actually was, at Fort Donelson, with no wagon transport to speak of, and with a very large sick-list, as he informed Halleck the same day, in his "daily report."[35]

Grant received this petulant message with Cullum's explanation and comment, "Evidently, the General supposes you on the Tennessee,"[36] on March 2, and at once ordered his main body back to Fort Henry.[37]

On March 3, Halleck learned from Cullum that Grant had "just returned from Nashville on the 28th of February."[38] It

---

[33] W. R. 7:944; W. R. 7:668.
[34] W. R. 7:674.
[35] W. R. 7:674.
[36] W. R. 7:677.
[37] S. O., No. 14, W. R. 7:678.
[38] W. R. 7:676.

was perhaps unfortunate for them both that during the preceding
week so many of Halleck's hopes and plans had gone awry, leaving the elderly general in an ugly mood.

McClellan, Secretary Stanton, and the President had all refused
to accede to his "Give me command . . . in the West!"
McClellan had reproved him for not reporting "often or fully
enough." Foote, commanding the fleet, was not complying with
his orders,[39] besides getting him into trouble with the President [40]
and McClellan.[41] But toward none of these could he afford to
show anger.

Grant had been a model subordinate, but Halleck's growing
vexation demanded an outlet and Halleck vented it upon Grant,
who, because of his—to Halleck's mind—too spectacular capture
of Donelson had been made a major-general ahead of Buell, thus
wrecking Halleck's design to coax Buell to come and be his vice-
regent over half of what was to be Halleck's enlarged kingdom.
Further, the various miscarriages and conflict of orders had made
Grant seem to be growing too assertive. Lastly, though indubi-
tably first, in Halleck's motives, a scapegoat was needed for all
the sins of the Department of the Missouri, and here was one
at hand.

In this mood Halleck wrote McClellan: "I have had no communication with General Grant for more than a week. He left
his command without my authority [42] and went to Nashville. His
army seems to be as much demoralized by the victory of Fort Donelson as was that of the Potomac by the defeat of Bull Run." [43]

And now for the fine Italian dagger:

[39] N. R. 22:637, 639.
[40] Wise to Halleck, N. R. 22:641.
[41] McClellan to Halleck, N. R. 22:631.
[42] Halleck overlooked in writing this that his own order had assigned Grant
to command the District of West Tennessee; Grant was not outside his district.
[43] Mch. 3, W. R. 7:679.

It is hard to censure a successful general immediately after a victory, but I think he richly deserves it. I can get no returns, no reports, no information of any kind from him. Satisfied with his victory, he sits down and enjoys it without any regard to the future.[44] I am worn out and tired with this neglect and inefficiency. C. F. Smith is almost the only officer equal to the emergency.

One must not blame Halleck too much for this. He probably regretted it later on. Self-restraint in personal relations and euphemistic letter-writing was not then the commonplace that it is to-day; a spade was a spade. Besides, Halleck had all the lawyer's instinct, when casting blame, to turn district attorney and make a real case of it. Further, he had never known Grant, probably had never seen him except in the strained ten-minute interview in which Grant had proposed the Henry expedition.

But what can be said for McClellan, who, according to King's statement, had been Grant's "comrade of the Mexican War days, his guest for some weeks at Fort Vancouver," [45] and therefore must have known him? Was he ready to sacrifice Grant in his closer friend Buell's interests? Or was he merely, uncritically, falling into Halleck's trap and ready to believe any slander against his former host? The reader must judge from his reply: "Do not hesitate to arrest him at once if the good of the service requires it, and place C. F. Smith in command. You are at liberty to regard this as a positive order if it will smooth your way." [46]

---

[44] Nicolay and Hay in describing Halleck after Corinth say that there he "imitated the conduct that he wrongfully imputed to Grant after Donelson." See "Abraham Lincoln," Vol. V, p. 351.

[45] Charles King: "The True Ulysses S. Grant," p. 144.

[46] McClellan to Halleck, Mch. 3, 6 P.M., W. R. 7:680. For these two messages, Grant's secretary, Badeau, searched the War Department after the war, by Grant's order. He finally obtained "after long research and repeated efforts" Halleck's telegram, but did not find McClellan's reply. The foot-note on p. 65, Vol. I, of Badeau's "Military History of U. S. Grant," makes one suppose that Grant refused to believe McClellan had authorized his arrest, but blamed Halleck for the whole affair.

Halleck had cooled off considerably by the next morning, perhaps realizing that if Grant were placed in arrest there would have
to be a court-martial and then "questions by the defense" which
might prove decidedly embarrassing. He therefore explained
matters to McClellan by the simple expedient of attributing
Grant's "neglect of my often-repeated orders" to drunkenness, or
as he put it: "A rumor has just reached me that . . . Grant has
resumed his former bad habits." [47]

The use of strong drink being as much in vogue as the use of
strong language, in those days, Halleck's letter continues, "I do
not deem it advisable to arrest him at present, but have placed
General Smith in command of the expedition up the Tennessee."

On March 4, Halleck, armed with the authority of the Commanding General of the Army and the Secretary of War, telegraphed: "Major-General U. S. Grant, Fort Henry: You will
place Major-General C. F. Smith in command of expedition,
and remain yourself at Fort Henry. Why do you not obey my
orders to report strength and positions of your command?" [48]

Grant replied to this from Fort Donelson, temperately and
with dignity:

Your dispatch of yesterday is just received. Troops will be sent,
under command of Major-General Smith as directed. I had prepared a different plan, intending General Smith to command the
forces which would go to Paris and Humboldt,[49] while I would command the expedition upon Eastport, Corinth and Jackson in person.
Information this morning, however, would have changed my plan,
even if your orders had not done it. Forces going to Eastport must
go prepared to meet a force of 20,000 men. This will take all my

[47] Halleck to McClellan, Mch. 4, W. R. 7:682. The much mooted question
of drunkenness on Grant's part during the Civil War has not been considered
pertinent to the subject of this study. There is no official record either for or
against. The contemporary gossip concerning it may not have had any more substantial basis than the accusation with which Halleck tried to veil his own deficiency of information.
[48] W. R. 11:3.
[49] This referred to orders of Halleck to Grant on Mch. 1. W. R. 7:674.

available troops after garrisoning Clarksville, Forts Donelson and Henry. . . .

I am not aware of ever having disobeyed any order from head-quarters—certainly never intended such a thing. I have reported almost daily the condition of my command and reported every position occupied. . . . My reports have nearly all been made to General Cullum, chief of staff, and it may be that many of them were not thought of sufficient importance to forward more than a telegraphic synopsis of.[50]

The letter gives a brief summary of Grant's strength: forty-six infantry regiments, three cavalry regiments, and ten light batteries.

On March 5, Halleck sent further instructions to Grant, for Smith's expedition, indicating that he intended Smith to operate under Grant's supervision and orders.[51] The next day, however, he sent Grant a disagreeable telegram and letter, each of which was destined to produce a violent reaction. The telegram read:

General McClellan directs that you report daily the number and positions of the forces under your command. Your neglect of repeated orders to report the strength of your command has created great dissatisfaction and seriously interfered with military plans. Your going to Nashville without authority, and when your presence with your troops was of the utmost importance, was a matter of very serious complaint at Washington, so much so that I was advised to arrest you on your return.[52]

Grant replied on the seventh, this time from Fort Henry, in a despatch not free from heat:

Your dispatch of yesterday just received. I did all I could to get you returns of the strength of my command. Every move I made was reported daily to your chief of staff, who must have failed to keep you properly posted. I have done my very best to obey

[50] W. R. 11:4.
[51] W. R. 11:7.
[52] Halleck to Grant, Mch. 6, W. R. 11:15.

orders and to carry out the interests of the service. If my course is not satisfactory, remove me at once. I do not wish to impede in any way the success of our arms. I have averaged writing more than once a day since leaving Cairo to keep you informed of my position, and it is no fault of mine if you have not received my letters. My going to Nashville was strictly intended for the good of the service, and not to gratify any desire of my own.

Believing sincerely that I must have enemies between you and myself who are trying to impair my usefulness, I respectfully ask to be relieved from further duty in the department.[53]

Halleck replied to Grant on the eighth, still nursing his wrath:

You are mistaken. There is no enemy between you and me. There is no letter of yours stating the number and position of your command since capture of Fort Donelson. General McClellan has asked for it repeatedly with reference to ulterior movements, but I could not give him the information. He is out of all patience waiting for it. Answer by telegraph in general terms.[54]

Grant, growing more indignant, replied:

Your dispatch . . . just received. I will do all in my power to advance the expedition now started. You had a better chance of knowing my strength whilst surrounding Fort Donelson than I had. Troops were reporting daily, by your order, and immediately assigned to brigades. There were no orders received from you until the 28th February to make out returns, and I made every effort to get them in as early as possible. I have always been ready to move anywhere, regardless of consequences to myself, but with a disposition to take the best care of the troops under my command. I renew my application to be relieved from further duty. Returns have been sent.[55]

The last of Halleck's bombshells, his letter of the sixth, reached Grant on the eleventh. It inclosed an unsigned letter, addressed to Judge Davis, alleging frauds in the disposal of captured prop-

[53] W. R. 11:15.
[54] W. R. 7:21.
[55] Mch. 9, W. R. 11:21.

erty at Forts Henry and Donelson,[56] which in ordinary circumstances would simply be referred to the commander concerned "for investigation and report."

But Halleck, evidently prejudging the case, concluded his letter of inclosure with a stinging rebuke:

The want of order and discipline and the numerous irregularities in your command since the capture of Fort Donelson are matters of general notoriety, and have attracted the serious attention of the authorities at Washington. Unless these things are immediately corrected I am directed to relieve you of the command.[57]

This was the last straw; Grant answered it not by letter but by telegraph:

Yours . . . enclosing an anonymous letter . . . speaking of frauds committed against Government, is just received. I refer you to my orders to suppress marauding as the only reply necessary. There is such a disposition to find fault with me that I again ask to be relieved from further duty until I can be placed right in the estimation of those higher in authority.[58]

President Lincoln now learned of the affair and dropped, with unerring aim, his own bomb. From the Adjutant General, Halleck received the following letter:

It has been reported that soon after the battle of Fort Donelson, Brigadier-General Grant left his command without leave. By direction of the President, the Secretary of War desires you to ascertain and report whether General Grant left his command at any time without proper authority, and if so, for how long; whether he has made to you proper reports and returns of his force; whether he has committed any acts which were unauthorized or not in accordance with military subordination or propriety, and, if so, what.[59]

[56] W. R. 11:14.
[57] Halleck to Grant, Mch. 6, W. R. 11:13.
[58] Grant to Halleck, Mch. 11, W. R. 11:30.
[59] Mch. 10, W. R. 7:683.

Halleck was now cornered; he must either withdraw his charges against Grant or be prepared to prove them. He had reached his goal. The President had given him command in the West.[60] McClellan was no longer in the picture, having been relieved from the general command. An alibi for his own poor staff work was therefore no longer needed. Besides, the more Halleck had probed into it, the more Grant's admirable conduct had stood out. An official investigation would certainly show Halleck himself in a poor light. Clearly, he must make his peace.

To explain the matter to the President without exactly eating his own words or admitting that he himself had been at fault, was relatively easy for one of his legal training and experience. He stated that Grant had gone to Nashville with "good intentions" and acted with "praiseworthy but mistaken zeal." He recommended "that no further notice be taken of it . . . His failure to make returns . . . has been explained . . . There never has been any want of military subordination . . . All these irregularities have now been remedied." [61]

The President, having rubbed out the friction between the two ranking generals in the new Department of the Mississippi, was easily satisfied. To calm Grant, who had now asked three times to be relieved, was not so easy, yet not beyond Halleck's powers, since he had tact and understood Grant's mentality, if not his ability, fairly well.

Halleck wrote:

Your letter of the 5th, just received, contains the first and only information of your actual forces. If you have reported them before I have not seen them. General McClellan has repeatedly ordered me to report to him daily the number and position of your forces. This I could not do, and the fault certainly was not mine, for I telegraphed to you time and again for the information but could get

---

[60] War Order No. 3, Mch. 11, W. R. 11:28.
[61] Halleck's report to Adjutant General, Mch. 15, W. R. 7:683.

no answer.[62] This certainly indicated a great want of order and system in your command, the blame of which was partially thrown on me, and perhaps justly, as it is the duty of every commander to compel those under him to obey orders and enforce discipline. Don't let such neglect occur again, for it is equally discreditable to you and to me. I really felt ashamed to telegraph back to Washington time and again that I was unable to give the strength of your command.

But to business. I think the guns and stores at Clarksville should be brought down to Paducah. We require no garrison there. Fragmentary regiments . . . will be sufficient to garrison Fort Donelson. The same for Fort Henry. All other troops should be sent up the Tennessee, as rapidly as possible. As soon as these things are arranged you will hold yourself in readiness to take the command. There will probably be some desperate fighting in that vicinity, and we must be prepared . . . I shall organize and send you re-enforcements as rapidly as possible, and when I get them under way I shall join you myself.[63]

This must have been a cheering letter to Grant. He says in his Memoirs that he was "virtually in arrest and without a command." [64] That is not true. He was never even in virtual arrest and never relieved of his command. Halleck had saved Grant's pride and prestige as well as the integrity of his command by directing Grant to "*send* Smith with the advance troops up the Tennessee." Smith was at no time taken from under command

[62] Grant in his Memoirs, Vol. I, p. 268, makes a point that the operator at the southern end of the telegraph line under construction from Paducah to Fort Henry proved to be a "rebel" and ran away with all the despatches to Grant. This may be true; but in that case what has become of the file copies at Department Headquarters? Grant, never critical of his superior, accepts Halleck's statement, knowing nothing of the routine of a department headquarters, but any one who does will question not Halleck's good faith but that his order, probably a blanket one to "telegraph all commanders for their returns" was carried out. The fault was clearly Halleck's, for a commander and no one else is responsible for his own staff. Moreover, the burden of proof was on him to produce the file copy of a single unanswered despatch. There is not one in the published official war records, and the files of despatches from the St. Louis headquarters are fairly complete.

[63] Halleck to Grant, Mch. 9, W. R. 11:22.

[64] Grant, I:270.

of Grant. The wound was not to his reputation, but a deeper one, to Grant's self-respect. That wound never healed; it played its part, perhaps an essential one. in the making of a great commander.

Keenly interested as he was in every move in the theater of war about him, and with intense patriotic zeal to play the part there that he felt capable of playing, Grant could no longer sulk in his tent, particularly when Halleck skilfully supplemented his apologetic letter of the ninth with the appeal in his telegram of the thirteenth: "You cannot be relieved from your command. There is no good reason for it . . . Instead of relieving you, I wish you as soon as your new army is in the field to assume the immediate command and lead it on to new victories." [65]

Ultimately, being temporarily placed in "obscuration," as it has been called, resulted in good for Grant and for his future. To learn to withstand without a quiver the shock of attacks from the rear—on his character, reputation, or prestige—is no less valuable training for the general than to learn to bear without fear the shocks of the enemy's attacks on his front. Further, there is from the fifth of March on, particularly after the eleventh, a change in the character of his reports and despatches. They become markedly more businesslike in tone; not only more frequent, but more clear and crisp. Reflecting on the affair, as he did on everything, he saw the need of better staff organization, and published in General Orders the assignment of duties among members of his routine and personal staff.[66] One result, not so pleasing, but perhaps useful in the position to which he was to be called, was the narrowing of the circle of those whom he chose to regard as friends, and a growing distrust, not at all innate, of the motives and actions of every one outside that circle.

[65] Halleck to Grant, W. R. 11:32.
[66] G. O., No. 21, Mch. 15, W. R. 11:41.

For Halleck, on the other hand, his own hasty giving way to anger, coupled with his hypocrisy in laying the onus for his acts on McClellan's shoulders, produced far-reaching consequences. Had he been a really strong man and with his own hand administered to Grant his dose of medicine, as he did successfully to both Buell and Pope later on, Grant in the end would probably have felt grateful to him for guiding him into the right path. But Grant was bound to find out Halleck's childish deception, eventually, and meantime Halleck, not being evil-minded, but merely a good man with an intriguing disposition, remained always fearful of being found out. Consequently, though he grew to admire Grant more and more as the war progressed, he could never feel at ease in his many later dealings with one to whom he had been unjust.

CHAPTER XVI

GRANT RESUMES COMMAND

*Man can sway the future only by foreseeing
through a clear understanding of the present to
what far off end matters are tending.—CÆSAR.*

HALLECK'S first directive, on March 1, for the expedition up
the Tennessee River gave as its main object "to destroy the
railroad bridge over Bear Creek, near Eastport, Mississippi, and
also the connections at Corinth [Mississippi], Jackson [Tennessee], and Humboldt [Tennessee]." [1]

The need for haste in the destruction was emphasized by Halleck in his despatch of the fifth and he added, "If successful, the
expedition will . . . encamp at Savannah [Tennessee], unless
threatened by superior numbers." [2]

On the sixth Sherman telegraphed Halleck, "A large force of
rebels have collected at Eastport . . . and also at Corinth . . .
estimated at 20,000." [3]

Halleck replied to this: "General Smith must advance with
great caution. If the enemy is in force at Corinth or Eastport,
our landing must be below." [4]

Smith started on the tenth with twenty-five thousand men,
escorted by two gunboats, and decided to make the rendezvous
of the expedition at Savannah on the northeast bank of the
Tennessee, a place ill suited for offensive operations, being on the

---

[1] W. R. 7:674.
[2] W. R. 11:7.
[3] W. R. 11:12.
[4] Halleck to Sherman and Grant, Mch. 6, W. R. 11:12.

wrong side of the river, but for that reason inaccessible to hostile attack.

The same day, March 10, Halleck notified Grant of the victory of Curtis over Van Dorn, at Pea Ridge, Arkansas, and that the "reserves intended for his [Curtis's] support" would now immediately be sent up the Tennessee, at the same time giving Grant the warning order to be ready himself "to take the general command." [5]

Grant, however, was busying himself with affairs in the immediate neighborhood of Fort Henry. The Confederate Governor of Tennessee had ordered a general conscription of men of military age throughout the State for the Confederate armies, and Grant sought to protect all the inhabitants he could against its enforcement. Confederate sentiment had never been strong in the State and had, besides, been greatly weakened by the Donelson victory. Grant therefore, on March 11, wrote Smith, "I think it exceedingly doubtful if I shall accept; certainly not until the object of the expedition is accomplished." [6]

He evidently had in mind that it would not be fair to Smith to supersede him in command until the first objects of the expedition, in point of time at least, the destruction of the railroad bridges and junctions, had been accomplished. Moreover, he was still piqued because of Halleck's harsh reprimands. Also Grant was sick during the two weeks of March 3–17, though he did not admit it until afterward [7] and forced himself in the meantime to deal with his responsibilities.

Whether Grant's reluctance to resume his front-line command was overcome by Halleck's reassuring telegram of the thirteenth (previously given) or whether Smith sent word that he was in-

[5] W. R. 11:26, 27.
[6] W. R. 11:29.
[7] W. R. 11:43.

capacitated by his wound and unable to command, there is nothing to indicate. The surprise expressed by Grant at Smith's landing his expedition at Savannah shows the diametrically opposite points of view of the two men: Smith anxious to obey every word of an order received, down to its last letter; Grant desirous only of achieving his assigned mission and ready to adopt any measures which promised to lead to success. However, Grant notified Halleck on the fourteenth of his willingness to "again assume command," but expressed a doubt about when he "should proceed up the river." [8]

Grant spent March 15 in reorganizing his staff, attending to local matters, and sending troops up the river. He now had, in addition to his three divisions at the surrender of Donelson, a fourth division, General Hurlbut's, composed of troops which reached him after the surrender; a fifth division, under Sherman, composed of new regiments collected at Paducah as a general reserve; and was to have added, a few days later, a sixth division, under Prentiss—the officer of Benton fame—composed also of chiefly new regiments gathered up from various parts as reinforcements.

Consequently having in immediate prospect, if not in hand, six divisions, or double his command at Donelson, Grant left Fort Henry on the sixteenth to rejoin his troops, feeling anything but timid, notwithstanding Halleck's injunction of that date: "As the enemy [at Corinth] is evidently in strong force, my instructions not to advance so as to bring on an engagement must be strictly obeyed." [9]

That the enemy might himself advance and bring on a "general engagement" evidently did not occur to Halleck any more than it did to Grant. In the same despatch Halleck stated that "Buell is moving in his [Smith's] direction."

[8] W. R. 11:36.
[9] W. R. 11:41.

Grant reached Savannah on March 17 and quickly grasped the state of affairs.

Sherman's division, the first to arrive, had reached Savannah on the eleventh. By Smith's direction Sherman had gone on up the river on the thirteenth, landed near Eastport to attempt to carry out the first-named of Halleck's objectives, the destruction of the Bear Creek bridge, but had been stopped by a "severe rainstorm" and resulting floods which carried away the bridges and made him give up the project.[10]

Another attempt had been made, by Lew Wallace's division (the 3d), to carry out Halleck's orders by destroying a long trestle near Purdy, on the Mobile and Ohio Railroad, with a small cavalry force landed at Crump's, supported by infantry.[11] The division had remained at Crump's.

The day before Grant's arrival at Savannah (March 16) Sherman had occupied, by Smith's order given at Sherman's suggestion, Pittsburg, Tennessee, with his own division (the 5th), and reinforced it with Hurlbut's division (the 4th) on March 17.[12]

Consequently, Grant found his five divisions posted:

1st and 2d—Savannah (north bank of Tennessee), 2d still on
    transports;
3d—Crump's (south bank, six miles up-stream);
4th and 5th—Pittsburg (south bank, nine miles up-stream).

Grant also received two reports from Sherman, one of which—concerning a frustrated cavalry raid on the Memphis road, attempted the night before—said, "I am satisfied we cannot reach the Memphis and Charleston Road without a considerable engagement, which is prohibited by General Halleck's instructions," [13] and the other:

[10] W. R. 10:8, 22, 30; 11:31, 34.
[11] W. R. 10:9, 11.
[12] W. R. 10:24, 25, 29; 109:224, 225.
[13] W. R. 10:24, 25.

I am strongly impressed with the importance of the [Pittsburg-Shiloh] position, both for its land advantages and its strategic position. The ground itself admits of easy defense by a small command, and yet affords admirable camping ground for a hundred thousand men. . . . The only drawback is that at this stage of water the space for landing is contracted too much for the immense fleet now here discharging.[14]

Grant's only information of the enemy, aside from Sherman's estimate just quoted, was the report from a spy sent out by Smith that Johnston's army had reached Corinth from Nashville and that he had there and in the vicinity 150,000 men, a number which was, as Grant said, "very much exaggerated."

Grant at once decided, without even seeing Pittsburg, to take Sherman's word for it and concentrate his army there, except McClernand's division (the 1st), which was left at Savannah—probably because Grant wanted Sherman, Smith being sick, to command the Shiloh camp.[15]

The day following his arrival, Grant spent in dealing with administrative matters and studied conditions somewhat, but wisely refrained from making a thorough appraisal of the situation or adopting positive measures beyond the immediate concentration of his forces near Pittsburg Landing. He said, however, on March 18, that while he had not been there "long enough to form much idea of the actual strength of the rebels," he felt "satisfied that they do not number 40,000 armed effective men at this time," [16] a shrewd estimate, close to the truth.

The next day, he inspected the camps at Crump's and Pittsburg, and satisfied himself that those two were the only feasible landing-places "west of the river" and so reported on March 19.[17]

[14] W. R. 10:27.
[15] Mch. 17, W. R. 11:42.
[16] W. R. 11:45.
[17] W. R. 11:48.

At Pittsburg he had an extended conference with Sherman, and while he was there Sherman received a spy report that the enemy was not "over 20,000 strong at Corinth, but has troops scattered at all stations and important points."

It evidently appeared to Grant that here was a golden opportunity for a sudden descent on Corinth, especially since Buell was "the party most expected by the rebels. They estimate his strength all the way from 20,000 to 150,000." Consequently, as Grant implied, they were giving little heed to his own lesser forces.

He was delighted beyond measure, therefore, to receive on his return to Savannah in the evening what naturally appeared to him an authorization for just such a move. Halleck's despatch of March 18 reads: "It is reported that the enemy has moved from Corinth, to cut off our transports below Savannah. If so, General Smith should immediately destroy railroad connection at Corinth." [18] While Grant knew Halleck's information about the enemy's move from Corinth was wrong, the counter-measure suggested was none the less both possible and inviting.

Grant answered Halleck at 11 P.M. the same evening (March 19): "Immediate preparations will be made to execute your perfectly feasible order. I will go in person, leaving General McClernand in command here." [19]

This despatch proved a little too cryptic for Halleck. Had Grant added something to the effect that though Halleck's information about the enemy's having moved from Corinth was incorrect, the Confederate troops were so scattered that a dash at Corinth with four divisions was "perfectly feasible," Halleck might not have approved, but he would at least have understood.

His answer effectually quashed any hopes of such a dash before Buell's arrival:

[18] W. R. 11:46.
[19] W. R. 11:49.

Your telegrams of yesterday received. I do not fully understand you. By all means keep your forces together until you connect with General Buell, who is now at Columbia [Tennessee], and will move on Waynesborough with three divisions. Don't let the enemy draw you into an engagement now. Wait till you are properly fortified and receive orders.[20]

Halleck all too evidently put his trust in victory in the "most battalions," unlike Grant, who asked only an even break in num-

Map of
SHILOH CAMPS
Given by Sherman to Buell
APRIL. 6, 1862.
FROM B.& L. VOL. I - 497

bers and trusted to his own will, and the right being on his side, to produce the victory.

Though nothing in the way of an offensive resulted from Halleck's message of the eighteenth, it hastened the concentration at Pittsburg, and it turned the minds of Grant and his subordinates toward preparation for offensive operations and away from any thought that the army might itself receive an attack.

[20] W. R. 11:50.

Grant did indeed have his chief of engineers, Colonel McPherson, lay out a defensive line,[21] which might be fortified, but nothing was done toward its construction. Also Sherman, as camp commander, ordered the divisional camps laid out so that the troops when formed would be in line of battle, at proper intervals, facing the enemy [22]—luckily enough for his side in the battle—but at the time he was careful to point out that this was to facilitate a quick forward movement.

Without waiting for Halleck's reply, which did not reach him until the twenty-second, Grant went boldly ahead, on the twentieth, making preparations for an offensive.

The landing facilities at Pittsburg were so limited, however, that the mere movement of troops to that point from Savannah occupied several days, during which the troops already there and at Crump's were ordered to be held in march readiness with ten days' rations, three "in haversacks," seven to be carried "on wagons," all "tents and personal baggage except what the men can carry" to be left behind.[23]

In the course of the second day of these hurried preparations, Grant got fresh intelligence of the enemy which made him hesitate. He informed Halleck that evening (March 21):

I have certain information that thirteen trains . . . arrived at Corinth on the 19th, with twenty cars to each train, all loaded with troops. This would indicate that Corinth cannot be taken without a general engagement, which, from your instructions, is to be avoided. This, taken in connection with the impassable state of the roads, has determined me not to move for the present without further orders.[24]

These thirteen train-loads of Confederate reinforcements—estimated by Grant at something over ten thousand—which would

[21] Grant I:274.
[22] Sherman, Orders, No. 15, par. 5; W. R. 11:50; Orders, No. 13; W. R. 10:28; to Lauman, W. R. 11:53.
[23] Orders to C. F. Smith and Wallace, Mch. 20, W. R. 11:52.
[24] W. R. 11:55.

give them thirty thousand at Corinth, with additional reinforcements within easy reach, combined with Halleck's message of the
twentieth, to "wait for Buell," brought to a close the first phase
of the expedition, in which Grant sought to execute alone the
mission assigned him.

Grant had sent two scouts to Buell on the nineteenth, with a
letter informing him that troops were being massed at Pittsburg.[25]
It was a week before they returned, as they had to go all the way
to Nashville, where Buell still remained; and Buell's answer when
it came gave no idea of the time his forces might be expected.[26]
Grant by no means sat in idleness while waiting for Buell. But
in looking back over the period, he probably wished that he had
reversed the order of his activities and done the reorganizing of
his divisional units a little earlier and the reconnaissances a
little later.

The story is best told by his daily correspondence.

On March 22 he wrote: "No movements making except to
advance General Sherman's division to prevent rebels from fortifying Pea Ridge. Weather here cold, with some snow." [27]

This move on Pea Ridge was evidently the result of a conference between Grant, Smith, and perhaps Sherman, because
Grant wrote Smith, "Commanding U. S. Forces, Pittsburg," the
next day (March 23): "Carry out your idea of occupying and
partially fortifying Pea Ridge. . . . I am clearly of the opinion
that the enemy are gathering strength at Corinth quite as rapidly
as we are here, and the sooner we attack the easier will be the
task of taking the place." [28]

On the twenty-fifth Grant sent Halleck a sketch map of Pitts-

[25] W. R. 11:47.
[26] W. R. 11:58.
[27] W. R. 11:57.
[28] W. R. 11:62.

burg. He added blithely enough: "General Wallace is six miles below, with a good road out, enabling them to form a junction with the main column, when a move is made, six or seven miles before reaching Corinth," [29] little witting that the question of the road by which Wallace was to join the main column was to lead to a controversy not to be settled for twenty-four years.[30]

On the twenty-sixth he reported: "My scouts are just in with a letter from General Buell. The three divisions coming this way are yet on east side of Duck River, detained bridge building. Rebel cavalry are scattered through from here to Nashville gathering supplies . . . No news from Corinth." [31]

The same day he organized newly arrived regiments as the 6th Division, under General Prentiss.[32]

On the twenty-seventh Grant visited "the different divisions at Pittsburg." He reported, "The health of the troops is materially improving under the influence of a genial sun which has blessed us for a few days past." [33]

The two reports of the twenty-eighth deal only with routine matters, except for a statement brought by a Union man who made his escape from Corinth that "the rebels have been . . . concentrating at Corinth," [34] a report which seems to have had but little significance for Grant himself.

On March 30 "some half dozen deserters from Corinth came in. One represents the number of troops there at seventy-five regiments, and the others say the whole number is usually represented at 80,000 men." [35] But the morale appeared to be poor. Grant added, "They describe the discontent as being very great

29 W. R. 109:230.
30 B. and L., I:607.
31 W. R. 11:67.
32 G. O., No. 36, W. R. 11:67.
33 W. R. 11:70.
34 W. R. 11:73.
35 W. R. 11:80.

among the troops and rations short. Many men will desert if an
opportunity occurs." He seemed not to know—or not to remember—that such statements by deserters need to be largely dis-
counted. Certainly Johnston's army, which only a week later was
to lose over ten thousand men, twenty-five per cent of its strength,
in an offensive action, was not seething with discontent, however
poor the rations.

His own command Grant reported as still improving under
the continuing "genial sun and influence of good water"—always
a vital factor in the well-being of troops.

On the thirty-first Halleck, disturbed by the lack of data, or
the vagueness of the data given in Grant's reports regarding the
enemy, telegraphed: "Give me more information about enemy's
number and positions. Your scouts and spies ought by this time
to have given you something approximating to the facts of
the case." [36]

As Grant's despatches had to go by steamer to Fort Henry to
be telegraphed from there, Halleck had probably not yet received
the reports of the twenty-eighth and thirtieth.

Grant's "return" of March 31 gives his "aggregate strength
present" up the Tennessee at 54,000, of which 2,000 were at Savannah, 9,000 at Crump's, leaving about 43,000 at the Pittsburg-
Shiloh camp.[37] This included, however, the sick, those in arrest,
etc., leaving the "present for duty" something under 40,000
officers and men.

Grant officially announced his headquarters as moved to Pittsburg on this day,[38] for the reason that McClernand claimed to
rank Smith as a major-general, and Grant did not wish McClernand to take command in an emergency. But, awaiting Buell's
arrival, he continued to sleep at Savannah and to maintain an
office there.

[36] W. R. 11:82.
[37] W. R. 11:84.
[38] G. O., No. 30, W. R. 11:84.

We find him growing restive under the prolonged inactivity; and he had on this day an added stimulus in the arrival of one of the armored gunboats, the *Cairo.*

On March 31 he wrote Halleck:

I have ordered her [the *Cairo*], with the two others, up the Tennessee to-morrow, to take and destroy the batteries established near Chickasaw. General Sherman accompanies, with [a detachment. His] instructions are not to engage any force that would likely make a stand against him, but if the batteries are unsupported . . . to take or destroy them.[39]

He also reported the arrival of two soldiers, sent ahead by Buell's leading troops, but they brought no message from Buell.

The next two days Grant spent in reviewing and reorganizing his divisions,[40] reapportioning the scanty cavalry and artillery units among the divisions and making them divisional troops instead of assigning them to brigades as he had done hitherto. This was in itself a wise and proper measure, but it was unfortunate for future events that it had not been done when he first announced his intention of doing it, to Smith on the twenty-fourth. [41] Some of the changes did not take place till the fourth or fifth of April, which interfered with proper reconnaissance by the cavalry before the battle on the days when it would have been most valuable, and in several cases put the artillery in commands and in terrain strange to them. Another self-imposed handicap for the battle about to open was the reassignment to other commands of newly promoted brigadiers,[42] giving the men, in several instances, superior commanders hitherto unknown to them.

As a result of his reviews, Grant found "the men in excellent condition, and as a general thing well clothed." [43]

[39] W. R. 11:82.
[40] S. O., No. 16, W. R. 11:88; G. O., No. 33, W. R. 11:87.
[41] W. R. 11:62.
[42] S. O., No. 43, W. R. 11:88.
[43] Grant's report, Apr. 3, W. R. 10:84.

He related the result of the gunboat expedition up the Tennessee, which found that the Confederate batteries previously at Chickasaw had been removed. Regarding the enemy, he wrote: "Nothing is learned from Corinth very reliable. Deserters occasionally come in, but all that can be learned from them that is reliable is that the force there is large and increasing."

And with his mind ever bent toward the moral factors, in the enemy's as well as in his own army, rather than upon mere numbers, he characteristically added: "They [the deserters] do not describe the feeling of the men as at all hopeful; on the contrary, say that many would desert if they could."

Grant, in this matter, did not put two and two together; he remembered well enough in his own command the depressing effect on his men of prolonged garrison duty at Cairo, and the magical improvement in their morale resulting from orders for a move on Belmont or Fort Henry; his imagination failed to picture what would be the electrical effect on Johnston's troops, who thus far had done nothing but retreat, of orders to advance and fight. Also we see from this that he had not yet discovered the first inkling of the fact that the chief value of information from deserters and prisoners is to make it possible to reconstruct the enemy's "order of battle," the only safe basis for estimating his strength and intentions.

On the night of April 2-3, Sherman made an ingenious "hammer-and-anvil" scoop before the outposts,[44] with cavalry and infantry, to catch prisoners. One wonders whether Grant or Sherman conceived the idea, and if it were not the forerunner of the hammer-and-anvil tactics of the Wilderness campaign in 1864. The Confederate pickets were warned, however, and only a single prisoner was brought in,[45] from whom apparently nothing was gleaned.

[44] Report, W. R. 10:86; Orders, W. R. 11:87.
[45] W. R. 11:90.

On the fourth Grant was to review the 6th Division (Prentiss), the last to be organized, but canceled the order.[46] He seems to have been apprehensive on this day of an attack on the 3d Division at Crump's and took measures accordingly.[47]

In the late afternoon there occurred an affair of the outposts of Sherman's division which afforded Grant the last of several opportunities to discover the nearness to his camp of the main forces of the enemy, and his intentions. Men of Sherman's pickets "imprudently advanced" and were captured. Sherman, hearing of it, pursued and brought back ten prisoners, sending them to Grant.[48] Grant heard the firing and rode to the front, but on meeting General W. H. L. Wallace and Colonel McPherson, and being reassured by them that all was well along the front, returned to the landing. On the way, in the darkness, Grant's horse slipped and fell, badly wrenching the general's ankle,[49] so that, in addition to its other ill luck, the Union army had to fight its decisive battle of the West under a commander on crutches—or on horseback, for luckily he could still ride.

Grant made a report on the fourth, but it is not of record and it is doubtful if it contained any additional information. On the fifth, despite his sprained ankle, he appears to have gone to Pittsburg in accordance with his note to Sherman on the fourth.[50]

He received a letter from Buell dated the fourth, announcing that he would reach Savannah "to-morrow." [51] Grant seems carelessly not to have noted that it was dated the day before, and sent an answer to Buell that he would be in Savannah to meet him "to-morrow," the sixth.[52]

In the afternoon Grant rode out to Nelson's division. Colonel

[46] W. R. 109:232.
[47] Instructions to W. H. L. Wallace and Sherman, W. R. 11:91.
[48] W. R. 10:89; W. R. 11:93.
[49] Grant I:276.
[50] W. R. 11:9. See also Ammen's "Diary," W. R. 10:330.
[51] W. R. 11:91.
[52] W. R. 11:93.

Ammen, commanding one of Nelson's brigades which had reached Savannah toward noon and gone into camp, wrote in his diary:

About 3 P.M., General Grant and General Nelson came to my tent. General Grant declined to dismount, as he had an engagement. In answer to my remark that our troops were not fatigued and could march on to Pittsburg Landing, Tennessee, if necessary, General Grant said:

"You cannot march through the swamps; make the troops comfortable; I will send boats for you Monday or Tuesday or some time early in the week. There will be no fight at Pittsburg Landing; we will have to go to Corinth, where the rebels are fortified. If they come to attack us, we can whip them, as I have more than twice as many troops as I had at Fort Donelson . . ." General Buell arrived about sundown.[53]

But, unfortunately, Grant did not know of Buell's arrival, and—the last of the seeming ill luck—they did not meet, though this was not through Buell's fault, as Grant's letter had expressly stated that he would meet him "to-morrow" and Nelson had doubtless told him that Grant had an engagement that evening.

Looking back over Grant's three weeks with his army before Shiloh, particularly during the second phase, after he had received Halleck's final injunction to await Buell's arrival, one cannot but be struck by his quiet but strong influence; by his unceasing efforts to prepare his army for the approaching crisis, despite his persistent refusal to give the slightest credence to any signs that pointed to the enemy's bringing on the decision of arms. Half his army had been at Fort Donelson and knew him; the other half was new, and needed to meet him face to face. The opportunities came in the reviews—without question, of supreme importance.

Soldiers are the severest and truest critics of their general. Others may believe; they know! But they want to look him in the eye and judge him, each man for himself; it is their traditional right, which the review accords them. If the soldier accepts the general as his chosen leader, he will do more than his duty for him; if not, he will do his duty only. What other armies in history have ever taken the losses of the armies of Grant and Johnston at Shiloh and still held their ground? Of forces of equal length of training, there are none!

And that is why the credit for the hard fighting—and for the victory if it be won—belongs to the general. The general accords it to the soldier, but the soldier returns the palm to the general. Self-styled critics may blow hot and cold with praise and blame. The soldier heeds them not; he fights for his general because he knows him to be what he is; therefore, more than any other, the soldier recognizes that it is the general's will which gains whatever of success fortune may bring.

Grant's dreams the night before the battle could not have troubled him, if indeed he could sleep despite the pain of the sprained ankle. How care-free he was is shown by his report of the fifth: "I have scarcely the faintest idea of an attack (general one) being made upon us, but will be prepared should such a thing take place." [54]

This statement has been the sport of many a wag, because of the stupid conception that preparation for battle means trenches and abatis. Grant referred to the essential elements, which were that he felt full confidence in himself and his men and knew that his officers and men trusted him, and in that sense he spoke the truth, and was prepared.

Many writers, particularly those who regard Grant as merely the child of good fortune, have asserted not only that C. F. Smith was the better general of the two, but that Grant in reality owed

[54] W. R. 10:89.

his success at Fort Donelson to Smith's kindly guidance, and his success at Shiloh to Smith's preparation for it. Granting these two premises, the conclusion inevitably follows that Smith did Grant a third good service by conveniently dying, since had he lived he, instead of Grant, would have ended in command of the Union armies.

The data by which to judge of Smith's generalship are scanty, and in reality Smith's ability to command an independent force in battle never came to the test. He did, of course, command a division at Fort Donelson, and did it admirably. But it is a well-recognized fact that a subordinate command of even a division or a corps, immediately under a superior who is present, is not so good a test of a commander as is the independent command of a regiment or even of a mere battalion acting alone.

As a disciplinarian Smith ranked high, and a board sent to investigate his command at Paducah pronounced it the best disciplined in the department. He himself reported, on his reconnaissance from Paducah on January 15, outrages committed by his men in "killing hogs and poultry despite every precaution taken by myself and brigade and regimental commanders." If those were the only "outrages," his discipline—of volunteers— was indeed excellent.

Smith knew his tactics, fortunately for Grant—at Donelson at least—and lived up to them. Further, like the older-time eighteenth-century soldier he was, he believed in obeying orders literally and in having them obeyed literally. Grant, on the other hand, both practised from the start of his career and taught his subordinates the exercise of "independent initiative," [55] which is, to be governed not necessarily by your commander's written in-

---

[55] An early example of this is Grant's order of November 3, 1861, to Oglesby (W. R. 3:268): "The object . . . is to destroy this [enemy] force, and the manner of doing it is left largely to your discretion."

structions, but by what you think he would order if he were present and knew all the circumstances known to you.

One example of this difference is the more striking because both were acting under virtually identical orders: at Belmont, west of the Mississippi, by Grant; on the reconnaissance conducted by General Paine, under Smith's instructions, toward Columbus, east of the Mississippi.

Grant considered the "mission" to be accomplished was the right thing to be done in the circumstances and did not hesitate to depart from both the letter and the spirit of his orders, the better to carry out the real purpose his superior had in view.[56] He wrote Smith—not then under his command—what he was going to do and asked Smith's coöperation. Did Smith, to aid Grant, depart one jot from his very precise orders? No indeed! But the fact is that General Paine, who commanded Smith's "demonstration" main column, did depart from orders, with the intention of aiding Grant, by marching on Milburn when he heard Grant's firing at Belmont,[57] instead of on Melvin where he had been instructed to go. By marching on Milburn he really did give the semblance of advancing on Columbus. Upon Paine's return Smith expressed in writing "surprise" at and "disapprobation" of Paine's departure from "precise and distinct orders" and declared his "intention to ask for a legal investigation." [58] The matter was finally quashed and Paine removed to Cairo.

Another example of Smith's narrow construction of orders is his conduct of the Tennessee expedition. Its main objects, as stated by Halleck to Grant, were "To destroy the railroad bridge . . . near Eastport, Mississippi, and also the connections at Corinth, Jackson, and Humboldt." [59] On the fifth Halleck added:

---

[56] W. R. 3:267 et seq.
[57] W. R. 3:302, 303.
[58] Newsham to Paine, W. R. 3:303.
[59] Halleck to Grant, W. R. 7:674.

"There should be no delay in destroying the bridge, etc. . . . If successful the expedition will . . . encamp at Savannah." [60]

Grant in his letter to Halleck of March 14 said, "The troops [of Smith's expedition] were debarked at Savannah; why I do not know," and in a postscript he added, "General Smith's landing at Savannah indicates fortifications have been encountered above that point and the enemy in force." [61]

No one who has traced the history of the two men in the official war records can doubt the reason. There were no fortifications "above that point," as Grant mistakenly but naturally inferred. With his mind fixed on the *mission* of the expedition, only fortifications would have stopped Grant's getting on toward its accomplishment. But Smith, in contrast, would stop only in the one town mentioned in Halleck's despatch as the ultimate locale for his troops.

Unquestionably, Smith was loved and trusted by his friends, Grant included, and had a wonderful prestige with and command over his men. His charge at Fort Donelson proved that. But it may be doubted if an officer with Smith's ideas of what might be termed the passive or unreflecting obedience to orders, would ultimately have been successful as an army commander.

To Halleck is due the credit of having given Grant an entirely free hand in the organization of his command prior to the Fort Henry expedition. His instructions concerning this read:

You will organize your command into brigades and divisions, or columns, precisely as you may deem best for the public service, and will from time to time change this organization as you may deem the public service requires, without the slightest regard to political influences or to the orders and instructions you may have heretofore

[60] W. R. 10:7.
[61] W. R. 11:36.

received. In this matter the good of the service, and not the wishes of politico-military officers, is to be consulted.[62]

On receipt of this order, Grant organized his 1st Division under McClernand, consisting of two brigades, but without divisional troops, the cavalry and artillery units being assigned to brigades. Smith similarly organized his Paducah command into the 2d Division. Later, after Donelson, Grant recognized the desirability of making the cavalry and artillery units divisional instead of brigade troops.

Apparently it did not occur to Grant at Shiloh that his six divisions might have been handled far more effectively by him had he organized them into three army corps of two divisions each. Could he have made his own selection of corps commanders, he might have considered this. But as matters stood, the corps would have had to be commanded by the three seniors present, McClernand, Lew Wallace, and C. F. Smith. Smith being sick, such a measure would have left McClernand and Lew Wallace as the two corps commanders, for which responsibilities they were far from being ripe. Experience in this matter proves that where corps commanders are not qualified for their commands, they are merely in the way. Therefore we cannot blame Grant for overburdening himself by organizing in such a manner as to have to deal with six separate division commanders, instead of a lesser number of corps commanders. In the circumstances, he probably made a safer decision.

On March 15, preparatory to resuming immediate command of the forces up the Tennessee, Grant issued a staff-organization order.[63]

Captain Rawlins, adjutant-general, assisted by Captain Rowley, A.D.C., was given "charge of the books of records, consolidating

---

[62] Halleck to Grant, Jan. 30, W. R. 7:572.
[63] W. R. 11:41.

returns, and forwarding all documents to their proper destination." Captain Hillyer, A.D.C., was made responsible for seeing "that returns are furnished by division and other commanders." Captain Lagow, A.D.C., and Colonel John Riggin, Jr., were to "act upon applications for passes . . . also, have a care to the amount of supplies on hand . . . commissary . . . coal, forage, etc."

Colonel Webster, "chief of staff and engineers," was recognized as "the adviser of the general commanding," and was to give his attention "to any portion of duties that may not receive proper attention." Captain Hawkins was made inspecting quartermaster and commissary.

An analysis of this order shows that whereas the staff branches dealing with administration and supply were well covered, two of the most important branches of the modern staff organization were left unprovided for—Operations and Intelligence—except in so far as Colonel Webster was to "give his attention to any portion of duties that may not receive proper attention."

It is axiomatic that any organization which leaves the commander duties that must be performed by himself is a faulty one; and it will be noted in the above organization that precisely those functions in exercising which Grant had had the least experience were the ones in which he did not provide for staff assistants.

In the matter of Intelligence, Grant had found at Cairo the time and means to keep himself excellently informed of the enemy's strength, morale, location, and intentions, and also to give not a little attention to essential counter-espionage matters. It is interesting to follow the reasons for the breakdown of his Intelligence at Shiloh.

At Cairo he had obtained information from returning prisoners of war, from friendly civilians traveling to and fro between the two sides, and from spies; but the idea of combat-intelligence, particularly the systematic questioning of prisoners of war and deserters, did not present itself to him. Later on, especially in the Army of the Potomac, this was reduced to what might be termed an exact science.

It is interesting to recall in this connection that neglect to make full use of the information to be obtained from prisoners repeated itself during the World War, in the British and French armies, in which, as with us during the Civil War, it was not until the second or third year that effective combat-intelligence became organized.

Grant does not appear to have had many spies; but excellent service was rendered by those he had. During the Donelson campaign one of Grant's spies visited Nashville, Decatur, and Memphis, and returned and reported, at Donelson on February 25, that Beauregard was in Columbus, which had been ordered evacuated—valuable information had it been acted upon by Halleck.

Had Grant at this time been informed of Halleck's intentions, he would doubtless have sent spies ahead, up the Tennessee. But kept in the dark as he was, regarding future plans, he naturally used his spies on his immediate flanks, east of the Cumberland and west of the Tennessee.[64]

Until the time of Smith's departure up the Tennessee on March 11, Grant seems to have had correct information of the Confederate strength at Corinth. However, during the period of Smith's command at Savannah, March 11–17, Grant either sent no spies up the river or had bad luck with them. It may have been because he was sick[65] or because of discouragement induced by Halleck's repeated reprimanding despatches, but whatever the reason, we find him on the eighteenth, at Savannah, reporting for

[64] Grant to Halleck, Mch. 10, W. R. 11:25; Mch. 11, W. R. 11:29. One of Grant's spies evidently returned to Fort Henry and reported there to Colonel Lowe, Mch. 28 (W. R. 11:74).
[65] Grant to Sherman, Mch. 17, W. R. 11:43.

the first time in his career as a general that he has not yet "much idea of the actual strength of the rebels," though he feels "satisfied they do not number forty thousand armed effective men at this time."

At Savannah, Grant found himself in hostile country and under the necessity not only of keeping informed regarding events in his immediate vicinity but of getting into communication with Buell's approaching column—something that occupied the time of two of his most skilled scouts from March 19 to 26,[66] when it would have been most useful to have them in Corinth instead. Shortly afterward he appears to have had at least one spy in Corinth; but unhappily for the general, this spy was unable to return until April 9, two days after the battle,[67] though he then brought valuable information.

The Confederate main body did not move out from Corinth until April 2, so prior to that date prisoners would not have had much information to give. However, on April 3, Sherman captured an enemy picket and sent him "forthwith for General Grant to question as he is pretty intelligent." Again, on April 5, the night before the attack, Sherman sent Grant "ten prisoners of war." [68]

Had these prisoners been separated and questioned by trained examiners, so that Grant might have known with certainty, as he would then have done by midnight of April 5-6, what he learned only at nine o'clock the following morning, the story of Shiloh would doubtless have made very different reading. Quite possibly it was owing to Grant's sprained ankle, the result of his horse falling upon him and the pain it caused him, that this examination was neglected.

Once again we see that Grant was quick to learn, since we find

[66] Grant's report, W. R. 11:47, 67.
[67] Grant's report, W. R. 11:99.
[68] Report of Sherman, W. R. 11:90, 93.

him two days later, on the ninth, "confirming information" through statements of prisoners.[69] However, the use of prisoners to confirm "the enemy order of battle" and "units present" was not to come until later.

Grant was destined to learn much in the course of the war regarding the problem of subsisting an army off the country in enemy territory, and it is interesting to find him, after Donelson, pursuing his study of this problem, begun during his brief stay at Ironton. With his practised eye, from his experiences as regimental supply officer in the Mexican War, he estimated the subsistence captured at Donelson as sufficient to last his command twenty days, that is to say, seven hundred thousand rations, though deficient in coffee.[70]

On March 1 he wrote Halleck:

My command is now suffering from camp dysentery, the result (according to report of surgeons) of being compelled to live on salt meat. I have had this country scoured for miles for beef cattle, but without being able to obtain them. The contractors . . . say they have the cattle but are unable to procure the transportation.[71]

Ever thoughtful of his men, he did not trust to his own or to higher staffs for the automatic supply of his army, but issued his own orders for the quantity of rations to be forwarded for troops sent up the river.[72]

Later on, at Savannah, he learned of a cache of a hundred thousand pounds of bacon collected for the Confederate army, twenty miles down the river, and he sent a major with a detachment to bring it in, to serve to his troops.[73]

[69] W. R. 11:99.
[70] Report, W. R. 7:637.
[71] W. R. 7:675.
[72] G. O., No. 21, W. R. 11:31.
[73] W. R. 11:63, 70.

CHAPTER XVII

SHILOH—THE BATTLE

When a man boasts of having made no mistakes in war, he convinces me that he has not made war long.—TURENNE.

HAD Albert Sidney Johnston had Grant's educational advantages—that is, had he learned the technique of command step by step, through actual operations in the field and in battle, beginning with forces of lesser size, so as to master gradually the difficulties of handling forty thousand men—or had he had experienced subordinates or a trained staff such as helped out inexperienced generals in the World War, he would undoubtedly have proved a great commander and have won many victories, of which Shiloh would have been one.

At Shiloh, Johnston proved that he possessed a forceful character, the power to inspire his men with confidence, a sense of strategic and tactical values, every natural qualification necessary for success, but lacked the technical knowledge of how to march his forty thousand men to a battle-field twenty-three miles out, and how to put them into action on their arrival. Realizing his own deficiency in this respect, he entrusted these details to his subordinates, Beauregard and Bragg, who pretended to know how to do such things, but did not.

The concentration of his divided army at Corinth was strategically correct and had been skilfully and quickly effected, by rail and marching. The week following his arrival at Corinth, on March 24, he had spent in reorganizing, equipping, and arming his men, and his organization, into three army corps, was excellent. The decision to march and attack Grant before Buell arrived was one of which no trained military man will disapprove. This decision was made on the evening of April 2, the plan being to utilize the two following days for the twenty-mile march to the place selected for deployment, and to attack on the morning of the third day. Faulty march orders together with poor staff work combined to delay the completion of the deployment until the late afternoon of April 5. Johnston wisely deferred his attack till the next morning.

The attack formation was as deplorable as had been the march order, three corps being formed in three successive lines, each corps in a single line, at half-mile distances. This formation led to the intermingling not only of the three corps but of divisional, brigade, and regimental units within the corps, as the battle developed, resulting in the loss of any general control, and to the substitution of a hundred detached "soldiers' fights" (which might lead in any direction but the right one) for a single battle fought under the direction of the commander. Johnston did, afterward, assign his corps leaders to different sectors, in fact took one himself and lost his life leading a brigade charge, but though they put in reserves and conducted detached combats here and there, any systematic battle-guidance was impossible.

This fact bespeaks all the more honor to the brave officers and men who notwithstanding the complete breakdown of their high command fought out their hundred-odd separate battles through two days of continuous combat with a gallantry seldom equaled and never surpassed. No other page of American history shines so brightly, and it was fitting that the end should be a drawn battle.

It was held a discovery of the World War that a higher head-quarters could function to advantage in two or more places at the same time. Grant, however, was a leap ahead of his time in many ways, and on that account was often misunderstood by the more conventionally minded. In modern terminology Grant's Pittsburg office would now be called, depending upon its organization, an "advanced headquarters" or "post of command." The staff officers at either headquarters who are competent to give orders in the name of the commander if he is present, are of course equally competent to do so during his absence; being, presumably, familiar with his plans and policy.

There is no rigid rule about the amount of independent initiative generals shall allow their individual staff members. Some give much, a few delegate but little authority; but it is safe to say that if the general does not trust an officer's judgment and his loyalty in carrying out faithfully his commander's established policy, he does not keep that officer with him long, in a general-staff capacity at least. What McPherson's position would now be called is "general staff officer" or "assistant chief of staff in charge of advanced headquarters." At that time McPherson was simply Grant's chief of engineers.

This explanation is made for the simple reason that many writers ignorant of military matters have assumed that the Union Army went un-commanded until Grant reached the field, and that whatever credit there might be for the victory, it was due to the behavior of the division commanders. The division commanders did, certainly, display exemplary initiative, but no more than should be expected of those entrusted with such commands.

Thus the formations for defense of the front-line commands of Sherman and Prentiss upon notice of the attack required no orders; nor did the formation of the second-line troops in support, those of McClernand and Hurlbut, and their employment

JAMES BIRDSEYE McPHERSON
(1828–64)

either to reinforce the first line or to receive it as it fell back, according to the tactical situation as it developed in each locality. The only question in doubt, which could not be settled by a division commander, was the employment of the 2d Division of Smith, now commanded by W. H. L. Wallace, obviously the higher commander's reserve, since it was in the third line, in rear. That could be moved only by authority of Grant or his staff representative.

Grant did, in fact, on April 4, as has been mentioned, give W. H. L. Wallace contingent orders in case the 3d Division of Lew Wallace should be attacked. But McPherson's presence with W. H. L. Wallace, on the nights of April 4–5 and 5–6 rather indicates that Grant was entrusting McPherson with the chief's highest responsibility in an emergency—the employment of his reserve.

The trust was, happily, placed in competent hands. It is of course possible that Grant had given McPherson precise instructions, but the chief's high praise of him in his report[1] combined with the fact that he was promoted from lieutenant-colonel to brigadier in May and to major-general in October, and in December of the same year given command of a corps under Grant, indicates a notable performance of duty.

The data on the subject are far from complete, owing to W. H. L. Wallace's being mortally wounded in the first day's battle, and the absence of reports from two brigades and several regiments of his division because the commanders had been killed or wounded. But it is clear that McPherson,[2] after sending, or directing W. H. L. Wallace to send, one regiment to guard the

---

[1] "Lieutenant Colonel McPherson . . . deserves more than passing notice for his activity and courage . . . During the two days' battle he was constantly in the saddle, leading troops as they arrived to points where their services were required." W. R. 10:110.

[2] Reports of Compton, Morton, Powell, W. R. 10:160, 161.

Snake Creek bridge and another with the divisional cavalry as a right-flank covering detachment, marched with the remainder of the division to a point in rear of the center, whence he could equally well fill gaps in the line between the right groupment (Sherman's line reinforced by McClernand's) and the center

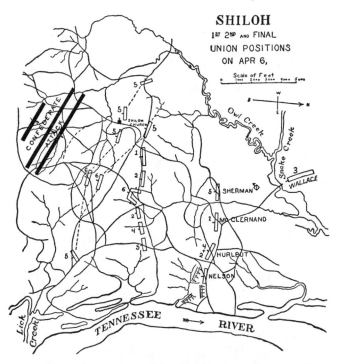

and extreme left, Stuart's brigade. McPherson then, after personal reconnaissances to see if and where reserves were needed, conducted them to their places in the line as became an accomplished general-staff officer and No. I graduate of his class at West Point. He was, in fact, engaged in the task of organizing a defensive line between center and right when Grant came on the field.

Let us now follow Grant in his approach to the field of battle.

He rises early and breakfasts at six.[3] Horses for himself and his staff have been ordered, that he may ride out on the Waynesboro road to meet Buell. Distant firing is heard. Without waiting to finish breakfast, Grant and the staff, with their horses, go directly down to the headquarters despatch-boat *Tigress*. While the boat is getting up steam, Grant dictates, to two members of his staff, messages to two of Buell's division commanders. To Nelson, already in Savannah, he says: "An attack having been made on our forces, you will move your entire command to the river opposite Pittsburg. You can obtain a guide easily in the village."[4] To Wood: "You will move your command with the utmost dispatch to the river at this point [Savannah], where steamboats will be in waiting to transport you to Pittsburg."

While his staff officers are writing these messages, Grant himself writes one to Buell:

Heavy firing is heard up the river, indicating plainly that an attack has been made upon our most advanced positions. I have been looking for this, but did not believe the attack could be made before Monday or Tuesday. This necessitates my joining the forces up the river instead of meeting you to-day, as I had contemplated. I have directed General Nelson to move to the river with his division. He can march to opposite Pittsburg.[5]

---

[3] W. R. 10:184.   [4] W. R. 11:95.

[5] W. R. 109:232. It may seem difficult to reconcile the statement, "I have been looking for this," etc., with his previously expressed views, if we assume Grant to mean by it that he has been looking for a combined attack by every man Johnston could rake and scrape between the Cumberland and the Mississippi. If, however, we recall his orders of Apr. 4 to both Sherman and W. H. L. Wallace (2d Division) to be prepared in case of an attack to go to assist Lew Wallace's 3d Division, more or less isolated at Crump's Landing, and take it in the sense that Grant has been expecting a minor surprise attack on his one detached division and supposes that is what has come, it accords with both what he has written and the measures he has taken. It should be remembered that he has had no word from Pittsburg, has no telegraph line there, and that the sound of firing would come from the same direction from either Pittsburg or Crump's. This view is further borne out by McPherson's report, W. R. 10:181.

At about 7 A.M. the boat bearing Grant and his staff started; at 7:30 it reached Crump's. Lew Wallace, expecting Grant, was waiting on a boat at the landing. It was clear to Grant now, from the sound of the firing, that the attack was not on Wallace, but on the main camp. It is probable, however, that at this time there was a lull in the firing, just after Sherman and Prentiss had fallen back from their first "parade-ground" positions, and the Confederate troops, as was only human, paused to have a look at the captured camps and a bite to eat where it was possible, before continuing the advance. Perhaps none begrudged it to them. After their three days of living on "cooked rations carried in haversacks" they certainly would fight all the better for it afterward.

But whether this was a mere lull in the battle or the end of the affair, Grant was not to be stampeded into hasty action until he knew more. Hence his word to Wallace, in passing, was: "Get your troops under arms and have them ready to move at a moment's notice." [6]

At about 8 A.M. the boat docks at Pittsburg. Grant and his staff mount their horses and ride toward the firing. As they reach the top of the bluffs two regiments are found (the 15th and 16th Iowa) [7] newly arrived and under orders to join Prentiss's division. Grant has an aid direct the two colonels to form line to round up stragglers, protect the landing, and hold themselves in reserve. Rather a complex order for raw, freshly arrived colonels, but it is soon to be followed by another, not so complex, and seemingly not so important, though one cannot be positive about that.

But Grant has not stopped. He rides on a half-mile and meets W. H. L. Wallace, who tells him what he knows:

"Prentiss is attacked and falling back on Hurlbut, who has formed in line. Sherman is falling back. McClernand is sup-

[6] W. R. 10:185; 10:178; 10:175.
[7] W. R. 10:286.

porting him; I have been posted here by your orders, issued by McPherson, as a central reserve to be used to fill in the gaps between our center and right or left. McPherson is up now posting my First Brigade, but ought to be back soon and can tell you better how things are." [8]

Grant has heard enough to know that Johnston with his "not over forty thousand" (Grant is not sure now that it is not over a hundred thousand) is driving at him and driving hard. It is a rude awakening; it is not so easy as it was yesterday to say, "If they come to attack us, we can whip them!" What he thinks is what every honest commander thinks in such circumstances: "I got my troops into this mess; it is up to me to get them out of it. What is the first thing to be done?"

Externally imperturbable as ever, he turns to Rawlins, his adjutant-general, and directs, "Send Baxter in the *Tigress* to tell Wallace [Lew] to march up at once." [9] To a supply officer of his staff he says, "Fill some wagons with ammunition and send up to the troops."

Now what? It seems to Grant that the center is being well handled by McPherson. The next point of importance is the right; to make secure the Snake Creek crossing for the approach of Lew Wallace. Grant goes to Snake Creek bridge. There he finds two regiments and four troops. He inquires if any of the cavalry officers know the road to Crump's. One does! The general directs him, "Ride there and tell General Wallace to hurry forward with all possible despatch."

Grant was to wish later that he had taken the two minutes necessary to have the order written and authenticated by a member of his staff; but that was one of the lessons he was to learn in this battle.

From the bridge he turns toward the front and, shortly before

[8] McPherson, W. R. 10:181.
[9] Rowley, W. R. 10:179; Rawlins, W. R. 10:185.

10 A.M., finds Sherman, just as the latter's division is being hard pressed in its second position along the Purdy road. Let Sherman describe the interview:

> After some general conversation he remarked that I was doing right in stubbornly opposing the progress of the enemy, and in answer to my inquiry as to cartridges told me he had anticipated their want and made orders accordingly. He then said his presence was more needed over on the left.[10]

That simply narrated conversation may not seem worth much to one who has not had his own battle experiences, but to those who have shared their thoughts with another under fire, and can read between the lines, it is redolent of the mutual confidence and reliance which were an inspiration to both men. It is neither play-acting nor much typewriting that wins battles, but trust of just that sort, given and reciprocated.

On Sherman's left, Grant finds McClernand. He respects but does not like McClernand, who for seven months has been of the same rank as Grant and all the time remained his second-in-command, through Belmont, Fort Henry, Fort Donelson, a painful position for one who aspires to be a leader! But McClernand is a good fighter and has qualities which Grant appreciates and uses, and, precisely because Grant does not like him he especially desires to be fair and just, more than just, to him in every event.

Neither of them ever mentioned the interview and we know of it only by its results. McClernand asked for reinforcements and got them—got Grant's last two regiments in reserve, the 15th and 16th Iowa, stationed at the landing at 8 A.M. to do triple duty.[11] There is no clue by which to judge whether Grant so easily and so early gave up his last reserve in hand because he saw with

---

[10] W. R. 109:559.
[11] W. R. 10:286, 288.

his own eyes that the situation demanded it or because he thought McClernand's morale was low and needed bracing or for the very human reason that, not liking McClernand, he did not wish to admit to him that he had no reserves that could be spared at that time, as he might easily, for example, have been willing to admit to Sherman.

But in any event, to speak from the technical military point of view, Grant's right, covering the crossing of Snake Creek which was being held open for Lew Wallace, was his critical side. There can be no question, therefore, that his reserve was employed correctly as to place, and since the question of the moment of its employment must, as a question of judgment, be left to the man on the spot, no just critic can impeach Grant's decision, whatever the motive to which we may ascribe it.

Grant's next stop was with Prentiss, and is recorded in that general's report as having been shortly after 10 A.M. Driven back from his first position in front of his camps, Prentiss had taken up an excellent position in rear, connecting with Hurlbut on his left, and the gap between his line and McClernand's was promptly filled by McPherson from W. H. L. Wallace's reserves, now become supports. Here Prentiss was assailed by a strong Confederate attack, and successfully repulsed it just as Grant came up. His report reads: "I exhibited to him [Grant] the disposition of my entire force, which disposition received his commendation, and I received my final orders, which were to maintain that position at all hazards." [12]

Whether Grant in giving that order, so vital for the final success, had a prevision of what it meant, or merely saw in what became known as the "hornets' nest" a naturally strong position capable of being tenaciously defended by relatively raw troops, takes us once more into the field of speculation.

[12] W. R. 10:278.

Grant's report [13] contains nothing regarding Prentiss but the same praise he gives the other division commanders, except Sherman, of whom special mention is made. In his Memoirs, however, he says in seeming mild reproof: "In one of the backward moves on the 6th, the division commanded by General Prentiss did not fall back with the others. This left his flanks exposed and enabled the enemy to capture him with about twenty-two hundred of his officers and men." [14]

Did Grant forget in writing this? Or didn't he mean "at all hazards"? Of course there is to be said that at the time he gave the order he was expecting the divisions of both Lew Wallace and Nelson within a few hours. But whichever view be taken, the order is unassailably logical.

Grant probably went from Prentiss to Hurlbut, next on the left, but of that, or his going to Stuart's brigade on the extreme left, there is no record, save the statement in his Memoirs, "I was with each of the division commanders that day, several times." [15]

We next find him with W. H. L. Wallace and McPherson, whom he now sees for the first time in the battle, at the post of what is left of the reserve. Grant can see that the troops right and left of Prentiss are being hard pressed. He directs an orderly to ride to the right to see if Lew Wallace is yet in sight. Then— it is not far—he rides to the river landing to see if Nelson has yet come. There is no sign of him. The log hut Grant has been using as an office is right there; he steps in and pens this note:

Commanding Officer Advance Forces (Buell's Army), near Pittsburg:

The attack on my forces has been very spirited from early this morning. The appearance of fresh troops in the field now would have a powerful effect, both by inspiring our men and disheartening

[13] W. R. 10:110.
[14] Grant I:280.
[15] Grant I:281.

the enemy. If you will get upon the field, leaving all your baggage on the east bank of the river, it will be more to our advantage, and possibly save the day to us. The rebel forces are estimated at over 100,000 men. My headquarters will be in the log building on the top of the hill, where you will be furnished a staff officer to guide you to your place on the field.[16]

It is easy to see from the note, with its phraseology so reminiscent of the one to Foote, before Donelson on February 15, the heavy burden of responsibility Grant was carrying. But he could not pause. He mounted and again rode to the right with his staff. It was now shortly after noon.

Captain Rowley, Grant's aide-de-camp, wrote:

As we were riding towards the right of the line, a cavalry officer rode up and reported to General Grant, stating that General [Lew] Wallace had positively refused to come up unless he should receive *written* orders. After hearing the report General Grant turned to me, saying, "Captain, you will proceed to Crump's Landing and say to General Wallace that it is my orders that he bring his division up *at once*." [17]

By Rawlins's account,[18] Grant, after this incident, turned and rode back to the landing, again hoping to find Nelson's division arriving. At 1 P.M. we find him aboard his boat, the *Tigress*. There Buell, who has just appeared, seeks him, to ask him to send transports to Savannah to bring up Crittenden's division. Grant and Buell have little in common; each is glad to see the other on this occasion, but neither desires to prolong the interview.[19] Grant soon leaves, and finding Baxter, asks him what Wallace said when he received Grant's orders. Baxter replies, "he appeared delighted! . . . He must now be near the point he was ordered." [20]

[16] W. R. 11:95.
[17] W. R. 10:179.
[18] W. R. 10:186.
[19] "Buell" in B. and L. I:493.
[20] W. R. 10:186.

Grant, therefore, having pointed out to McPherson where he wants Wallace to go in support of Prentiss—and without question the proper place for him—about 2:30 P.M. sends McPherson and Rawlins to meet Wallace and conduct him to his place on the field.[21]

Thereafter we lose our attendant scribes and though we at times catch glimpses of Grant, we can no longer follow him on his lonely traverse of the battle-field.

To sum up the first two phases, not of the battle itself but of Grant's leadership in the battle:

The first, or staff-control phase of the deployment and location of reserves, is well conducted. Great credit is due to Sherman and Smith, in the first instance for their excellent judgment in locating the camps, keeping the tactical situation in mind; also to the division commanders for their commendable and proper initiative in both the first and second line; and not least to Lieutenant-Colonel McPherson, for boldly handling the whole situation as it should be handled until Grant arrived. Yet the credit for all these reverts to Grant. He had so organized and trained his staff as to make them possible. Three of his division commanders had served under him seven months. He had, so to speak, brought them up, taught them what to do on their own, and what to await orders for; that the other three, who were new, so quickly grasped his policy and what he expected of them is all the more credit to him, showing as it does the strength of the *esprit de corps* which he had created.

In the second phase, it is difficult to see how Grant could have more successfully conducted the affair than he did. As a result of his previous instructions and training he found his army already automatically disposed for defense. There remained only

[21] W. R. 10:181.

for him to do what he could to provide for, and if possible accelerate, the movements of all available reinforcements for his side then in the vicinity and to keep his defensive organization oiled and running smoothly.

This he accomplished by his visits to his division commanders, to see if they understood what to do, if they had what they needed in the way of troops and ammunition, and if they were "playing the game" with their flanking neighbors. The division commander is essentially the director of the fighting of his unit, and nothing is to be gained by a higher commander's stepping in and interfering unless the situation has gotten out of hand.

Perhaps in some of these visits nothing occurred but a nod of the head or a look in the eye; yet that nod or look might well, between men who understood and trusted each other, by conveying a sense of appreciation, of approval, or of congratulation, mean more to a tired and anxious division commander than several regiments of reinforcements; it might well make that subtle balance that so often oscillates between success and failure incline toward the side of success. Further, one cannot have followed Grant's career and character thus far and have any doubt that when division commanders needed any words of suggestion, correction, or explanation, the general gave them with his blunt but kindly straightforwardness.

Between the hours of two and four there appears to have been, if not a lull, at least a lessening in the ardor of the Confederate attack; it would have been a miracle had there not been. The men were tired and hungry, and not too well equipped, and the captured Union camps, with their food and prospects for very desirable plunder were a powerful magnet for those who could break away from their units. In the dense growth of the numerous wood patches, that was easy under the conditions. Considering their training and discipline, and with the intermingling of units owing to the faulty deployment, the Confederate army showed a cohesion and persistency in its attack which were really marvelous, and an enduring tribute to its commander.

It is of interest to note how the opposing commanders applied themselves when they realized this weakening of the attacking power on the Confederate side and of the power of resistance on the Union. Johnston sought to infuse spirit into the attack locally, led a brigade in a charge against a weak spot, and was killed. Grant, on the other hand, had gone through the morning expecting from hour to hour to see the arrival of his hoped-for reinforcements—Lew Wallace and Nelson—to restore the threatened equilibrium. But, since they did not come, the desperate state of affairs became more and more clear. The division commanders were good fighters, but they could not be everywhere, and more generals as well as more troops were needed.

Grant from this time on begins to take a hand in dealing with local tactical situations along the line. Not like Johnston, indeed, leading a charge; that is not the commander's duty as Grant sees it, no matter how stirring the appeal to throw himself into it. Grant is guided in all his acts by a stern, unbending sense of duty to his country and to his men; and that duty calls for putting forth his full powers of mind and will to exercise the central control and coördination of the combined efforts without which all must be lost.

Thus we find him toward 3 P.M. again at the Snake Creek bridge, anxiously looking for Lew Wallace, but on not finding him, giving directions for the disposition of the two infantry regiments there for the better safeguarding of the bridge and to keep the crossing open for Wallace.[22]

___

[22] Reports, Compton, 14th Missouri, W. R. 10:160; Morton, 81st Ohio, W. R. 10:161.

At 3 P.M., Grant again rode to see Sherman and found his division and McClernand's having a hard time of it.[23] After this he must again have ridden to the left, perhaps by way of the landing, since about this time, if not earlier, he gave to his chief of staff, Colonel Webster, who was an artilleryman, the additional rôle of chief of artillery with the mission to build up, near it, an artillery reserve as the nucleus for the ultimate defense of the landing, should it come to that.

Between 4 P.M. and 5 P.M. is the crucial period. The last ounce of effort is being exerted by the Confederates to drive the Union forces back to the banks of the Tennessee. They succeed in forcing back Grant's right wing slightly, and in outflanking his left wing. But Prentiss in the center, with a few reinforcing regiments, carries out his orders to hold the center, the "hornets' nest," at "all hazards." Becoming isolated by the falling back of the Union troops on both his right and his left, Prentiss bends back his flanks and organizes his position for all-round defense.

By this development, though the Union line is greatly contracted as it falls back toward the apex of the angle between Snake Creek and the Tennessee River, there is left a gap in the Union center which just now there are no troops to fill. This is the time for the Confederate high command to assert itself and give the attack a proper direction. Shall the troops turn, surround and "pinch out" Prentiss in his "hornets' nest," or ignore him and, leaving a handful of troops to contain Prentiss, push on with all their might in a last attempt to carry Snake Creek bridge and the landing and thus cut off all possibility of Union reinforcements?

There are but two hours of daylight remaining; manifestly there can be but one answer. The landing must be carried in those two hours; that is their only hope. But, unfortunately for them, the Confederate high command has ceased to function in

[23] Report, Sherman, W. R. 10:250.

the hundred or more separate battles going on. Each local leader is doing what he pleases and in the mêlée the magnet presented by Prentiss, now cut off and virtually surrounded, proves to have an irresistible power of attraction for all the remaining Confederate troops in that part of the field. They might so easily carry the last Union strongholds, but instead they devote the last of their energies for the day and use up the remaining daylight in hammering at the "hornets' nest" where toward 6 P.M. Prentiss and his two thousand remaining men are finally forced to surrender.

While all this was going on Grant was once more, between four and five o'clock, with Sherman.

In a letter to Professor H. Coppée, two years later, Sherman wrote:

About 5 P.M., before sunset, General Grant came again to me, and, after hearing my report of matters, explained to me the situation of affairs on the left, which were not as favorable. Still the enemy had failed to reach the landing of the boats. We agreed that the enemy had expended the furors of his attack, and we estimated our loss and approximated our strength, including Lew Wallace's fresh division, expected each minute, and he then ordered me to get all things ready, and at daylight the next day to assume the offensive. That was before General Buell had arrived but he was known to be near at hand. . . .

I remember the fact the better from General Grant's anecdote of the Donelson battle, which he told me then for the first time, that at a certain period of the battle he saw that either side was ready to give way if the other showed a bold front, and he determined to do that very thing, to advance on the enemy, when as he prognosticated the enemy surrendered.[24]

Adam Badeau gives us the same picture, evidently based on conversations with Grant at City Point or elsewhere in 1864 and 1865:

[24] June 13, 1864, W. R. 109:559.

I have often heard him declare that there comes a time in every hard-fought battle, when both armies are nearly or quite exhausted, and it seems impossible for either to do more; this he believed the turning-point; whichever after first renews the fight is sure to win. He could not urge his jaded troops that night [April 6] into any further assault, but his resolution was unshaken, and although Buell's advance was not yet across the river, he gave positive orders to take the initiative in the morning. To Sherman, he told the story of the Donelson battle . . . At 4 P.M., on the 6th of April he thought the appearances the same.[25]

This vital lesson for the military commander, Napoleon learned at the Battle of Marengo, a battle which was in many ways strikingly similar to that of Shiloh, including the pivotal retreat from the right and the deferred entry of the division of Desaix after the battle was believed won by the Austrians, comparable to the division of Lew Wallace in Grant's case. Napoleon describes this, in a statement much like Grant's, in a conversation with St. Cyr:

He [Napoleon] replied to me that he held no preference either for an attack on the center or against the flanks; that he held it as a principle to engage the enemy with as many means of combat as possible; that when the corps nearest the enemy became engaged he let them carry on, without too much concerning himself over their good or bad chances; that he merely exercised great care not to yield too easily to the demands for reinforcements on the part of their commanders . . . He added that it was only towards the end of the day when he saw that the tired enemy had put into play the greater part of his forces, that he assembled whatever he had been able to conserve in the way of reserves, to launch on the field of battle a strong mass of infantry, of cavalry and of artillery, that the enemy not having anticipated this, he brought about what he named an *event* [*événement*] and that by this means he had nearly always gained the victory.[26]

[25] "Military History of U. S. Grant," Vol. I, p. 85.
[26] St. Cyr's Memoirs, Vol. IV, p. 41.

This effect of fresh reserves entering the combat at the moment when the soldiers on both sides are exhausted and susceptible (as a psychological crowd) to being swept off the field in panic, Grant had seen demonstrated, against him at Belmont, in his favor at Donelson; and he was to see it once again at Shiloh. From then on it entered into all his military calculations.

And while it does not in the least detract from the credit due him for appreciating and mastering this vital lesson of war, yet it may be well to recall that Grant's great teacher, Experience, favored him by causing him in his first three fights to engage an almost equal enemy under almost equal conditions, so that the truth was ground into his very soul; whereas some Civil War generals, such as McClellan, Pope, Burnside, and others, popularly deemed favored by fortune in having easy initial victories, were later mentally quite unprepared when suddenly confronted with a real battle crisis on a large scale.

The Battle of the Wilderness, in 1864, was perhaps the real turning-point of the war, certainly in the last phase; Grant's preparation for dealing with it tactically came to him at Belmont, Donelson, and above all at Shiloh.

CHAPTER XVIII

SHILOH—AND AFTER

By experience it is become known unto me
that victory over the foe proceedeth not from the
greatness of armies, nor defeat from inferiority in
numbers; for conquest is obtained only by skilful
and judicious measures.—TIMUR.

WE left Grant, in the last chapter, late on the afternoon of
Sunday, April 6, discussing the battle with Sherman, and
his plan for winning it by taking advantage of the psychological
moment to stem and turn the tide. There remained the none too
easy task of carrying that plan into execution.

Let us take a look at the situation as it appeared to the correspondent of the "Cincinnati Gazette," who evidently was near
the landing:

We have reached the last act in the tragedy of Sunday. It is
half-past four o'clock. Our front line of divisions has been lost
since half-past ten. Our reserve line is now gone, too. The rebels
occupy the camps of every division save that of W. H. L. Wallace.
Our whole army is crowded in the region of Wallace's camps, and
to a circuit of one-half to two-thirds of a mile around the Landing.
We have been falling back all day. We can do it no more. The
next repulse puts us into the river, and there are not transports enough
to cross a single division till the enemy would be upon us.

Lew Wallace's division might turn the tide for us—it is made
of fighting men—but where is it? Why has it not been thundering
on the right for three hours past? We do not know yet that it was
not ordered up till noon. Buell is coming, but he has been doing
it all day, and all last week. His advance-guard is across the river

now, waiting ferriage; but what is an advance-guard, with sixty thousand victorious foes in front of us? We have lost nearly all our camps and camp equipage. We have lost nearly half our field artillery. We have lost a division general and two or three regiments of our soldiers as prisoners. We have lost—how dreadfully we are afraid to think—in killed and wounded. The hospitals are full to overflowing. A long ridge bluff is set apart for surgical uses. It is covered with the maimed, the dead and dying. And our men are discouraged by prolonged defeat. Nothing but the most energetic exertion, on the part of the officers, prevents them from becoming demoralized . . .

Meanwhile there is a lull in the firing. . . . Let us embrace the opportunity, and look about the Landing. We pass the old-log house, lately post-office, now full of wounded and surgeons . . . General Grant and staff are in a group beside it. The General is confident, "We can hold them off till to-morrow; then they'll be exhausted, and we'll go at them with fresh troops. . . ."

On the bluffs above the river is a sight that may well make our cheeks tingle. There are not less than five thousand skulkers lining the banks! Ask them why they don't go to their places in the line; "Oh! our regiment is all cut to pieces. . . ."

Officers are around among them, trying to hunt up their men, storming, coaxing, commanding—cursing I am afraid.[1]

It will be noted that the single bright spot in the mind of the correspondent was the optimism of the Union commander, who saw beyond the dark clouds the coming victory, although the end of the defensive action had not yet come. Toward 6 P.M. troops on the extreme Confederate right wing gathered impetus for a last attack to gain possession of the bluffs immediately above the landing. For some time past, however, Colonel Webster, Grant's chief of staff and chief of artillery, had been gathering reserve artillery and had succeeded in collecting a battery of one hundred guns to defend the heights above the landing, which

---

[1] Moore IV:393.

now became the extreme left flank of what was left of the Union army.

As infantry supports for these batteries the remnants of Stuart's brigade—which had fallen back shortly after five o'clock, and remnants of the 2d, 4th, and 6th divisions, had been gathered up by General Hurlbut, who was given command of the left wing. This part of the line was further reinforced by the leading regiments of Nelson's division, which appeared toward dark and were posted there by Grant himself.

The Confederate commander Beauregard, as dusk approached, gave orders to break off the combat and assemble the troops for the night. As a matter of fact, the Confederate army could do nothing else. Units were badly mixed and the field was covered with stragglers. Order could be produced out of this chaos by daylight only; if it were not effected before dark the reorganization of the command would be impossible. It is to the greatest credit of the Confederate leaders that they were able to maintain the cohesion of their force as well as they did in the circumstances. The troops withdrew and many of them succeeded in finding in the captured Union camps quarters for the night and shelter from the heavy rains which fell. Beauregard appears to have passed the night in Sherman's headquarters near Shiloh church, where after a council of war he decided to renew the attack in the morning.

Grant himself, sharing the hardships of his troops, slept during the night under a tree near his log-hut headquarters.

During the night the divisions of Crittenden, Wood, and McCook reached Pittsburg by steamer from Savannah and were formed by Buell on the left for an advance against the Confederate right. The Union gunboats, which had come into action to assist the Union left in the last phase of the battle near the landing on Sunday, kept up an intermittent fire on the enemy, with the idea of breaking up the rest of the Confederate troops. However, the men on both sides were too weary to be greatly troubled by occasional gun-fire.

Early on the morning of the seventh Grant issued orders to his own army to take the offensive and recapture their former camps. He does not appear to have issued anything in the nature of orders to Buell, who saw clearly for himself the golden opportunity that was presented by the arrival of four reinforcing divisions of his army and of the division of Lew Wallace, which was at last on the field. In this phase of the battle Grant, lacking now two of his division commanders—Prentiss captured and W. H. L. Wallace wounded—took an even more active part in the tactical direction of brigades and regiments than he had taken on the sixth, and we find him ordering advances and charges all along the line.

With the Union superiority there was never any doubt about the result, yet the advance was by no means easy. The Confederate army, elated by its successes of the day before and hopeful of completing its victory, fought its hardest, and till mid-afternoon the field was as hotly contested as on the first day. But as the day waned it became apparent that the weight of battalions was against them, and the Southern lines began to give way. Toward half-past four the most advanced Union camps of Sherman and Prentiss had been regained and the question of whether or not further pursuit should be undertaken came to Grant for decision.

Grant has been blamed by many critics for his failure to order a pursuit from the battle-field, particularly in the light of the information afterward gained that the Confederate retreat on Corinth had degenerated into a rout in which guns and wagons were abandoned in the heavy mud. However, there is to be said

that the severity with which he is blamed by his critics is generally in increased ratio to their lack of understanding of military
operations. Taking the situation as it existed at 4 P.M. on April
7, and considering the information actually possessed by Grant,
there was nothing to justify his pushing his troops beyond the line
already gained.

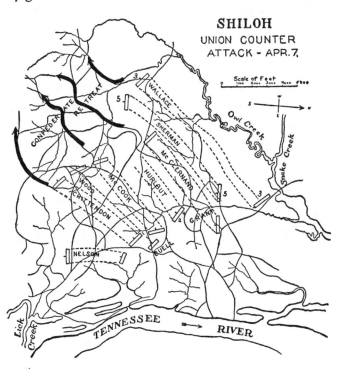

SHILOH
UNION COUNTER
ATTACK - APR. 7.

Two days of hard fighting for his men with an uncomfortable
night in between, spent without cover in the rain, could not well
be followed with orders for an active pursuit. Had Buell's army
been fought, as it should have been, with three divisions in the
line and one in reserve, a fresh division on the evening of the
seventh might have completed the destruction of the Confederate

forces; but Buell's troops had all of them made forced marches
on the sixth and done hard fighting on the seventh, and they were
scarcely more effective at the end of the day than were Grant's.

Had Grant assumed command of Buell's army, he might justly
be blamed for the too early commitment of Buell's forces to the
general action. But as the second day's battle was fought on the
basis of mutual coöperation, the blame must rest on Buell and
not Grant.

Mistakes at Shiloh in the actual fighting were negligible; at
least it is as absurd to find fault with the leaders' tactics, which
were the best they knew, as to blame the troops for speaking
English instead of French.

The Battle of Shiloh became an object of more controversy
and dispute than perhaps any other battle of the war, not excepting Gettysburg. The press, then as always, looking for "good
stories" and at the time not restrained by either censorship or by
patriotic motives from publishing tales reflecting on its own
armies and army commanders, was seeking only for dramatic copy.

Thus we find Grant almost universally condemned for allowing his army to be "surprised." As typical of what became for
a time the accepted tradition, we may take the narrative published
in the "Cincinnati Gazette":

The first wild cries from the pickets rushing in, and the few
scattering shots that preceded their arrival, aroused the regiments to
a sense of their peril; an instant afterward, shells were hurtling
through the tents, while, before there was time for thought of preparation, there came rushing through the woods, with lines of battle
sweeping the whole fronts of the division-camps and bending down
on either flank, the fine, dashing, compact columns of the enemy.

Into the just-aroused camps thronged the rebel regiments, firing
sharp volleys as they came and springing toward our laggards with
the bayonet. Some were shot down as they were running, without

weapons, hatless, coatless, toward the river. The searching bullets found other poor unfortunates in their tents, and there, all unheeding now, they still slumbered, while the unseen foe rushed on. Others fell, as they were disentangling themselves from the flaps that formed the doors to their tents; others as they were buckling on their accoutrements; a few, it was even said, as they were vainly trying to impress on the cruelly-exultant enemy their readiness to surrender.

Officers were wounded in their beds, and left for dead . . . and on Monday evening were found . . still able to tell the tale.

Such were the fearful disasters that opened the rebel onset on the lines of Prentiss's division. Similar were the fates of Hildebrand's brigade in Sherman's division . . .[2]

Such was the press report that spread over the country. Naturally, in every camp there are always some asleep in their tents in the daytime: the sick; those up at night, on guard or other duty. But that is not the picture given. It is distinctly that of a surprised camp. The correspondent does not pretend to have been an eye-witness, for he was at Crump's when the fighting began, and the battle was already some hours old when he came up by boat to Pittsburg, since, according to him, "the west bank of the river was lined with the usual fugitives from action" upon his arrival.

Let us now review the facts:

General Prentiss, pursuant to Grant's instructions, sent forward "the usual advance-guard," [3] on the eve of the battle; also a special outpost at the left, which was not usual. "In view of information received" from the outpost commander, General Prentiss sent forward a half-regiment under Colonel Moore. "About seven o'clock . . . Moore returned, reporting some activity in front." On receiving this report, Prentiss strengthened his advance posts, "extending the picket lines to the front a distance

[2] Moore IV:388.
[3] W. R. 10:277.

of a mile and a half, at the same time extending and doubling the lines of the grand guard [outpost reserve]."

At three o'clock on the morning of the battle, Colonel Moore again went forward with half his regiment as special support for the outpost, and "at break of day the advance pickets were driven in, whereupon Colonel Moore pushed forward and engaged the enemy's advance," despatching a messenger to Prentiss asking that the balance of his regiment be sent to him, which was done.

Prentiss at once, as he says, "ordered the entire force into line" and advanced the rest of the 1st Brigade well to the front. "Shortly before 6 o'clock," Moore being wounded, "his regiment commenced falling back. . . . Hereupon the entire force . . . was advanced to the extreme front."

Later, being outflanked, Prentiss fell back on a second position in front of his camp, and at 9:05 A.M.—after three hours of fighting—fell back to his third position, the "hornets' nest," where Grant visited him at 10 A.M., and which position he held until his surrender at 5:30 P.M.

Prentiss's narrative, as above given, is substantiated by the reports of subordinates, written independently. Colonel Van Horn [4] gives 7 A.M. as the hour when the division fell back from the first line, some distance in front of its encampment, to its second position, still in front of its encampment. These reports naturally render absurd the idea of any troop organizations being surprised in their tents. The reports of the colonels of Hildebrand's brigade of Sherman's division are to similar effect.

There was much criticism in the press at the time, and has been much by writers since, because the Shiloh camp had not been entrenched. Usually the same writers blame Halleck in the subsequent advance to Corinth for delaying his movement by entrenching every camp occupied. Later in the war any commander would

4 W. R. 10:284.

undoubtedly have entrenched in the circumstances; but there is to be remarked on this subject that had entrenchments been constructed at Shiloh, the consequences might easily have been a lost battle for the North. The troops were on an offensive mission, imbued with the spirit of victory of Fort Donelson. Aside from the depressing effect on the morale of the men from the severe physical labor connected with the construction of entrenchments, they would certainly have lost their idea that their commander was unafraid, and that therefore they should be unafraid, of meeting the enemy in the open.

There is to be said on this subject, further, that troops driven out of an entrenched line are seldom capable of making a stand in the open afterward. That Albert Sidney Johnston, with his picked troops, would have been able to penetrate at one or more points and carry an entrenched line four miles long there can be little question.

Of course, had the Shiloh camp really been effectively entrenched, Johnston, in his own country, would have had complete information and would not have attacked at all, but would, by threatening to cut Grant off by a movement to the river below Shiloh, have maneuvered to compel him to come out of his entrenchments. In other words, Grant had no business being at Shiloh at all if he was afraid of fighting Johnston on equal terms. That the moral value of the victory, to the North, was the greater in the circumstances is undeniable.

But these criticisms in the press of the period regarding Grant's conduct of the battle, of his absence from the battlefield at the start, of his surprise, of his lack of entrenchments, and of his failure to pursue, did not end the matter. Buell's Army of the Ohio firmly believed that the Army of the Tennessee had all run away—had they not seen them skulking behind the banks of the river?—and that they themselves had arrived in the nick of time to rescue them from the pursuing Confederates, who, happily, had tarried to loot the Union camps before pushing Grant's men into the river.

But, for some unaccountable reason, Grant's Army of the Tennessee refused to be grateful for its rescue by the Army of the Ohio. More and more as time passed did they refuse to admit their desperate plight. They were willing to share with Buell's army the honors of the second day of the counter-attack, but not to concede having been rescued in the first day's battle.

After the war Buell became the champion of his army's claims, and in 1885, when public interest in the Civil War began to revive, wrote an able article entitled "Shiloh Reviewed," [5] in which he says:

Indeed, the want of cohesion and concert in the Union ranks is conspicuously indicated in the official reports. A regiment is rarely overcome in front, but falls back because the regiment on its right or left has done so, and exposed its flank. . . .
This outflanking, so common in the Union reports at Shiloh, is not a mere excuse of the inferior commanders. It is the practical consequence of the absence of a common head and the judicious use of reserves to counteract reverses and preserve the front of battle. The want of a general direction is seen also in the distribution of Hurlbut's and Wallace's divisions.

Still more definitely attacking Grant's leadership in the battle, Buell, at the close of his article, says:

The record is silent and tradition adverse to any marked influence that he exerted upon the fortune of the day. . . . If he could have done anything in the beginning, he was not on the ground in time. . . . But he was one of the many there who would have resisted while resistance could avail.

[5] B. and L. I:487–536.

In one sense Buell is correct in his criticism and he might have applied it to Donelson as well as Shiloh: neither battle was won primarily by Grant on the battle-field. That is to say, had Grant joined his army as a stranger a day or two before either battle—assuming his troops to have had their training of less than a year under some other or others of the hundred Union generals of the time—such intellectual guidance as he was able to give it would probably not of itself have brought the success.

But war differs from chess, in that while chess remains the same whether the pieces played with be wood or ivory, in war soldiers are imbued in more or less mysterious ways with the spirit of victory or of failure, the spirit of loyalty and trust or of questioning and doubt, by their commanders. Hence while in the game it is a matter solely of the brains of the player, in war it is a matter of the spirit and the initiative which the commander has infused into his men, as much as it is the orders given on the field, that decides the result. For this reason it is that a Grant, a Lee, a Frederick, or a Napoleon, will accomplish time and again the seemingly impossible. Thus, even granting Buell's premise that Grant exerted but trifling personal influence over events on the battle-field itself, nevertheless the credit for the victory must still remain with Grant.

Buell himself was to experience the difference in this respect—though he never realized it—between the faith Grant's men had in him and that which Buell was able to inspire in his own Army of the Ohio, in his very next battle, Perryville, which, with its sequel, closed his career of active command.

In wars between nations a strong sense of moral superiority—or the reverse—may set up a tide of feeling which the personality of a leader cannot greatly change. But in our Civil War the soldier material, with slight local differences, was virtually the same. The men of each side were, moreover, with equal sincerity convinced that their cause was "right." Hence it was left to each leader to mold his men as best he knew how.

Thus in the East, Lee and Jackson, with their insight into the soldier mind, more than overcame the disparity in numbers which was against them, so long as they were fighting against a McClellan, a Pope, a Burnside or a Hooker. In the West, Grant possessed this insight; so did Albert Sidney Johnston; that was why Shiloh was one of the hardest-fought battles of all time.

There is to be noted in this connection that the troops that broke and fled from the field at Shiloh, the newly joined regiments of Prentiss, Sherman, and Hurlbut, were precisely those that, owing to Halleck's side-tracking of Grant during the obscuration period, had not yet learned to respond to his confidence in them and to his faith in victory, the faith that is "the substance of things hoped for, the evidence of things not seen."

While the bitter criticism in the contemporary press, and later of carping critics both civilian and military, put Grant on the defensive regarding his conduct of the battle, and caused his friends and apologists Richardson, Coppée, and Badeau, and later himself (in 1885) to seek to justify all his actions before, during, and after the battle; and while this defense was undertaken in a tone far from being apologetic, there is no question that Shiloh afforded Grant the most important tactical lessons of his military career—lessons which by reason of his subsequent period of enforced inactivity he was, perhaps fortunately, given ample leisure to mark, learn, and inwardly digest.

The foremost of these lessons was that stability of character in the commander, and faith in himself and in his troops, while of primary importance in the winning of victories, are not alone sufficient with larger forces, as they so often are with forces of less size. With larger forces, there are required also knowledge and technique.

If Grant could have recorded for us, as Napoleon so conveniently did after Marengo,[6] his study of his own faults in the battle, and how to remedy them, it would have made one of the most fascinating books of all time. But he was still not sufficiently introspective to be conscious of his own mental processes. This fact is shown in his Memoirs.

The Battle of Shiloh must ever remain the apex of that classical and heroic struggle which Rudyard Kipling aptly dubbed "The Epic of the Anglo Saxon race," and no one can deny that it was magnificently fought on both sides by the commanders, as well as by the officers and men, who put into it all their might and knowledge; yet it was not war—at least not modern war, quite apart from the matter of weapons in use. No modern general-staff intelligence section could be forgiven for the total ignorance which existed in each army concerning the other.

As for the operations, no modern general would be forgiven for a failure to provide for a regular and systematic deployment of his command in the circumstances in which the army of Grant was placed at Shiloh, whether an attack were anticipated or not. Further, under the conditions, operations and supply sections between them should have organized the facilities for the systematic reinforcement of the Shiloh force by Buell's approaching troops

---

[6] Napoleon's reports of the Battle of Marengo enable the student to follow both his intensive study of that battle and the lessons he gleaned from it. His first report, forwarded to the Directory soon after the battle, represents the main facts, doctored to the best of his ability at the time, to conserve his own reputation. Two years later, as a result of his study of the battle, being then First Consul, he wrote a second report, changing his story to conform to his later ideas of how the battle should have been fought. This he sent to the Bureau of Archives, ordering his previous report destroyed. Two years later, after he had made himself emperor, he was still studying this battle and had evolved still further ideas on how it should have been fought. These ideas he incorporated in a third report which was duly sent to the archives, to be substituted for the previous report, which was in its turn ordered destroyed. The Bureau of Archives, however, merely filed all three reports, and a century later all three were published in the volume of "documents" pertaining to the Marengo campaign, edited by the Historical Section of the French General Staff.

whatever might happen. Grant appears to have had sufficient steamers for the simultaneous transportation of the troops of two divisions. Had these means of river transport been properly organized, there is no reason why he should not have had on the field of Shiloh before noon the divisions of both Nelson and Lew Wallace, as completely fresh battle reserves; and, in addition, two more divisions of Buell by mid-afternoon.

In the actual fighting the weak links were due to the lack of organization of liaison on the battle-field. Had Grant known before the battle what he learned from it, concerning all these matters, its story would have been very different.

One criticism, however, Grant cannot escape. Despite the fact that Buell exercised an independent command,[7] Grant was the senior and alone responsible for victory or defeat. By military regulations, as well as by custom, he should have taken command of Buell and his divisions and used them for the best interests of the Union cause. That he would have done so had Buell not shown every evidence of complying with his intentions—namely to attack on the morning of April 7—there is little doubt. Grant, however, was in a new position, that of exercising command over two armies, and doubtless also was impelled by motives of delicacy to a hesitancy to assume the command over another who, although now his junior in rank, was his equal in assignment, and who until a short time before had not only been his senior but a department commander.

The lessons which have to be learned by a commander of armies are exceedingly complex and it is not to be expected that they can be mastered in a day.

Halleck decided after Shiloh to join the armies of Buell and Grant on the Tennessee and assume command. He reached Pitts-

---

[7] Grant probably had not received Halleck's order placing Buell under his command in the event of a battle.

burg Landing on April 11, and the next day issued an order thanking Buell and Grant and their respective armies for "the bravery and endurance with which they sustained the general attacks of the enemy on the 6th, and for the heroic manner in which, on the 7th instant, they defeated and routed the entire rebel army."

The same order announced that Grant and Buell "will retain the immediate command of their respective armies in the field."

The day following, Halleck issued an order to Grant that "immediate and active measures must be taken to put your command in condition to resist another attack by the enemy."

This order would indicate that Halleck was not pleased with the condition of Grant's army as compared with Buell's. There was much more cordiality between Halleck and Buell than between Halleck and Grant, and the result naturally was that, with their more limited experience, they were disposed to blame Grant for many of the occurrences at Shiloh which, had they known more, they would have realized are inevitable when forces of forty thousand men on a side engage in a two days' battle.

Ten days later, Pope's Army of the Mississippi arrived and was encamped on the left of the combined army, at Hamburg, Tennessee. Halleck thereupon organized his forces, to be composed of the right wing (Grant), center (Buell), and left wing (Pope). Various routine orders and reports passed during the next ten days between Halleck and Grant. A week later the army was directed to begin its advance on Corinth, on April 29. For this movement, Halleck's Special Orders, No. 31, changed the organization slightly by renaming his three armies as three army corps.[8] In the advance of the twenty-ninth, in pursuance of Halleck's orders, it is interesting to note that, while Buell and Pope promptly rendered detailed reports of the movement, the

8 W. R. 11:138.

records contain no report whatever from Grant. Whether this is the reason for the change in organization, or whether Halleck felt that so exalted a person as he ought to have a "second in command," as Albert Sidney Johnston had had in the advance on Shiloh, there is no evidence to determine. At any rate, Thomas, on April 30, was assigned to command the right wing, while the divisions of McClernand and Lew Wallace, presumably for the reason that they both ranked Thomas, were detached from the right wing and constituted as the reserve, under command of McClernand. By this order [9] both the right wing and the reserve were to remain parts of the Army of the Tennessee, which Grant was still to command in addition to being Halleck's second in command. In an accompanying letter on the same date [10] Halleck requested Grant, in view of his new assignment, to move his head-quarters over nearer to Halleck's own. It is quite possible, in fact only natural, that Halleck, a master of theory but lacking practical experience with troops, felt that he needed in that capacity just such a man as Grant to assist him.

The new assignment proved awkward, for Grant evidently did not fit into Halleck's scheme. He never before had been second in command. Even in the Mexican War he was quartermaster and, while nominally a staff officer, in reality the commander of trains and other quartermaster detachments. Following his duty as quartermaster, he commanded a company; after that, his next military command was a regiment. He nowhere before in his experience had filled the rôle of general adviser, proposer of plans and general courtier, laughing at his chief's jokes, cheering the chief up when he was sad, and pointing out in a tactful way the reasons why the said chief should do this and should not do that, while at the same time not letting anybody suspect—especially

[9] S. O. 30; W. R. 11:144.
[10] W. R. 109:245.

not the chief—that he, the subordinate, was the power behind the throne. Beauregard had been eminently suited for such a rôle. The duty proved not only unwelcome to Grant but impossible for him. He was essentially a man of action and of decision. He acted very largely on his intuition or, if the term be preferred, his subconscious reasoning, which he could not explain to another or perhaps even justify.

On Halleck's part there was, of course, the dark cloud of his lie to Grant regarding the origin of the complaints made against him, after Donelson, to the War Department, which probably made it uncomfortable for him even to see Grant unnecessarily. It is perhaps a little too strong to say that Grant proved persona non grata to Halleck, but the two officers, with such wide differences in their careers in civil life, had totally different points of view.

It should not be overlooked, in analyzing the conditions, that Halleck was reputed to be and no doubt believed himself to be a strategist of high order. He had at his finger-tips all the formal rules of the geometrical strategy of the eighteenth century, from the use of "interior lines" to the "strategic penetration of a wing." Grant, fortunately for his country, had never blinded his vision with these rules, which as formulated were so inapplicable to the Civil War. Hence he could not even discuss with Halleck the strategical ideas which presented themselves to his chief's mind, for the two men did not use the same vocabulary.

Thus, as the campaign of Corinth wore on through its dull course, Grant inevitably became more and more of a figurehead, and, because of the delaying effect of sending orders to the right wing and reserve through Grant as Commander of the Army of the Tennessee, Halleck, on May 12, discontinued the practice, although Grant was not nominally relieved of his command.[11]

[11] W. R. 11:182.

The importance of this period in the evolution of Grant the strategist cannot be overestimated. Grant so intensely concentrated his whole attention on the duty facing him at the moment that he tended to lose all perspective about outside matters; and if we consider him as destined to command all the armies of the United States two years later, we can see how fortunate it was that he should have been given periods of relative inactivity for study and reflection, when he did not have his entire mind occupied each day—as it had been from the time he reached Cairo onward—with petty details appertaining to a purely local situation. That he found this period of inactivity on the outer plane unwelcome, and was on the point of quitting his post altogether shortly before it terminated, need neither surprise us nor change our opinion. Sherman in his Memoirs gives this pathetic picture of his visit to Grant's headquarters not long before Halleck received the order calling him to Washington:

A short time before leaving Corinth I rode from my camp to General Halleck's headquarters . . . where we sat and gossiped for some time, when he mentioned to me casually that General Grant was going away the next morning. I inquired the cause, and he said that he did not know, but that Grant had applied for a thirty days' leave, which had been given him. Of course we all knew that he was chafing under the slights of his anomalous position, and I determined to see him on my way back. . . . I found him seated on a camp-stool, with papers on a rude camp-table; he seemed to be employed in assorting letters, and tying them up with red tape into convenient bundles. After passing the usual compliments, I inquired if it were true that he was going away. He said, "Yes." I then inquired the reason, and he said. "Sherman, you know. You know that I am in the way here. I have stood it as long as I can, and can endure it no longer" . . . I then begged him to stay, illustrating his case by my own. . . .

I argued with him that, if he went away, events would go right along, and he would be left out; whereas, if he remained, some happy accident might restore him to favor and his true place. He certainly appreciated my friendly advice, and promised to wait awhile; at all events, not to go without seeing me again, or communicating with me. Very soon after this . . . I received a note from him, saying that he had reconsidered his intention, and would remain.[12]

On June 10, Halleck revoked his order organizing his army into right wing, center, and left wing, which had been made solely for the advance on Corinth,[13] and shortly after Grant applied for and obtained permission to remove his headquarters to Memphis. With an escort of cavalry, he reached there on June 23. This gave him his first experience in dealing with an out-and-out Confederate community, as up to this time he had been only in fortifications such as Fort Henry, Dover (Fort Donelson), Shiloh, and Corinth, where there was no civilian population. From his Memoirs, Grant appears to have found much food for thought in the tenacity of the convictions of the citizens of Memphis and their refusal to conceal their sympathies or to admit that the Southern cause was yet hopeless.

Grant's stay in Memphis was of three weeks' duration, after which he was recalled by Halleck to Corinth: informed that Halleck had been ordered to Washington; and that he, Grant, would be left in command of his former District of West Tennessee comprising the part of the State of Tennessee west of the Cumberland River and, of course, the State of Mississippi as far south as he might penetrate.

---

12 W. T. Sherman, "Memoirs," Vol. I, p. 282.
13 W. R. 11:288.

CHAPTER XIX

GRANT ENTERS A LARGER FIELD

> In war . . . the commander of an immense
> whole finds himself in a constant whirlpool of
> false and true information, of mistakes committed
> through fear, through negligence, through precip-
> itation, of contraventions of his authority, either
> from mistaken or correct motives, from ill will,
> true or false sense of duty, indolence or exhaus-
> tion, of accidents which no mortal could have
> foreseen.—CLAUSEWITZ.

TO understand the situation confronting Grant upon Halleck's departure from Corinth for Washington, we must
briefly review events of the preceding three months.

After the Battle of Shiloh, Beauregard had retired on Corinth,
where desperate attempts were made by the Confederates to
gather sufficient force from the trans-Mississippi States to check
the Union advance. In the meantime Farragut had succeeded in
capturing the forts at the mouth of the Mississippi and opening
the way for Butler's troops, unopposed, to occupy New Orleans.
As a movement from here northward could be easily prevented,
the Union occupation of this city, while a severe blow to the Confederacy—New Orleans being as it was at that time the largest
commercial city in the South and second in importance only to
New York in the whole United States—had the immediate effect
of releasing additional troops to reinforce Beauregard's army at
Corinth.

Beauregard was fully committed to an active defense of
Corinth and sought during Halleck's approach to find some open-

GRANT AT MEMPHIS
November, 1862

ing favorable for an attack. But Halleck's cautious measures and policy of constantly keeping his forces entrenched gave him no opportunity. Finally, when Halleck's forces had reached the environs of Corinth, Beauregard's courage failed him, even for conducting a defense of the town, although it was strongly fortified. His retreat without a battle was a bitter disappointment to President Davis, who, shortly after, replaced him in command by General Bragg.

It will be seen from this that Halleck's success thus far had not been so empty a one as it is made to appear by some critics. His measures after he reached Corinth are not so easily to be justified. Beauregard had gone southward to Holly Springs, Mississippi. Instead of following him Halleck became imbued with the idea that the important strategic point of the West had been gained and that all that remained was to hold it and extend the line eastward to embrace East Tennessee—at least as far as Chattanooga. He failed to recognize that the Confederate railways, while important for the Confederacy, were not available as lines of communication and supply for the Union army unless they were strongly guarded at every vulnerable point, since small cavalry detachments in their own country could so easily burn the bridges and tear up the tracks.

He determined upon the policy of leaving the Confederate main army south of Corinth to its own devices, and of detaching from his own forces Buell's army—which, before Shiloh, he had been so insistent should come West to reinforce his own—to march eastward on Chattanooga. Unfortunately for the result, Buell was further directed to repair the Memphis and Charleston Railroad and to keep it open as his line of supply. This proved difficult from the start, and eventually impossible.

Buell's departure gave Bragg his opportunity. As soon as he heard of it he started northward with the idea of regaining possession of Kentucky and Tennessee and also of drawing Buell away from eastern Tennessee. Bragg left Van Dorn in command of a part of his army, to oppose Halleck in Corinth.

Therefore when Grant was called to command in Corinth, upon Halleck's departure for Washington, he found himself with some nine divisions in occupation of a great stretch of hostile country, from Decatur, Alabama, on the east to Memphis on the west, with many posts in rear which had to be occupied, including Cairo, Columbus, and Fort Donelson. And since the low stage of water in the Tennessee River during the summer months prevented the use of river transportation for supplying his army, the railway from Columbus, Kentucky, to Corinth had to be maintained and therefore heavily guarded. Considering existing conditions, his forces at this time did not admit of undertaking any serious offensive operations. Besides, he had been simply left in charge for the time being, to carry on without any particular instructions.

In fact his situation here was almost a repetition of that when he first went to Cairo, though on a larger scale with regard to both forces and territory. Grant had now more divisions than at Cairo he had had brigades, and a much greater extent of territory to cover; and, in addition, he had the problem of maintaining a railroad line of communications.

In this larger field, developments in a way repeated those at Cairo. At the start, as in the first phase at Cairo, we find him making many detachments and occupying extensive lines. In the second phase, in which at Cairo he had two regiments detached from his command, he now lost two of his divisions, which had to be sent to reinforce Buell, and later a third division. In consequence of this reduction, Grant, again as he had done at Cairo, learned to distinguish the posts essential to be occupied from those which were not so; to study how to make the most of every unit under his command; to guard his broad front, on the defensive—than which there is no better training, particularly for a commander with an aggressive disposition.

In the course of the summer months Van Dorn's army at Holly Springs, Mississippi, had been considerably reinforced, and upon learning that Grant's forces had been depleted to reinforce Buell, Van Dorn sought an opportunity of wresting western Tennessee from the Union occupation. As Grant drew in his forces westward from Decatur toward Corinth, Van Dorn, with a detachment under General Price, seized Iuka, Mississippi, a few miles eastward from Corinth, which had been left guarded by a single regiment. Grant sought to retaliate with a "nutcracker" attack by means of large columns which should march simultaneously from the north and south, while he himself attempted, from a central point on the railroad, to coördinate the advance of the two columns. The plan failed wretchedly, for the reason that the methods of coördination were inappropriate to the larger forces in the more difficult theater, but the failure taught Grant another vital lesson—that methods successful with a regiment or a brigade are by no means necessarily so with a division or an army corps; also, that there is no more assurance that a major-general, simply because he is duly commissioned in that grade, will always do the right thing under stress than there is that a major will do it.

This Iuka affair occurred on September 19. On October 4, Van Dorn was bold enough to attack Grant's principal post at Corinth. Grant's organization of his forces at this time was: the Army of the Mississippi, under Rosecrans, at Corinth; two divisions, under Sherman, at Memphis; two divisions, under Ord, guarding the line of communications, with headquarters at Jackson, Tennessee, where Grant also had his headquarters.

Grant—although he knew of Van Dorn's coming attack—

reposing the same confidence in Rosecrans that he had in Sherman, did not go to Corinth to take personal charge of the defense of that post, but sent what reinforcements he could to Rosecrans and left him in command.

In the ensuing battle, Rosecrans conducted a brilliant defense and decisively defeated Van Dorn. The results gained, however, did not satisfy Grant, who had directed an immediate pursuit to reap the full fruits of victory. Rosecrans did pursue, but after too great a delay for the pursuit to be made effective.

The consequences of this and other disagreements were, unhappily, an estrangement between the two officers, of which there was no outward evidence at the time, since Rosecrans shortly after was ordered North to replace Buell in command of the Army of the Cumberland, but which resulted in Grant's substituting Thomas for Rosecrans, as commander of that army, a year later at Chattanooga.

Following the failure of the immediate pursuit, Grant did not feel strong enough, notwithstanding the success gained at Corinth, to begin at once offensive operations. But he began to plan for them, and, recognizing that the logical next step in the conquest of the South was the capture of Vicksburg, the last great Confederate stronghold on the Mississippi, he proposed to Halleck on October 26:

As situated now, with no more troops, I can do nothing but defend my positions, and do not feel at liberty to abandon any of them without first consulting you. I would suggest, however, the destruction of the railroads to all points of the compass from Corinth, by the removal of the rails to this place [Jackson, Tennessee] or Columbus, and the opening of the road from Humboldt [Tennessee] to Memphis. The Corinth forces I would move to Grand Junction [Tennessee], and add to them the Bolivar [Tennessee] forces except a small garrison there. With small re-enforcements at Memphis I think I would be able to move down the Mississippi Central road and cause the evacuation of Vicksburg and to be able to capture or destroy all the boats in the Yazoo River. I am ready, however, to do with all my might whatever you may direct, without criticism.[1]

Halleck replied to this on November 3:

I approve of your plan of advancing upon the enemy as soon as you are strong enough for that purpose. The Minnesota and Wisconsin regiments should join you very soon, and the Governor of Illinois has promised ten regiments this week. I have directed General Curtis to re-enforce Helena [Arkansas], and if they cannot operate on Little Rock [Arkansas] they can cross the river and threaten Grenada. I hope for an active campaign on the Mississippi this fall. A large force will ascend the river from New Orleans.[2]

Two days later, Halleck telegraphed, "Had not troops sent to re-enforce you better go to Memphis hereafter? I hope to give you 20,000 additional men in a few days."

On November 9, Grant informed Halleck: "Re-enforcements are arriving very slowly. If they do not come on more rapidly I will attack as I am. But one regiment has yet reached Memphis." [3]

Halleck replied to this the day following, giving Grant a new idea of his Mississippi problem:

Five regiments and one battery left Illinois for Memphis last week. Six or seven more will leave this week. Others will be sent from Ohio and Kentucky. Memphis will be made the depot of a joint military and naval expedition on Vicksburg.

Grant could not understand exactly what this meant and asked:

Am I to understand that I lie still here while an expedition is fitted out from Memphis, or do you want me to push as far south as possible? Am I to have Sherman move subject to my order, or is

1 W. R. 25:296.
2 W. R. 24:467.
3 W. R. 24:468.

he and his forces reserved for some special service? Will not more forces be sent here?

Halleck's answer to this gave Grant the command in full and left to him entire liberty of action: "You have command of all troops sent to your department, and have permission to fight the enemy where you please."

It is significant that all these despatches following Halleck's being called to Washington in command indicate that Halleck had personally the highest regard for Grant and showed full readiness to comply wherever possible with his requests and expressed wishes. This would seem to indicate that he had all the time had a very much higher opinion of Grant and respect for his judgment than he had ever admitted to Grant himself, or even allowed him to suspect. Halleck, being very much older than Grant, may have had the trait so common in older men, of regarding a man only a few years younger than himself as a mere youth and fit subject for fatherly correction and a certain amount of suppression as necessary in order not to spoil him.

There is, none the less, the possibility that Mr. Lincoln was back of these despatches giving Grant entire freedom of choice and full responsibility, inasmuch as Halleck is stated by Nicolay and Hay to have hesitated to settle questions himself and put everything up squarely to the President after Pope's failure at the second Battle of Bull Run. However, that Halleck, whether personally responsible for the above messages or not, entertained high respect for Grant's character is shown by his letter to Sherman, with whom he had been from the start upon far more intimate and cordial terms socially:

I am sorry to say that many of the generals commanding armies exhibit a very bad spirit. They seek rather to embarrass the Government and make reputations for themselves than to put down the rebellion. General Grant and a few others are most honorable exceptions.[4]

The "campaign of the Mississippi Central Railroad" was brought to a summary conclusion by the capture and destruction of Grant's principal advanced depot of supplies accumulated by his army at Holly Springs. At the same time the line of communications was interrupted at various other points and the means of transportation as a result were inadequate to supply his advanced forces. Grant at this time had to choose between cutting loose from his base and going forward, depending upon food supplies that could be picked up in the country itself, or turning back upon his base, Memphis. The thing he could not do was to remain stationary, since an army the size of his could not draw its supplies from the same locality for more than a few days. It had to move in order to exist.

Whether Grant at this time seriously contemplated going forward to Vicksburg, or whether his statement in the Memoirs to that effect is merely one of those possibilities which are always so clear after the event, it is hard to say. It is also a question whether his reserve ammunition also had been captured and destroyed at Holly Springs. That was one necessity which the hostile country could not supply, and if that were lost, then indeed Grant could only retreat.

It may be that he was influenced to retire by news that reached him about this time regarding the full import of the appearance of the new corps of McClernand on the Mississippi and its relation to the operations of himself and Sherman, which will be considered later.

In any event, as it stands, this campaign—the march from Corinth southward to Grenada, Mississippi, and back, unopposed as it was by the weaker forces of Pemberton, except for cavalry raids on Grant's rear and line of communications—must take its place in Grant's evolution as an important training period in which he had the experience of maneuvering a larger force in a larger theater.

Nor must the non-military reader make the mistake of assuming that the handling of forces so much larger in the field than Grant had hitherto been accustomed to, merely involves a little more work for the staff. In reality it is an altogether different task, requiring a practised hand and a sure technique. Grant had been given his first opportunity, from which in the circumstances and because of his discontent he may not have profited as well as he might had he studied more thoroughly the technique of Halleck's exercise of command in the advance on Corinth, instead of fretting over not being given personally any active function to perform. Nevertheless he could not help gaining his initial insight into some of the factors; and just as before his Fort Henry campaign he had been afforded the opportunity of learning to maneuver his troops in the delta between the Tennessee and Mississippi rivers, so now he could learn and have his staff learn the technique of a far more difficult problem, in kind as well as in degree—that of dealing with the larger forces which had to be employed to meet the ever increasing size of opposing Confederate armies and the increasing skill of Confederate leaders.

Whether one is disposed to believe that Grant's education as a higher commander was deliberately planned by some guiding intelligence or that it was purely accidental, it cannot be gainsaid that had some able schoolmaster in the military art, such as the elder Moltke, arranged the course of training for an apt pupil, he could not have done so in any more simple, orderly, and progressive manner than that which the natural course of events provided for Grant during the Civil War.

CHAPTER XX

VICKSBURG

To hold out against all, one must have faith in
one's own intuition and judgment. This often appears at the moment mere obstinacy, but in reality
it is the force of mind and of character that we
call firmness.—CLAUSEWITZ.

IN November, General Grant's first intention had been to have Sherman advance from Memphis southward against Grenada, Mississippi, in conjunction with his own movement from La Grange, Tennessee. When, however, he received Halleck's telegram saying that Memphis would be made the base for joint naval and land operations against Vicksburg, he determined to send Sherman back to Memphis in order to operate in two columns: one on the river against the front of Vicksburg; the other overland against Jackson, Mississippi, which would cut off Vicksburg from the rear. This plan resulted in Sherman's eventual first assault at Chickasaw Bluffs.

At the time of the adoption of this plan Pemberton's army was in front of Grant's on the Yallabusha River and it was agreed between Grant and Sherman that if this army moved to oppose Sherman, Grant would promptly advance against Vicksburg from the rear; while if Pemberton should remain in front of Grant, Sherman would take advantage of the absence of Pemberton to assault Vicksburg from the front. The unfortunate capture of Grant's base at Holly Springs, resulting in the two weeks' interruption of his lines of communication with Sherman, left Grant without the means of informing Sherman of the disaster to his supply reserves and his consequent inability to carry out his part of the plan agreed upon. This breakdown of the communications between them, on the other hand, gave Sherman the idea that Grant had abandoned his communications and determined to march on the rear against Vicksburg, thereby rendering it more imperative than ever for Sherman to attack on the Vicksburg front, in order to keep Pemberton from throwing his whole forces against the advance of Grant. The result was the severe repulse of Sherman's attack at Chickasaw Bluffs on December 29.

General McClernand now appeared on the scene, wielding the authority of the President "to command the Mississippi River expedition" under Grant's direction. The situation was awkward. Neither Grant, Sherman, nor Porter, the naval commander, had confidence in the ability or judgment of McClernand, whom they considered merely a clever politician who sought some easy military success as a stepping-stone to the Presidency. Sherman made the best of it and guided McClernand by his advice, which was the more easy because McClernand had learned at Shiloh to rely on Sherman's more mature judgment.

When Grant reached Memphis and determined to throw his whole force against Vicksburg by way of the river, abandoning the overland attempt, he soon saw the necessity of going, himself, to take command, as he was the only officer in his department senior to McClernand.

In the meantime McClernand, guided by Sherman, had moved against the "Post of Arkansas," a short distance up the Arkansas River, occupied by a force of five thousand Confederates which finally capitulated on January 11. It is amusing to note that Grant in a despatch to the War Department severely blamed McClernand for this move which later, when he discovered that Sherman had advised and virtually directed the operation, he fully justified as an essential preliminary to subsequent operations against Vicksburg.

On January 30, Grant joined the army on the west bank of the Mississippi before Vicksburg and assumed personal command, to the complete dissatisfaction of McClernand, who desired that Grant should deal with the other army corps commanders only through him, under the plea that the President had placed him in command, "under Grant's direction." Grant, however, fully sustained by decisions from Washington on this point, kept McClernand in his place as simply one of the corps commanders, until the friction between them, and McClernand's antagonizing of the commanders and officers of other corps belonging to the Army of the Tennessee, rendered impossible his further retention.

McClernand's career is a perfect illustration of failure through almost a single fault of policy. He appears to have been a man of force, of a certain degree of offensive spirit, of presence of mind, of initiative, and of constantly growing appreciation of military operations. But his success was tainted from the start by his failure to be personally loyal to his immediate superior and this was the direct cause of the wreck of his military career, from which even the best wishes and personal endeavors of the President in his behalf could not save him.[1] The same may be said of Rosecrans,[2] while Grant and Sherman are examples of officers who fit themselves into the picture by perfect loyalty throughout to their immediate superiors, regardless of the personal shortcomings of these superiors or seeming injustice on their part.

Upon his arrival Grant found McClernand engaged in the construction of a canal for the purpose of passing a gunboat and transport fleet to a point in the river below Vicksburg, to enable

[1] W. R. 109:431, 437.
[2] See letters, W. R. 25:283, 287.

the flanking movement to be made against that fortress from the south side. Various plans were proposed for penetrating through the bayous and swamps north of Vicksburg to the high bluffs in rear giving access to the mainland. Grant tried them all without success. Just when he conceived his ultimate plan and how long he was in working it out, is not clear. Richardson quotes a lady connected with the sanitary commission who spent much time at the front during these months:

On board the head-quarters boat at Milliken's Bend, a lively gathering of officers and ladies had assembled. Cards and music were the order of the evening. Grant sat in the ladies' cabin, leaning upon a table covered with innumerable maps and routes to Vicksburg, wholly absorbed in contemplation of the great work before him. He paid no attention to what was going on around, neither did any one dare to interrupt him. For hours he sat thus, until the loved and lamented McPherson stepped up to him with a glass of liquor in his hand, and said, "General, this won't do; you are injuring yourself; join with us in a few toasts, and throw this burden off your mind." Looking up and smiling, he replied: "Mac, you know your whisky won't help me to think; give me a dozen of the best cigars you can find, and, if the ladies will excuse me for smoking, I think by the time I have finished them I shall have this job pretty nearly planned." Thus he sat; and when the company retired we left him there, still smoking and thinking.[3]

Grant's plan was to move his army overland to the river opposite Grand Gulf; then for Porter's fleet to run the gantlet of the Vicksburg batteries, protected as best they could be by cotton-bales, to a point on the river near Grand Gulf where ended the Confederate line of river fortifications. The movement of his troops southward west of the river was begun the latter part of March and was screened by Grierson's cavalry raid from the north in rear of Vicksburg to Banks's command on the south, and fur-

[3] Richardson 295.

ther by a feint undertaken by Sherman to hold Pemberton's main body north of Vicksburg. The march of Grant's troops was made in the worst season of the year, when the roads were soft and spongy from recent floods. Wagon-trains were often mired in the bad roads and had to be pulled out by hand, as did also the guns.

Grant first planned to cross to the east bank in the vicinity of Grand Gulf, hoping that the gunboats, having successfully run the Vicksburg batteries, could as readily reduce the Grand Gulf batteries as they had those of Fort Henry. However, this proved impossible and he then determined to move farther to the south, run by the Grand Gulf batteries with his fleet, and cross the river below. The crossing was eventually effected at Bruinsburg, Mississippi, on April 30, and on May 1 his leading troops met the enemy at Thompson's Hills, where after a sharp skirmish the Confederates were defeated and retreated across Bayou Pierre, burning the bridges behind them.

Grant promptly occupied Port Gibson and crossed the bayou by a ponton bridge. On May 3 he entered Grand Gulf, which the Confederates had evacuated, and made it a temporary base from which to renew his supplies and ammunition. Here he waited the arrival of Sherman, who, having accomplished his mission of holding Pemberton's main forces on the north, joined him at Grand Gulf on May 6.

Leaving Sherman at Grand Gulf, Grant moved out on the seventh with the XIIIth Corps and XVIIth Corps under, respectively, McClernand and McPherson, to give the impression of an advance against Vicksburg by the Black River route, of which, to mislead the enemy, all the ferries were closely guarded.

On the ninth the XVIIth Corps pushed on to Utica; on the tenth the XIIIth Corps marched to Five Mile Creek; on the eleventh the XVth Corps (Sherman) passed the XIIIth and camped at Auburn, followed by the XIIIth, which took the road to Hall's

Ferry on the Black River. On the same day Grant informed the War Department that they would not hear from him for five days, and abandoned his line of communications and base at Grand Gulf.

On the twelfth the XIIIth Corps drove the enemy's pickets at Hall's Ferry while the XVth Corps engaged the enemy on Fourteen Mile Creek near Auburn and after some sharp fighting pushed him back to Raymond. The XVIIth Corps advanced on Raymond by another road and met the enemy southwest of that village, defeating him and driving him toward Jackson. The XVIIth Corps then marched north on Clinton, which it reached May 13. The XVIIth Corps and XVth Corps then marched against Jackson, while the XIIIth covered their rear at Raymond. The advance against Jackson on the fourteenth was continued in a heavy rain-storm and along miry roads, the troops marching nearly fourteen miles.

The Confederate general Joseph E. Johnston, now in command of troops in the western theater, had placed his reserve at Jackson, whence, in view of Grant's successful moves, he had directed Pemberton to abandon Vicksburg and join him. Grant's two corps promptly attacked and drove Johnston's forces eastward out of the city. May 15 was spent by part of Grant's forces in the destruction of the military supplies, the shops, railroads, and bridges in and about Jackson; and, learning that Pemberton was marching westward toward Jackson, Grant ordered the XVIIth Corps back to Clinton, while the XIIIth Corps was ordered northward from Raymond and reached Bolton on the fifteenth, capturing the Confederate garrison at that point.

On the sixteenth the XIIIth Corps moved toward Edwards Station, accompanied on the north by the XVIIth, which encountered the Confederates and gained the victory of Champion's Hill, driving the Confederates across the Black River. The same day the XVth Corps, abandoning Jackson, reached Bolton and, by noon on the seventeenth, Bridgeport on the Black River. Pemberton now sought to defend the line of the Black River. Grant succeeded, however, in effecting a crossing on May 17 and the next day, five days after breaking his communications with Grand Gulf, he was before Vicksburg with his three corps, with his communications reopened by the possession of Walnut Hills on the Yazoo River, and the Confederates completely cut off from the hope of escape, in a campaign as brief and as brilliant as is to be found in military annals.

The ensuing siege followed the usual course of such operations and ended in the surrender of Pemberton's army, thirty thousand men.

A few days after Vicksburg President Lincoln wrote his congratulations to Grant, with delightful simplicity and straightforwardness:

MY DEAR GENERAL: I do not remember that you and I ever met personally. I write this now as a grateful acknowledgment for the almost inestimable service you have done the country. I wish to say a word further. When you first reached the vicinity of Vicksburg, I thought you should do what you finally did—march the troops across the neck, run the batteries with the transports, and thus go below; and I never had any faith, except a general hope that you knew better than I, that the Yazoo Pass expedition and the like could succeed. When you got below and took Port Gibson, Grand Gulf, and vicinity, I thought you should go down the river and join General Banks; and when you turned northward, east of the Big Black, I feared it was a mistake. I now wish to make the personal acknowledgment that you were right and I was wrong.[4]

Grant's reply to this is equally simple and pleasing:

SIR: The bearer of this, Lieut. Col. J. A. Rawlins, is the assistant adjutant-general of the Army of the Tennessee. Colonel Rawlins

4 W. R. 109:406.

has been connected with this army and with me in every engagement from the battle of Belmont to the surrender of Vicksburg. Colonel Rawlins goes to Washington now by my order as bearer of the reports of the campaign just ended, and rolls and paroles of prisoners captured. Any information desired of any matter connected with this department, from his official position he can give better probably than any other officer in it. I would be pleased if you could give Colonel Rawlins an interview, and I know in asking this you will feel relieved when I tell you he has not a favor to ask for himself or any other living being. Even in my position it is a great luxury to meet a gentleman who has no ax to grind, and I can appreciate that it is infinitely more so in yours.[5]

A further proof, if one were needed, of Lincoln's genuine esteem for Grant, following Vicksburg, was that while he had been made Major-General of Volunteers after Donelson, Lincoln now gave him the highest military office in his power to bestow, under existing law—that of Major-General in the Regular Army.

[5] W. R. 109:416.

CHAPTER XXI

CHATTANOOGA

*The essential quality of the general is firmness,
and that is a gift from heaven.—*NAPOLEON.

AFTER Vicksburg Grant had sent Sherman again to Jackson,
the capital of the State, to drive Johnston's army, the only
Confederate force left in this theater of war (after the fall of Port
Hudson, Louisiana, to Banks on July 9) entirely out of Mississippi. The mission was speedily accomplished.

Grant hoped now to undertake an expedition to capture
Mobile. But the President, who with his broader vision was
troubled by the French occupation of Mexico and possible com-
plications therefrom, felt as greater the need of occupying the line
of the Rio Grande. Hence the many reinforcements, which had
been sent from every possible quarter to aid Grant in his Vicksburg undertaking, were recalled and detached, some to Banks,
in command at New Orleans, others to aid Rosecrans, hard pressed
in eastern Tennessee.

Thus Grant was again left inactive for a period, but this time
under no cloud and with nothing to disturb the complete calmness
of his reflections on the future conduct of the war. Yet physically
he was ever active and unresting. Not content to remain idly in
Vicksburg, nor yet willing to deprive Sherman of whatever credit
might be gained from driving Johnston wholly away from the
region, by accompanying him on that mission, we find him on
August 23 at Memphis, and later in the same month going to New
Orleans for a conference with Banks.

Here Banks tendered Grant a review of his old XIIIth Corps, the nucleus of which had been the regiments under Grant at Belmont, Donelson, Shiloh, and Vicksburg—a happy reunion for both Grant and his men, also, though neither knew it, to be their last meeting in wartime.

Here there occurred another physical mishap, similar to the one preceding Shiloh. Butler, out of compliment to Grant's fine horsemanship, had assigned him a spirited horse, which, after the review, became unmanageable, dashed against a carriage, and "fell heavily with his whole weight on Grant's leg and hip." [1] This stopped Grant's wanderings for a time, as the general was confined to his bed for two weeks and was still compelled to use crutches on October 9, when at Vicksburg he was notified by Halleck: "It is the wish of the Secretary of War that as soon as General Grant is able to take the field, he will come to Cairo and report by telegraph." [2]

There is always hope for a country in which public opinion has come to recognize that while a real general is often seen in a well-tailored uniform and sitting on a horse, neither the horse nor the uniform matters very much, provided that certain qualities and characteristics of the general are in order.

Thus in Prussia in 1864, when the elder Moltke had reached the ordinary retirement age of sixty-four and applied to retire because old and no longer physically vigorous, Bismarck encouraged him to remain, with the result that the Austro-Prussian War was won by Moltke aged sixty-six, and the Franco-German War by the same general, aged seventy. Conversely, in a later instance, in 1905, when von Schlieffen was thrown from his horse and incapacitated for further riding, the German Kaiser would not permit him to remain at the head of the German Army, and

[1] Richardson 349.
[2] W. R. 53:55, 375.

thereby lost for Germany one of her chances of winning the World War.

In the South African War, after the young and lusty generals had all failed, public opinion in England demanded the sending out of the seventy-year-old but proven Lord Roberts, whose arrival speedily righted matters for the British.

In 1861 the "man on horseback" idea of a general had been so strong in America that the experienced and skilful Scott was, because aged and infirm, side-tracked in favor of McDowell and the youthful McClellan. The results were the Union reverses at Bull Run and the Peninsula. There is scarcely the shadow of a doubt that could Lincoln have had Scott carried along on a litter borne on the shoulders of relays of able-bodied men—as Louis XV did Marshal Saxe at the Battle of Fontenoy—the Army of the Potomac under Scott would have captured Richmond with the same promptitude that he had captured Mexico City.

By the fall of 1863, however, the heavy casualties and numerous disappointments and reverses had brought home the lesson to the people that neither glittering uniforms nor prancing steeds were vital factors, and it was realized that a Grant on crutches— or even on a litter—was more certain to produce the desired victory if placed in command than any other generals, however physically fit the others.

Grant left at once, and at Cairo was further directed to proceed to Indianapolis, where took place his initial meeting with that first of the great American Secretaries of War to whom the country owes so much—Stanton. Secretary Stanton and Grant went together from Indianapolis to Louisville, whence Stanton returned to Washington and Grant to the danger-point of his new and enlarged command.

The Secretary of War had offered Grant his choice of two orders. Both organized the three departments of the Ohio, the

Cumberland, and the Tennessee into a single command under the title of "Military Division of the Mississippi," with Grant in command. One order left Rosecrans in command of the Department and Army of the Cumberland; the other substituted Thomas, who at the time was a corps commander in Rosecrans's army. In view of his distrust of Rosecrans, based on the latter's insubordination at Corinth the year preceding, Grant chose the second of the orders submitted. He at once assumed command of his new territorial division at Louisville, on October 18, directed Rosecrans to turn over the command of his army to Thomas; and the latter to hold Chattanooga at all hazards.

Grant reached Chattanooga on October 23, and found the troops there on half rations owing to the army's being cut off, by the Confederate occupation of Lookout Mountain, from direct river and railroad communication with its base, Nashville. However, plans for driving the Confederates back were already in being, and the troops to execute them available, for the prompt opening of what became known as the new "cracker line."

Grant's rôle at Chattanooga, at least in the initial phase, was like that of Marshal Oyama at the Battle of Liao-Yang. There his chief of staff presented to Oyama the plan for an elaborate and dangerous turning movement. The marshal inquired if the plan had received due consideration by the general staff and been approved, and was informed that it had. "Very well," said he, "I approve it. Give the necessary orders for carrying it out." The next day Oyama's chief of staff again came to him and said the general staff had decided that the plan was too dangerous to be carried out. Marshal Oyama replied: "You told me the plan was the best you could devise. I assume the danger and the responsibility for carrying it out. The general staff has nothing more to do with it except to give the necessary orders."

This incident, which even if not true is one of those that ought to be, perfectly typifies Grant's rôle at Chattanooga. The situation that had overtaken the Army of the Cumberland under Rosecrans, who had allowed himself to be shut up and nearly surrounded in the city of Chattanooga, had been mainly produced by a lack of confidence which had infected not only the garrison of Nashville but the reinforcements consisting of two army corps under Hooker, brought from the East to assist it. Every one knew perfectly what ought to be done, but there was lacking "the will to power." That this was so is no reflection on the able and experienced officers present.

Plans were submitted by Thomas and the members of his capable staff and were promptly approved by Grant and ordered carried into execution. The plans called for the attack by Hooker with his two corps on the shoulder of Lookout Mountain, to re-open a proper line of supply for the army and enable it to secure full rations instead of the half rations it had been receiving. Hooker's sentiments when he received the order for his corps to open up the proposed new "cracker line" are described by Howard:

I never saw Hooker apparently so apprehensive of disaster. He said: "Why, Howard, Longstreet is up on that Lookout range with at least 10,000 fighting men. We will be obliged to make a flank march along the side and base of the mountain. I shall have scarcely so many men, and must take care of my trains. It is a very hazardous operation, and almost certain to procure us a defeat." [3]

Howard adds, giving his own opinion:

A few days later, after a nearer survey of the country around Chattanooga, I saw that Hooker had good reasons for his surmises; for Lookout was like the Grecian Acropolis at Athens—a place for the most extended observations, quite unassailable if defended by a few men well posted, and fine grounds for well-chosen sorties.

[3] "Autobiography of Oliver Otis Howard," Vol. I, p. 458.

Had the same orders for so difficult a movement been received by Hooker from a Rosecrans or a Thomas, there would have been presented innumerable reasons why they could not be carried out; but coming from Grant, they had to be. It is all a matter of war psychology.

Some writers argue indefinitely over the question of who originated this or that plan, and appear to think that the proposer of a military plan has the same right to the credit for its successful execution, provided he can prove his authorship, that the inventor of a new mechanical device has to royalties upon his invention when it has been patented. Thus we find Buell, in later years, exceedingly disgruntled because Halleck fails to concede that he first suggested the Fort Henry plan. Many critics seem to think that because Grant adopted the plans of others, and appeared to have no originality at Chattanooga, he was a mere figurehead, and that the credit should be distributed among the original authors of the various parts of the plans adopted.

Any such view, whether held by a civilian or an unprofessionally minded officer, is so at variance with the conceptions of a professional military man that it is hard for one side to see the point of view of the other. All military plans are exceedingly simple in their nature. Roughly speaking, on the offensive one has the choice of attacking on the right flank, the left flank, or the center, or maneuvering against the rear. Probably every one in the army and every one cognizant of conditions has a plan which he believes to be the right one, yet of thousands who have these plans there may not be a man capable of executing any one of them successfully.

Generally speaking, there is a question whether of two plans under consideration it is better to adopt the one which, while promising less decisive results in the end, is more sure of attainment, or that which involves greater risk, but also, if successful, assures more important results. The choice between these plans must depend upon the general himself, his confidence in his men, his knowledge of their confidence in him, and, on some occasions, still more upon the political conditions in rear: whether it is better for his Government to play safe and be content with lesser results or whether the political situation is so desperate as to demand the staking of everything upon a single throw of the dice to gain "all or nothing," as Lee did in the Seven Days' Battles at Richmond in 1862, and as the French considered doing in May, 1918. Only the general, and he only if he be a real general, can weigh all these factors in their proper proportions, since he alone has complete knowledge at the time of the case in all its ramifications.

It will be seen from this that while originality is something that every one admires, a general who refused to carry out any plan unless he could prove that he himself had originated it would be the man least deserving of trust as a military commander.

In Grant's case the question of copyright on ideas and military plans troubled him not at all during the war itself. He liked to have his staff, and friends such as Sherman, sit in his tent and talk over the campaigns and possible plans and their relative merits and risks, taking no part in the discussion himself and apparently paying no heed to it; though whether it was from the proposals thus presented to his calm and unruffled mind that he formulated his plans, or whether they merely provided him with the external words in which to embody his own visions gathered from the invisible, each must judge for himself. In any case, when the decision was forthcoming, it came out, more and more as the war progressed, with a torrent of energy, and was speedily clothed by Grant himself in concise and forceful orders.

Friends of Rawlins have claimed for him an integral part in Grant's success, going so far as to say, as Badeau did in his conversation with Henry Adams, that Grant and Rawlins together formed a sort of dual personality which could function only when united as a whole. Undoubtedly Rawlins, a simple country lawyer possessing no whit of military knowledge at the outbreak of the war, was a happy choice on the part of Grant for his adjutant-general. But the assertion that he was essential to Grant's success can best be answered by asking whether McClellan would have been any more successful if he could have had Rawlins as adjutant-general or Grant any less so if he had had Seth Williams. The considered answer must be "no" in both cases. Nor is it any less to be expected of a general able, as Grant was, to train an army and infuse into it the spirit of victory, that he should also be able to train a man with the proper stuff in him to act efficiently as his adjutant-general or chief of staff.

The operations about Chattanooga and Grant's relations to them possess their chief interest for us on the psychological side.

Hooker's success in his undertaking—in spite of his initial misgivings regarding it—was complete and the "hunger period" of the Army of the Cumberland was at an end, which betterment naturally was accompanied by an enormous rise in morale in the Northern army.

President Davis came at this time on a visit to Bragg and was probably personally responsible for the detaching of Longstreet's corps for a movement on Knoxville, Tennessee (which was being held by Burnside's corps), in the hope of driving Burnside out of the upper Tennessee Valley and reopening the direct railway connection between eastern Tennessee and Richmond. Grant sought to take advantage of Longstreet's departure by ordering Thomas to attack the lines of Bragg in his front. Thomas, however, did not feel strong enough to do this and Grant had to wait for the arrival of his own former Army of the Tennessee, now under Sherman, which even before Grant's arrival had been

GRANT ON LOOKOUT MOUNTAIN
(Brady Photograph)

ordered to march overland from Memphis by way of Decatur, Alabama, on Chattanooga.

On Monday, November 23, Grant ordered Thomas to make a reconnaissance in force on Orchard Knob, the center of the Confederate lines in front of Nashville. This being successful, Grant directed the positions to be held.

Grant's detractors, ever seeking to point out errors and misconceptions on his part, have taken the circumstance that the movement against Orchard Knob was ordered merely as a reconnaissance as an indication of Grant's "blundering short-sightedness," and the result as merely another example of the good luck which attended his dispositions. A more correct judgment would appear to be that Grant underestimated the offensive spirit still remaining in the Army of the Cumberland after its unfortunate defeat at Chickamauga and the long-drawn-out siege at Chattanooga following. Nevertheless no military man will disagree with him in the circumstances for playing very safe and preferring to eat his own words, if necessary, by converting an ordered reconnaissance into a successful attack rather than risk a possible lowering of morale in Thomas's army by ordering an attack in the first place and having afterward to convert it into a reconnaissance.

The day following, Grant directed an advance against the Confederate lines on Lookout Mountain. Once more the troops did more than their orders called for by also capturing the summit. There is little question that Grant the psychologist was fully alive to the delight and pride of the soldier in accomplishing more than is called for by the orders, and as little question that Grant cared nothing at all at the time for the effect on his own reputation, however sensitive he may have become subsequently to criticisms on this and other points.

Bragg had now completely evacuated the Lookout Mountain area, but remained south and east of Chattanooga on Missionary

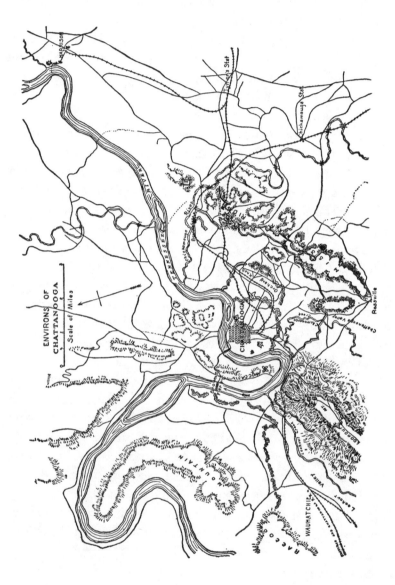

Ridge, which was strongly entrenched and held both along its crest and at its base. The Army of the Tennessee having arrived, Grant directed Sherman to attack the Confederate right, advancing from the north on Missionary Ridge, while Thomas, in front of the Confederate lines, was to make a demonstration against the front of Missionary Ridge to hold the Confederates in position and prevent their massing against the flanking move of Sherman.

This movement was the cause of somewhat acrimonious rivalry between the armies of the Tennessee and Cumberland, the men of the Cumberland believing that they were intended by Grant's plan to play the rôle of "holding the bag," the scene being laid so that Sherman with Grant's former army should gather in the honors of defeating or capturing Bragg's forces. If such had been Grant's plan, it was completely circumvented by difficulties of terrain which prevented Sherman from effectively carrying out his mission on his front, while in Thomas's army what had been intended as merely a demonstration resulted in a victorious charge undertaken by the troops themselves which sufficed to complete the utter dislodgment and rout of Bragg's troops, leaving Sherman's army very much in a position of "holding the bag."

Grant is represented by Fullerton and others as having been very indignant when he saw the charge being made by the troops of Thomas up the slopes of Missionary Ridge, and demanding to know who gave those orders and intimating that "somebody will suffer for this"—all of which was taken to indicate that Grant was jealous of Thomas's men gaining the credit he had planned should be reaped by his own Army of the Tennessee. But it should not be lost to view that Grant's words, even if correctly quoted, are more open to the interpretation that he was fearful lest so difficult an assault, undertaken prematurely as it was before

Sherman had gained a position from which he could coöperate, should result in failure. There was all the more danger of this as Grant had left the center virtually denuded of reserves to meet such a disaster as might follow the failure of an assault.

Such questions can never be answered by mere reasoning or by circumstantial evidence.

As has before been remarked, Grant was never conscious of his own mental processes, but his powers can be summed up under two heads: (1) The ability to make military decisions, though how he made them he never knew, he simply made them; (2) the indomitable force necessary to carry them into execution, again he scarcely knew or could explain afterward how.

Grant's subsequent attempts in "The Century" articles and in his Memoirs to explain why or how he did things are frequently little in accord with the facts where these are known, as, for example (see Appendix), his decision, suddenly made the night before, to attack the enemy at Belmont; and at Donelson the equally sudden decision made—as asserted in the Memoirs—upon finding one of the Confederate prisoners with three days' rations in his knapsack, which indicated a plan by the Confederates to escape, whereas actually the Confederates had no thought at that time of escaping and none of their men had either knapsacks or three days' rations, as is overwhelmingly established by contemporaneous evidence. It is not too much to say that the historical student of to-day, while he may never be able with the source material now available to reconstruct Grant's actual mental processes, can much more nearly approximate what they must have been, from his actual deeds and orders, than could Grant himself in later years with his blurring memories of events—Grant who had no memory at all of the operations of his own mind, since he had not been conscious of them at the time.

Having disposed of Bragg's army for the immediate present,

Grant now gave his attention to raising the siege of Burnside's forces at Knoxville by Longstreet, and Sherman with the Army of the Tennessee was ordered on that mission. Longstreet, seeing the inevitable, promptly retreated eastward and, on December 7, Grant was able to announce the relief of Knoxville.

The closing in of winter prevented further offensive operations in this theater and while Grant's army settled down in its winter quarters Grant himself was afforded another quiescent period in which to prepare himself for the coming final struggle. He seems to have been as little moved, either intellectually or emotionally, by what was now said in his favor as he had previously been by the obloquy formerly heaped upon him for his alleged short-comings at Shiloh and in the first failures in the Vicksburg campaign. Only one thing mattered to him: what his immediate superior thought about it. None the less he was probably as pleased in a minor way to receive the resolution of Congress— the first to be carried in its December session in 1863—that "a medal be struck for General Grant, and a vote of thanks be given to him and the officers of his army," as he had been to receive the innumerable boxes of cigars sent him after Donelson when the newspapers had informed the public that he was a constant smoker.

CHAPTER XXII

GRANT AS STRATEGIST

In order to seize the material forces, operations
are directed against those points at which those
resources are chiefly concentrated.—CLAUSEWITZ.

IT is not the author's purpose, in this book, merely to add one
more to the many volumes describing the campaigns and
battles of the Civil War. These have been thoroughly and com-
petently dealt with more than once. In connection with Grant,
the earlier battles possess a special interest for us, showing as they
do under critical examination his growth from tactical immaturity
to mastery. These are precisely the ones which have not been
covered by general writers, because of their lesser importance.

So far as actual combat was concerned, Shiloh may be said to
have completed Grant's tactical education, in the sense that tactics
is the art of employing troops for the winning of battles. He had
yet to learn the art of strategy—the art of combining battles for
the purposes of the war. In this larger field he was unaided, and
perhaps fortunately, by any bookish knowledge of the subject.
Had he been so primed he might have ended as another Halleck,
his mind perplexed, bemuddled by the hopeless task of reconciling
the principles of eighteenth-century geometric strategy with the
conditions of the Civil War.

It is interesting to know that Sherman, in several letters to
Grant, himself mentions his doubts of Grant's ability to deal with
strategic problems, owing to his lack of book knowledge on the

subject, but later on confesses that the man's splendid common sense seems to have supplied the deficiency.

In this book we shall merely outline the later events in which Grant participated, to bring out the growth of his strategic conceptions and to show how he applied them toward ending the war. The extreme gravity of his problem is perhaps not always realized. Seldom in history has a revolt of equal magnitude failed to establish the independence of the rebellious group. It is in precisely a war of this nature, where one side seeks to extinguish the complete autonomy of the other, that the passion for freedom inherent in the human breast creates the strongest feeling on the part of the "rebels." At the same time—and this is also the case in no inconsiderable measure in the Civil War—the cause of the group in revolt cannot but excite the sympathy of many individuals belonging to the opposing group.

Further, the theater was a difficult one and favored the South in many ways—though by no means in all, as the course of the Shiloh campaign showed.

Considering the purpose for which the North was fighting the war—namely, to restore the Union and bring back, as was so often said, "the erring Sister States into the fold"—the mere winning of a battle or the securing of any particular locality would by no means end the matter—a fact too little recognized by public opinion in the earlier years of the war. What was most dreaded by many professional military men on both sides was that the conflict might degenerate eventually into a guerrilla warfare.

That this sort of warfare would have been evolved had the striking victories of Grant's summer campaign of 1864 been gained by the North in 1862, or even in 1863, there is little doubt. There was needed something deeper than the mere driving back of the Confederate armies. To convince the Confederate population that peace was desirable, it was necessary to change their

mental attitude in two respects. Their conviction that they could
never again feel themselves at one with the United States had to
be overcome; and their faith in the possibility—even the barest
possibility—of the ultimate success of their cause had to be
dissipated.

There was the further consideration in Grant's mind that the
accomplishment of these war aims on the part of the North
should not be attained through unnecessarily harsh measures which
might postpone or even defeat the restoration of the Union by
adding to the existing bitterness in the Southern population. In
this regard we must thank the leaders on both sides, particularly
Generals Polk, Grant, Price, and Frémont for their joint refusal,
no matter what else happened, to permit the war to degenerate
into the savagery of guerrilla fighting.

The strategic map used by Grant and marked by him with red
and blue lines is perhaps the most interesting document which
has come down to us from the Civil War.[1] The upper red line
shows the line occupied by the North at the outset of the war;
the lower red lines indicate the territory still in possession of the
Confederacy in the winter of 1863–64. The blue lines indicate
the lines of advance under consideration by Grant; the blue circles
are the strategic objectives or communication centers vital for
the preservation of the Confederate economic structure. This map
brings out clearly the enormous advantage accruing to the North
from possession of the entire Mississippi and the resulting first
great cleavage of the Confederacy.

On January 15, Grant outlined to Halleck his plans for the
coming campaign in the Military Division of the Mississippi:

Sherman has gone down the Mississippi to collect at Vicksburg
all the force that can be spared for a separate movement from the

---

[1] See attached map.

Mississippi. . . . The Red River and all the streams west of the Mississippi are now too low for navigation. I shall direct Sherman, therefore, to move out to Meridian [Mississippi] with his spare force (the cavalry going from Corinth) and destroy the roads east and south of these so effectually that the enemy will not attempt to rebuild them during the rebellion. He will then return, unless the opportunity of going into Mobile [Alabama] with the force he has appears perfectly plain. Owing to the large number of veterans furloughed I will not be able to do more at Chattanooga than to threaten an advance and try to detain the force now in Thomas' front. . . .

I look upon the next line for me to secure to be that from Chattanooga to Mobile, Montgomery [Alabama] and Atlanta [Georgia], being the important intermediate points. To do this large supplies must be secured on the Tennessee River, so as to be independent of the railroads from here to the Tennessee for a considerable length of time. Mobile would be a second base. The destruction which Sherman will do to the roads around Meridian will be of material importance to us in preventing the enemy from drawing supplies from Mississippi and in clearing that section of all large bodies of rebel troops. I do not look upon any points except Mobile, in the south, and the Tennessee, in the north, as presenting practicable starting-points from which to operate against Atlanta and Montgomery. They are objectionable as starting-points to be all under one command, from the fact that the time it will take to communicate from one to the other will be so great; but Sherman or McPherson, one of whom would be intrusted with the distant command, are officers of such experience and reliability that all objection on this score except that of enabling the two armies to act as a unit, would be removed. . . .

Heretofore, I have abstained from suggesting what might be done in other commands than my own in coöperation with it, or even to think much over the matter; but as you have kindly asked me in your letter of January 8, only just received, for an interchange of views on our present situation, I will write you again in a day or two, going outside of my own operations.[2]

2 W. R. 58:100.

On January 19, 1864, Grant presented his first proposal to
Halleck, in response to Halleck's invitation:

I would respectfully suggest whether an abandonment of all
previously attempted lines to Richmond is not advisable, and in lieu
of these one be taken farther south.   I would suggest Raleigh, N. C.,
as the objective point and Suffolk [Virginia] as the starting point.
Raleigh once secured, I would make New Berne [North Carolina]
the base of supplies until Wilmington [North Carolina] is secured.
    A moving force of 60,000 men would probably be required to
start on such an expedition.   This force would not have to be increased unless Lee should withdraw from his present position.   In
that case the necessity for so large a force on the Potomac would not
exist.   A force moving from Suffolk would destroy first of all the
roads about Weldon [North Carolina], or even as far north as Hicksford [Virginia].   From Weldon to Raleigh they would scarcely meet
with serious opposition.   Once there, the most interior line of railway still left to the enemy, in fact the only one they would then
have, would be so threatened as to force him to use a large portion
of his army in guarding it.   This would virtually force an evacuation
of Virginia and indirectly of East Tennessee.   It would throw our
armies into new fields, where they could partially live upon the country and would reduce the stores of the enemy.   It would cause thousands of the North Carolina troops to desert and return to their
homes.   It would give us possession of many negroes who are now
indirectly aiding the rebellion.   It would draw the enemy from
campaigns of their own choosing, and for which they are prepared,
to new lines of operations never expected to become necessary.   It
would effectually blockade Wilmington, the port now of more value
to the enemy than all the balance of their sea-coast.   It would enable
operations to commence at once by removing the war to a more
southern climate, instead of months of inactivity in winter quarters.
Other advantages might be cited which would be likely to grow out
of this plan, but these are enough.   From your better opportunities
of studying the country and the armies that would be involved in
this plan, you will be better able to judge of the practicability of
it than I possibly can.   I have written this in accordance with what

I understand to be an invitation from you to express my views about military operations, and not to insist that any plan of mine should be carried out. Whatever course is agreed upon, I shall always believe is at least intended for the best, and until fully tested will hope to have it prove so.[3]

While the disastrous effect on the Confederate economic structure of the occupation of Raleigh is unquestionable, this plan shows that Grant did not fully realize at the time he proposed it the difficulties in the way of its execution. An army to advance from Suffolk on Raleigh would have to be prepared to meet forces which could be readily thrown against it, from both Lee's Army of Virginia and Johnston's Army of Tennessee. Unless a strong army were maintained, in both northern Virginia and Tennessee, there was every prospect that 1864 would witness fresh Confederate incursions, with the resultant loss of the advantages gained by the North in the campaigns of 1863.

Whether Grant later recognized the weakness of his own plan or laid it aside in accord with President Lincoln's views, communicated to him either directly or through Halleck, is not established. But it may well be that when faced with the actual responsibility for the decision he saw its difficulties of execution, which were not so clear to him when he was merely advising another where the next cleavage into the Confederate economic system could best be made.

In Grant's proposed plans for his own campaign we find expressed the idea of a second great cleavage of the Confederacy to follow that of the Mississippi. It is interesting to consider its probable economic results, but as it was never carried out, these results must remain problematic. However, there is little question that in Grant's mind it was aimed at the economic system of the Confederacy and its lines of intercommunication, as Grant saw

[3] W. R. 58:41; 60:394.

these at the time. The first part of his letter of January 15 is taken up with a discussion of Longstreet's flanking position in East Tennessee, the strategic advantages of which to the Confederates Grant fully realized and did his best to counteract by driving Longstreet out.

Sherman's part in the campaign outlined by Grant to Halleck was well carried out. On February 6, he reached Jackson, Mississippi,[4] and on February 14, Meridian. From there Sherman destroyed the railroads "south below Quitman, east to Cuba Station, 20 miles north to Lauderdale Springs, and west all the way back to Jackson." His destructive work in other directions also was satisfactory to Grant and served the purpose intended.

On March 10, 1864, occurred the momentous turning-point in the conduct of military affairs on the side of the North. Grant, having been appointed and confirmed as lieutenant-general, was assigned by the President to the command of the Armies of the United States, while Halleck on the same date was relieved from duty as General-in-Chief, and two days later was assigned to duty in Washington, as Chief of Staff of the Army.

At this point it is well to stop and to consider the economic structure of the Confederacy.

Within the limits of the Confederate territory remaining east of the Mississippi lay the heart of the South, still pulsating with vigor. Grant's problem was to find where lay the more vulnerable points, the attack on which would yield the greatest results with the least expenditure of time and effort on the part of the North.

This problem had three closely related aspects: (1) The vulnerable points and their location (primarily the centers of production of food, clothing, and all other articles necessary for the existence of the population and the maintenance of the armies);

[4] W. R. 57:173.

(2) the military geography of the country, with its means of communication open for the passage and supply of advancing armies (roads, railroads, rivers, and the like); (3) the opposition to be expected from Confederate armies, considering their organization, numbers, and the means necessary for their existence with respect to territorial recruitment, supply, and lines of communication.

In the absence of available records for many of the eleven Confederate States, the whole subject of the strength of the Confederate man-power is a difficult one and can only be approximated by calculation and conjecture.

By the census of 1860 the military population (from eighteen to forty-five years of age) of the eleven seceding States, taken as twenty per cent of the total white population, was 1,042,000, to which should be added 200,000 for boys attaining military age between 1861 and 1865. In addition the border States Kentucky and Missouri supplied 19,000 to the Southern Armies, not including Price's Missouri militia.

In considering the statistical data concerning man-power it is instructive to take the States by groups, as they were successively cut off and isolated, to get a true picture, since though the war in the detached groups still continued in a more or less guerrilla stage, it had no influence on the main result. (See table on page 314.)

Actual man-power in 1864 cannot, however, be determined from Census data alone; allowance must be made for losses.

The Confederate "killed and died of wounds" for the war numbered 73,000. The total number of deaths from disease and other causes has been estimated as 200,000 [5] but, at the same ratio as in the North of killed and died of wounds to deaths from other causes, would be 240,000, which is probably more nearly correct, giving a total loss for the war of 313,000. By January,

[5] S. H. S. P. 7:288.

CONFEDERATE AND SLAVE-SOLDING STATES

		Estimated military population	*Furnished to Confederacy*
Eastern States finally isolated by Sherman's march	Va. (less W. Va.)	160,000 [1]	153,875 [4]
	N. C.	126,000	121,038 [5]
	S. C.	58,000	60,127 [6]
		344,000	
States cut off by Sherman's march	Ga.	118,000	106,157 [6]
	Ala.	105,000	90,857 [6]
	Miss.	75,000	66,982 [6]
	Fla.	15,000	15,000 [7]
		657,000	
Trans-Mississippi States cut off by taking of Vicksburg, 1863	La.	71,000	55,820 [8]
	Ark.	65,000	
	Tex.	84,000	
		877,000	
States cut off by Donelson-Shiloh campaign	Tenn.	165,000 [2]	
	Ky.	184,000 [3]	
	Mo.	212,000 [3]	
Total man-power of slave States (except Maryland)		1,438,000	

[1] West Virginia supplied the Union armies 31,000 men. Total military population of the original State of Virginia, 200,000, of which 191,000 participated on the two sides; these figures are probably an under-statement.
[2] Tennessee joined the Confederacy, but furnished 31,000 men to Union Army. Fox 554.
[3] Kentucky and Missouri did not join the Confederacy, but furnished 19,000 Confederate troops, besides numerous militia troops for local operations.
[4] W. R. 129 : 102.
[5] S. H. S. P. 14 : 508.
[6] W. R. 129 : 102.
[7] S. H. S. P. 27 : 118.
[8] S. H. S. P. 20 : 152.

1864, the loss had probably reached 250,000. The total wounded have been estimated at 200,000, and the prisoners at the same number. However, many of the wounded recovered and resumed their places in the ranks and, until Grant came into chief command, the prisoners were exchanged, so that the permanent losses from "wounded and missing" probably did not exceed 100,000 for the first three years of war.

The Southern percentage of the military population available for conscription differed from the Northern for two reasons: (1) The greater part of the country was agricultural and hence there did not have to be many exemptions for "essential industries"; (2) the large slave population sufficed in the main for the agricultural labor needs.

Thus the actual number of total "enrolled" probably exceeded the usual percentage of the military population in several of the Eastern States, especially after the military age limits had been lowered to sixteen years from eighteen and raised from forty-five years to fifty-five.

However, the main cause of loss was from desertion. From the more closely settled parts of the Eastern and Central States the desertion rate was low, but among conscripts from sparsely settled regions, and in the Western and border States, where deep enthusiasm for the war was lacking, it was very high. Particularly was this the case with men from the regions on the border and in the West coming under the ever extending control of the Union armies.

As the problem presented itself to Grant, who had been a witness to the cooling of the ardor of the rebellious populations in Tennessee and Mississippi, as the Union armies had advanced into those States, if the war fervor of Georgia could be similarly cooled, the effective armies of the Confederacy would have a remaining military population of not exceeding 250,000 to draw on, since whatever the war leaders in Richmond might hope, the men of Georgia, Alabama, and Mississippi could not fail to see that the Confederacy was a lost cause and that the victorious consummation of the Northern effort to preserve the Union was only a question of time.

Just what estimate Grant made of the Confederate man-power is not known, but it is clear that his calculations proved to him that if the Northern man-power were judiciously employed he would have a superiority of two to one, which was none too much to permit what the situation demanded—the undertaking of two simultaneous but widely separated major offensives.

The Confederate problem of war finance was most difficult. The Southern States had three chief means of getting funds: (1) Export of cotton and tobacco; (2) foreign loans; (3) domestic loans.

The first of these was crippled by the blockade, and increasingly so with the successive occupation of the Southern ports. The value of the cotton crop during the war years was estimated at considerably more than a half-billion dollars, a large sum for those days. Nor up to 1864 had the cotton-growing areas yet been materially disturbed by the ravages of military operations. Foreign loans had been possible at the outset, but as the Union armies continued to regain more and more territory in the West the indecisive victories of Lee in the East did not suffice to sustain this source of credit. The possibilities in the way of domestic loans were soon exhausted; the chief assets of the South being farm-lands and slaves, neither of which could readily be turned into cash in wartime.

As these sources of financial stability began to wane, the chief considerations for the Northern leaders became the continued checking of the export of Confederate cotton and tobacco, and keeping the Confederates from winning a victory which might lead to foreign recognition and hence reopen the possibility of securing foreign loans. The consequences of having to resort to the issuing of worthless scrip in lieu of currency, and of having to impress needed supplies from unwilling owners, were bound to be a speedy and final drying up of the remaining sources of supply.

From Vicksburg onward, Grant had had daily borne in on him some phase of the Confederate financial problems; hence when it fell to him to make strategic plans he needed no assistance in correctly estimating this factor.

Prior to the Civil War cotton and tobacco had been found so much more profitable than other crops that the main efforts of the planters had been directed to the production of these. The South furnished a far greater proportion of the world's cotton supply than it does to-day, and British cotton factories were almost wholly dependent upon the Southern States for their raw materials. It was on this fact that Mr. Davis and his advisers relied largely in their hopes for the support and assistance of the British Government in the war. Two thirds of the cotton produced east of the Mississippi River was raised in Mississippi and Alabama, while two thirds of the remainder was raised in Georgia; only one eighth of the whole being raised in North and South Carolina. Thus to gain quick control of the bulk of the cotton crop or at least deprive the Confederacy of the power to export this valuable source of income, it was only necessary to occupy Mobile and the line of Chattanooga-Atlanta-Savannah, which line will be found indicated in blue upon Grant's map.

The South, it is true, raised other farm products for home consumption; but only in the northernmost parts of the slave States, namely northwestern Virginia, Tennessee, and Kentucky, could wheat be grown to advantage. Before the war this was obtained for a large part of the South from the Northwest, brought down by the easy and economical trade routes afforded by the Missis-

sippi, Tennessee, and Cumberland rivers, and thence distributed
by railroads to the interior.

In 1864 the State of Georgia had become the principal reliance
of the Confederacy for its food supply as regards cereals, while
Florida had become the last reserve for the supply of meat. The
Carolinas were barely self-sustaining, and while Virginia was,
normally, an exporter of foodstuffs, her supplies had been so depleted by the requirements of the various armies, and the arable
land so overrun by those armies, that the State was no longer even
self-supporting and afforded no surplus for Lee's army. Northern
Alabama was reported in the spring of 1864 as almost destitute
of subsistence, for the reason that the Northern raids had so
interfered with the cultivation of the land, while the Confederate
cavalry, stationed in the vicinity for the protection of the country,
had been an extra drain on its resources.

About Mobile and in southern Alabama conditions were better.
But this fact was probably due to the accumulation there of commissary supplies to meet the possibility of having to undergo a
siege.

The central portion of Mississippi and other parts not directly
under Union control had had their surplus so heavily drawn on
by 1864 that the State barely afforded provisions for its own population, and it became in consequence increasingly difficult for the
Southern forces to secure supplies there, although the southern
counties were still an important source of meat supply and the
lower western counties produced sugar and molasses. All
through 1864 large numbers of beeves were obtained from the
trans-Mississippi States by swimming them across the river at
points unguarded by the Union army or fleet.

It will thus be seen that the food supply of the Confederacy by
the beginning of 1864 had become a most serious question,
Georgia being the principal reliance for cereals, Florida for meat,

with the somewhat problematical additions to be expected from
ships running the blockade and from the trans-Mississippi. For
securing what was to be had from Georgia, Florida, Alabama,
Mississippi, and the trans-Mississippi States, Virginia and the
other Eastern States were of course dependent upon the remaining, far from adequate, primitive railroad lines of the period.

Metal resources also had been developed, but these had by
no means been exploited prior to the Civil War to any considerable extent, except in the northernmost regions of Virginia,
Kentucky, and Tennessee, most of which, particularly those in
western Virginia (now West Virginia), Kentucky, and western
Tennessee, early came into the control of the Northern armies.
Under the low tariff of the period, steel, iron, and other manufactured goods had been imported from England more cheaply
than they could be produced, particularly in the South. Naturally,
with the blockade the South found it difficult, increasingly so as
the war progressed, to supply its metal requirements, and the
Confederate Ordnance Department displayed extraordinary resourcefulness and powers of organization in creating and developing factories and arsenals for the production of arms and ammunition, as shown by their locations given in the table on page 320.

It will be seen in the campaigns of 1864 and 1865, that each
one of the production centers named in this table was made an
objective by Grant.

While the South was at the time the world's center for the
production of raw cotton, yet it had at the outbreak of the war
almost no textile factories, every plantation having its own looms,
operated by negroes, for the making of rude home-spun cloth.
This was why the Confederate troops were so poorly clothed.

With respect to woolen goods, the South was even worse off,
both for raw materials and for manufacturing facilities. Some
wool was obtained from the sheep-raising country west of the

LOCATION OF IMPORTANT CONFEDERATE RESOURCES

	Va.	N. C.	S. C.	Ga.	Ala.
Arsenals and depots, at some of which small arms, ammunition and equipage were manufactured	Richmond	Fayetteville, Asheville	Charleston, Columbia	Augusta, Savannah, Athens, Macon, Atlanta, Columbus	Selma, Montgomery, Tallahassee
Powder mills.........	....	Raleigh (State plant)	Pendleton, Walhalla	Augusta (Main source)	....
Chemicals, sulphuric acid, etc...........	....	Charlotte	....	....	....
Niter, for making saltpeter [1]	....	Greensboro	Columbia, Charleston (niter beds)	Savannah, Augusta (niter beds)	Mobile, Selma (niter beds)
Charcoal (from cottonwood trees)	....	....	Savannah River	....	....
Sulphur [2]...........	....	....	....	....	....
Lead [3]...............	Wytheville	....	....	....	....
Heavy artillery.......	Richmond	....	....	....	Selma
Field artillery, made and repaired	Richmond	....	....	Augusta, Rome	....
Small arms..........	Richmond	Fayetteville	....	....	....
Caps and primers.....	Richmond	....	....	Atlanta	....
Accoutrements.......	....	....	....	Largely at Macon	....
Artillery ammunition.	Richmond	....	....	....	....
Laboratory at which copper, lead, and zinc were smelted [4]	Petersburg	....	....	....	....
Foundries and rolling-mills	Richmond	....	....	Atlanta, Macon	Selma
Important machine-shops	Lynchburg, later moved to Danville	....	....	Atlanta, later moved to Columbus	....
New fields of iron-production	....	....	....	....	Bibb and Shelby counties

[1] Much niter was obtained through the blockade. Nitrous earth was dug from under old houses, barns, cellars, etc. Greensboro was the center of this kind of production. The niter beds were started in 1861. They had nearly matured in 1864. The end of the war prevented their profitable use.

[2] A sufficient supply of sulphur (several hundred tons) was secured early in the war at New Orleans, where it had been collected for sugar-refining.

[3] A great deal of good lead was secured by picking over the battle-fields.

[4] The principal source of copper seems to have been, prior to 1864, the Ducktown mines in east Tennessee. Some ore seems also to have been obtained from Jonesboro in the same region. When this section fell under Federal influence, the Confederates were driven to ravish of their copper the turpentine and whisky stills, found quite generally in certain sections.

Mississippi—even in 1864 small quantities of it were still smuggled across—but as the war went on, the shortage of woolen cloth became so great that woolen overcoats and blankets were no longer to be had even for Lee's army. This made anything in the way of winter campaigns almost impossible for the South and was a handicap on the initiative of Southern leaders greater than is sometimes realized.

The railroads of the South naturally followed the lines of the greatest production of the valuable crops, cotton and tobacco. These lines led chiefly from the important production centers to the nearest distribution point—usually on the coast. The connection of these interior-to-coast lines with one another and with the North had been, before the war, of minor use and importance, and had been the last to develop. It had not been foreseen that it was precisely those roads connecting Richmond-Chattanooga-Memphis in the Northern Confederate territory and Richmond-Atlanta-Vicksburg in the central area that would now become most vital lines for the prosecution of the war; as in the North the railway lines from New York and Washington west to Chicago, Cincinnati, and St. Louis similarly became.

During the war the railway net of the South had rapidly deteriorated because of the difficulty of maintenance, the inadequate supply of rolling stock, and the impossibility of replacing that which was destroyed or worn out. As long as the Southern armies were moving in a theater of war which afforded for them temporarily adequate food supplies, the railroads could meet their other needs. But after the Virginia food supplies had been exhausted, which was the case by 1864, and Lee's army pinned down to one locality, the transportation requirements became greater than the tiny cars, poor engines, and badly laid track of those days could meet. Naturally, the railway system broke down under the strain.

The Railroad Construction Department did indeed, in 1865, attempt the replacement of cars; but engines could not be made within the Confederacy, nor was there any possibility of manufacturing new rails to replace those destroyed by Sherman and others. The only railroad construction during the war was that rendered necessary by strict military requirements; usually this was limited to the repair of sections of the road destroyed by Union raids. For the repairs or laying of new branch lines it was necessary to take up the track on branch lines of lesser importance, as the only possible method of securing rails.

From the foregoing study of Confederate resources, it will be seen that the State of Virginia, while constituting one center of vulnerability of primary importance as to munitions and wealth, was by 1864 of less importance to the Confederacy in the matter of food, from which aspect Georgia, part of North Carolina, and Alabama had become the de facto important regions since the destruction of the great wheat areas of northern Virginia, incident to the campaigns of the preceding years. Thus the mere driving of Lee's army southward out of Virginia, instead of weakening the Confederacy from the point of view of food, would really strengthen it, as the Confederate armies would then be nearer their food sources, within closer supporting distance of one another, while the disproportion in forces, so greatly in favor of the North, would largely be overcome by the difficulty met by the Northern armies in maintaining long lines of communication through hostile territory. Thus it was more than desirable—in fact, a necessity— for Grant to hold Lee in Virginia while at the same time occupying the most important food and industrial areas in the Central States still left to the Confederacy.

From the point of view of munitions, arsenals and factories for the manufacture of arms and ammunition had been constructed: for the Eastern armies, around Richmond; and for the

GRANT AND HIS GENERALS

From original painting by Balling

(See pages 324 and 378)

Western troops, at Atlanta, Georgia, and Selma, Alabama; and the occupation of Georgia not only would in itself result in the capture and destruction of the principal sources of ordnance supply for the West, but would render it impossible for the ordnance requirements of Lee's army to be met in case it should be compelled to fall back from Virginia. In a sense the Confederacy at this time may be likened to a turtle, of which Virginia was the protruding head. Merely to drive Lee out of Virginia would only cause the turtle to withdraw into its shell, where it would be less vulnerable than before.

The problem as it presented itself to Grant, on his taking command of all the armies, was both an offensive and defensive one. He must naturally defend his own territory of the North, and at the same time retain possession of Southern territory already under Union military control; but also he must proceed to attack in an aggressive and efficient manner what was left of the Confederacy. It was really both a land and sea problem, as the Northern command of the sea made possible the transporting of armies to any accessible points desired on the Southern coast.

Although the offensive phase of the undertaking was the one by which Grant's success was bound to be measured by public opinion, its defensive phase was one which could not be neglected. The Confederate generals by this time had become experts and were ready to take advantage of the least opportunity that might present itself for an invasion of the North. Quite aside from the aspect of Northern home politics, which forbade the taking of any risks in this direction, there was the added reason that if Lee could show himself still able to undertake an invasion of Northern territory in the fourth year of the war, as he had done in the second and third years, there was danger that the ultimate reestablishment of the Union might be jeopardized through the recognition of the Confederacy by foreign European powers.

Then, too, 1864 was the year of the Presidential election, and

if the armies of the Union were to fail to protect Northern territory during this year, there was but little hope for the election
of a President on a platform of carrying on the war. The peace-
at-any-price advocates in the North who were in favor of giving
the South the political independence it desired, if only the war
could be stopped, grew more powerful with every evidence of
Confederate strength, and no such evidence could be stronger in
its effect than an invasion of Maryland, Pennsylvania, or Kentucky.

In such circumstances, even though seaboard lines of operation
might offer more important and more easily obtainable results,
they could be followed only if the North were able to gather the
necessary military strength, both to protect her own soil and to
collect over and above that the large armies necessary for the
coastal operations. For this reason, Grant was compelled to
accept it as the basic principle of his strategy that his strongest
effort must be directly to the front against the land side of the
territory left to the Confederacy. The existence of the Georgia
Central Railroad made a penetration of Georgia from the north
more easily feasible than any other line between Virginia and the
Mississippi.

Only in two cases did Grant plan large operations by sea: one
the attack by Banks on Mobile, having the prospect of an advance
on Atlanta in connection with Sherman's operation on that city
from the side of Chattanooga; and the other, the sending of
Butler's corps to coöperate with Meade's army by effecting a landing at City Point, on the south side of the James. It is true that
other coastal expeditions were made later with a view to completing the destruction of any possible outlets left to the Confederacy
for foreign commerce, yet at the start Grant limited those quite
properly to expeditions supplementary to the advance of the two
main armies.

CHAPTER XXIII

GRANT'S FINAL CAMPAIGN

> But as soon as difficulties arise, and that must
> always happen when great results are at stake,
> then the machine, the army itself, begins to offer
> a sort of passive resistance, and to overcome this
> the commander must have great force of will.
> —CLAUSEWITZ.

TO secure that preponderance of man-power so essential for his bold designs, Grant's first efforts after assuming command of the armies were directed toward gathering into the front line of the armies every man who could be spared from the rear areas. The generals commanding departments, at New York City, Cincinnati, St. Louis, and St. Paul, and even the commander of the defenses of Washington, were ordered to forward all surplus troops, particularly infantry, to the front.[1]

There was a certain reluctance on the part of some of the commanders to meet this demand, the more difficult to overcome since it had in the end to be left to their judgment how many men could be spared; and that judgment was inevitably circumscribed by their respective local points of view, rather than broadened by ideas of the requirements of the whole nation. Rosecrans, in St. Louis, did not wish to part with any of his forces, and put forward various excuses, such as hostile secret societies, barely covered up insurrections, as reasons for requiring every man he had.[2] This particular failing Grant had the less patience with since he him-

[1] W. R. 60:733, 770, 826, 882, 879, 913, 925, 1008; W. R. 62:740.
[2] Eventually he was replaced by Dodge, who at once released 15,000 troops from that department to reinforce Thomas at Nashville.

self never had objected to parting with an officer or a unit at any time if in the opinion of his superior the public service demanded it.

The next element in Grant's strategical efforts was to secure coördination and coöperation between the several forces employed and at the same time the direction of every ounce of Northern military strength against the hostile Confederate forces. This is made clear in nearly all of his orders.

To Meade:

So far as practicable, all the armies are to move together and toward one common center.[3]

To Butler:

In the spring campaign . . . it is proposed to have coöperative action of all the armies in the field, as far as the object can be accomplished.[4]

To Sigel:

In the spring campaign it is desirable to bring into the field all the troops possible. From the extended line you have to guard no troops can be taken from you except to act directly from your line toward the enemy. In this way you must occupy the attention of a large force, and thereby hold them from re-enforcing elsewhere.[5]

To Sherman:

It is my design, if the enemy keep quiet and allow me to take the initiative in the spring campaign, to work all parts of the army together and somewhat toward a common center.[6]

To Banks:

Lose no time in making a demonstration to be followed by an attack upon Mobile. . . . It is intended that your movements shall be coöperative with movements elsewhere, and you cannot now start too soon.

I would much rather the Red River expedition had never been begun than that you should be detained one day after the first of May in commencing your movement east of the Mississippi. . . . No matter what you may have in contemplation, commence your concentration, to be followed without delay by your advance on Mobile.[7]

In his final report in 1865 Grant summed up as follows his efforts to secure coördination in the movements of all the armies:

From an early period of the rebellion I had been impressed with the idea that active and continuous operations of all the troops that could be brought into the field, regardless of season and weather, were necessary to a speedy termination of the war. The resources of the enemy and his numerical strength were far inferior to ours; but as an offset to this, we had a vast territory with a population hostile to the Government, to garrison, and long lines of river and railroad communications to protect, to enable us to supply the operating armies.

The armies in the East and West acted independently and without concert, like a balky team, no two ever pulling together, enabling the enemy to use to great advantage his interior lines of communication for transporting troops east to west, re-enforcing the army most vigorously pressed, and to furlough large numbers, during seasons of inactivity on our part, to go to their homes and do the work of producing for the support of their armies. It was a question of whether our numerical strength and resources were not more than balanced by these disadvantages and the enemy's superior position.

From the first, I was firm in the conviction that no peace could be had that would be stable and conducive to the happiness of the people, both North and South, until the military power of the rebellion was entirely broken. I therefore determined, first, to use the greatest number of troops practicable against the armed force of the enemy, preventing him from using the same force at different seasons against first one and then another of our armies, and the possibility of repose for refitting and producing necessary supplies for carrying on resistance; second, to hammer continuously against the armed force of the enemy and his resources, until by mere attrition, if in no other way, there should be nothing left to him but an equal submission with the loyal section of our common country to the constitution and laws of the land. These views have been kept constantly in mind, and orders given and campaigns made to carry them out.[8]

In the above passage, it is not clear whether Grant meant to imply that he thought he was introducing a new idea into the conduct of the war, or merely more effective management: in other words, whether the "balky team" simile was aimed at the failure of the driver—the President—to direct or the balking mules—the generals—to respond to his direction. As a matter of fact, Lincoln's endeavors along this line, which doubtless Grant did not know of, had been constant throughout; and had he had in command of the Northern line of departments in 1861 a Grant, a Sherman, and a Sheridan to carry out his orders, instead of a McClellan, a Frémont, and a Buell, there would have been a rather different outcome of the earlier campaigns.

Even in the final campaign some of the army "teams" were quite as balky under Grant as they had been before his period of general command: Banks, Butler, Sigel, Hunter, and some of the Western commanders were far from proving able to profit from his ideas of coördination, excellent as these were.

There is further to be pointed out with regard to Grant's plans of campaign that the main and almost the exclusive pressure was to be directed against the major part of what was left to the Confederacy east of the Mississippi. Except for protective measures in Missouri and the holding of a central post in Arkansas to prevent fresh outbreaks from gaining material impetus, the trans-

[8] July 22, 1865, W. R. 67:12.

Mississippi States were to be left for later attention. The sound logic of this solution cannot be disputed.

In this central theater the two main Confederate armies were correctly placed to cover the two areas of greatest value for the maintenance of the forces in the field. But it must be remarked that not soon enough, if at all, did President Davis come to a realization of the preponderating importance of the Georgia area over that of Virginia for the attainment of his ultimate objective—the existence of the Confederacy.

The location of the Southern armies facing Chattanooga and Washington, in view of the defensive requirements which Grant could never afford to neglect, naturally influenced the direction of his own offensive policy. Of necessity, these armies had to be contained, if not forced back; and, to avoid duplication of effort, it was easier to combine the offensive against the Confederate resources with a tactical offensive against their two main masses, commanded respectively by Lee and Johnston. It is clear, however, that Grant's first thought was for the strategic offensive against the economic resources, and that the tactical offensives against the Confederate covering armies were merely the immediate means toward the main strategic accomplishment. That Grant recognized that the situation which called for two co-equal major offensives at the same time was most unusual, and provided the Confederates, with their shorter interior lines of reinforcement, with an opportunity, is shown by his letter to Sherman of April 19:

What I now want more particularly to say is, that if the two main attacks, yours and the one from here [Virginia], should promise great success, the enemy may, in a fit of desperation, abandon one part of their line of defense and throw their whole strength upon a single army, believing that a defeat with one victory to sustain them is better than a defeat all along their line; and hoping, too, at the same time, that the army meeting with no resistance will rest perfectly satisfied with their laurels, having penetrated to a given point south, thereby enabling them to throw their force, first, upon one and then on the other. . . . My directions, then, would be, if the enemy in your front show signs of joining Lee, follow him up to the full extent of your ability. I will prevent the concentration of Lee upon your front if it is in the power of this army to do it. . . .[9]

All of which is but the logical carrying out of the basic idea of coördination.

Let us now consider in detail the plans for the final campaign, which was so successfully to end the war. In the Virginia theater the main attack was to be directed against Lee's army and combined with three secondary attacks. The largest and most important of these subsidiary movements was to be conducted along the south side of the James by Butler; the second to be pushed south, east from Beverly, but was later changed so that the movement was made in a southwestern direction along the Shenandoah Valley; the third to be southeast from Charleston, West Virginia. It will be seen that these lines of operation were convergent in direction; and, excepting that of Butler, they converted into offensive-use forces necessary to cover Northern territory.

The main attack was to be made by Major-General Meade's Army of the Potomac, at that time in the vicinity of Culpeper Court-House. In his directive for Meade's army, Grant assigned Meade his objective as "Lee's Army," using the expression, "Wherever Lee goes, there you will go also." [10]

It is significant that these same words were used by President Lincoln in a message to Hooker in the spring of 1863. Whether Grant got the expression from Lincoln or both men reached the same sound conclusion regarding the correct strategy for the war independently is an interesting question.

[9] W. R. 59:409.
[10] W. R. 60:827.

The direction of Grant's main attack with his Eastern army has been criticized as faulty, on the ground of the time, effort, and losses spent in moving from the Rapidan to the James, instead of going there directly by sea. The critics entirely overlook the difference between the conditions when McClellan moved his army from Washington to Fortress Monroe in 1862 and those in the spring of 1864 at the time Grant was placed in command. In 1862 the Confederate army was ill-organized as to transportation, of inferior attacking power, and commanded by the defensively minded and at that time inexperienced general Joseph E. Johnston. In 1864 the same army, commanded by the able and quick-witted Lee, made such a course one of madness. General Grant expressed this thought in his instructions to Butler, already quoted in part: "The necessity for covering Washington with the Army of the Potomac and of covering your [Butler's] department with your army makes it impossible to unite these forces at the beginning of any move." [11]

One of Grant's objects was to unite his armies in this immediate theater, but in a manner which should render it certain that in case Lee's army were again to attempt an invasion of the North, in 1864, the army of Meade would be close enough to follow and destroy it. There was the added consideration in Grant's mind that the overland route provided the only means of attacking Lee's army outside the fortifications which, in the three years of war, had been built completely to surround the city of Richmond. As has been seen, Grant never welcomed the prospect of siege operations if any operations of open warfare were presented as an alternative.

Looking back on the campaign of 1864 in Virginia, it is difficult to suggest any solution which would have brought the same results any more quickly or at less cost. Not only was the

[11] W. R. 60:794.

"attrition" on Lee's army such as to put an end to any further idea on his part of serious offensive operations northward, but at the same time the theater of war in northern Virginia was so broken up through the destruction of crops and railroads as to render impossible in any event the movement of any considerable Confederate force northward. Lee did, indeed, send Early with a corps through the Shenandoah Valley, as an offensive gesture, but that was a move easily met by Grant, and the answer to it was forthcoming at once—the orders to Sheridan to destroy the crops and resources in the Shenandoah Valley so as to make the repetition of even that much of an offensive by the Confederates impossible in the future.

But if in Grant's conception Lee's army was the first objective of Meade's army, the major secondary attack, that of Butler, was Richmond, and the purpose of it entirely economic.

By 1864 the supply of Lee's Army of Northern Virginia had become a railroad problem, since there were no longer sufficient supplies of food to be had in Virginia itself. Quite aside from the question of sentiment and prestige connected with the holding of Richmond and vicinity, there was the added reason of the coal and metal supply and important manufacturing plants and arsenals located at and near that city. Further, except for the James River Canal, and the Virginia and East Tennessee Railroad with its branches, which were otherwise provided for in Grant's scheme, every line of approach to Richmond from the South would be controlled by Butler's attack, if that were successful. That this thought was uppermost in Grant's mind when he ordered Butler's movement, and that he knew if the attack were successful it would compel Lee to fall back into or beyond Richmond, is clear from his instructions to Butler on April 18:

Should Lee, however, fall back into Richmond, I will follow up and make a junction with your army on the James River. Could I be certain that you will be able to invest Richmond on the south side, so as to have your left resting on the James above the city, I would form the junction there.[12]

Had Butler been Sherman, McPherson, or Sheridan, instead of Butler, and accomplished his mission, there would have been but two alternatives remaining for Lee—surrender or escape into Georgia. However, as before indicated, in war we have to use the personalities we have, we cannot create new ones. Because of Butler's wide political influence Grant could not afford to supersede him. He therefore hoped for the best and gave Butler instructions to collect all the troops of his own department (Virginia and North Carolina) that could be spared from garrison duty, estimated at twenty thousand men, to which force was to be added an additional ten thousand from the coast of South Carolina. With the thirty thousand thus obtained [13] he was to move from the mouth of the York River by water on the night of May 4, his cavalry leaving from Suffolk against the railroads in the direction of Hicksford.

Butler himself was to land at Bermuda Hundred and after fortifying the neck of that little peninsula, begin his operations against Richmond from the south side. He began his operations on schedule time, but the fact that he was a sheep in a wolf's hide, and not a wolf, soon showed itself. Beauregard, with an improvised force gathered up from the defenses of Richmond and points south, defeated him in the battle of Drury's Bluff, and in less than two weeks from the time of his departure Butler was back within the cover of his Bermuda Hundred entrenchments, where, as Grant picturesquely says, he was as completely shut off from further operations against Richmond as if he had been "in a bottle tightly corked."

[12] W. R. 60:904.
[13] W. R. 60:794.

Butler did not even accomplish the secondary mission assigned him: "If you cannot carry the city, at least detain as large a force there as possible." [14] His failure to attain this object was felt by Grant on the North Anna when Pickett and Kemper arrived there to reinforce Lee, and later when Hoke reached Cold Harbor and very nearly took that important point away from Sheridan.

However, Grant did not therefore abandon his original purpose of bringing about a junction between Meade's army and Butler's in case Lee should fall back upon Richmond, as he was forced to do. This junction enabled Grant to combine in one spot and with a single army groupment both his economic objectives in Virginia and his military objective, Lee's army. His further purpose—the destruction of the James River Canal and the Virginia and East Tennessee Railroad—was not accomplished until March, 1865. As soon as this was done by Stoneman, the Army of the Potomac, which since June, 1864, had been perseveringly reaching westward from the east side of Petersburg and grasping, one by one, the railroads leading into Richmond from the south, at last laid hold of the only one remaining to the Confederacy—the South-Side. When that happened, Lee was forced to abandon Richmond and retreat, only to find himself cut off by Sheridan at Appomattox and almost immediately surrounded by Meade's closely pursuing army.

Turning now to the other secondary attacks in the Eastern theater, there is to be said that they appear to have been made not so much with the expectation of any distinct individual campaign successes as with the idea of using every possible man actively against the Confederacy. Grant wrote Sherman on April 4:

With the long line of railroad Sigel has to protect [Baltimore and Ohio] he can spare no troops, except to move directly to his front. In this way he must get through to inflict great damage on

[14] W. R. 60:904.

the enemy, or the enemy must detach from one of his armies a large force to prevent it. In other words, if Sigel can't skin himself he can hold a leg while some one else skins.[15]

It is interesting to note that this latter expression is evidently borrowed from Mr. Lincoln, who when Grant explained to him his plan and outline, replied with the same figure of speech, to show that he was entirely in accord with Grant's leading idea.

The main object of the expedition in West Virginia was economic, the destruction of the Virginia and East Tennessee Railroad being the first aim, though the destruction of anything that could be of use to the enemy in prolonging the war also was directed.[16] In this area there were important resources of the South: the lead-mines at Wytheville, the iron-works at Fincastle, and the salt-mine at Saltville. Grant, however, assigned as the secondary mission—in case the primary one could not be accomplished—the containing of a large force to prevent it from reinforcing the enemy elsewhere.

The original plan for the utilization of the troops in West Virginia and the Shenandoah Valley was to collect a force of not less than eight thousand infantry, three batteries, and fifteen hundred picked cavalry, at Beverly, under Ord, to move south to Covington, thence to the easiest point of access on the Virginia and East Tennessee Railroad.[17] At the same time, Crook was to advance from Charleston, West Virginia, throwing his infantry southward to prevent the enemy from coming through the mountain gap, while his cavalry was to march to the Virginia and East Tennessee Railroad, after reaching which he was to move eastward, destroying the railroad, and effect a junction with Ord.

[15] W. R. 59:245.
[16] W. R. 60:765.
[17] Grant to Sigel, Mch. 29, W. R. 60:765; Apr. 15, W. R. 60:874; Grant-Ord, Mch. 29, W. R. 60:758.

The orders left matters largely in Ord's hands after Crook reached the railroad, but if he were able to get as far east as Lynchburg, which it was hoped would be the case, he was expected by subsisting on the country for a time to establish a base on the James. In this event he was not to consider a retreat, without further orders.

The plan was not carried out in the manner intended, though the objectives remained unchanged. Averell moved south from Charleston, West Virginia, early in May, with the cavalry of Crook's command, on Saltville. Crook himself moved simultaneously from Charleston, by Fayetteville, along the line of the Kanawha River. He had a skirmish at Princeton on May 6; a fair-sized battle at Cloyd's Mountain, in which he was the victor; and a skirmish at the New River bridge of the Virginia and East Tennessee Railroad on May 10. The bridge was destroyed. Crook then started in retreat and reached Union on May 15.

Averell with the cavalry had marched to Saltville, where he found the enemy in some force, moved up the railroad to Wytheville, where he had a skirmish, moved to Dublin, crossed the New River on the twelfth and after spending a short time destroying the railroad toward Christiansburg, joined Crook at Union on the fifteenth. The combined force then moved to Meadow Bridge on the nineteenth, having nothing to its credit except the destruction of the railroad bridge at New River and of a short piece of track. Neither the salt-works at Saltville nor the lead-mines at Wytheville had been touched, nor had the presence of these forces in the Alleghany Mountains at Meadow Bridge been of any real use in the execution of Grant's designs.

The Beverly expedition had in the meantime been abandoned. Ord had been relieved at his own request and Sigel in his place was assigned the other subordinate attack, but, with Grant's permission, changed the line of advance to one up the Shenandoah.

He assembled his command at Winchester and moved to New-market, where he was attacked and beaten by the combined Southern forces of Breckenridge, Echols, and Imboden, and promptly retreated to Strasburg, having accomplished less than nothing.

The immediate result of this failure was felt by the Army of the Potomac when it reached the North Anna on May 23 and found that Breckenridge had arrived there to join Lee. Imboden and Echols, however, were left in the valley to prevent the return southward of Sigel.

It will thus be seen that all of the secondary attacks in the East ordered by Grant had broken down without having accomplished anything advantageous to the Union cause, except the indirect one of having brought about the concentration against Meade's army of nearly the entire Confederate force in this theater. Yet Grant was apparently content with this result and he attributed no blame to any one. As Porter says: "Grant's mind seemed always more concerned about preventing disasters to the armies of his distant commanders than to the troops under his own personal direction. . . . His self-reliance was so great that he always felt that he could take ample care of himself." Regarding Butler's force, Grant could and did, on nearing Richmond, make use of one corps of his command by transferring it by boat up the York River as a reinforcement for the Army of the Potomac, prior to its attack at Cold Harbor on June 3.

In the Shenandoah Valley, however, Grant determined to make further efforts. Hunter replaced Sigel in command of the Department of West Virginia on May 19, while the army of Meade was at Spottsylvania. Grant was in some doubt concerning what directions to give Hunter,[18] but finally determined—on the ground that the enemy, and in particular Lee's army, was rely-

[18] Grant-Halleck, May 20, W. R. 70:500; May 25, 70:536.

ing largely for supplies on what could be brought over the branch road leading to Staunton—to have him move on Staunton. Later when Meade reached the North Anna, Grant expanded this idea and desired Hunter to get to Charlottesville, if possible to Lynchburg, destroying the railroads and canal beyond the possibility of repair for weeks, and then to make his way back to his base, or possibly to join the Army of the Potomac by way of Gordonsville.

By June 6, after the deadlock at Cold Harbor, Grant had decided to send Sheridan, with two divisions of the cavalry corps, from Cold Harbor to Charlottesville, to continue the destruction of the Virginia Central Railroad, already begun by the Army of the Potomac on the North Anna.

Hunter's part in this new plan was to be, in case the order was received between Staunton and Lynchburg, to turn east at once and advance until he reached the Lynchburg branch of the Virginia Central Railroad, then to move eastward along that line, destroying it thoroughly, until he joined Sheridan, when both were to rejoin the Army of the Potomac.[19]

This change in plan was not because of the diminished importance in Grant's mind of the occupation of Lynchburg or of the destruction of the canal, but because Grant feared that Hunter would not be able to reach it. He left it to Hunter to decide finally whether he should go there or not.

Hunter left Strasburg on May 26, reached Staunton on June 6, where he was joined by Crook and Averell from Meadow Bridge. Thence his route lay through Lexington to Lynchburg, which he reached about June 16, meeting with little resistance and having accomplished the destruction of a considerable quantity of Confederate supplies of all kinds. By this time, however, the situation had changed, through the failure of Meade's army in its attacks at Cold Harbor, with the result that Lee could now

[19] June 6, W. R. 70:598.

afford to detach troops from his Army of Northern Virginia to prevent further inroads in the western part of the State. The consequence was that Hunter, on his arrival in Lynchburg, found not only that the division of Breckenridge had already reached there, but that Early's corps, detached from Lee's army, was on its way. He could only retreat, but did so in an unfortunate direction, on Charleston, West Virginia, which he reached June 30. From there his troops were returned to Parkersburg by river and to Cumberland by railroad, but too late to meet the emergency caused by his abandonment of his assigned theater of war, and in a false direction.

Early, one of Lee's able corps commanders, after a short pursuit of Hunter found the way left open for an advance against Washington. He therefore turned to the northeast, up the Shenandoah, reached Winchester on July 2, demonstrated at Maryland Heights against Sigel, who was in command there, and who again promptly fled and was again relieved of his command. Early then crossed the Potomac, brushed aside Lew Wallace and his hastily collected troops at Monocacy Junction, and arrived before the defenses at Washington on July 10.

The diversion was important and made at an opportune moment for the South. The armies of Meade and Lee were locked in their final grapple at Petersburg and Grant was compelled to detach troops for the defense of Washington. This, however, he now could do easily and quickly, utilizing river transportation.

Early, finding the opportunity for the capture of Washington had passed with the arrival of Wright's corps, retired on July 12 by Leesburg and established himself in the Shenandoah. Sheridan was then sent by Grant to take command of the Union forces in the valley. During the autumn of 1864, Sheridan and Early had several engagements, but without particular strategic consequences. The vital factor, so far as the war was concerned, was that Sheridan occupied himself, pursuant to Grant's orders, in carrying out systematically the destruction of the food resources of the country, the conservation of which, as also the gathering in of the fall crops, had been one of the principal objects of Lee in sending Early to the Shenandoah.

This campaign, however, was interrupted by the winter, and active operations suspended until March, 1865, when Sheridan started south from Winchester with all of the cavalry of his army. This time the Confederates were completely driven out of the valley and Sheridan continued by Waynesboro to the James River Canal, the cutting of which had been for so long one of Grant's most desired objectives, after which he joined the Army of the Potomac by the north side of Richmond in time to take part in the pursuit of Lee's army which ended at Appomattox.

While the early failures in the Shenandoah Valley and western Virginia were due to the incompetence of the commanders, the defeat of Hunter and the subsequent operations of Early's corps were a direct result of Grant's own failure at Cold Harbor. Had he not attacked there or had he attacked and made good, Lee could not have detached forces, as he did subsequently, to carry the war again into Maryland, though this time with a detachment and not with his main forces. We see from this the larger strategic consequences which often follow tactical decisions. A single tactical failure, in combined operations, may result in an entire shift from offensive to defensive, and in an entire theater of war.

Although the James River Canal remained untouched until March, 1865, two other of Grant's economic objectives were attained through a raid made by Stoneman in December, 1864.

To get a complete picture of the strategic situation in 1864 and 1865, one should really consider all the movements collectively as they occurred in both the East and the West. However, in outlining them it is easier to take these theaters up separately as has already been done for the East.

In the West, Sherman had succeeded Grant in command of the Military Division of the Mississippi upon Grant's call to the chief command. Grant and Sherman had, in their new relationship, the advantage not only of deep personal sympathy but of a thorough understanding of each other; both were thoroughly impersonal in their thoughts, and loyal to the core to the cause of the Union regardless of what happened to themselves individually; and each knew that the other shared in this respect his own qualities. This background of mutual understanding and common ideals made possible more complete coördination in the two principal theaters of war than has probably ever before taken place between a commanding general and his principal subordinate.

On taking over his new command, Sherman began at once large-scale preparations for the opening of the spring campaign of 1864. His prospective field army consisted of the Army of the Ohio, gathered around Knoxville; the Army of the Cumberland, about Chattanooga; and the Army of the Tennessee, near Huntsville, Alabama.

The Confederate main force opposed to Sherman, under Joseph E. Johnston, was opposite Chattanooga at Dalton, Longstreet, who had been for so long in East Tennessee, having been withdrawn to join Lee in Virginia before the campaign opened.

Grant explained to Sherman in his directive of April 4, his part in the campaign:

I have sent orders to Banks . . . to finish up his present expedition against Shreveport with all dispatch; to turn over the defense of the Red River to General Steele and the navy, and return your troops to you and his own to New Orleans; to abandon all of Texas except the Rio Grande, and to hold that with not to exceed 4,000 men; to reduce the number of troops on the Mississippi to the lowest number necessary to hold it, and to collect from his command not less than 25,000 men; to this I will add 5,000 from Missouri. With this force he is to commence operations against Mobile as soon as he can. It will be impossible for him to commence too early. . . .

You I propose to move against Johnston's army, to break it up and to get into the interior of the enemy's country as far as you can, inflicting all the damage you can against their war resources.

I do not propose to lay down for you a plan of campaign, but simply to lay down the work it is desirable to have done, and leave you free to execute in your own way.[20]

With this directive Grant also provided Sherman a copy of his own map of the general theater of war, the lines of operation marked in blue.

In this plan we note a slight variation from that proposed by Grant in January, at the time he expected to remain in command of the Division of the Mississippi. At that time he had proposed to cut off the west wing of the Confederacy with a line from Chattanooga through Atlanta and Selma to Mobile, operating from the Tennessee River. Now he had decided to start cleavages from two directions simultaneously: a main attack from Chattanooga; a secondary attack from Mobile.[21]

The Red River campaign upon which Banks was engaged under instructions from Halleck written early in January [22] was destined to interfere with the course of the second of these cleavages. On April 8, Banks was badly beaten in the Battle of Mansfield, Louisiana, and retreated to Alexandria, Louisiana, which he reached on April 25. There there was a long delay, due to difficulties in getting the gunboats down the Red River. Later the retreat was continued down the river to Simmesport, where Banks was relieved by Canby on May 9.

20 W. R. 59:245. The letter is in Grant's own handwriting.
21 See also Grant to Banks, Mch. 31, W. R. 61:11.
22 W. R. 62:55.

Coming from Little Rock, Arkansas, Steele advanced, on March 23, by Pine Bluff and Elkins Ferry on Camden, which he reached on April 16, after Banks's defeat at Mansfield. Supply difficulties and news of Banks's retreat caused him to decide to retreat also and he returned to Little Rock on May 3.

The complete breakdown of the operations of Banks and Steele west of the Mississippi caused Grant to decide to abandon for the time being the attempt to use their troops for a secondary cleavage east of the Mississippi.[23] However, Canby, in an expedition from New Orleans, succeeded in capturing Forts Gaines and Morgan, commanding the entrance to Mobile Bay, and in putting an end to blockade-running from that harbor.

In March, 1865, operations were again resumed against Mobile by Canby and Steele jointly, the latter advancing from Pensacola. The city was evacuated by Confederate troops on April 11, and the campaign resulted in the final surrender of all Confederate forces in Alabama, Mississippi, and east Louisiana, under Taylor, at Citronelle, Alabama, on May 4, 1865.

Left to bear the main burden of the attack of Confederate forces in the central theater, owing to Banks's failure up the Red River, Sherman moved on schedule time from Chattanooga on Dalton, Georgia. Johnston did not feel strong enough to oppose Sherman by an active defense, but merely fought delaying actions, and when outflanking was threatened by Sherman's superior forces, retreated to positions in rear on Atlanta.

As Sherman advanced he complied fully with that part of Grant's directive which called for the destruction of the enemy's war resources, by means of cavalry expeditions east and west of the line of advance. In connection with the movement on Atlanta it is interesting to note the strategical use of the Confederate

[23] Grant to Halleck, Apr. 29, W. R. 63:331.

cavalry in the attempt to stop Sherman's advance by means of cavalry raids undertaken in his rear.[24] The first of these was Wheeler's raid through northern Georgia and eastern Tennessee (August 10 to September 9, 1864), in which he attacked the Union line of communication south of Chattanooga and later between Chattanooga and Nashville. Following this raid, Forrest, starting from Verona, Mississippi, on September 16, moved by Florence and Athens, in Alabama, and Fayetteville, Columbia, and Spring Hill, Tennessee, thence back to Corinth, Mississippi.

The Confederate commanders regarded these raids as highly important in their results, whereas from the larger point of view they annoyed merely the commander of the line of communications, and caused no real discomfort to Sherman or the main armies. This is in complete contrast to the raids of the Union cavalry at the same time, which resulted in the progressive destruction of the economic resources of the country.

On July 18, 1864, Hood was placed by President Davis in command of the Army of the Tennessee, hence these cavalry raids are chargeable to him and not to Johnston. On September 29, the Army of the Tennessee under Hood left Palmetto, Georgia, on a raid of its own, hoping to draw Sherman after him, as in 1862 Bragg had drawn Buell from Corinth northward nearly to Louisville. Sherman did follow Hood for a time, but finally decided to send Thomas back to Nashville to gather up a force to stop him there, and continued upon his chief task of destroying the war resources in this main and central part of the Confederacy.

Hood finally reached Franklin, Tennessee, on November 30, and Nashville on December 15, where he was attacked and decisively defeated by Thomas. His army then retreated to Tuscumbia, Alabama, and moved thence by rail to Corinth, where he was replaced on January 2 by Taylor, who surrendered to Canby four months later.

[24] W. R. 74:951.

That Sherman's accomplishment of his mission and subsequent advance to Savannah, Georgia, in order to obtain a new base on the sea, was rendered easier by Hood's movement northward, there can be no question. Hood and President Davis undoubtedly had in mind the repetition of the Antietam and Gettysburg campaigns by Lee in the East, both of which had promptly drawn the Union Army of the Potomac northward in pursuit. They failed to recognize the difference between the shorter movement over the good roads in the Eastern theater in summer, and the longer one over the poorer roads in the Southern theater in winter.

The Savannah campaign, Sherman's answer to Hood's march against his line of communications on Chattanooga, was a brilliant conception, though merely a logical sequence to Grant's general instructions. Sherman, having obtained Grant's approval, cut loose from Atlanta on November 12 and marched across Georgia on a broad front, devastating the country. The railroads were torn up, not only in the path of the army but by means of cavalry far on both flanks. The food and forage necessary for the army were taken and what could not be consumed was carried along or destroyed. More than ten thousand horses and mules were impressed. Sherman estimated that this expedition cost the State of Georgia something like $100,000,000.

On December 21, Sherman entered Savannah and obtained his sea base. In January, 1865, he left Savannah on a march northward through the Carolinas in which he was opposed once more by Joseph E. Johnston, who was at this time in the position of being a "general without an army," other than a handful of levies gathered with extreme difficulty. As soon as he heard of Lee's surrender, Johnston surrendered to Sherman, on April 26, 1865. Sherman then marched his army to Washington, where he joined with the Army of the Potomac in the grand final review, May 24, 1865.

During the last campaign Grant ordered various minor operations for special reasons, of which mere mention will be made.
Butler having been sent to capture Fort Fisher, controlling the
port of Wilmington, North Carolina, in December, 1864, and
having failed in his attempt, Terry was sent there and succeeded
in making the capture January 15, 1865. The taking of this fort
closed the final door by which blockade-runners could still reach
the Confederacy. The cavalry raids ordered by Grant in connection with the operations of the Army of the Potomac have been
endlessly discussed and not a little misunderstood. It has even
been suggested that Sheridan's first raid in Virginia was ordered
by Grant more to stop a quarrel between Meade and Sheridan
than for any other reason.

These raids on the Union side can be correctly interpreted only
in connection with Grant's economic strategy directed against the
resources of the Confederacy; either in general, as seems to have
been the case with the seven raids conducted by Sheridan in person, or for some particular object, as was the case with General
Stoneman's raid in southwestern Virginia in December, 1864.

The final raid on a large scale was conducted by Wilson
through northern Alabama and south-central Georgia, incidental
to which was the capture of Mr. Davis, the Confederate President,
at Irwinsville, Georgia, on May 10, 1865.

It has commonly been supposed that these raids were suggested by the Confederate ones, initiated by Stuart earlier in the
war, but an examination of the respective intentions of Grant
and Lee will show that this was not the case. While Lee's object
in despatching Stuart upon his various raids was solely tactical,
Grant's object was strategic and was in the end accomplished and
hence fully justified; whereas the soundness in principle of the
raids ordered by Lee and executed by Stuart must remain in question—in fact, they have been most generally condemned.

No one can follow the course of Grant's final campaign, in 1864–65, without being impressed by the contrast between his masterly plan and its sorry execution by so many of the subordinate leaders. The reason is not far to seek. War, merely by itself, is the poorest of schools in which to learn how to make war. No man can become fit to lead an army merely by being assigned to do so; and in no other profession would the mere conferring of a degree without previous study be expected to supply mastery of the subject. Only a long course of lessons can do this. That, out of three million combatants, four years of civil war produced only *one* Grant is the best proof of this. Genius he undoubtedly had. Most probably others had it also. To Grant alone, however, appears to have been given the opportunity for the balanced development of that genius through the solving, during his career, of an orderly sequence of progressively arranged problems.

His armies in the West, commanded by officers who had had the benefit of being trained and guided in their earlier experience by Grant himself, responded nobly to their allotted tasks and assured ultimate success to the strategic plan; but in the East, capable, trained executives were in general lacking. The strategic success, won in spite of the tactical breakdowns of Grant's principal army, is all the greater proof of the essential soundness of his strategic conception. The situation did not call for desperate gambling, but for certainty of success.

To Grant, with his trained vision and sound thinking, the country is more indebted for its unity to-day than to any other man save only Lincoln.

CHAPTER XXIV

GRANT AND HIS ARMY COMMANDERS

> The military machine, the army and all belong-
> ing to it, is in fact simple and easy to manage.
> But let us reflect that no part of it is in one piece,
> that each piece is composed entirely of individuals,
> each of whom keeps up his own friction in all
> directions.—CLAUSEWITZ.

WHEN General Scott, on the occasion of their first meeting after the war, presented Grant with his autobiography inscribed, "From the oldest to the greatest American general," he was paying no idle or formal compliment. Scott, in addition to his brilliant conduct of the Mexican War, had himself borne the weight of the supreme command in the early part of the Civil War, and thus was more capable than any other man of his time, save Lincoln, of appreciating the burden of Grant's final command and his successful execution of its manifold responsibilities.

By many writers a military force acting independently is considered an army whether that force be composed of ten thousand or a million men, so that not infrequently we find comparisons drawn which ignore the fact that one general was carrying a donkey's load, the other an elephant's.

Broadly speaking, there are three degrees of difficulty in military leadership:

(A) Corps command—up to 60,000;
(B) Army command—60,000 to 200,000;
(C) Group-of-armies command—200,000 to 10,000,000.

From Dodge's "Recollections"

William Tecumseh Sherman
(1820–91)

From B. & L.

George Henry Thomas
(1816–70)

From B. & L.

George Gordon Meade
(1815–72)

GRANT'S ARMY COMMANDERS

Each additional thousand of men adds to the responsibilities of the general; and when his command outgrows a corps in size, so that he can no longer think in terms of divisions, his task changes not only in complexity but in kind. Commercially speaking, it is the difference between running a small corner grocery and managing a department store. If his command is enlarged beyond the army size, so that it must be handled as groups of armies, the problem changes again, as if the department-store manager had suddenly been put at the head of a world-wide oil company, with questions not merely more complex but entirely new to solve. Thus we can never be certain that the commander of a corps-size force, however ably he has handled it, will also succeed with an army; the percentage of those who fail is too large. Even Napoleon, who had done well with a corps (1796–1800) and an army (1805–1809), failed lamentably when confronted with the problems of a group of armies (1811–1812).

Grant, in fact, is the first commander known in history to deal successfully with the army of a million in size. Others may improve on the methods of the pathfinder; they must still remain his followers.

The characteristic most obviously essential in a higher commander is, of course, great force of will; but even more vitally necessary is the power so to kindle in his immediate subordinates his own spirit that his desires become to them no mere orders but real inspirations impelling them to put forth their utmost. Grant's ability to do this is clearly evidenced in his relationships with his army commanders.

Meade's attitude toward Grant is clearly brought out by his letters to his wife,[1] which form a most illuminating commentary upon the 1864–65 campaign. Before Grant's arrival on March 8, 1864, Meade wrote:

[1] "Life and Letters of George Gordon Meade," Vol. II, pp. 176–271.

Grant is to be in Washington to-night, and as he is to be com-
mander-in-chief and responsible for the doings of the Army of the
Potomac, he may desire to have his own man in command, particularly as I understand he is indoctrinated with the notion of the superiority of the Western armies, and that the failure of the Army of the
Potomac to accomplish anything is due to their commanders.

During the spring campaign Meade's regard for Grant grew
until Petersburg was reached. From then on he appears to have
been hurt by the honors and favors shown to other commanders,
and particularly the assignment of Sheridan to the independent
command in the Shenandoah Valley, which Grant himself had
contemplated giving Meade and which Meade greatly desired.
After that, apparently, Meade questioned Grant's fairness.

Three days after Appomattox Meade wrote his wife:

Your indignation at the exaggerated praise given to certain officers, and the ignoring of others, is quite natural. . . . I have the
consciousness that I have fully performed my duty, and have done
my full share of the brilliant work just completed; but if the press
is determined to ignore this, and the people are determined, after
four years' experience of press lying, to believe what the newspapers
say, I don't see there is anything for us but to submit and be resigned.
Grant I do not consider so criminal; it is partly ignorance and partly
selfishness which prevents his being aware of the effects of his acts.[2]

We cannot but feel here two elements in Meade's character
which were detrimental to his career as an army commander.
One was his muffled resentment of the non-recognition of his
services, and the other his personal ambition—the desire to gain
honors rather for himself than for his Army of the Potomac. He
added, concerning Sheridan, "His determination to absorb the
credit of everything done is so manifest as to have attracted the
attention of the whole army." One reading these quoted pas-

[2] Meade II:271.

sages suspects that the writer saw in Grant and Sheridan merely the reflection of his own mentality and was prevented thereby from recognizing the impersonal patriotism and loyalty which stand out so clearly in the contemporary records of Grant's words and deeds.

As for Grant's attitude toward the Army of the Potomac, it is interesting to note that the accusation that Grant attributed to its commanders the "failure of the Army of the Potomac to accomplish anything" was not borne out by the facts. He wrote Washburne shortly after Vicksburg, regarding the possibility of his being ordered to command that army: "My going could do no possible good. They have there able officers who have been brought up with that army; and to import a commander to place over them, certainly could produce no good." [3]

Grant's letter continues, showing that his judgment did not apply to the Army of the Potomac alone:

Whilst I would not positively disobey an order, I would have objected most vehemently to taking that command, or any other, except the one I have. I can do more with this army than it would be possible for me to do with any other, without time to make the same acquaintance with others I have with this. I know that the soldiers of the Army of the Tennessee can be relied on to the fullest extent. I believe I know the exact capacity of every general in my command to command troops, and just where to place them to get from them their best services. This is a matter of no small consequence.

This reluctance to command personally the Army of the Potomac naturally disappeared after Grant's assignment to command all the armies of the United States, since in those circumstances his presence with an army became a compliment to it and an implied recognition of the importance of its work.

[3] Richardson 345.

The story of the failure of the Army of the Potomac to respond in full measure to Grant's demands upon it constitutes one of the most interesting pages of Civil War history. While the blame must remain partly upon the shoulders of Grant, yet it is lessened, with regard to him, by the fact that the conduct of war in all the theaters was in his hands and he could not, even if he would, give the Army of the Potomac more than its proper share of his attention. This fact is often overlooked by critics who judge of Grant in 1864 exclusively by the single campaign of the army with which he established his headquarters, instead of viewing it, as is the only just way, in its relations with all the campaigns in both the Eastern and Western theaters, which was, after all, the only aspect that properly should have concerned him at that time.

Grant began the campaign by giving Meade quite as much independence in the execution of his directives as he would have given Sherman. While Meade appreciated this and the implied compliment, he failed to recognize the fact that he could best serve by proving his own ability to conduct the offensive campaign desired and thereby relieve Grant's mind of all consideration of details, leaving it free for larger responsibility. Instead of doing this Meade began to consult Grant on the first day of the Wilderness battle as to what he desired to have done. Grant naturally had his views and communicated them. This led eventually to a division of responsibility, for the tactical conduct of the Army of the Potomac, which proved in the end most unfortunate.

Directly to command the Army of the Potomac, Grant had neither the time nor the wish. But when the army commander came to him to ask him whether he wanted this or that done, and how he wanted it done, he could not refuse him an answer.

It does not seem too much to say that the situation was one in which Meade had an opportunity to distinguish himself far beyond that of either Sherman or Sheridan. Had he thrown himself heart and soul into the task of accomplishing what Grant desired, without troubling the General of the Armies with any details, as Sherman or Sheridan would have done in his place, his services would not in the end have failed to receive proper recognition and reward. But Meade did not see matters in that light. He was so anxious to please Grant that he came more and more to consult him as the campaign progressed.

The more Grant was consulted, naturally the more danger there was that Meade would get a partial, not a complete, idea of his wishes; hence; having begun to concern himself with details, Grant was obliged more and more to continue to do so. He recognized the difficulties of Meade's position and was entirely sympathetic toward him. In the course of the move on Petersburg he wrote Stanton recommending that both Meade and Sherman be made major-generals in the regular army, and added, "I should not like to see one of these appointments made at this time without the other." However, after Meade's failure to accomplish anything at Petersburg had convinced Grant that Meade preferred the rôle of liaison-officer between the General of the Armies and the Army of the Potomac rather than that of army commander, Grant simply made the best of it.

For Gettysburg, Meade had indeed deserved well of his country and fully earned there the promotion which in later years he came so ardently to crave. But the judgment of history cannot concede that in 1864 he fully met the responsibilities which faced him; had he done so, the war might easily have been shortened nearly a year.

The relationship between Grant and Sherman is best summed up in the despatches which passed between them after the capture of Atlanta by Sherman's armies. Grant notified Sherman:

I have just received your dispatch announcing the capture of Atlanta. In honor of your great victory I have ordered a salute to be fired with shotted guns from every battery bearing upon the enemy. The salute will be fired within an hour, amidst great rejoicing.[4]

Sherman's response reads: "I have always felt that you would take personally more pleasure in my success than in your own, and I reciprocate the feeling to the fullest extent."

These despatches were not a mere exchange of courtesies; both came from the heart. It is impossible to decide which is the more admirable, Sherman's supreme trust in Grant's loyalty to him, or the sterling qualities in Grant which nurtured that trust.

Following the Civil War the friends of General Thomas became very hostile toward Grant for his treatment of Thomas during the siege of Nashville. Thomas had the merit of inspiring intense loyalty in all who came under his command; his subordinates universally believed that he was the greatest general developed in the war and resented Grant's imputations of his slowness and lack of enterprise.

The case of Thomas at Nashville reminds one strongly of Grant's own case at Donelson while the Triumvirate were attempting to decide among them the course to be pursued by Grant's forces. The difference was that Thomas was in telegraphic communication throughout the period of the siege with his three superiors, Secretary Stanton, Halleck, and Grant. Mr. Lincoln himself appears not to have participated in the affair save as he influenced the despatches sent by Stanton and Halleck. Space does not permit the correspondence to be given in its entirety,[5] but the leading despatches suffice to give a striking picture of the conflict of views held by the man on the spot and his superiors in the East.

---

[4] Grant to Sherman (From City Point, Sept. 2), W. R. 72:87; *ibid.* 76:808.
[5] For the whole correspondence see W. R. 94:3–143.

On December 1, Thomas summed up the results of the battle
of Franklin and gave his intentions:

> I therefore think it best to wait here until Wilson can equip all
> his cavalry. If Hood attacks me here, he will be more seriously
> damaged than he was yesterday; if he remains until Wilson gets
> equipped, I can whip him and will move against him at once.

Stanton telegraphed Grant, in reference to the above, the
day following:

> The President feels solicitous about the disposition of General
> Thomas to lay in fortifications for an indefinite period "until Wilson
> gets equipments." This looks like the McClellan and Rosecrans
> strategy of do nothing and let the rebels raid the country. The
> President wishes you to consider the matter.

Whether Grant came to the same conclusion independently
or was led by this message to send one or both of his despatches
to Thomas is not evident. Grant replied to Stanton the same
day: "Immediately upon receipt of Thomas' dispatch I sent him
a dispatch which no doubt you read as it passed through the
office." His two despatches to Thomas on this day read:

> (1) If Hood is permitted to remain quietly about Nashville, you
> will lose all the road back to Chattanooga, and possibly have to aban-
> don the line of the Tennessee. Should he attack you it is all well,
> but if he does not you should attack him before he fortifies. Arm
> and put in the trenches your quartermaster employés, citizens, etc.
> (2) With your citizen employés armed, you can move out of
> Nashville with all your army and force the enemy to retire or fight
> upon ground of your own choosing. After the repulse of Hood at
> Franklin, it looks to me that instead of falling back to Nashville,
> we should have taken the offensive against the enemy where he was.
> At this distance, however, I may err as to the best method of dealing
> with the enemy. You will now suffer incalculable injury upon your
> railroads, if Hood is not speedily disposed of. Put forth, therefore,

every possible exertion to attain this end. Should you get him to retreating, give him no peace.

The same day Thomas acknowledged receipt of these two despatches, explained the situation in some detail, and added:

I now have infantry enough to assume the offensive, if I had more cavalry, and will take the field anyhow as soon as the remainder of General McCook's division of cavalry reaches here, which I hope it will do in two or three days . . . I earnestly hope, however, that in a few more days I shall be able to give him a fight.

On December 5, Grant despatched the following to Thomas:

Is there not danger of Forrest moving down the Cumberland to where he can cross it? It seems to me whilst you should be getting up your cavalry as rapidly as possible to look after Forrest, Hood should be attacked where he is. Time strengthens him, in all probability, as much as it does you.

The same evening Thomas reported: "I have been along my entire line to-day. The enemy has not advanced at all since the 3d instant. If I can perfect my arrangements I shall move against the advanced position of the enemy on the 7th instant."

An interesting side-light is thrown on the differences between Thomas's views and those held in the East, by the despatches between Major Eckert, in charge of the War Department telegraph service, and his subordinate, Captain Van Duzer, at Nashville, who during this period was sending in his own despatches to his chief, which, however, immediately reached Lincoln and Stanton in Washington, and probably Grant. Van Duzer telegraphed at the same time as the last quoted despatch from Thomas: " General Thomas works on hypothesis that Hood is here with whole force," but went on to give details which suggested that the general was mistaken in this belief.

Thomas's three days now being up, General Grant telegraphed him on December 6: "Attack Hood at once, and wait no longer for a remount of your cavalry. There is great danger of delay resulting in a campaign back to the Ohio River."

The same evening, Thomas replied to Grant's two last telegrams, of the fifth and sixth: (1—8 P.M.) "As soon as I can get up a respectable force of cavalry I will march against Hood. . . . I hope to have some 6,000 or 8,000 cavalry mounted in three days from this time"; (2—9 P.M.) "I will make the necessary dispositions and attack Hood at once, agreeably to your order, though I believe it will be hazardous with the small force of cavalry now at my service."

The next morning Stanton telegraphed Grant: "Thomas seems unwilling to attack because it is hazardous, as if all war was anything but hazardous. If he waits for Wilson to get ready, Gabriel will be blowing his last horn."

Grant replied: "You probably saw my order to Thomas to attack. If he does not do it promptly, I would recommend superseding him by Schofield, leaving Thomas subordinate." Whatever Grant's justification for this despatch, the sending of it could only seem to admirers of the Jove-like Thomas a sacrilegious act.

The same day, Thomas telegraphed Grant regarding another matter, but did not mention his own intentions, which omission probably irritated Grant still more. The day following, December 8, Halleck telegraphed Grant: "If you wish General Thomas relieved . . . give the order. . . . The responsibility, however, will be yours, as no one here, so far as I am informed, wishes General Thomas' removal."

Grant, before he could have received this despatch, however, had already sent Thomas an encouraging message (at 8:30 P.M.):

Why not attack at once? . . . Now is one of the finest opportunities ever presented of destroying one of the three armies of the enemy. If destroyed, he can never replace it. Use the means at your command, and you can do this and cause a rejoicing that will resound from one end of the land to another.

An hour later he replied to Halleck's telegram: "I want General Thomas reminded of the importance of immediate action. I sent him a dispatch this evening which will probably urge him on. I would not say relieve him until I hear further from him."

Thomas's report of the same evening again gave no inkling of his intentions except that he was not yet ready.

On the ninth, Grant, thoroughly roused, asked of Halleck, "Please telegraph order relieving him [General Thomas] at once and placing Schofield in command." Halleck had the order prepared, but, ever friendly toward Thomas, instead of sending it, tried to incite that officer to a more active policy: "General Grant expresses much dissatisfaction at your delay in attacking the enemy. If you wait till General Wilson mounts all his cavalry, you will wait till doomsday, for the waste equals the supply."

Thomas replied to Grant:

I had nearly completed my preparations to attack the enemy tomorrow morning, but a terrible storm of freezing rain has come on to-day [Dec. 9] . . . I am, therefore, compelled to wait for the storm to break . . . Halleck informs me that you are very much dissatisfied with my delay in attacking. I can only say I have done all in my power to prepare, and if you should deem it necessary to relieve me I shall submit without a murmur.

One does not know whether more greatly to admire the fine spirit of loyalty and impersonality in the above despatch or the like spirit in Grant's answer to it:

I have as much confidence in your conducting a battle rightly as I have in any other officer; but it has seemed to me that you have been slow, and I have had no explanation of affairs to convince me otherwise. . . . I telegraphed to suspend the order relieving you until we should hear further. I hope most sincerely that there will be no necessity of repeating the orders, and that the facts will show that you have been right all the time.

On the tenth, Thomas telegraphed, "The sleet . . . still continues, rendering offensive operations extremely hazardous, if not impossible."

In justice to Grant we must add that during this period he was making every endeavor to send Thomas reinforcements from all possible quarters, both infantry and cavalry. On the eleventh he sent his last telegram:

If you delay attack longer the mortifying spectacle will be witnessed of a rebel army moving for the Ohio River, and you will be forced to act, accepting such weather as you find. Let there be no further delay. Hood cannot stand even a drawn battle so far from his supplies of ordnance stores. If he retreats and you follow, he must lose his material and much of his army. I am in hopes of receiving a dispatch from you to-day announcing that you have moved. Delay no longer for weather or re-enforcements.

Naturally, the above messages have to be interpreted in accordance with the conventionalities of the day. On the part of Grant, they display an outspokenness which Thomas found disconcerting, and he complained, according to Wilson, that he was being treated like a child. But we must remember that while they did not pass from friend to close friend, as would be the case of despatches between Grant and Sherman, they were between West Point comrades and old regular army officers both imbued with the ideal of loyalty, and placing devotion to duty before all personal considerations; and in this sense it is impossible not to admire the frank sincerity with which Grant tried to impress upon Thomas his views regarding the policy the good of the country required. Nor can we fail to admire the fine spirit with which Thomas yielded his own judgment to that of his superior in his final despatch of December 11, before the attack: "I will obey the order as promptly as possible, however much I may regret it, as the attack will have to be made under every disadvantage."

CHAPTER XXV

GRANT AND LEE

Two stars keep not their motion in one sphere.
—SHAKSPERE.

THE opposing commanders who were at the head of the Northern and Southern armies at the close of the war, were widely different in character. Lee was to the manor born and remained the patrician, alike in affluence and power and in the relative poverty and obscurity of his later years. Grant, on the contrary, was essentially a man of the people—one of the common ones of the kind Lincoln once said the Lord must have loved because he made so many of them.

The appeal of the two opposing commanders to their men was as different as the men themselves. The Confederate soldier had that veneration for Lee which the fighting man always has for the commander who is a real aristocrat. To his troops Lee was at least a demigod, whose life was worth more than all their lives put together and whose orders it became a pious and sacred as well as a military duty to obey.

Grant made no such appeal. Had he tried to pretend to the part he would doubtless have failed, as have so many commanders before and since; but by being honest, straightforward, fair, looking out for the interests and welfare of his men, and assuming no grand airs, he won their regard and they did what he wanted.

After all, soldiers, like some other people of republican tendencies, see certain advantages in having a leader who is distinctly human like themselves; he may make more mistakes; but if he evidently does his best, and is sincere and gives of himself, they readily overlook those mistakes. Nevertheless, despite his simple outlook on life, Grant was not without a certain gentle dignity which became him admirably both during the war and in after years when honors were showered upon him.

The contrast between the generalship of the two leaders was as great as between their personalities. Neither was a school-trained commander in the staff-college sense; but both had been trained by war itself and each had become rounded and developed as was to be expected. Lee had begun the Civil War with a great advantage over Grant—his staff experience under Scott in Mexico. As time went on, however, Lee was not favored with the same depth and variety of experience as came to Grant. While Grant was still grappling with the tactical and administrative problems of a petty commander, learning one by one the simple lessons which Fate so admirably graduated in difficulty for him, Lee had begun, after his first skirmish in West Virginia, as President Davis's military adviser, and had stepped from that post to the active command of the principal Confederate army, which command he held to the end. In this rôle of army commander he acquired a marvelous technique and gained for himself and his army a series of successes unsurpassed for their brilliance in tactical annals.

But when Lee came to fight Grant, the charm was broken. The reason why, Lee never understood; and he never was able to penetrate Grant's plans or moves. The reason was that, while Lee was fighting only the Army of the Potomac, Grant was not fighting Lee merely; his vision was a much broader one: he was fighting the Confederacy—Lee was merely one of the many obstacles standing in the way of restoration of the Union. That

Grant never lost this point of view is evident from his despatches as well as from his recorded table talk at the time.

Lee's failure to penetrate Grant's designs during the spring campaign of 1864 is wholly to be accounted for by this difference of outlook in the two leaders, and not in any sense by any personal falling off of the Confederate general's mental capacity as a most skilful army commander. Toward the end Lee gradually began to sense Grant's aims; but too late to be able to stem the flood or further to prolong the war. The story is told in his despatches to President Davis.[1]

It is an impressive conclusion to Grant's final campaign that, just as he had out-thought Lee in his strategic aims, so he surprised him in the surrender. Lee came to him thinking in the old terms of victor and vanquished; he found himself and his men received and treated not as rebel prisoners but as sons returning to their rightful political home—two of Meade's corps went hungry for several days that their Southern brothers might be fed.

[1] See Lee's confidential despatches.

GRANT AT CITY POINT, 1864

APPENDICES

APPENDIX A

BELMONT IN THE MEMOIRS

Voluntary memory, the memory of the intellect,
only gives inexact facsimiles of the past which do
not resemble the past any more than bad paintings
resemble springtime.—MARCEL PROUST.

No act of Grant's life compels more our admiration of his superb will-power and unflinching sense of duty than when, in spite of illness and advancing years, he forced himself to the writing of his Memoirs in order to meet the financial difficulties which had overtaken him. But while the Memoirs, with their directness and simplicity, will deservedly survive, a critical examination of them reveals that in the stirring occurrences of the twenty years which had elapsed since the war Grant had forgotten, or had retained but dim memories of, both the events of the Civil War and what he had himself written at the time regarding them.

Belmont is a convenient example; let us begin by summarizing his original statements regarding the affair and then examine the Memoirs in the light of these and other contemporary data:

(1) Grant's first message after Belmont was oral, sent by Colonel Wallace at Bird's Point to Colonel Oglesby, commanding column at Bloomfield, and received the evening of the day following the battle. It will be recalled that on the sixth, Grant, who had not yet learned to measure time and distance, sent orders to Oglesby, then at Bloomfield, to join him at Belmont; it was necessary, therefore, to inform him at once of the result. Oglesby has not incorporated the message in his report, but he communicated it to Colonel Perczel, who has: "Our friends [Grant's forces] had engaged the enemy at Belmont and . . . been routed." [1]

[1] W. R. 3:257.

This was the simple fact, important for the subordinate to know since he must now retreat at once—which he of course did.

(2) Grant's next message was to Smith, also the evening after the battle. It explained simply, "They had eleven regiments against our three thousand men," and left Smith to infer the result.[2]

(3) The report to the Adjutant-General of the Department was sent on the evening of the seventh. This time Grant presented only the brighter aspect of the affair, as it appeared to him that same evening, overlooking the fact that the Confederate side also would be published far and wide:

We met the rebels . . . two and a half miles from Belmont and drove them, step by step, into their camp and across the river. We burned their tents and started on our return with all their artillery. . . . The rebels recrossed the river and followed in our rear to place of embarkation. Losses heavy on both sides.[3]

(4) The day after the battle Grant saw only the victory and forgot the dark hours of the Confederate counter-attack and pursuit. From this altered point of view, he wrote his congratulatory order to be read to his troops, stressing the "hotly contested" battle and "gallantry" of the troops, but saying nothing of the events.[4] He could not delude his own men; they had been there and knew what had happened; the events were fresh in their minds.

(5) He wrote, also on the eighth, a second message to Smith, giving him the silver lining to the cloud: "The victory was complete," with details: the captured cannon, burned tents, one hundred and thirty prisoners, heavier Confederate than Union casualties.[5]

(6) The same day he similarly informed the Adjutant-General: "The victory was complete," etc., with the added justification: "Prisoners taken report that a large force was prepared to start to join Price. This move [of Grant's on Belmont] will no doubt defeat this move [of Confederate troops to join Price].

[2] Nov. 7, W. R. 4:346.
[3] Nov. 7, W. R. 111:506.
[4] W. R. 3:274.
[5] W. R. 4:346.

The prisoners may have said so. In answer to leading questions prisoners of war are likely to assent to almost anything, but their information, to judge from all that is known of Confederate plans, was not true. Neither Polk nor Johnston had given the slightest indication of any intention to reinforce Price from Columbus at this time.

(7) On the eighth Grant sent the good news to his father. In this letter he describes the expedition as a "reconnaissance toward Columbus" and for the first time defined its object, which he says was "to prevent the enemy from sending a force into Missouri to cut off troops I had sent there for a special purpose, and to prevent reinforcing Price." [6]

(8) On November 12, in his third official but first detailed report, he inverted the order of these objectives: "The object of the expedition was to prevent the enemy from sending out reinforcements to Price's army in Missouri and also from cutting off columns that I had been directed to send out from this place and Cape Girardeau in pursuit of Jeff. Thompson." [7]

In this report, evidently to meet the most serious and obvious criticism made of his dispositions for the attack—his failure to hold out a reserve—the transport guard is renamed a "reserve." That it was not so named at the time is fully substantiated by the reports —of Colonel Dougherty, who received the order; [8] of Captain Dietrich, to whom it was immediately transmitted; and of Colonel Lauman, who was either present when the order was given or had it at once communicated to him, since it concerned two companies of his regiment. The order sent to Dietrich by an aid subsequently converted the "transport guard" into a sort of left-flank guard, but a "reserve" it never became in fact, nor was it so named.[9]

(9) The next dated report is that in the official records ("War

[6] Moore III:287.
[7] Moore III:278.
[8] W. R. 3:291, 295, 296.
[9] The correspondent of the "Louisville Journal," also mentions Dietrich's command as "left . . . to guard the steamboats" (Moore III:288). General McClernand does also, W. R. 3:293.

of the Rebellion," No. 3, page 267) headed "Cairo, November 17, 1861," but since this is doubtless the substituted report which Coppée mentions as having been submitted on June 26, 1865, to the Secretary of War "to take the place of the old one," [10] it must be received with double caution.

(10) There is, however, another contemporary report by Grant, dated November 20,[11] in reality a letter of transmittal for the reports of subordinates, but which gives further details.

Thus we see that Grant's story of Belmont in his Memoirs was at least his eleventh account of that affair, all but the first having been committed by him to writing.

Let us now glance briefly at the criticisms disparaging to the conduct of the Union forces at Belmont. For the period immediately following the battle we may take the statement by the Cairo correspondent of the "Louisville Journal," written a few days after the battle, which evidently expresses Grant's own views, because the correspondent mentions being "shown a letter in General Grant's quarters to-day . . . directing him [Grant] to move only against Belmont" and is writing in a strain distinctly favorable to Grant:

It might be well to notice here the underhanded antagonism evident in many of our prominent journals to the Union cause, in pronouncing—even in the face of positive evidence to the contrary—every action in which our troops are engaged . . . to be positive defeats and repulses. We have a notable instance of this determination to embarrass and disparage our army in the recent editorials of the Chicago Tribune and other journals, in relation to this Belmont fight.[12]

In the "Military History of Ulysses S. Grant," by Badeau, Grant's secretary, first published in 1867, we find reflected Grant's evident irritation under this criticism of Belmont which refused to die down during the war:

The country, however, knowing none of the objects of the movement [against Belmont] and seeing only that troops had advanced and then

---

[10] Coppée, Henry, "Grant and His Campaigns," footnote, p. 34.
[11] W. R. 3:272.
[12] Moore III:288.

retired, regarded the affair as a disaster, while the enemy, of course, heralded it for a rebel victory. Long after, many who looked upon Grant as one of the greatest of soldiers, declared he should be forgiven for Belmont.

Now, neither in 1865, when he wrote his substituted report, pre-dated "November 17, 1861," nor twenty years later when he composed his Memoirs, was Grant in any mood to be "forgiven for Belmont," or, for that matter, to be "forgiven" for anything else; his convictions remolding his memories supplied the corrections necessary for explanation.

Regarding Belmont he wrote:

I had no orders which contemplated an attack by the National troops, nor did I intend anything of the kind when I started out from Cairo; but after we started I saw that the officers and men were elated at the prospect of at last having the opportunity of doing what they had volunteered to do—fight the enemies of their country. I did not see how I could maintain discipline or retain the confidence of my command if we should return to Cairo without an effort to do something. Columbus, besides being fortified, contained a garrison much more numerous than the force I had with me. It would not do, therefore, to attack that point. About two o'clock on the morning of the 7th I learned that the enemy was crossing troops from Columbus to the west bank to be despatched, presumably, after Oglesby. I knew there was a small camp of Confederates at Belmont, immediately opposite Columbus, and I speedily resolved to push down the river, land on the Missouri side, capture Belmont, break up the camp, and return.[13]

In other words, Grant, according to his Memoirs, had had no orders to attack, nor had he intended to attack, but was led to do so by the eagerness of his men to fight; and made up his mind speedily after getting, at 2 A.M., the information, which, incidentally, was quite erroneous and considering the source, not stated in the Memoirs, not to be taken seriously.

Grant's is a picturesque account and a real dramatization of history; but let us check up on a few of its statements.

[13] Grant I:220.

If Grant did not intend to attack at Belmont, what did he intend doing? There were not many things he could do and it may be as well briefly to consider his other possible courses of action:

(1) Not to land anywhere, but return to Cairo;
(2) To land on the Kentucky shore, march on Columbus, returning without attacking;
(3) To land on the Missouri shore and

    (a) march toward Belmont, but retire without attacking;
    (b) establish a camp;
    (c) reëmbark;
    (d) land and march to join Oglesby.

With these hypotheses in mind, let us examine Grant's contemporary writings.

Grant wrote to Smith on November 5:

> I am now fitting out an expedition to menace Belmont. If you can make a demonstration toward Columbus at the same time . . . it would probably keep the enemy from throwing over the river much more forces than they now have there, and might enable me to drive those they now have there out of Missouri.[14]

This message excludes any intention of (2) a landing on the Kentucky shore. It also excludes (1) not landing, as how otherwise could he hope to drive the enemy "out of Missouri"? As to the alternatives under (3), to land on the Missouri shore, let us turn to his orders to Oglesby of November 6, written before he left Cairo.[15] Oglesby, it will be recalled, had been sent with a reinforced brigade southwest from Bird's Point (via Commerce) to Sikeston, in pursuit of the Missouri chieftain Jeff Thompson. Grant orders Oglesby: "On receipt of this turn your command to New Madrid. When you arrive at the nearest point to Columbus, from which there is a road to that place, communicate with me at Belmont."

Thus, by giving an independent brigade commander, so to speak, his post-office address at Belmont, and further directing him to march

14 W. R. 3:273.
15 W. R. 3:269.

past Belmont on New Madrid (where so small a force was bound to be cut off, unless protected by some intervening force at or near Belmont), Grant clearly established his intention before leaving Cairo to land for a shorter or longer time at or near Belmont. By another order of the same date, to Colonel Plummer, commanding at Cape Girardeau, a side-light is cast on Grant's intention in writing the order last mentioned:

From On Board Transport near Columbus, Kentucky, November 7 [before the battle]. When I gave directions for the expedition from Cape Girardeau [against Thompson] I expected the force from Bird's Point to protect them from the South and the whole to meet at Bloomfield or be within striking distance. Requiring Colonel Oglesby's command with me, however, I have sent a messenger after it to him in this direction. This will leave your command wholly unprotected from this quarter; hence the necessity of having it [Plummer's detachment] stronger than first designed.[16]

And, as if to deny any sudden change of purpose, Grant goes on to explain that "I should have dispatched to you immediately to prevent the expedition continuing as it was," but "I felt that he was strong enough and did not think of a portion of his command being withdrawn."

What Oglesby thought when he received the November 6 orders (on November 8 at Bloomfield) is best described by his subordinate Colonel Perczel in his report:

At noon on the 8th, Colonel Oglesby arrived with his forces, and gave me orders to be in readiness to march in two hours. His first intention was to push after Thompson [who had retreated without fighting]; his second [evidently after receipt of Grant's order of the sixth] to march toward New Madrid; and his third [evidently after further study of the order of the 6th or talk with the messenger who had brought it] to march toward Belmont, across Nigger Wool Swamp. He gave me orders to march in the last-named direction, promising to follow the next morning. I marched out and encamped at Bessy's Mill.

In the night [of November 8–9] I received a letter from Colonel Oglesby, informing me that [evidently the message sent by General Grant

16 W. R. 3:259.

or his staff officer] our friends had engaged the enemy at Belmont, and that they had been routed, and his [Oglesby's] determination to return to his detachment via Cape Girardeau.[17]

Colonel Oglesby's report supplies the information of how the news was received: "Through Colonel [W.H.L.] Wallace, I received your verbal order to return to Bird's Point." [18]

These data cannot but suggest that what Grant had in mind at the time he informed Smith on November 5, 1861, "It might enable me to drive those [the enemy forces] they now have out of Missouri," was far from being a sort of pleasure excursion on transports down the river and up again without a fight, which is the impression given in his Memoirs. On the contrary, it seems that he had visions of reclaiming the western bank of the Mississippi River (in the State of Missouri), then held by the Confederates from Belmont to New Madrid. Far from suddenly deciding to land to rescue the Oglesby column, Grant, as he wrote Colonel Plummer, now required Oglesby's command with him. Grant's statements of purpose made immediately after the event may be excused as wartime propaganda, but his earnest admirers cannot but regret that he was led twenty years later to distort the facts in this and other instances, an innocent victim to the tricks of memory.

Looking at it from a purely professional point of view, the Belmont expedition, in principle, needed no apology. Grant was ordered to make a demonstration to prevent troops being detached from Columbus. The surest way to do that was to attack a detached outpost not easily to be supported by the Confederates, if (a) Smith would make a feint on Columbus on the Kentucky shore, or if (b) the Union gunboats were able to prevent the crossing of troops. Looking back on it and knowing the exact situation, it is not easy to find a better solution of the problem than Grant's.

In matters of detail Grant's memory is, as is to be expected, equally faulty.

---

[17] W. R. 3:258.
[18] W. R. 3:256.

He states in his Memoirs that he had with him at Belmont two guns. He had six—according to the report of Captain Taylor,[19] and a private letter from a member of Taylor's battery.[20]

He says in his narrative: "When the debarkation commenced I took a regiment down the river to post it as a guard against surprise. At that time I had no staff-officer who could be trusted with that duty." The "guard" was not a regiment, but five companies. It was not posted when the debarkation "commenced," but after the debarkation had been completed and after the last troops to arrive had been formed in line.[21] Left behind *after* the troops had marched away from the landing, Captain Dietrich received orders from one of Grant's aids where to go! [22] Clearly Grant is visualizing in his Memoirs not what took place, but what he wishes he had done or what he would have done if he had it to do over!

The Memoirs continue, "Up to this time [the posting of the transport guard] the enemy had evidently failed to divine our intentions." General Polk had received news of the landing "shortly after" daybreak. He had at once notified Colonel Tappan, commanding at Belmont (who received the news "about 7 A.M."), and ordered Pillow to cross the river with four regiments and take charge. It was the skirmishers sent out by Pillow that Grant first encountered.[23] In this instance Grant naturally had hoped that his intentions might be longer unknown to the enemy, and in his memory the hope displaces the fact which a simple analysis would have shown him.

"The officers and men engaged at Belmont were then under fire for the first time." The twenty-second had been in two engagements.[24] "This [fighting] continued, growing fiercer and fiercer, for about four hours." The fighting began about ten; the camp was

[19] W. R. 3:290.
[20] Moore III:293.
[21] See report of Col. Dougherty, W. R. 3:291, and Capt. Dietrich, W. R. 3:294.
[22] W. R. 3:294.
[23] Reports of Polk, Pillow, Tappan, W. R. 3:306, 325, 355.
[24] W. R. 3:137, 198.

captured shortly after twelve.[25] Grant is making a good story of it!

Grant gives us this picture of the capture of the Confederate camp by his men:

> At this point they became demoralized from their victory. . . . The moment the camp was reached our men laid down their arms and commenced rummaging the tents to pick up trophies. . . . I tried to get them to turn their [captured] guns upon the loaded steamers above. . . My efforts were in vain. At last I directed my staff-officers to set fire to the camps.

The idea seems to be to blame the rawness of the troops for the failure to follow up the victory. Grant tries in vain (so he tells us) to get the men who captured the Confederate guns to turn the guns on the crowded steamers bringing reinforcements. As a last resort, he directs his staff officers to set fire to the camps.

Let us compare this with the facts [26] :

Buford says, "While these deeds [the capture of the camp] were being enacted you [McClernand] rode into our midst and it was by your order that my regiment fired the camp."

If so, did McClernand originate the order or did he receive it from Grant, to transmit to his brigade?

Fouke writes, "After the defeat of the enemy at the camp, I caused my colors to be planted, my drums to beat, and rallied my regiment in position at the point where we were first attacked by the reinforcement of the enemy."

Logan says simply, "After we had taken the camp and burned it," implying, though not definitely stating, that his men had participated in the burning.

Dougherty tells us, "After assisting in the destruction of the rebel camp and property not movable . . . the order to retire . . . was received." He does not say from whom he received the order. It may be noticed, however, that he uses the phraseology of Grant's two official reports, "destruction of property that cannot be moved."

[25] Reports of Trask, Winslow, Butler, Tappan, Miller, Wright, W. R. 3:333–363; Walke, N. R. 22:401.

[26] W. R. 3:284.

Lauman [27] led his men *through* the camp to the river and up the river road, where he was wounded. In his report he says, "In the meantime our men had received orders to burn and destroy the camp and property."

McClernand merely states, "The enemy's tents were set on fire." [28]

Thus, of the five regimental commanders, three (two by direct statement) received orders to burn the camp, one (Lauman) pursued the enemy to and up the river; and one (Fouke) rallied and re-formed his regiment—to which commendable initiative, probably, is due the escape of Grant's force from the envelopment attempted by Polk's reinforcing troops.

We cannot escape the conclusion, in the light of these reports, that while at the time Grant's goal was to "burn the camp" and he set all hands to do it (he wrote his father the next day, "We burned everything possible, and started back, having accomplished all that we went for and even more" [29]), with his maturing judgment, and looking back, he saw the burning as a mistake. The enemy and not the camp should have been and remained the objective; the burning, if done, should have been done by a detail, not by the whole command, which could only lead to disorder. The border lines between the "should have been" and "might have" and "what was" had, not unnaturally, faded out.

But most amusing is the artillery episode of the Memoirs. Grant, to fire on the enemy transports, did not need personally to direct infantrymen with a captured gun—which they never understand how to range or aim. He had Taylor's battery of four six-pounder guns and two twelve-pounder howitzers, and the river was only eight hundred yards wide. Why did he not send or give orders to Taylor, who was right there?

As a matter of fact, McClernand tells us he did order "a section of Taylor's battery . . . down near the river and opened fire upon them [the enemy's steamers]." The Confederate reports tell us the

[27] W. R. 3:296.
[28] W. R. 3:280.
[29] Moore III:287.

fire of these guns was extremely effective and that the further movement of troops across the river had to be suspended for the time being, and until the fire ceased.

One cannot but wonder whether or not Grant at the time knew about the steamers or the battery firing at them, and suspect that he is subconsciously apologizing for something that should have been done, and was done, but that he did not know had been done, by explaining that he tried to do it and failed.

Least satisfying of all in his Memoirs is Grant's account of the retreat and reëmbarkation. In the advance he had accompanied the center regiment (Logan) and given Logan orders.[30] Later, he was with McClernand, who was with Fouke [31] on Logan's right, when his horse was shot in the third charge.[32] Thereafter the only mention of Grant in the reports is in connection with the order given or sent to Dougherty "to retire." [33] The commander of the so-called "transport guard," Captain Dietrich, mentions receiving orders "to march the detachment on board" after "all our forces had about been reëmbarked," but does not state from whom the orders came.

Grant's story of his personal search for the guard, personal reconnaissance of the enemy's pursuing force, and dramatic boarding of the transport—mounted by a single plank—in the absence of the slightest corroborating testimony, and in view of the highly unsatisfactory nature of his whole narrative, is not to be taken seriously. One remembers that even Frederick the Great ran away in his first battle and only learned later that his army had gained the victory.

In the return up the river, it is doubtful if Grant knew that Buford's regiment had been left behind, cut off, because it was McClernand who landed higher up and waited for them, ordering Walke, with his gunboats, to assist.[34] Apparently Grant was occupied with other matters: sending orders for the return of the Oglesby column

[30] W. R. 3:288.
[31] W. R. 3:286.
[32] W. R. 3:279.
[33] W. R. 3:293.
[34] W. R. 3:276, 281.

and providing for the safety of the column sent down the Kentucky side of the Mississippi from Fort Holt, which he subsequently ordered the gunboats to assist if need be.

These "old-soldier camp-fire stories" of the Memoirs—which, because of their wide variance from the established facts, is all they can be called—should in no wise detract from Grant's reputation for generalship in the war, or suggest doubt of his candor or of his honest intentions at the time the Memoirs were written. What he knew how to do, he did well. What he did badly or wrongly, he learned to avoid. Had other generals been as willing to profit from their own mistakes, the war would have been won without Lincoln's having to wait for Grant's tactical and strategic education to be fully completed.

The only object, then, in bringing out the unreliability of these Memoir tales, is to protest against their wide acceptance as the Gospel of the Civil War, by so many historical writers who have swallowed them whole without investigating to determine their historical worth. This has tended to the establishment of an accepted tradition regarding Grant which has not redounded to his credit, but has served to make of him an irresponsible creature of fortune and child of fate, instead of what he was, a man of strong character who knew in reality very little about the military profession in 1861, but who had fine soldierly qualities and an open mind, and who in his quickness to learn was ahead of his compeers. His comrades-in-arms of to-day owe it to him and to themselves to clear away these cobwebs which have served not to add to but to detract from his reputation.

APPENDIX B

Balling's Painting of "Grant and His Generals"

Balling seems to have secured authority of the executive branch of the Government for his painting, to have visited the various generals in the field during the last year of the war, and to have sketched them in their field uniforms and on their war-mounts as actually equipped. Hence this group of portraits is more than mere artist's fancy. The arrangement of the generals—to the left of Grant, in the front rank, his principal army commanders; on the two flanks, also in the front rank, his trusted detachment commanders, Sheridan, Terry, and Schofield—must have been suggested by Grant himself.

The original painting, two by three feet in size, was completed soon after the war and the artist sought in vain amid the turmoil of the times to secure the authorization of Congress to paint an enlargement for the Capitol. Finally, broken in health and spirit, he tried to borrow money on which to exist while painting an enlargement on his own account, but before he could have been satisfied with it the enlargement was seized by his creditors.

The original "Grant and His Generals," has been photographed by Bachrach—it is believed for the first time—for this book. Grant is depicted riding his favorite war-horse, named after the city which presented it to him—"Cincinnati."

A SHORT BIBLIOGRAPHY

WORKS OF REFERENCE

American Encyclopedia. D. Appleton and Company, New York, 1860–63; 16 vols.

Gives a convenient bird's-eye view of fundamental conditions during the Civil War period. Its supplements, "The American Annual Encyclopedia" for the years 1861–65, give valuable contemporaneous data free from the bias of later prejudices.

Eighth Census of the United States (1860). Government Printing Office, Washington, D. C.

Gives a valuable statistical summary of conditions in the United States as a whole and by States and Counties at the outbreak of the Civil War. The volumes on "Population," "Agriculture," and "Manufacturing" are particularly illuminating.

War of the Rebellion: Official Records. Government Printing Office, Washington, D. C., 1880–1901; 128 vols. (Cited in foot-notes as "W. R."; reference being to serial number and page.)

The only sound basis for a study of the Civil War.

Official Records of the Union and Confederate Navies in the War of the Rebellion. Government Printing Office, Washington, D. C., 1894—not completed. (Cited in foot-notes as "N. R."; reference being to serial number and page.)

A valuable supplement to the war records.

Report of the Congressional Committee on the Conduct of the War. Government Printing Office, Washington, D. C., 1863, 1865–66; 5 vols.

Another valuable supplement to the war records.

The Rebellion Record: A Diary of American Events. G. P. Putnam, New York, 1861–69; 12 vols.

Documents, narratives, etc., published contemporaneously during the war period. Contains much information not to be found in the official war records.

Southern Historical Society Papers. Richmond, Va., 1876–1909. (Cited in foot-notes as "S. H. S. P.")
Contain data of much value.

Abraham Lincoln: A History, by John G. Nicolay and John Hay. Century Co., New York, 1890; 12 vols.
Indispensable for the study of the Civil War.

Lee's Dispatches. G. P. Putnam's Sons, New York, 1915.
Contains many important letters not found in the war records.

Donelson Campaign Sources. Army Service Schools Press, Fort Leavenworth, 1912.
A Service School publication which contains some original material.

Sherman Letters. Charles Scribner's Sons, New York, 1894.
Wartime correspondence between General and Senator Sherman.

Battles and Leaders of the Civil War. Century Co., New York, 1887; 4 vols.
Contains valuable data.

HISTORIES AND NARRATIVES

Atkinson, C. F. *Grant's Campaigns of 1864 and 1865.* Hugh Rees, London, 1908.
A thoughtful and very valuable study of the last campaign of the Army of the Potomac.

Badeau, Adam. *Military History of U. S. Grant.* D. Appleton and Company, New York, 1881; 3 vols.
A valuable study containing important data, but highly colored in favor of Grant and representing his views long after the events.

Coolidge, Louis A. *Ulysses S. Grant.* Houghton Mifflin Company, Boston, 1917, 1922.
An able study featuring Grant as President but giving a pleasing appreciation of his war service.

Coppée, Henry. *Grant and His Campaigns.* Charles B. Richardson, New York, 1866.
Written by a West Point graduate and based on intelligent study of the records. Contains much original matter.

Cramer, Jesse Grant. *Letters of Ulysses S. Grant.* G. P. Putnam's Sons, New York, 1912.
Grant's wartime letters to his father and younger sister; of personal interest.

Dana, C. A. *Recollections of the Civil War.* D. Appleton and Company, New York, 1898.
A delightful narrative, but composed late in the author's life and based mainly on recollections.

Dodge, Gen. G. M. *Personal Recollections of Pres. Lincoln, Gen. U. S. Grant, and William T. Sherman.* Monarch Printing Co., Council Bluffs, Iowa, 1914; privately printed.
Gives interesting sidelights on Grant; by a trusted subordinate and close personal friend.

Fiske, John. *The Mississippi Valley in the Civil War.* Houghton Mifflin Company, Boston, 1901.
A general history of the Western campaigns.

Force, Gen. M. F. *From Fort Henry to Corinth.* Charles Scribner's Sons, New York, 1881.
An excellent introduction to the study of this campaign.

Fuller, Col. J. F. C. *The Generalship of Ulysses S. Grant.* Dodd, Mead & Company, New York, 1929.
A thoughtful study.

Garland, Hamlin. *Ulysses S. Grant, His Life and Character.* The Macmillan Company, New York, 1898, 1920.
Is based on wide research and contains interesting documents.

Grant, U. S. *Personal Memoirs.* Century Co., New York, 1885, 1895; 2 vols.
References are to the second edition; for estimate see Appendix.

Greene, Gen. F. W. *The Mississippi.* Charles Scribner's Sons, New York, 1899.
A keen bird's eye view of the operations in this theater of war.

Hart, B. H. Liddell. *Sherman, Soldier, Realist, American.* Dodd, Mead & Company, New York, 1929.
A work highly recommended but somewhat colored in justification of Sherman.

Howard, Gen. O. O. *Autobiography of Oliver Otis Howard.* The Baker and Taylor Co., New York, 1907; 2 vols.
Based on a wartime diary and valuable.

Howell, Col. Willey. *Lieut.-General Grant's Campaign of 1864–65.* (Military Historian and Economist, Vol. I.) Harvard University Press, Cambridge, Mass., 1916.

The pioneer study of the economic factors of this campaign. Has been largely drawn upon in Chapters XXII and XXIII of the present work.

Humphreys, Gen. A. *The Virginia Campaign of '64 and '65.* Charles Scribner's Sons, New York, 1899.
An indispensable work for the study of this campaign, by the able Chief of Staff of the Army of the Potomac.

King, Gen. Charles. *The True Ulysses S. Grant.* J. B. Lippincott Company, Philadelphia, 1914.
Another book by a West Point graduate which gives a vivid personal portrayal based on wide research and contains data not found elsewhere.

Meade, George. *Life and Letters of George Gordon Meade.* Charles Scribner's Sons, New York, 1913.
Contains valuable contemporary documents.

Porter, Gen. Horace. *Campaigning with Grant.* Century Co., New York, 1897.
Gives a picture of daily routine and performance of staff duty at Grant's headquarters during the Virginia campaign of 1864–65 and interesting personal glimpses of Grant.

Richardson, Albert D. *A Personal History of Ulysses S. Grant.* American Publishing Co., Hartford, Conn., 1869.
The work of a war correspondent who spent much time at Grant's headquarters, highly anecdotal and not always reliable, but giving valuable original material.

Schouler, James. *History of the United States of America under the Constitution.* Dodd, Mead & Company, New York, 1899; 7 vols.
Vol. VI of this history covers the period 1861–65 and gives an admirable critical survey of the Civil War.

Sherman, Gen. W. T. *Memoirs.* C. L. Webster & Co., New York, 1890; 2 vols.
Honest, blunt, delightful; but not always accurate.

Wilson, Gen. J. H. *Under the Old Flag.* D. Appleton and Company, New York, 1912; 2 vols.
Interesting reminiscences, comments and critiques, by Grant's one-time staff officer.

Wister, Owen. *Ulysses S. Grant.* Small, Maynard & Co., Boston, 1909.
All too brief, but a classical introduction to the study of Grant.

INDEX

Adams, Henry, 300
Alcorn, Gen., 115, 149, 151
Alexander, Col., 9
Alexandria, La., 342
Ammen, Col., 228
Appomattox, 334, 340, 350
Arkansas, Confederate organization in, 33, 39
Athens, Ala., 344
Atlanta, 309, 324, 342, 343, 345
Auburn, Miss., 289, 290
Averell, Gen. W. W., 336, 338

Badeau, Adam, 254, 268, 299, 366
Banks, Gen. N. P., 288, 293, 294, 324, 326, 328, 341, 342, 343
Battle of Chickamauga, 9, 301
  Cloyd's Mountain, 336
  Belmont, 86–100, 363–375
  Bull Run, 282
  Fort Donelson, 18, 170
  Fort Henry, 158
  Iuka, Miss., 280
  Lookout Mountain, 301
  Mansfield, La., 342, 343
  Missionary Ridge, 303
  Monroe, 6
  Seven Days', at Richmond, 299
  Shiloh, 7, 18, 29, 238, 256
  Stone's River, 9
  The Wilderness, 256
Bayou Pierre, 289
Baxter, Capt., 123, 124, 155, 245, 249
Bear Creek, 214, 217
Beauregard, Gen. Pierre G. T., 235, 238, 259, 273, 276, 277, 333
Belle of Memphis, 85
Belmont, battle of, 86–100, 363–375
Belmont, Mo., 26, 44, 54, 55, 56, 62, 63, 66, 72, 79, 85, 86, 101, 118, 124, 125, 156, 157, 160, 164, 231, 292
Benton, Mo., 25, 27, 74
Bermuda Hundred, 333
Bertrand, Mo., 119
Beverly, Va., 330, 335
Bird's Point, Mo., 20, 26, 54, 60, 62,

66, 72, 81, 82, 118, 119, 120, 121, 144, 363
Black River, 290, 291
Bland, Col., 25
Blandville, Ky., 62, 68, 81, 145
Bloomfield, Mo., 38, 74, 363
Bolivar, Tenn., 280
Bolton, Miss., 290, 291
Bowen, Gen., 148, 149
Bowling Green, Ky., 73, 76, 79, 131, 136, 137, 138, 140, 149, 154, 180, 181, 187, 190, 200
Bragg, Gen. B., 238, 278, 300, 301, 302, 344
Breckenridge, Gen., 337, 339
Bridgeport, Miss., 291
Bruinsburg, Miss., 289
Brunot, Mo., 19
Buckner, Gen. Simon B., 54, 76, 79, 136, 171, 174
Buel, Col. W. H., 127
Buell, Gen. D. C., 73, 118, 131, 132–145, 152, 178, 192, 200–228, 239, 243, 249, 254, 259, 260, 261, 262, 265, 266, 271, 277, 280, 298, 328
Buell-Halleck duel of despatches over Forts Henry and Donelson, 178–213
Buford, Col., 87, 89, 91, 102, 103, 104, 106, 107, 372
Bull Run, battle of, 282
Burnside, Gen. Ambrose E., 256, 268, 300, 305
Butler, Gen. Benjamin F., 276, 294, 324, 326, 328, 330, 332, 333, 334, 337, 346

Cairo, gunboat, 225
Cairo, Ill., 6, 13, 18, 20, 26, 30, 38, 44, 48, 53, 54, 58, 60, 61, 67, 68, 77, 78, 83, 85, 98, 99, 102, 110, 112, 117, 118, 120, 124, 125, 127, 129, 133, 136, 138, 139, 146, 155, 162, 164, 174, 180, 190, 195, 198, 199, 226, 234, 278, 294
Caledonia, Mo., 15

Camden, 343
Camp Beauregard, 111, 149, 150
Camp Holt, 120
Camp Johnston, 88, 93
Camp Yates, 4
Canby, Gen. Edward R. S., 342, 343, 344
Cape Girardeau, 24–28, 38, 54, 55, 60, 72, 73, 74, 81, 82, 114, 365, 369
Carlin, Col., 75, 81
Carondelet, gunboat, 167
Centerville, Mo., 16, 17, 24
Chalk Bluffs, Ky., 58
Champion's Hill, 290
Chancellor, transport, 94
Charleston, Mo., 25, 54, 66, 68, 72, 73, 81, 87, 119, 121
Charleston, West Va., 330, 335, 336, 339
Charm, The, 92, 103
Chattanooga, 277, 280, 296, 302, 341–344, 355
Cheatham, Gen., 97, 109
Chicago, 42
Chickamauga, 301
Chickamauga, battle of, 9
Chickasaw Bluffs, 285, 286
Chickasaw, Tenn., 225, 226
Christiansburg, 336
Cincinnati, 48
"Cincinnati Gazette," quoted, 257, 262
Citronelle, Ala., 343
City Point, 324
Civil War, analysis of the causes of, 41 *et seq.*
Clarksville, 188, 196, 199, 200, 202, 211
Clinton, Miss., 290
Cloyd's Mountain, battle of, 336
Coathe's Mill, 145
Cold Harbor, 334, 337, 338, 340
Columbia, Tenn., 220, 344
Columbus, Ky., 54, 55, 56, 57, 61, 63, 64, 66, 67, 69, 70, 72, 73, 74, 75, 76, 79, 80, 83, 97, 102, 105, 111, 115, 116, 118, 133, 135, 139, 145, 146, 147, 148, 152, 154, 158, 231, 335, 278, 365
Commerce, Mo., 25
Conestoga, gunboat, 48, 63, 64, 73, 161
Confederacy, the: military organization of the Mississippi valley, 32–40; failure to recognize economic factors, 50; comparative wealth of, 51; man-power of, 53; forces in Kentucky, 67; the economic structure of, 312; military population of, 313; losses—killed and

wounded, 313; man-power, 315; loss from desertion, 315; Grant's estimate of resources, 316; war finance, 316; cotton and tobacco crops, 317; food supply, 318; metal resources, 319; manufactures, 319, 320; railroads, 321
Confederate States, wealth of, 51
Confederate commanders, 35–40
Confederate regiments: Arkansas—13th, 88, 89. Tennessee—2d, 92; 13th, 108
Corinth, Miss., 214, 218, 219, 221, 222, 223, 226, 235, 238, 239, 260, 273, 275, 276, 278, 279, 280, 283, 284, 344
Coppée, Prof. Henry, 254, 268, 366
Cotton crop of the South, 316
Covington, 335
Crittenden, Gen. T. L., 249, 259
Crook, Gen., 335, 336, 338
Crump's Landing, Tenn., 217, 221, 244, 249
Cuba Station, Miss., 312
Cullum, Gen., 197, 200, 201
Culpeper Court-House, 330
Cumberland River operations, 166–200
Curtis, Gen., 113, 114, 126, 215, 281

D. G. Taylor, The, 127
Dallas, Mo., 25
Dalton, Ga., 341, 343
Davis, Jefferson, 31, 32, 35, 37, 44, 53, 55, 56, 67, 96, 97, 99, 277, 300, 329, 344, 345, 346, 361
Decatur, Ala., 235, 278
Dietrich, Capt., 365, 371, 374
Dollin, Col., 88
Dougherty, Col. Henry, 85, 86, 87, 88, 95, 105, 365, 372
Dover, Ky., 166, 168, 170, 178, 182, 183, 188
Drury's Bluff, 333
Dublin, 336
Duck River, 223

Eads, James B., 47
Early, Gen. Jubal, 332, 339, 340
Eastport, Miss., 214, 231
Echols, Gen., 337
Eckert, Major, 356
Eddyville, Ky., 77
Edwards Station, Miss., 290
Elkins Ferry, 343
Elliott's Mills, Ky., 69, 145
Essex, gunboat, 161

Farm products of the Confederacy, 317
Farragut, Admiral David G., 276
Fayetteville, Tenn., 336, 344
Financial problem of the Confederacy, 316
Fincastle, 335
Florence, Ala., 188, 344
Florida, Mo., 6
Floyd, Gen., 169, 171, 176
Fontenoy, battle of, 295
Food supply of the Confederacy, 318
Foote, Commodore, A. H., 48, 58, 83, 84, 98, 118, 124, 141, 152, 153, 154, 157, 158, 161, 164, 168, 171, 174, 183, 190, 195, 197, 201, 202, 204, 249
Forrest, Gen. N. B., 176, 344, 356
Fort Donelson, 63, 154, 158, 160, 161, 162, 163, 164 et seq., 228, 230, 232, 255, 256, 265, 278, 354
Fort Donelson, battle of, 166–176
Fort Fisher, 346
Fort Gaines, 343
Fort Heiman, 156, 157
Fort Henry, 107, 156, 163, 178, 188, 224, 232, 289
Fort Henry, plans for attack on, 142–154
Fort Holt, 61, 62, 65, 72, 98, 115, 136, 144
Fort Jefferson, 62, 65, 68, 70, 71, 87, 146
Fort Morgan, 343
Fort Sumter, 46, 47
Fortress Columbus, 148
Fortress Monroe, 331
Foulke, Col., 108, 372, 374
Four Mile Creek, 290
Fox, G. V., Asst. Sec. Navy, 83
Franklin, Tenn., 344, 355
Fredericktown, Mo., 17, 19, 24, 75, 76
Frémont, Gen. John C., 7, 8, 11, 13, 16, 17, 18, 19, 20, 24, 25, 26, 27, 28, 38, 48, 54, 58, 60, 61, 62, 63, 64, 65, 66, 67, 68, 71, 72, 73, 75, 81, 82, 83, 98, 124, 125, 201, 308, 328

Gordonsville, 338
Grand Gulf, 288, 289, 290, 291
Grant, Gen. Ulysses S., adviser to Gov. Yates, 4; organizes 21st Illinois Regt., 4; appointed colonel, 4; as a regimental commander, 6–10; made brigadier-general, 11; at Pilot Knob, 11–19; superseded by Gen. Prentiss, 19; in command at Jefferson City, 20–23; the Prentiss affair at Benton, 27; assumes command of Southeastern Missouri District, 30; realizes importance of Mississippi River operations, 45; occupies Paducah, Ky., 58; rebuffed by Gen. Frémont, 60; activities in Kentucky, 63 et seq.; forces under his command, 67; the Belmont engagement, 85–101; negotiates for exchange of prisoners, 102–109; first uses term "the enemy," 111; applies economic pressure, 112; as a disciplinarian, 116–121; reports to Gen. Halleck, 118, 119, 121, 122, 126; problem of supplies, 123; relations with superiors, 124–129; the Fort Henry plan, 154; up the Tennessee River, 155; captures Fort Henry, 158; crosses to the Cumberland, 165; invests Fort Donelson, 167; the Fort Henry campaign, 179; after Fort Henry, 183; during Fort Donelson campaign, 187; after fall of Fort Donelson, 191, 199; differences with Gen. Halleck, 193; Halleck's instructions, 195; further friction, 202–213; superseded by Gen. Smith, 206; Halleck explains, 210–212; command restored, 214; prepares for Tennessee River expedition, 216–221; waiting for Buell, 222–227; strength of forces, 224; associations with Gen. C. F. Smith, 228; use of spies, 235; before Shiloh, 241; at the Battle of Shiloh, 241–249; leadership, 250; the last Confederate attack, 258; Union counter-attacks, 259; criticisms of the battle, 262–269; under Halleck's command, 271–275; at Corinth, 277; the Mississippi campaign, 281–284; investment and capture of Vicksburg, 285–291; Grant and President Lincoln, 291; commissioned Major-General, 292; contemplates capture of Mobile, 293; given broader command, 296; at Chattanooga, 296–300; Lookout Mountain, 301; relieves Knoxville, 305; as a strategist, 307–312; his strategic map, 308; plan for the Mississippi campaign, 309; presents new plan for capture of Richmond, 310; his résumé of the problem on assuming chief command, 323; sea operations planned, 324; orders to secure coöperation, 326; final report,

327; strategy for final campaign, 329;
in the East, 330–340; in the West,
341–346; first to command an army
of a million, 349; Meade's attitude,
349; relations with Sherman, 353;
with Thomas, 354; Grant and Lee,
360; analysis of the Belmont engagement as described in the "Memoirs,"
363–375
Greenville, Mo., 14, 19, 24, 81
Grenada, Miss., 283, 285
Grierson, Gen., 288
Gunboats on the Mississippi, 46, 47, 48

Halleck, Gen. Henry W., 13, 20, 29,
38, 49, 117, 118, 123, 125, 151, 154,
158, 163, 217, 228, 231, 237, 264,
268, 278, 280, 284, 298, 312, 342,
354, 357, 358; assumes command of
the Western Department, 111; receives reports from Gen. Grant, 118,
119, 121, 122, 126; questions Grant's
authority to exchange prisoners, 127–
129; plans active operations in Missouri, 130; relations with Gen.
McClellan, 131–140; with Gen. Buell,
134–138; orders Grant to open campaign in Tennessee, 143; interview
with Grant, 151–153; the triumvirate—Halleck, Buell, McClellan,
and their duel of despatches, 178–213;
orders Tennessee River expedition,
214; receives Grant's reports, 217–
225; gives Grant free hand, 232;
assumes command after battle of
Shiloh, 270–275; advances on Corinth,
271; relinquishes command and returns to Washington, 275; caution before Corinth, 277; the problem of
the Mississippi, 281; evinces high respect for Grant, 282; receives Grant's
plans for Mississippi campaign, 308;
Grant's suggestion for Richmond campaign, 310; relieved from duty as
General-in-Chief, 312
Halleck-Buell duel of despatches over
Forts Henry and Donelson, 178–213
Hall's Ferry, 290
Hannibal and St. Joseph Railroad, 6
Hannibal, Mo., 6
Hardee, Gen. William J., 14, 17, 33,
36, 38, 76, 97, 126
Harris, Gen. Tom, 5, 6, 7
Harris, Governor of Tennessee, 54, 55,
56, 57
Hatch, Col., 109

Hawkins, Capt., 234
Hay and Nicolay, 282
Hecker, Col., 19, 62
Heiman, Col., 158, 160
Helena, Ark., 281
Hickman, Ky., 55, 58, 114
Hicksford, Va., 310, 333
Hildebrand, Gen., 264
Hillyer, Capt., 104, 234
Hitchcock, Gen., 185, 192
Hoke, Gen., 334
Hollins, Commander, 147
Holly Springs, Miss., 277, 279, 283, 285
Holt, Col., 186
Hood, Gen. J. B., 12, 344, 345, 355,
356, 357, 359
Hooker, Gen. Joseph, 268, 297, 300,
330
Hopkinsville, Ill., 118
Howard, Gen. O. O., 297
Hurlbut, Gen. S. A., 216, 217, 240,
242, 244, 247, 248, 259, 266, 268
Humboldt, Tenn., 214, 231, 288
Hunter, Gen., 110, 185, 192, 328, 337,
338, 339
Huntsville, Ala., 341

Illinois, volunteers enrolled, 43
Imboden, Gen., 337
Indian Ford, 81, 82
Indian Territory, Confederate organiza-
tion in, 33
Indiana, volunteers enrolled, 43
Iowa, volunteers enrolled, 43
Ironton, Mo., 6, 9, 11, 14, 15, 18, 19,
21, 22, 24, 25, 26, 27, 37, 38, 61,
72, 75, 81, 87
Irwinsville, Ga., 346
Island No. 10, 79
Iuka, battle of, 280

J. D. Perry, The, 114
Jackson, Governor of Missouri, 34, 96
Jackson, Miss., 290, 291, 312
Jackson, Mo., 26, 27, 61
Jackson, Tenn., 214, 231, 279, 280
Jackson, "Stonewall," 268
James River Canal, 332, 334, 340
Jefferson City, Mo., 20, 23
Jefferson Barracks, 8
Johnson, Gen. Bushrod, 171
Johnston, Gen. Albert Sidney, 73, 74,
76, 79, 80, 97, 99, 148, 149, 150,
159, 169, 218, 224, 229, 238, 245,
265, 268, 272, 365

Johnston, Gen. Joseph E., 290, 293, 329, 341, 342, 343, 344, 345
Jonesborough, 121

Kemper, Gen., 334
Kentucky, importance of to the Confederacy, 50; neutrality of, 51; joins the North, 51; invaded by Confederates, 54; legislature adopts Union resolution, 57; early campaign in, 62–79
King, Gen. Charles, 205
Knoxville, 305, 341

"Lady Davis," Confederate big gun, 93, 99
Lagow, Capt., 234
La Grange, Tenn., 285
Lauderdale Springs, 312
Lauman, Col., 70, 87, 168, 365, 373
Lee, Gen. Robert E., 24, 268, 310, 329, 332, 334, 339, 345, 346, 360–362
Leesburg, 339
Lexington, gunboat, 48, 61, 62, 63
Lexington, Mo., 71, 80
Liao-Yang, battle of, 296
Lincoln, Abraham, 20, 44, 45, 57, 100, 134, 135, 136, 145, 192, 200, 209, 291, 293, 295, 300, 335, 354, 356, 360
Little Rock, 281, 343
Logan, Gen. John A., 88, 172, 372
Longstreet, Gen. James, 297, 300, 305, 312, 341
Lookout Mountain, 296–301
Losses in Confederate armies, 313
Louisville, 344
Louisville and Nashville Railroad, 97
Lowe, Col., 74
Lynchburg, 336, 338, 339
Lyon. Gen., 17, 20, 33, 96

Magoffin, Governor of Kentucky, 53, 57, 58
Man-power of the Confederacy, 53, 314
Man-power of the North, 53
Mansfield, La., battle of, 342, 343
McArthur, Gen. J., 26, 169, 172
McClellan, Gen. George B., 14, 45, 48, 101, 123, 130, 132, 133, 134, 137, 138, 139, 140, 143, 152, 154, 175, 178, 192, 198, 204, 213, 256, 268, 295, 300, 328, 331
McClernand, Gen. J. A., 85, 86, 88, 94, 102, 116, 118, 121, 145, 155, 156, 157, 168, 169, 171, 173, 175, 218, 219, 224, 233, 240, 242, 244, 246, 253, 272, 283, 286, 287, 372, 373, 374
McCook, Gen. A. McD., 259
McCook, Gen. E. M., 356
McCullough, Gen. Benjamin, 33, 34, 37
McDowell, Gen. Irvin, 295
McKeever, Adjt.-Gen., 82
McPherson, Col. J. B., 163, 221, 227, 240, 241, 244, 245, 247, 248, 250, 289, 333
Marengo, battle of, 255, 269
Marks, Col., 94
Marsh, Col., 26
Maryland Heights, 339
Mattoon, Ill., 4
Mayfield, Ky., 69, 79, 111, 145
Meade, Gen. George G., 324, 326, 330, 331, 334, 337, 338, 339, 346, 349–353
Meadow Bridge, 336, 338
Meigs, Quartermaster-General, 124
Memphis, 154, 235, 275, 279, 280, 281, 285, 286
Memphis and Charleston Railroad, 217, 277
Memphis, The, 104
Meridian, Miss., 309, 312
Metal resources of the Confederacy, 319
Mexico, French occupation of, 293
Milburn, Ky., 231
Miller, Lieut.-Col., 150
Milliken's Bend, 288
Mill Springs, Ky., 140
Minnesota, resolution concerning Mississippi River, 43
Minnesota, volunteers enrolled, 43
Missionary Ridge, battle of, 303
Mississippi Central Railroad campaign, 283
Mississippi River, its rôle in the Civil War, 41–49
Missouri and the Confederacy, 39
Missouri as a border state, 50
Missouri, Jackson, Governor of, 34
Missouri National Guard, 34
Mobile, 293, 309, 324, 342, 343
Mobile and Ohio Railroad, 217
Moltke, Count von, 294
Monocacy Junction, 339
Monroe, Mo., 6, 7
Montgomery, Ala., 309
Montgomery City, Mo., 7
Moore, Col., 263, 264
Mulligan, Col., 71
Murdoch, Col., 116

Naples, Ill., 5
Napoleon, 255, 269, 349
Nashville, 79, 132, 191, 199, 200, 202, 218, 222, 223, 235, 296, 344, 354
National Guard of Missouri, 34
Naval operations in the Mississippi River, 46 *et seq.*
Neely's Landing, 121
Nelson, Gen., 191, 202, 227, 228, 243, 259, 270
New Berne, 310
New England, volunteers enrolled, 43
New Era, gunboat, 97
New Madrid, Mo., 32, 73, 80, 85, 114, 118, 368, 369, 370
Newmarket, 337
New Orleans, 80, 276, 293, 341, 343
New River skirmish, 336
New York State, volunteers enrolled, 43
Nicolay and Hay, 282
Norfolk, Ky., 62, 64, 66, 70, 71, 72, 81, 87
North Anna River, 337, 338
Northern States, man-power of, 53
Northern States, wealth of, 51

Oglesby, Col., 65, 66, 68, 70, 71, 72, 82, 85, 117, 121, 172, 363, 368, 369, 370
Orchard Knob, 301
Ord, Gen., 279, 335, 336
Owensboro, Ky., 70
Oyama, Marshal, 296

Paducah, Ky., 51, 58, 60, 61, 63, 64, 66, 67, 68, 73, 74, 83, 85, 97, 126, 129, 130, 133, 136, 138, 139, 145, 147, 199, 201, 211, 230, 233
Paine, Gen., 145, 231
Palmetto, Ga., 344
Palmyra, Mo., 6
Parkersburg, 339
Pea Ridge, Ark., 215
Pea Ridge, Tenn., 222
Pearce, Gen. N. Bart, 34, 37
Pemberton, Gen., 284, 285, 289, 290
Pennsylvania, volunteers enrolled, 43
Pensacola, 343
Perczel, Col., 369
Petersburg, 339, 350
Phelps, Lieut., 161, 164
Pickett, Gen. George E., 334
Pillow, Gen. Gideon J., 32, 33, 36, 38, 55, 83, 86, 87, 89, 90, 91, 97, 100, 103, 164, 171, 173, 174, 371

Pilot Knob, 11, 81
Pine Bluff, 343
Pinkerton, Allen, 14
Pittsburg Landing, 50, 217–227, 259
Platte City, The, 111
Plummer, Col., 76, 82, 369
Polk, Capt., 103
Polk, Gen. Leonidas, 32, 33, 35, 54, 55, 56, 57, 58, 61, 66, 67, 68, 70, 74, 78, 79, 80, 86, 93, 97, 98, 99, 100, 102, 103, 104, 105, 106, 107, 119, 120, 127, 144, 148, 149, 150, 159, 160, 308, 365, 371
Pope, Gen. John, 7, 8, 20, 21, 72, 124, 126, 256, 268, 271, 282
Port Gibson, 289
Port Hudson, 293
Porter, Commodore W. D., 83, 84, 97, 146, 286, 288
Porter, Gen. Fitz-John, 29
"Post of Arkansas," 286
Potosi, Mo., 16, 17
Prentiss, Gen., 19, 24, 29, 55, 216, 223, 226, 240, 244, 247, 248, 250, 253, 254, 260, 263, 264, 268
Price, Gen. Sterling, 34, 37, 66, 75, 80, 96, 143, 147, 217, 218, 221, 222, 223, 227, 279, 308, 365
Princeton, West Va., 336
Puntney's Bend, 146
Purdy, Tenn., 217

Railroads of the Confederacy, 321
Raleigh, 310
Ramsey, Governor of Wisconsin, 43
Rawlins, Col. J. A., 233, 245, 249, 291, 299
Raymond, Miss., 290
Reynolds, Gov. T. C., 80
Richardson, Albert D., 162, 176, 268
Richmond, 310, 332, 337
Riggen, Col. John, 234
Rodgers, Commander John, 47, 48, 55, 61 *note*
Roosevelt, Theodore, 184
Rosecrans, Gen. William S., 279, 287, 293, 296, 297, 325, 355
Ross, Col., 62, 116
Rowley, Capt., 233, 249

St. François River, 81, 82
St. Genevieve, Mo., 24
St. Joseph, Mo., 37
St. Louis, 5, 7, 19, 21, 24, 77, 83, 84, 110, 112, 113, 120, 125, 127, 147, 151, 200

St. Louis-Ironton Railroad, 24, 39, 75
St. Louis-Rollo Railroad, 39
Salt River, Mo., 6
Saltville, Va., 335, 336
Savannah, Ga, 345
Savannah, Tenn., 214, 215, 216, 217,
  218, 221, 227, 235, 236, 237, 249,
  259
Saxe, Marshal, 295
Schofield, Gen. John McA., 358
Scott, Gen. Winfield, 36, 45, 68, 128,
  182, 295, 348
Selma, 342
Seven Days' Battles, 299
Shawneetown, Ill., 117, 118
Shenandoah Valley, 330, 332, 337, 339,
  340
Sheridan, Gen. Philip, 328, 332, 333,
  334, 338, 339, 340, 346, 350
Sherman, Gen. William T., 73, 76, 118,
  185, 198, 214, 217, 218, 219, 221,
  222, 226, 227, 236, 240, 242, 244,
  246, 253, 254, 257, 260, 268, 274,
  279, 285, 286, 287, 289, 293, 303,
  305, 306, 308, 312, 326, 328, 333,
  334, 341, 342, 345, 353
Sherman's march to the sea, 312, 345
Shiloh, 228, 229
Shiloh, battle of, 7, 18, 29, 238, 256,
  262-270
Sigel, Gen. Franz, 116, 326, 328, 334,
  336, 337, 339
Sikeston, Mo., 74, 85
Simmesport, La., 342
Smith, Col. R. F., 6, 25
Smith, Gen. C. F., 60, 63, 69, 71, 76,
  77, 82, 98, 126, 128, 132, 136, 142,
  144, 145, 147, 156, 157, 175, 192,
  195, 198, 205, 206, 207, 214, 216,
  217, 218, 219, 222, 229, 233, 235,
  364, 368
Smith, Francis M., 108
Snake Creek, 253
Spottsylvania, 337
Springfield, Ill., 4, 77
Springfield, Mo., 17, 81
Spring Hill, Tenn., 344
Stanton, Edwin M., 183, 200, 202, 204,
  294, 295, 354, 355, 356, 357
States' rights doctrine, 41
Staunton, 338
Steele, Gen., 341, 343
Stephens, Alexander H., 50
Stewart, Capt., 121
Stoneman, Gen., 340, 346
Stone's River, battle of, 9

Strasburg, 337, 338
Stembel, Commander, 62, 63
Stuart, Gen. David, 242, 248, 259
Stuart, Gen. J. E. B., 346
Suffolk, Va., 310, 333

Tappan, Col., 86, 88, 89, 91, 108, 371
Taylor, Capt., 371
Taylor, Gen. Richard, 343
Taylor, Gen. Zachary, 36
Tate, Sam, 36
Tennessee, as a border State, 50
Tennessee, Confederate organization in,
  32
Tennessee River operations, 155-160,
  214
Terry, Gen., 346
Thomas, Gen. George H., 140, 280,
  296, 297, 300, 301, 303, 344, 354-
  359
Thompson, Gen. M. Jefferson, 32, 37,
  38, 61, 62, 72, 73, 74, 75, 76, 79,
  81, 82, 97, 110, 119, 365, 368
Thompson's Hills, 289
Tigress, despatch-boat, 243, 245, 249
Tilghman, Gen., 158
Transportation, prior to Civil War, 42-
  44
Trask, Capt., 92
Turchin, Col., 62
Tuscumbia, Ala., 344
Twiggs, Gen. David E., 32, 34, 47
Tyler, Col., 94
Tyler, river gunboat, 48

Union City, Ky., 74, 111
Union regiments: Illinois —7th, 27, 88;
  16th, 6; 21st, 4, 6, 7, 19; 22d, 87;
  27th, 87, 89, 102, 107; 31st, 88.
  Iowa—7th, 87, 94; 15th, 246; 16th,
  246

Van Dorn, Gen., 215, 278, 279, 280
Van Duzer, Capt., 356
Van Horn, Col., 264
Verona, Miss., 344
Vicksburg, 38, 50, 280, 281, 351; in-
  vestment and capture of, 285-291
Virginia and East Tennessee Railroad,
  332, 334, 335
Virginia Central Railroad, 338
Virginia, final campaign planned, 330
Virginia's importance to the Confed-
  eracy, 322
Volunteers, percentage enrolled in vari-
  ous States, 43

Waagner, Col., 26, 54, 55, 61, 62, 63, 64, 68, 69
Walke, Commander, 77, 84, 94, 167
Wallace, Gen. Lew, 118, 168, 173, 217, 223, 233, 241, 244, 245, 247, 248, 249, 250, 252, 255, 257, 260, 266, 270, 272, 339
Wallace, Gen. W. H. L., 66, 118, 172, 175, 227, 244, 247, 248, 257, 260, 363
Walnut Hills, 291
Washburne, Congressman, 4
Washington, D. C., threatened, 339
Waynesboro, Va., 340
Waynesborough, Tenn., 220
Wealth, comparative, of the North and the Confederacy, 51
Webster, Col., 104, 156, 234, 253, 258
Weldon, N. C., 310
Welles, Gideon, 47, 118
West Point Military Academy, 35
Wheeler, Gen. Joseph, 344
White River, 82

Wilderness, battle of, 256
Williams, Seth, 300
Wilmington, N. C., 310, 346
Wilson, Gen., 346, 357, 358
Wilson's Creek, 33, 37, 71, 96
Winchester, 337, 339, 340
Wisconsin, reliance on Mississippi River route, 43
Wisconsin, volunteers enrolled, 43
Wood, Gen., 243, 259
Wright, Col., J. V., 108
Wright, Col. Marcus J., 109
Wright, Gen., 339
Wytheville, Va., 335, 336

Yallabusha River, 285
Yankee, gunboat, 63
Yates, Richard, Governor of Illinois, 4
Yazoo River, 291
Yazoo, The, 104

Zollicoffer, Gen., 54, 140

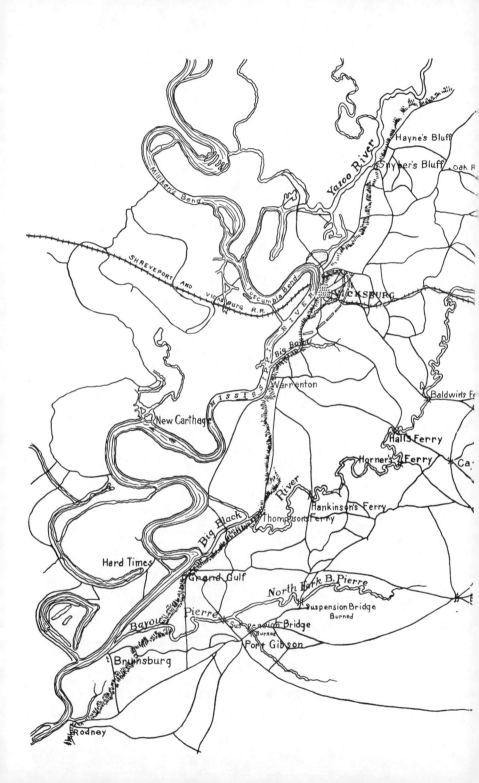

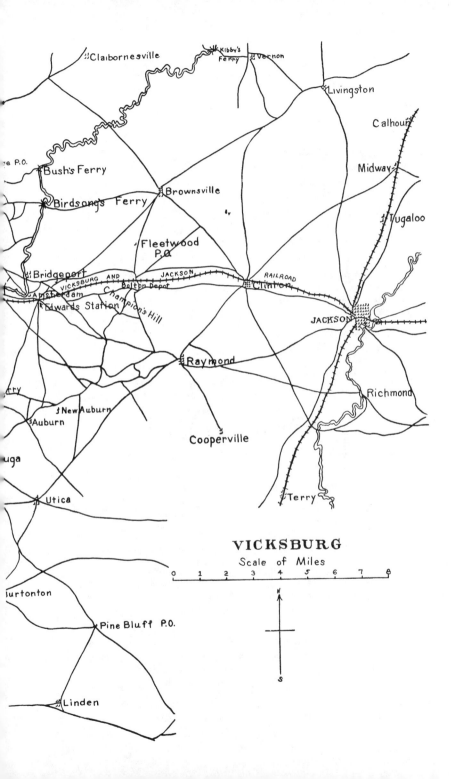

VICKSBURG

Scale of Miles

0 1 2 3 4 5 6 7 8

Claibornesville   Kibby's Ferry   Vernon

Livingston

Calhoun

Midway

Bush's Ferry

Birdsong's Ferry

Brownsville

Tugaloo

Fleetwood P.O.

Bridgeport

VICKSBURG AND JACKSON RAILROAD

Bolton Depot

Clinton

Amsterdam

Champion's Hill

Edwards Station

JACKSON

Raymond

Richmond

New Auburn

Auburn

Cooperville

Terry

Utica

urtonton

Pine Bluff P.O.

Linden

N

S

Other titles of interest

ABRAHAM LINCOLN
His Speeches and Writings
Edited by Roy P. Basler
Preface by Carl Sandburg
888 pp., 6 illus.
80404-2 $19.95

THE ANNALS OF THE
CIVIL WAR
Written by Leading Participants
North and South
New introd. by Gary W. Gallagher
808 pp., 56 illus.
80606-1 $19.95

BATTLE-PIECES AND
ASPECTS OF THE WAR
Herman Melville
New introd. by Lee Rust Brown
282 pp.
80655-X $13.95

BY SEA AND BY RIVER
A Naval History of the Civil War
Bern Anderson
344 pp., 20 illus.
80367-4 $13.95

CAMPAIGNING WITH GRANT
General Horace Porter
New introduction by
William S. McFeely
632 pp., 32 illus.
80277-5 $12.95

THE CIVIL WAR DAY BY DAY
An Almanac 1861-1865
E. B. Long with Barbara Long
1,135 pp., 8 pages of maps
80255-4 $19.95

A CIVIL WAR TREASURY
Being a Miscellany of Arms and
Artillery, Facts and Figures,
Legends and Lore, Muses and
Minstrels, Personalities and People
Albert A. Nofi
431 pp. 80622-3 $15.95

PERSONAL MEMOIRS OF
U.S. GRANT
New introduction by
William S. McFeely
Critical Notes by E. B. Long
xxxi + 608 pp.
80172-8 $15.95

SHERMAN
Soldier, Realist, American
B. H. Liddell Hart
New foreword by Jay Luvaas
480 pp., 11 maps
80507-3 $15.95

THE STORY OF THE
CONFEDERACY
Robert Selph Henry
526 pp.
80370-4 $14.95

TRAGIC YEARS 1860-1865
A Documentary History of the
American Civil War
Paul M. Angle and
Earl Schenck Miers
1108 pp.
80462-X $23.95

PERSONAL MEMOIRS OF
P. H. SHERIDAN
New introduction by Jeffry D. Wert
560 pp., 16 illus., 16 maps
80487-5 $15.95

SHERMAN'S BATTLE FOR
ATLANTA
General Jacob D. Cox
New introd. by Brooks D. Simpson
294 pp., 7 maps
80588-X $12.95

SHERMAN'S MARCH TO THE SEA,
Hood's Tennessee Campaign & the
Carolina Campaigns of 1865
General Jacob D. Cox
New introduction by
Brooks D. Simpson
289 pp., 10 maps
80587-1 $12.95